Applied Econometrics Association Series

General Editors: **Jean H.P. Paelinck**, Emeritus Professor, Erasmus University, Rotterdam; and **Henri Serbat**, University of Paris 2

The vital importance of econometrics for understanding economic phenomena is increasingly recognized in every field of economics.

The discipline is based on 'scientific processes which aim to identify, explain and forecast economic phenomena using formalised tools to produce, measure, structure and model the information' (Gérard Duru and Henri Serbat, 1991).

The Applied Econometrics Association, established 1974, seeks to develop the use of econometric tools by regular updates on the state of the art and the progress made in each specific field, and so to further the transformation of unconnected facts into pertinent information for use in analysis and decision-making.

The series was conceived to form a set of working references for advanced students and researchers in each specific field, as well as a guide to development across the discipline more broadly.

This exchange of knowledge will be continued permanently by the opening of a debate site on the Internet (http;/www.aea.fed-eco.org).

Titles include:

Serge Allegrezza and Anne Dubrocard (*editors*)
INTERNET ECONOMETRICS

Patrick-Yves Badillo and Jean-Baptiste Lesourd (*editors*)
THE MEDIA INDUSTRIES AND THEIR MARKETS
Quantitative Analyses

Françoise Bourdon and Jean Bourdon (*editors*)
WAGE ECONOMETRICS AND MODELLING

Fabrizio Carlevaro and Jean-Baptiste Lesourt (*editors*)
MEASURING AND ACCOUNTING ENVIRONMENTAL NUISANCES AND SERVICES

Arthur Getis, Jeśus Mur and Henry G. Zoller (*editors*)
SPATIAL ECONOMETRICS AND SPATIAL STATISTICS

Siv S. Gustafsson and Danièle E. Meulders (*editors*)
GENDER AND THE LABOUR MARKET
Econometric Evidence of Obstacles to Achieving Gender Equality

Hans Heijke and Joan Muysken (*editors*)
EDUCATION AND TRAINING IN A KNOWLEDGE-BASED ECONOMY

Pavlos Karadeloglou (*editor*)
EXCHANGE-RATE POLICY IN EUROPE

Pavlos Karadeloglou and Virginie Terraza (*editors*)
EXCHANGE RATES AND MACROECONOMIC DYNAMICS

Applied Econometrics Association
**Series Standing Order ISBN 978–0–333–91990–3 (cased) and 978–0–333–71460–7
(paperback)**
(*outside North America only*)

You can receive future titles in this series as they are published by placing a standing order.
Please contact your bookseller or, in case of difficulty, write to us at the address below with
your name and address, the title of the series and one of the ISBNs quoted above.

Customer Services Department, Macmillan Distribution Ltd, Houndmills, Basingstoke,
Hampshire RG21 6XS, England

Internet Econometrics

Edited by

Serge Allegrezza
Director General, National Statistical Office of Luxembourg

and

Anne Dubrocard
Head of Research Unit, National Statistical Office of Luxembourg

First published 2012 by
PALGRAVE MACMILLAN

Palgrave Macmillan in the UK is an imprint of Macmillan Publishers Limited,
registered in England, company number 785998, of Houndmills, Basingstoke,
Hampshire RG21 6XS.

Palgrave Macmillan in the US is a division of St Martin's Press LLC,
175 Fifth Avenue, New York, NY 10010.

Palgrave Macmillan is the global academic imprint of the above companies
and has companies and representatives throughout the world.

Palgrave® and Macmillan® are registered trademarks in the United States,
the United Kingdom, Europe and other countries.

ISBN: 978–0–230–36292–5

This book is printed on paper suitable for recycling and made from fully
managed and sustained forest sources. Logging, pulping and manufacturing
processes are expected to conform to the environmental regulations of the
country of origin.

A catalogue record for this book is available from the British Library.

A catalog record for this book is available from the Library of Congress.

Contents

Part II Determinants of Demand for ICT

Tables

Appendix tables

Figures

Appendix figure

Acknowledgments

This book is the result of work submitted to the conference on Internet Use and Impact held in Marseille in November 2009. H. Serbat and the Applied Econometric Association gave us the opportunity to valorize works undertaken during the conference and authors who have accepted to submit a paper version reviewed of their contributions.

The book would not have been possible without the help of the 2009 research team based at STATEC Luxembourg, namely Anna-Leena Asikainen, Giovanni Mangiarotti, Leila Ben-Aoun, and Chiara Peroni, for their readings and suggestions in order to identify a consistent set of contributions and recommendations.

Thanks also to Olga Chapovaliouk for her contribution in preparing the document for publication and Valentina Biagini for assistance in normalizing layout of the preliminary version of the book.

Contributors

Serge Allegrezza is Vice President of the Social and Economic Council (Conseil économique et social) since January 2009. He is General Director for Economic Studies and heads the Competitiveness Observatory (Ministry of Economic and Foreign Trade). He is also Head of the LU delegation at the Economic Policy Committee (EPC) of the EU since 2004. In addition, Allegrezza is also Scientific Adviser to the Centre de Recherche Public Henri Tudor, Chairman of the Board of LuxTrust Inc., and Chairman of the Economic and Social Council, Luxembourg, since 2009. He has been General Director of the National Statistical Institute and Economic Studies (Service central de la statistique et des études économiques, STATEC) at Luxembourg since April 2003 and was previously Conseiller de Gouvernement 1ère classe at the Ministry of Economics of Luxembourg where he was responsible for internal market policy and then for general economic policy from 1991 to 2003. Allegrezza has a PhD in applied economics.

Mohamed Ayadi is Professor of Econometrics and Quantitative Economics at the University of Tunis. He is Head of the Economics Department at the Tunis High School of Business, and is also a member and supervisor at the UAQUAP research unit at the same institution. He is the author of a number of scientific articles in the fields of econometric and statistical modeling, consumer behavior and public economic policies, welfare and poverty analysis, financial international economics and international trade, innovation and new products analyses. Ayadi has coordinated several projects for the World Bank, the African Union, and the Department of Research at the Tunisian Ministry of High Education.

Ergin Bayrak is an economist whose current research interests are in the areas of economics of media and communication industries, the economics of radio spectrum, economic literacy and entrepreneurship, and the economics of innovation. Bayrak has served as a Google Public Policy Fellow at the New America Foundation, and as a Graduate Fellow at the Center for Communication Law and Policy. He is also a research associate at the Center for Risk and Economic Analysis of Terrorism Events (USA).

Leila Ben Aoun is a research economist at National Statistical Institute and Economic Studies (Service central de la statistique et des études économiques, STATEC) at Luxembourg. She graduated in Economics and Econometrics at the Université de la Méditerranée in Marseille and has a diploma from GREQAM (Groupement de Recherche en Economie Quantitative d'Aix Marseille, France). Her current research focuses on the influence of new technologies on productivity and business performance.

Adel Ben Youssef is Assistant Professor at the University of Nice Sophia-Antipolis, France. He is a member of the GREDEG-CNRS Research Centre. He has held the post of Associate Professor and Research Fellow at the EDHEC Business School and taught for several years at Supélec Paris, a leading engineering school in France. Youssef has been Visiting Professor in universities such as University of Wuhan (China), University of Hanoi (Vietnam), Cairo University (Egypt), Mundiapolis University (Morocco), ESSEC Tunis (Tunisia), UOC Barcelona in Spain and MBI (Algeria). His principal research interests are environmental economics, industrial economics, digital economics, and Mediterranean economics.

Teruyuki Bunno is Professor of Business Management, Faculty of Business Administration, Kinki University, Osaka, Japan. Bunno's major areas of specialty include innovation theory, lifecycle of firms, and new business creations. His current research focuses on the roles of human resources in firms' dynamics. He is a board member of the Japan Academy of Small Business Studies and the Kansai Association for Venture and Entrepreneur Studies.

David Castillo-Merino is Lecturer of Accounting and Finance at the Department of Economics and Business at the Open University of Catalonia (UOC). He is a member of the Information & Communication Technologies Interdisciplinary Research Group (i2TIC at IN3-UOC). His research interests and areas of expertise include the economics of intangible assets, the finance of firms' innovation, and e-learning and he has authored books and papers in these areas. He is also a part of European eLene-EE project on the economics of e-learning.

Sophia P. Dimelis is Professor at the Athens University of Economics and Business in Athens, Greece. She holds a PhD in Economics from the University of Pittsburgh, USA. Her main research interests are in the areas of applied econometrics and time-series. Her current research is based on empirical econometric analysis in the areas of foreign direct investment, information and communication technologies, knowledge capital, firm productivity, and growth.

Anne Dubrocard is Head of the Research Unit at National Statistical Institute and Economic Studies (Service central de la statistique et des études économiques, STATEC) in Luxembourg. She holds a PhD in Economics from the Ecole des Hautes Etudes en Sciences Sociales, France. Coming from the business consulting and insurance sectors, she put together a research team supported by the Observatoire de la Compétitivité. STATEC Research Unit is involved in extensive research regarding productivity and firm performance in Luxembourg and is aimed at developing econometric studies measuring the impact of innovation and information and communication technologies on competitiveness.

Alex Durand has been an econometric data and foresight analyst at CRP Henri Tudor since 2003. He holds a PhD in Economics from the University Paris II – Panthéon-Assas. On completion of his PhD, he pursued his career as an economist in Luxembourg. His research revolves around structural indicators for small open economies and the use of data mining tools for marketing innovation and strategic management.

Alexia Gaudeul is a post-doctoral research fellow at the Graduate School of Human Behaviour in Social and Economic Change (GSBC) at the Friedrich Schiller University in Jena, Germany. Her research interests include the internet, open-source software, and media industries. She has worked on the economics of intermediation on the Internet, written a case study of the LaTeX open-source typesetting software, and is now researching the concept of consumer choice when faced with confusing offers.

Walid Hadhri is a post-doctoral fellow at Paris-Sud 11 University. He is a member of the ADIS Research Centre located at the Jean Monnet Faculty in Paris, and a member of the UAQUAP research unit located at the Tunis High School of Business. He is also part of European eLene-EE project on the economics of e-learning, where he is a teaching assistant.

Hiroki Idota is Professor at Otemon Gakuin University, Faculty of Management, Osaka, Japan. His research interests include management information and innovation, and technology management.

Auguste K. Kouakou is Assistant Professor at the Department of Economics and Management at the University of Cocody-Abidjan, Côte d'Ivoire, and a member of the Ivorian Centre for Economic and Social

Research (CIRES), where he is Deputy Director of the research unit in microeconomics of development. He is also a member of the African Economic Research Consortium (AERC) based in Kenya. His research areas include telecommunication economics, energy economics, and industrial economics. He has published studies on the demand for mobile telephony in Côte d'Ivoire and has undertaken research reports within the AERC network.

Ana Jesús López is Professor of Statistics and Econometrics at the University of Oviedo, Spain. She has been a visiting fellow at several universities in Spain, UK, Cuba, and Hungary. Her research activities include the measurement of economic inequality, regional modeling and forecasting, and the socioeconomic impact of information and communication technologies (ICT). She has also worked as an expert evaluator for the European Commission Lifelong Learning Programme, through the Spanish National Agency (OAPEE).

Ludivine Martin is Research Fellow in Economics at the CEPS/INSTEAD, Luxembourg, and is a member of CREM-UMR CNRS 6211, University of Rennes 1, France. She has completed her PhD thesis in Economics at the University of Rennes 1 CREM. Her research interests are in the area of knowledge economy, the diffusion of ICT, outsourcing strategies, ICT and innovation, ICT use and motivations and well-being.

Laurence Mathieu is a researcher at eftec. She has several years of experience working on economics of natural resources and fisheries management. She is experienced in valuation methods, project appraisal, and statistical analysis, and has worked in both developed and developing countries. Since joining eftec in September 2010, she has contributed to various projects, with a particular focus on the economic valuation of marine and terrestrial ecosystem services. Previously, she was a research associate with the Overseas Development Group at UEA and at the Centre for Social and Economic Research on the Global Environment (CSERGE) focusing on fishery resource management and the valuation of water resources. She has also worked as a research associate at the Centre for Competition Policy at UEA, where her focus was on domestic energy consumption in the U.K. She holds a 'Maitrise' in Financial Economics from the University of Montpellier, France, and a Master's in Ecological Economics from the University of Edinburgh.

Masaru Ogawa is Associate Professor of Business at the Faculty of Business Administration, Kobegakuin University, Kobe, Japan. His areas of specialization include the economics of information and information security of Japanese universities. Ogawa's current research focuses on an evaluation of Japanese broadcasting and the information security policy of Japanese universities. He is a member of a working group that edited and published the *Sample Policies for Information Security Measure for Higher Education Institutions in Japan*, and was subsequently awarded the position of Chief Cabinet Secretary.

Sotiris K. Papaioannou is Research Fellow at the Center of Planning and Economic Research in Athens, Greece. His main research interests are in the areas of applied econometrics and economic growth. His current research is based on empirical aggregate and industry-level studies on economic growth, productivity, and information and communication technologies. He has published several articles in refereed journals and collective volumes. He has also presented his research at a number of international conferences and has served as a referee in various economic journals.

Chiara Peroni is Research Economist at STATEC. She has also held the position of Lecturer at the School of Economics at the University of East Anglia and at the University of Manchester, UK. Peroni holds a PhD in Economics and an MSc in Econometrics from the University of York. Her research interests are in the areas of applied econometrics and statistics, and she is the author of several scientific articles on the subject of empirical finance and networks and innovation economics.

Joost Poort is Senior Researcher at the Institute for Information Law, part of the University of Amsterdam, the Netherlands. Until mid-2011, he worked for SEO Economic Research, initially as a senior researcher and, since 2008, as head of the section for Regulation and Competition Policy. He has performed a wide variety of studies on market structure and regulation in various markets. Poort's research interests include energy and telecommunications, as well as the economics of copyright and the interface of culture, heritage, and economics.

Paul Rutten is a Visiting Professor in Creative Industries and Innovation at the Faculty of Applied Economics of Antwerp University, and an independent researcher. Previously, he has held the posts of Professor in Digital Media Studies at University Leiden, Senior Researcher and Consultant at TNO Strategy, Technology and Policy and Reader in Media and Entertainment Management at Inholland University of Professional Education.

Masatsugu Tsuji is Professor of Economics at the Graduate School of Applied Informatics, University of Hyogo, Kobe, Japan, Professor

Emeritus of Osaka University, and Visiting Professor of Carnegie Mellon University, Pittsburgh, USA, and National Cheng Kung University, Taiwan. His areas of research include the economics of information and telecommunications, and the economic evaluation of telemedicine. He received the Thammasat University Award from Thammasat University, Bangkok, Thailand, in June 2009.

María Rosalía Vicente is Associate Professor of Applied Economics at the University of Oviedo, Spain. She received her PhD in Economics in 2007 with a thesis on 'Metrics and Indicators of the Information Society: Approaching ICT Diffusion and the Digital Divide'. She has published several papers in scientific journals and has been a visiting researcher at the Massachusetts Institute of Technology and the OECD.

Marco Vincenzi is a PhD student in public policy at Heinz College, Carnegie Mellon University in Pittsburgh, USA. His research interests include the economics of technological innovation and international macroeconomics. His papers span a wide range of topics, including the role of multinationals in the diffusion of technology in Eastern Europe and the impact of economic reforms on Italian multinational firms in Latin America.

Introduction

The information and communication technologies (ICT) development that allowed Internet-based communication is often referred to as the fourth technological revolution. Just like steam and electricity, the diffusion of those 'general-purpose technologies' in all sectors of activity modifies not only the products, but also the organization of production and the way of life. Nevertheless, their 'added value is based on the manipulation and diffusion of ideas', which attribute radically different characteristics and properties. ICT and the Internet can be thought of in the context of network economy as they are characterized by constant fixed costs and small/negligible marginal costs; the wide use of these technologies impacts on markets' structure. Varian (2000) analyzed the relation between technology and market structure and concluded that the value creation process must be reconsidered. Indeed, the diffusion of ICT and network technologies changes the sharing of profits along the value chain, redesigns the physical firm's borders, as well as the way firms compete in the market. Brynjolfsson and Hitt (2000) give examples of those transformations and show how technical and organizational changes made possible by ICT cause vertical integration and/or redefinition of capabilities within companies. Many of these aspects are considered using the quantitative approaches collected in this volume.

Organization of the book

The chapters in this book consist of a selection of contributions submitted to the 98th International Conference of the Applied Econometric Association, entitled "Internet Uses and Impacts: Quantitative Analysis," organized in Marseille on 5–6 November 2009. Their aim

1

is to explore and deploy tools and methodology in order to measure phenomena embracing the different nature of ICT impacts. These approaches are grouped together in three parts. Part I makes an international comparison of ICT diffusion and impact on productivity at macro level. Part II examines determinants of household demand and adoption for ICT at micro level. Part III examines the supply side at micro level and highlight the impact of ICT on organization of production and products. The Parts II and III also emphasize the international comparison by using samples, collected in several geographical areas.

Part I: ICT and productivity

Data and methodology

At the macro level, standard growth accounting framework, as well as a technical inefficiency measurement based on a stochastic frontier, are used to compare and explain the gap between US and EU total factor productivity (TFP) growth. ICT is one of the possible answers explored across the first chapters. Vincenzi, in Chapter 1, proposes a measure of the impact of ICT on TFP and technical progress (looking at information technology, complementary capital and the transatlantic productivity divergence). Here, he re-examines the gap in productivity between the USA and Europe using US, French and Belgian data regarding investments in ICT. The notion of organizational capital is introduced into the production function estimated for three countries and 30 sectors of activity between 1993 and 2005. In Chapter 2, Dimelis and Papaioannou seek to find factors explaining how ICT is correlated with labor productivity growth, but not so clearly with the TFP growth. Using a selection of 17 countries providing data on ICT capital from 1990–2005, they analyze possible ICT effects in reducing aggregate technical inefficiency, paying particular attention to the ubiquity (the professional along with the private use) of ICT generating further externalities. Thus, ICT diffusion among firms and households seems to be a determinant for the competitiveness of nations. In order to have a clear picture of what is going on in Europe, therefore, in Chapter 3 Vicente and López present measures of diffusion of ICT and their usage in European households, comparing several ICT measurements obtained at regional level. Regional statistics on the information society provided by Eurostat are analyzed, applying principal components and cluster techniques to 216 regions belonging to 30 European countries.

Summary of main results

ICT had a significant impact on labor productivity growth in the USA and EU and accounts, in part, for the faster productivity growth witnessed in the USA during the late 1990s. However, its impact on technical progress and TFP growth has not been so clearly demonstrated. The fact that there are high levels of US investment in ICT, as well as, most significantly, the ability of industries and firms to derive greater output boosts from their investment explain how some of the divergence in TFP can be attributed to ICT. Theory suggests that TFP growth should be negatively correlated with contemporaneous investments in ICT capital because firms are diverting resources to install the new capital, whereas it should be positively associated with lagged investments in ICT capital. In Chapter 1, Vincenzi establishes that while the United States started to invest in ICT and in complementary capital in the late 1980s and continued throughout the 1990s, evidence has been found that France and Belgium delayed their wave of ICT investments until the late 1990. In addition, Vincenzi suggests a different conceptualization of 'complementary capital', suggesting that constrained supplies of skilled labor are a determining factor in the impact of ICT investment on productivity. In particular, he finds that complementary investments are necessary to fully exploit these technologies.

In Chapter 2, Dimelis and Papaioannou use a method that allows them to quantify the ICT impact in the reduction ofcross-country inefficiencies. They show that, on average, ICT contributed by more than 5 percent to the increase in technical efficiency across countries and over time. The efficiency estimates indicate that the most efficient countries are Belgium and the Netherlands, followed by the USA. However, it seems that several south European countries are less efficient and have not yet reached the efficiency levels of the most developed OECD countries. Finally, there is evidence to suggest that ICT acts as an enabler of productivity growth, including its TFP component – thus, economic growth and competitiveness. Appropriate indicators and measures of such phenomena are needed in order to support and inform policymaking. Vicente and López, in Chapter 3, analyze the range of Eurostat ICT indicators and conclude that the leaders in ICT adoption are Nordic territories, together with some British regions. In contrast, Eastern and Southern European countries lag behind. Furthermore, five ICT clusters are indentified across Europe, with 15 low-performing regions and 68 high-performing territories. In order to identify factors underlying the regions and countries gap, to the matter is studied at micro level. Data describing characteristics and behaviors of individuals and households, as well as firms and the business sector, are, respectively, mobilized in the two following parts.

Part II: Determinant of demand for ICT

Data and methodology

Because ICTs 'are reformulating the equation of aggregate productivity' (Faucheux et al., 2010), the measurement of their effects and the identification of spillover factors matter. A first approach consists in indentifying factors enhancing or hampering speed and spread of adoption and usage of ICT among people and households. A second range of studies aims to describe the demand function and measure the advantages of consumption and usage of Internet. Thus, in Chapter 4, Kouado considers the Côte d'Ivoire, and in Chapter 5, Walid Hadhri, Mohamed Ayadi and Adel Ben Youssef *consider* France, *aiming* to identify characteristics of users and non-users. *With regard to the Côte d'Ivoire*, data come from a survey conducted on behalf of the Telecommunications Agency of Côte d'Ivoire (ATCI) by the Ivorian Centre for Economic and Social Research (CIRES) with 1,500 households drawn under a two-stage sample selection with stratification. Hadhri et al. use different souces of statistics provided by French National Statistics (INSEE), the French postal and electronic communications regulatory authority (ARCEP) and l'Institut de l'Audiovisuel et des Télécommunications en Europe (IDATE). *Both chapters* base their estimates on the distinction between access and intensity of utilization. Kouakou estimates a simple logit model in order to discern factors behind the decision to adopt the Internet; then he considers the frequency of usage after having access to the network.

Frequency of use of the web, wherever it occurs, is estimated using the ordered logit model. Hadhri et al. estimate the decision of the Internet adoption using a simple probit model in which the dependant variable is the probability of deciding to adopt Internet. Second, Internet use estimation is based on the time that the individual spends online. The dependant variable represents the number of hours per week that individuals spend connected to the Internet. The two-step Heckman's method deployed allows differentiation between Internet adoption and access to frequency patterns and ability to solve the selection problem. In Chapter 6, Bayrak proposes also to measure benefits for the consumer. He focuses on consumers with home networks and highlights the different demand characteristics and welfare attainments of consumers who connect to the Internet through wireless networks from those who connect through other (wired) types of networks; the incremental consumer surplus from using wireless networks is measured. For highly time-intensive goods, the true cost of consumption includes the opportunity cost of time, in addition to very small market expenditures. Using the variation in time use and wage data is likely to give more accurate estimates of elasticities and welfare than using market price and consumption data. The data consist of a sample of 4,865 respondents who report to have some type of home network and are online at least monthly. This sample is selected from North American Consumer Technographics data from Forrester Research. Finally, a fourth demand function is estimated in order to measure the willingness of consumers to pay for a new service. In Chapter 7, Durand analyses the adoption of a service of electronic signature and digital identification card aimed at securing online transactions by Luxembourg inhabitants. He uses a survey conducted with 1,509 individuals from 16 to 74 years old.

The estimation of demand function and the elaboration of the models to capture the modalities of diffusion of ICT do not offer an exhaustive picture of uses and associated transformations. In particular, social networks play a new and crucial role in the process of innovation. To fully understand the social and economic changes, one needs to consider also new forms of social interactions based on Internet communities (for a complete overview of the economic characteristic of social network, see Gensollen, 2007). Quantitative analysis, proposed by Gaudeul, Peroni, and Mathieu in Chapter 8, explores the role of reciprocal attention in Internet communications. Properties of blogging networks are derived from a model where bloggers devote attention to others, produce content for others and exchange attention for content within their network of relations; as Gaudeul et al. put it: 'in a network, an agent that offers little content compared to others will need to compensate for this by devoting more attention to others in order to maintain her place in the network. Conversely, an agent that offers a lot of content compared to others will devote less attention to others.' The aim of the analysis is to demonstrate, first, that bloggers who display higher levels of content production and general blogging activity have more readers and, second, that bloggers with relatively more friends than readers produce less content than other bloggers. The predictions from the model are tested with a novel dataset from LiveJournal, a major blogging community. The database contains a number of measures of activity and involvement in social relations from data gathered on the activity of 2,767 bloggers drawn randomly from LiveJournal.

Summary of main results

The measurement of ICT effects and the identification of spillover factors give a better understanding of factors behind the spread of the service in the population. Age, location, type of employment, education and social capital are important factors in the decision to adopt the Internet network, in the Côte d'Ivoire as well as in France. Moreover, for France, findings confirm the fact that a higher education level, computer and Internet skills and lifestyle have a positive effect on Internet adoption. Those with higher levels of income and younger people are more willing to use Internet. Lifestyle, which indicates ICT and electronic tool use, positively correlate with Internet use. Indeed, using an ICT or electronic tool, such as a mobile phone, laptop, DVD player or digital camera influences positively the probability of adoption of the Internet. Finally, high-income people were more able to adopt Internet, but they spend less time online than low-income ones. This relies on time opportunity cost. Evaluating consumer surplus shows that French time opportunity cost is three times more important than connection cost. French households have found the Internet to be a valuable addition to their welfare levels. In 2005, the French consumer surplus ranged between $1,240 and $3,126, depending on the methodology applied (between $2,107 and $2,651 with the two-stage estimation method). Following Bayrak's estimation for USA, the consumer surplus from the Internet is around $7,000. With the most conservative estimate, consumers with wireless networks are found to be realizing, on average, $824 more consumer surplus from the use of the Internet, compared to wired network owners. Finally, measuring utility throughout non-monetary variables, blogger's activity has been found to be related to the size of that blogger's relational network and to the level of aggregate reciprocation within that network. Bloggers who do not adhere to reciprocity norms are found to have fewer readers than their activity might otherwise have predicted. Posting activity and intensity of interaction are positive determinants of network size; departures from aggregate reciprocity can be accounted for by content production; failure to reciprocate attention is sanctioned with a lower popularity than other measures of activity might normally warrant. These results suggest that bloggers who produce more content devote less attention to others. Furthermore, bloggers sanction deviations from the norm of reciprocity, which occur when a blogger does not return friendship as expected.

Beyond blogs, social networks, peer-to-peer and file sharing, new tools generate new individual behavior, redesigning business models. Thus, the last part of the book focuses on a piece of work analyzing Internet impact on specific businesses and markets.

Part III: New organizational business frontier

Data and methodology

Going back to the behavioral attitude seen throughout Internet worlds, in Chapter 9 Poort and Rutten analyze the impact of file sharing on business models in the music industry, providing a comprehensive overview. The production of recorded music, as well as that of films and games, is characterized by relatively high fixed costs and low marginal costs. As a result of digitization, the costs of reproduction and distribution of content have decreased dramatically, as well as the possibilities for copyright holders to control this process. The fact that file sharing gives free access to content is just one of the various reasons to engage in this activity, while interactions between file sharing and buying can be either positive, neutral or negative. A lot of source of information has been mobilized in order to draw a detailed picture of facts and trends. The study reviews relevant literature and draws on a range of secondary – particularly statistical – sources, as well as interviews of active uploaders and downloaders and a survey of a representative group of 1,500 Internet users, conducted by research agency Synovate in the Netherlands. Analyzing characteristics of and trends in the film, games and music industries and their respective markets related to file sharing highlights developments in the business models of the sectors and offers hints for identifying the possible implications of file sharing for consumer behavior in other markets in which this content is sold (and also the short- and longer-terms implications of these changes). As it can be seen throughout the analysis of the music industry, ICT impacts business models through the modification of consumption behaviors. It also impacts directly the internal and external organization of firms by allowing multiple shifting of the frontier of their activities. Indeed, to manage their activities effectively, firms choose to resort increasingly to outsourcing and/or offshoring of activities, both for the manufacture of products and for the inputs included in the production process. Moreover, technological changes favor the compatibility and tradability of many services across the world. In Chapter 10, Martin attempts to modelize the choice of whether to buy in ICT services and characterizes Luxembourgish firms which outsource some of their IT functions. A primary consideration, as firms are trying to minimizing costs, rests on the relative costs of producing in-house or purchasing services on the market. Second, the firm has to choose between sourcing from a foreign subsidiary or an independent outside firm. The dataset comes from the Luxembourg part of the 'ICT Usage and e-Commerce in Enterprises' survey (2007). Models tend to analyze the two contrasting effects that could be expected: either the firm's investment in ICT can reduce the cost of outsourcing and, thus, can favor it; or conversely, if the firm has skilled workers, the cost of managing in-house ICT services will be lower.

For Japan, Idota, Ogawa, Bunno, and Tsuji propose, in Chapter 11, to analyze the choice of outsourcing and/or offshoring implementing a bivariate probit. In order to improve performance and efficiency in all aspects of business activities, SMEs need to increasingly rely on ICT as a basis for organizational restructuring. The chapter is based on data collected from field surveys, a mail survey and in-depth interviews in two of Japan's most prominent SME clusters, located in Higashi-Osaka city in Osaka prefecture, and Ohta ward in the Tokyo metropolitan area. In 2004, questionnaires were sent to more than 6,000 SMEs in the two clusters, yielding nearly 1,200 responses mail surveys of selected high-ICT-adopting SMEs. In order to identify factors that promote ICT use among Japanese SMEs, an index of ICT usage using an analytic hierarchy process (AHP) is calculated. Ordinary least squares (OLS), logit and probit regression are implemented in order to predict ICT use and identify factors that promote ICT use, based on survey responses. For Catalan firms, Ben Youssef, Merino and Walid Hadhri propose to modelize, in Chapter 12, the intra-firm diffusion process, combining the well-established models of technological diffusion with an organizational and networking complementarities view and epidemic evolutionary approaches. Three econometric models are then tested. The first one is an ordered probit model estimating the probability of ICT adoption by firms. Second, a general model is built in order to explain intra-firm diffusion of ICT according to some specific tools, as well as to different business uses of these digital technologies. The database comes from a survey conducted in 2003 by the Catalan government of 2,038 enterprises. Thus, in order to promote ICT use and impact, better understanding of adoption of ICT by firms and their internal diffusion, as well as their link with innovation capacity, is needed in order to help their promotion. The generalized diffusion of ICTs, including their convergence with the Internet network and capabilities, increases the value of innovations and R&D investments of firms; furthermore, competitive pressure on the market of products in turn imposes more reactive organizational forms. In Chapter 13, Ben Aoun and Dubrocard highlight the complexity of this relationship between ICT and innovation at firm level, using an original sample of Luxembourgish firms.

Summary of main results

Chapter 9 establishes that music is steadily acquiring the characteristics of a public good, while live concerts constitute an ever-growing source of income for industry. Thus, new artists are gaining access to novel and accessible channels through which to market their wares, such as MySpace and YouTube, responding to the democratization of talent development. In order to survive, the industry must redesign its business model and is increasingly focusing on sponsorship contracts, 360-degree contracts and merchandising. These new value creation drivers include such initiatives as alliances between the mobile phone and music industries. At the same time one can see that file sharing impacts on the rest of the economy through spin-off revenues.

From the point of view of intra- and inter-firm reorganizations, Chapter 10 establishes that, for Luxembourg, firms' resources positively influence the probability of choosing the option of outsourcing and offshoring ICT activities. Concerning ICT investment, after the control of its potential endogeneity, one can observe that firms with the highest specific ICT needs choose to find these services from external suppliers or firms located abroad, especially when their ICT competencies measured by the presence of ICT/IT specialists is low. Conversely, other firms that have high ICT needs but that are associated with the employment of IT specialists don't seem to resort to external services providers. Finally, it appears that high trust in data transfer favors the choice of outsourcing ICT services. These results find echoes in Japanese studies (see Chapter 11), showing that information security is a major concern for large firms that want subcontractors to use the firms' ICT systems, with associated costs for complying with ICT demands. Finally, the lack of human resources to handle ICT and concern about security and privacy of data related to customers and business transactions are the main factors hampering ICT adoption. Moreover, the latest study emphasizes that the best way to promote ICT use among SMEs is to encourage top management to better understand, value and proactively pursue ICT. Once management adopts a positive perception of ICT, they can determine the exact ways in which they will implement ICT to meet their specific goals. Therefore, in Chapter 12, Ben Youssef et al. show that boosting ICT diffusion depth inside the firms does not depend only of the top management state of mind and willingness. Their results confirm the well-established literature. Thus, the main conclusion is that inter-firms ICT diffusion (i.e., investment in digital equipment) and depth of ICT adoption (i.e., spread of efficient digital uses) have different determinants, although they share some common traits based on the existence of complementary effects between digital technologies, innovation, organizational structure and workers' skills within a firm. Linking ICT adoption to innovation ability in Luxembourgish firms, it can be established that the probability of being innovative increases significantly with the size of firm, regardless of the type of innovation. This link between size and innovation ability is concave. R&D ratio expressed as R&D expenses over turnover has also a positive impact on probability of innovation (for every type other than marketing innovation). The most frequently significant variable representing ICT is the number of automatic links. Indeed, it is the only ICT variable with a positive impact for technological innovations; the percentage of highly qualified employees also contributes significantly and positively to explaining the probability of innovation for a product. Finally, on the one hand, ICTs constitute an aggregate of major innovations which, in turn, accelerate the process of innovation through new applications and new processes. As ICTs favor innovation, they improve all inputs' productivity. On the other hand, the innovation process accelerates and modifies the way to implement ICT in a process of co-invention, which renders the ICT more effective. Therefore, ICTs are closely related to the firms' ability to innovate, that is to say to introduce new products and services, new processes and new applications. In addition, sharing and knowledge transfer, as well as the development of real-time networks, foster scientific and technological innovation and make new practices and organizational arrangements possible. For example, e-management, e-business or e-commerce are themselves organizational innovation, and enhance firms' performance. Indeed, data at firm level evidence the impact of intangible organizational investments and innovation of products and services related to computers. These are necessary to make organizational structures coherent with technological capabilities.

References

ARCEP (Autorité de Régulation des Communications Electroniques et des Postes) (2005) 'Rapport d'activité de l'Autorité de Régulation des Communications Electroniques et Postales 2005'.

Brynjolfsson, E. and L.M. Hitt (2000) 'Beyond Computation: Information Technology, Organizational Transformation and Business Performance', *Journal of Economic Perspectives*, Vol. 14, No. 4, pp. 23–48.

Brousseau, E. and N. Curien (2007) *Internet and Digital Economics: Principles, Methods and Applications*, Cambridge: Cambridge University Press.

Faucheux, S., C. Hue and I. Nicolaï (2010) 'TIC et développement', Brussels: De Boeck.

Gensollen, M. (2007) 'Échanger: Comment le numérique modifie en profondeur les conditions de socialisation de l'échange', mimeo, available at http://www.gensollen.net/Gensollen_echanger_2007_05_enligne.pdf

IDATE (INSTITUT de l'AUDOVISUEL et des TELECOMMUNICATIONS en EUROPE) (2005) 'Use-IT: qui consomme quoi en 2015?'

REGULATION (EC) No 1006/2009 of the European Parliament and of the council official journal of the European Union.

Regulation (EC) No 808/2004 concerning Community statistics on the information society.

Varian, H.R. (2000) 'Market Structure in the Network Age', in E. Brynjolfsson and B. Kahin (eds), *Understanding the Digital Economy*, Cambridge, MA: MIT Press.

Part I
ICT and Productivity

1

Information Technology, Complementary Capital, and the Transatlantic Productivity Divergence

Marco Vincenzi

Introduction

In March 2000, all the heads of government and of states of the European Union (EU) gathered in Lisbon (Portugal) to develop a strategic plan for Europe for the next ten years. This plan was known as the Lisbon Agenda, and it sought to make the EU the world's most competitive economy within a decade. That decade has now nearly elapsed; few inside or outside or Europe would regard the Lisbon Agenda as a success. The main concern confronting European leaders in 2000 was the evident widening gap in economic performance between the USA and the European Union. After the gathering in Lisbon, a heated debate began about the future of the EU.

Many structural reforms have been proposed to close the widening gap in economic performance, but its causes remain imperfectly understood. The European Commission, in *The EU Economy: 2004 Review* (2004), pointed to the sharp acceleration in labor productivity per hour in the USA since the mid-1990s, a feat not matched by most of the European countries, as a primary factor behind the EU's worsening relative performance. After decades of convergence to US productivity levels, during which the EU countries enjoyed persistently higher rates of labor and TFP growth than the USA, labor productivity in the EU is on a trend growth path lower than the one in the USA, as shown in Figure 1.1.

Thus, the divergence in productivity is not limited to labor productivity. Other studies indicate that US TFP accelerated in the mid-1990s,

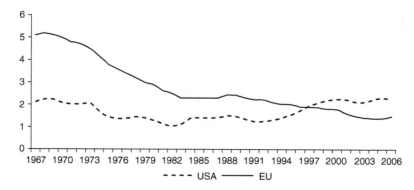

Figure 1. 1   Trend of labor productivity growth (per hour) (%change), EU Comm. 2007

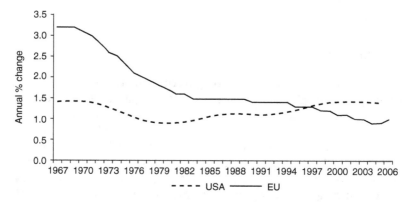

Figure 1. 2   Trend of total factor productivity growth, EU Comm. 2007

while in the European economies and in Japan, TFP growth decelerated (van Ark et al., 2002; Gust and Marquez, 2004). This poses an obvious challenge to European economies. To maintain growth in an environment of shrinking, aging workforces, steady and significant increases in productivity will be necessary. The divergence of US and European productivity trends suggests that Europe is now falling behind a technology frontier which it had been steadily pursuing for decades.

This chapter does not attempt to study, analyze, or evaluate the policy proposals that are part of the Lisbon Agenda, but it does seek to understand the nature of the transatlantic productivity divergence that motivated the Lisbon Agenda. It will focus on the role of information and communication technology (ICT) as a driver of this divergence. We will review a series of findings in the literature suggesting that the USA's improved relative performance is driven, in part, by its more effective utilization of ICT. Drawing (heavily) upon the work of Basu et al. (2003), we will lay out a theoretical framework in which the output elasticity of investment in ICT hardware (and packaged software) requires investment at the firm level in modification of the organizations' routines and activities in order to take full advantage of the capabilities inherent in the ICT system.[1] As Basu et al. (2003) note, this investment in complementary organizational capital is not measured in conventional datasets. However, the theoretical model we derive will suggest a way in which its presence can be inferred from more conventional data on TFP and ICT hardware investment. An important implication of the model is that increased investment in ICT hardware can coincide with an increase in investment in (unmeasured) complementary capital that actually lowers measured TFP growth in the short run, but brings about an increase in TFP growth in the longer run. Basu et al. (2003) apply an empirical specification similar to the one used in this chapter to UK data, with limited success. We apply an empirical specification based on Basu et al. (2003) to continental European economies. We find mixed evidence for the idea that Western European productivity growth could be (temporarily) undermeasured due to a process of accumulation of complementary capital in Western European economies.

Driven in part by the mixed results, we suggest a reinterpretation of the concept of complementary capital that emphasizes the role of customized software in mediating the impact of investment in ICT hardware on productivity. This interpretation suggests the importance of specialized workers with software engineering skills and points to the relative scarcity of such workers in Western Europe as a possible additional explanation for lower levels of ICT investment and lower measured output elasticities of ICT investment in Europe relative to the USA. Preliminary regressions suggest a positive correlation between measures of the intensity of software skills in the workforce and TFP growth. We sketch out a research strategy by which this tentative hypothesis could be further tested.

Literature review

For many years, productivity researchers searched in vain for evidence that increasingly intensive investment in ICT in the USA and in other advanced industrial technologies was bearing fruit in the form of enhanced labor and TFP As late as the mid-1990s, little convincing evidence of this had emerged – a conundrum dubbed the Solow Paradox.[2] This paradox was partially resolved later in the decade. After the mid-1990s, measured labor and TFP growth accelerated in the USA, but not in most other major industrial economies. An extensive literature has linked both productivity accelerations to ICT. The work of Jorgenson and Stiroh (1999, 2000) and Stiroh (2001) carefully and convincingly established this linkage for labor productivity and TFP within the ICT goods-producing sector. Theoretically, the linkage between ICT investment and labor productivity is clear. Rising productivity within the ICT manufacturing industries leads to substantial declines in ICT goods prices. Falling prices of ICT equipment, in turn, allow for a classical substitution effect between inputs, causing a change of the ratio K/L along a given production function. This is simple capital deepening, and it has no necessary implications for TFP growth outside the ICT goods-producing sector.

The work of Jorgenson and Stiroh shows the importance of high-tech industries for USA productivity growth during the period 1958–96. These are ICT-producing industries like industrial machinery and equipment, which includes computer production, and electronic and electrical equipment, which includes semiconductor production, as well as industries such as instruments and communications (respectively SIC 35, 36, 38 and 48). The obvious importance of the knowledge economy, in particular of ICT-producing industries, and the evident industrial dynamism of Silicon Valley in the 1990s, was certainly on the minds of the European policymakers pushing the Lisbon Agenda. In fact, there have been various (largely unsuccessful) attempts to replicate a knowledge hub in Europe during the 20th century.[3] But the work of Stiroh (2001) also points the importance of labor productivity growth in ICT-using industries. The labor productivity increases induced by falling ICT prices in these ICT-using industries were also quite important in explaining the USA's productivity miracle at the aggregate level, in part because these industries accounted for a larger fraction of total GDP than the ICT goods-producing industries.

These ICT-using industries appear to be critical in driving the measured productivity divergence between the USA and the EU. In their pioneering productivity comparison between the EU and the USA, van Ark et al. (2002) demonstrate this. Despite the visible industrial triumphs of Silicon Valley, van Ark et al. show that ICT-producing industries in both the USA and the EU are small parts of total GDP, and that they experienced broadly similar accelerations in productivity growth in the 1990s. The USA–EU divergence is driven by the differential trends in ICT-using service sectors, in particular retailing, wholesaling, and financial services. Van Ark et al. also show that these different trends remain even after accounting for the different ways in which European and USA statistical agencies attempt to account for quality change. These different trends are, on the surface, hard to explain if the principle mechanism is one of cheaper capital goods leading to capital deepening. ICT goods are widely traded internationally, and prices of the goods tend to follow broadly similar trends across countries. Why did substantial price decline in the USA lead to a greater surge in labor productivity than in the EU?

The mystery deepens as researchers have broadened their studies to cross-national comparisons of TFP growth (Bosworth and Triplett, 2002; Basu et al., 2001; Inklaar et al., 2007). It turns out that the USA has enjoyed superior TFP growth in the same sectors in which labor productivity has surged. The concentration of TFP movements in ICT-using service sectors suggests that something may be going on besides a simple capital deepening story.

Basu et al. (2003) add an illuminating theoretical framework and additional empirical evidence to these findings through a comparison of the UK and the US economy at industry level. They treat ICT as a general purpose technology (GPT). In this new setting, firms need substantial and costly co-investments in complementary capital to fully benefit from ICT investments. This implies that TFP is mismeasured. Indeed, in the production function, not all the inputs are observable (e.g., the service flow from intangible complementary capital), nor are all outputs observable (e.g., investments in complementary capital). Basu's characterization of ICT as a GPT seems quite plausible. According to Bresnahan and Trajtenberg (1995), characteristics of a GPT include:

1. Scope for improvement.
2. A variety of applications throughout the economy.
3. Complementarities with existing or potential new technologies.
4. Efforts or investments are required to use the GPT fruitfully.

Many GPTs of the past, such as the steam engine and electricity, have arguably met these requirements; we argue that ICT does also. If Basu et al.'s conceptualization is correct, then the absence of a measured productivity acceleration in Europe could simply reflect an accumulation of unmeasured complementary capital within European firms whose timing differs from that of the USA. Governmental intervention may be justified, when the socially desired level of R&D activity is higher than that practiced by enterprises. Nelson (1993) argues that when firms seek profits under nonquantifiable uncertainty, the aim of government policies is to provide conditions that support innovations by facilitating the diffusion of knowledge. Widespread knowledge is a key factor in the adoption of general-purpose technologies, where sector-specific technological improvements find applications in many other industries. These points will be developed in the next sections and in the conclusions.

Theoretical model

As discussed in the introduction, the novelty introduced by a GPT model lies in the fact that its effects goes well beyond the industry of production; substantial co-investments are required in order to fully benefit from its use.[4] The GPT, in this case, is the production of ICT capital at a continuously falling price, which is exogenous. Value added in industries that use ICT is

$$Q_{it} \equiv Y_{it} + A_{it} = F(Z_t\, G(K_{it}^{IT}, C_{it}), K_{it}^{NT}, L_{it}), \quad i = 1,...,N \qquad (1)$$

where
- F and G are homogeneous of degree 1 in their arguments;
- Z is a technology term that each industry takes as exogenous;
- K^{IT} is ICT capital, while K^{NT} is non-ICT capital rented by each industry in competitive, economy-wide markets.

The aggregate stocks of the two types of capital evolve as:

$$K_t^{JT} = I_t^{JT} + (1 - \delta^{JT})K_{t-1}^{JT} \quad \text{Where} \quad J = \{I, N\} \qquad (2)$$

where
- Y is the marketable output of each industry;
- C is the stock of complementary capital, while A is the investment flow (time and resource cost of training and creating new business structures).[5]

A and C are linked as follows:

$$C_{it} = A_{it} + (1 - \delta_C)C_{it-1} \qquad (3)$$

Now, it is important to notice that the marginal productivities of K^{IT} and C are closely linked, since the elasticity of substitution between the two inputs in the production of G is relatively small. So, when ICT capital price is falling, the incentive to accumulate C is strong in order to grasp the benefit of K^{IT}. Since A and C are unobserved, the main implication of a GPT model is that TFP is mismeasured. In order to see why, we start differentiating (1):

$$\Delta q = \frac{F_{K^{IT}} K^{IT}}{Q} \Delta k^{IT} + \frac{F_C C}{Q} \Delta c + \frac{F_{K^{NT}} K^{NT}}{Q} \Delta k^{NT} + \frac{F_L L}{Q} \Delta l + s_G \Delta z \tag{4}$$

Making Solow's assumptions of constant returns to scale (CRS) and perfect competition (PC), we have:

$$\frac{F_{K^{IT}} K^{IT}}{Q} + \frac{F_C C}{Q} + \frac{F_{K^{NT}} K^{NT}}{Q} + \frac{F_L L}{Q} = 1 \tag{5}$$

If we observed total output Q and knew the required rates of capital, we could find the elasticity of output with respect to complementary capital, C:

$$\frac{F_C C}{Q} = 1 - \frac{WL}{PQ} - \frac{P_K^{IT} K^{IT}}{PQ} - \frac{P_K^{NT} K^{NT}}{PQ} \tag{6}$$

Dividing both terms by measured output Y^{NT} and multiplying by Q, we have:

$$\frac{F_C C}{Y^{NT}} = \frac{Q}{Y^{NT}} - \frac{WL}{PY^{NT}} - \frac{P_K^{IT} K^{IT}}{PY^{NT}} - \frac{P_K^{NT} K^{NT}}{PY^{NT}}$$

Adding Solow's assumptions of CRS and PC to (4) gives us:

$$\Delta y^{NT} - \frac{P_K^{IT} K^{IT}}{PY^{NT}} \Delta k^{IT} - \frac{P_K^{NT} K^{NT}}{PY^{NT}} \Delta k^{NT} - \frac{F_L L}{Q} \Delta l$$

$$\equiv \Delta TFP = \frac{F_C C}{Y^{NT}} \Delta c - \frac{A}{Y^{NT}} \Delta a + s_G \Delta z \tag{7}$$

Equation (7) is an expression for the conventional Solow residual, where a biased estimate of TFP growth is caused by omitting complementary inputs. When unmeasured output is growing ($\Delta a > 0$), TFP is underestimated as resources are diverted to investment. When unmeasured input is growing ($\Delta c > 0$), TFP growth is overestimated. In steady state, ($\Delta a = \Delta c$) implies that:

$$\frac{C}{Y^{NT}} \left[F_C - \frac{A}{C} \right] g = \frac{C}{Y^{NT}} \left[(r^* + \delta_C) - \frac{g + \delta_C}{1 + g} \right] g$$

Where r^* is the steady-state real interest rate. In steady state, the mismeasurement is positive and thus TFP growth is lower than measured. Thus, the question now is how to estimate A and C, which are unobserved.

Suppose G takes a CES form:

$$G = \left[\alpha K^{IT\frac{\sigma-1}{\sigma}} + (1-\alpha)C^{\frac{\sigma-1}{\sigma}} \right]^{\frac{\sigma-1}{\sigma}}$$

The maximization problem of producing G at minimum cost leads us to:

$$\Delta c_t = \Delta k_t^{IT} + \sigma \Delta p_t^{IT} \tag{8}$$

where is Δp_t^{IT} the change in the relative rental rate of ICT capital to C-capital.

This equation implies a direct link between growth in complementary capital and growth of observed ICT capital.

Differentiating equation (8), we have:

$$\Delta a_t = \frac{C}{A} \left[\Delta c_t - \frac{(1-\delta_C)}{(1+g)} \Delta c_{t-1} \right]$$

Substituting the last equation and equation 8 into equation 7 gives us:

$$\Delta TFP = \left[\frac{F_C C}{Y^{NT}} - \frac{C}{Y^{NT}} \right] \left[\Delta k_t^{IT} + \sigma \Delta p_t^{IT} \right]$$
$$+ \left[\frac{C}{Y^{NT}} \frac{(1-\delta_C)}{(1+g)} \right] \left[\Delta k_{t-1}^{IT} + \sigma \Delta p_{t-1}^{IT} \right] + s_G \Delta z \tag{9}$$

This is a key equation, because it relates TFP growth to the importance of complementary capital accumulation. The first term is negative, since it is proportional to $(r^* + \delta - 1)$. The second term, however, is clearly positive. Hence, our GPT model implies that industries that invest in ICT have now a lower measured output, but they will have a higher one in the future. The main conclusion is that benefits from ICT investments show up in TFP growth with a time lag, which we need to estimate, while contemporaneous investments in ICT are negatively correlated with TFP growth. When we try to estimate equation (9), we have the difficulty that, in the long-run, industries will differ in their C/Y^{NT} ratio. To solve this issue, we find the first order conditions of the above maximization problem for the function G:

$$\frac{K^{IT}}{C} = \left[\left(\frac{1-\alpha}{\alpha}\right)^{\sigma}\right]\left(\frac{P_K}{P}\right)^{-\sigma}$$

Or

$$\frac{C}{Y^{NT}} = \frac{PC}{P_K K^{IT}} \frac{P_K K^{IT}}{PY^{NT}} = \left[\left(\frac{1-\alpha}{\alpha}\right)^{\sigma}\right]\left(\frac{P_K}{P}\right)^{1-\sigma} s_{K^{IT}}$$

In the Cobb-Douglas case, we have that the C/Y^{NT} ratio is proportional to the observed ICT share, so ceteris paribus the bias in complementary capital is more relevant in industries intensive in ICT use. Substituting the last equation into (9), gives us the equation that we have to test.

$$\Delta TFP = [F_C - 1]\beta\tilde{k}_t + \left[\frac{(1-\delta_C)}{(1+g)}\right]\beta\tilde{k}_{t-1} + s_G\Delta z \tag{10}$$

where $\tilde{k}_t = \left(\frac{P_K}{P}\right)^{1-\sigma} s_{K^{ICT}}\left[\Delta k_t^{ICT} + \sigma\Delta p_t^{ICT}\right]$ and $\beta = \left(\frac{1-\alpha}{\alpha}\right)^{\sigma}$

Data and caveats

For data on TFP growth and ICT investment in France, Belgium, and the USA, we use a dataset,[6] financed by the European Commission (Research Directorate General) and developed by the Groningen Growth and Development Centre (GGDC) (University of Groningen, the Netherlands). This dataset contains observations on TFP and on ICT capital services (computers, communication equipment, and software) and also on the share of ICT capital in total capital compensation from 1970–2005. This chapter uses data from 1993–2005 on 30 industries (two-digit SIC industry codes). A list of these industries is attached in the Appendix.

In regressions described later in the chapter, we will also use data on software professionals in the USA. These data come from the Occupational Employment Statistics (OES) Survey,[7] conducted by the Bureau of Labor Statistics, Department of Labor of the US Government. This chapter uses data from 1997–2001 on 24 industries (two-digit SIC industry codes). Computer scientists are under the Occupation Code 25000 for the years 1997–98 and under the code 150000 for the years 1999–2001.[8] A list of these industries is attached in the Appendix.

Finally, regarding the level of disaggregation of the observations, we wish we had data on ICT investments at firm level, but we have it only at a fairly aggregated industry level. These and other data limitations will complicate our inference.

Empirical evidence on the role of ICT

As shown in the introduction, the gap in productivity growth between the USA and many European countries has been widening since the mid-1990s. While Basu et al. explore the correlation between productivity growth and ICT capital growth in the 1990s in the UK and in the USA, we want to extend their analysis to two other countries (France and Belgium) and also to a more recent period in the USA which covers the early 2000s.

In order to implement Basu et al.'s framework, we must make some assumptions regarding the time frame over which ICT investments and, more importantly, investments in complementary capital fully reveal their effects on productivity. As Basu et al. (2003, p. 29) recognize, there is no theoretical reason for choosing one time lag over another one, because "time lags will depend on factors such as the time it takes to learn/innovate/reorganize, which depend on the adjustment cost associated with that complementary capital investment." In order to make consistent comparisons between the three countries, we use the same time lag for Belgium, France, and the USA; that is, a four-year time lag. From the theoretical section, we know that the general model of interest is:

$$TFP_{it} = \beta_0 + \beta_1 ICT_{it} + \beta_2 ICT_{it\text{-}4} + \beta_3 ICT_{it\text{-}8} + \cdots + \gamma_i + v_{it} \qquad (11)$$

where
- TFP is Total Factor Productivity in 2001–05;
- ICT capital in 2001–05, 1997–2001 and 1993–97;
- an industry-specific fixed effect (γ_i);
- t is the period 2001–05, t-4 is 1997–01 and t-8 is 1993–97;
- i = 1, 2, ..., 30 industries in the dataset.

This model might suffer from a heterogeneity bias due to the presence of an industry-specific effect (γ_i). In order to have accurate estimates, we must adopt a procedure to eliminate γ_i. Here, we choose first-differencing. First, we calculate the growth rate of TFP and ICT year after year, which is indeed a first-difference. In this way, we can eliminate the time-invariant industry-specific fixed effect (γ_i). Then, following Basu et al., we average the differences across years to minimize the impact of year-to-year fluctuations on our regressions with an arithmetic mean over the years in the period. Thus, we estimate the following econometric model:

$$\Delta TFP_{it} = \delta_0 + \beta_1 \dot{K}_{it} + \beta_2 \dot{K}_{it\text{-}4} + \beta_3 \dot{K}_{it\text{-}8} + \Delta \nu_{it} \qquad (12)$$

where

$$\dot{K} = S_{KICT} * \Delta K_{ICT}$$

We regress average industry TFP growth in the period from 2001–05 over contemporaneous share-weighted growth in ICT capital services (defined as computers, communication equipment, and software) in 2001–05, share-weighted growth in ICT capital services with one lag (1997–2001), and share-weighted growth in ICT capital services with two lags (1993–97). (ΔTFP_{it}) is calculated as the average of yearly TFP growth during the period 2001–05 in each of the 30 industries of the dataset. Shared ICT capital growth (κ) is given by average industry share of ICT capital in total capital compensation in the period considered (e.g., 2001–05) times average industry ICT capital growth in the same period (e.g., 2001–05). The second term (ΔK_{ICT}) is calculated as the average of yearly ICT capital growth during the period 2001–05 in each of the 30 industries of the dataset and then is multiplied by yearly share of ICT Capital (S_{KICT}).

Basu et al. apply this equation to their data, treating the output and contemporaneous and lagged input measures for each industry as a single observation, but one in which time-invariant fixed effects within industries have been differenced away. When we derive the dependent variable (ΔTFP_{it}) and the independent variables (ΔK_{ICT}), we are, indeed, differencing observations across years. We present results based on this treatment of the data, to generate results comparable to those of Basu et al. In the next section, we utilize different treatments of the data.

The objective of this regression is to determine whether productivity growth in 2001–05 is larger in industries that had rapid share-weighted ICT growth in the mid-1990s or in the late 1990s or in the early 2000s or, of course, in none of the above.

Statistics about the macro performance of Belgium, France, and USA during the period 1980–2005 and about the acceleration of TFP growth for the three countries in the 1990s is available in the Appendix. Table 1.1 shows a summary of the mean and the standard deviation across the 30 industries of all the variables, based on equation (11) and Figure 1.3

Table 1.1   Summary of the statistics for TFP growth and for ICT capital

	Belgium		France		USA	
	Mean	**S.D.**	**Mean**	**S.D.**	**Mean**	**S.D.**
$\Delta TFP^{2001-05}$	−0.041	0.749	0.399	1.048	1.097	1.498
$\dot{K}^{2001-05}$	1.606	1.508	0.8	0.756	1.11	1.366
$\dot{K}^{1997-01}$	2.981	3.025	1.496	1.221	2.425	2.576
$\dot{K}^{1993-97}$	1.858	2.189	0.656	0.56	1.765	1.627

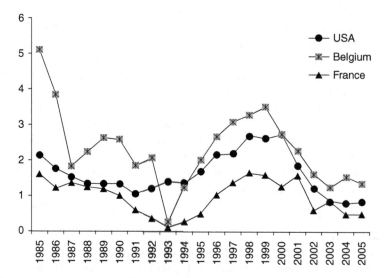

Figure 1.3   Contribution of ICT capital in Belgium, France, and USA (1985–2005) (% change)

Source: EU KLEMS.

shows the variation of the contribution of ICT capital in the three countries. Table 1.2 summarizes the results of the regressions with ΔTFP it as dependent variable and current and lagged share-weighted ICT capital growth as independent variables. Standard errors are in parentheses. The theory of a model of unmeasured complementary capital investment, developed in section 1.3 suggests that, controlling for lagged capital growth, ICT capital growth should be negatively correlated with contemporaneous TFP growth.

This is because while firms are making ICT investments, they are also diverting an increasing amount of worker time to installing the new

Table 1. 2 Effect of ICT capital growth on TFP growth

	Belgium	France	USA
C	−0.0757	0.5021	0.6441
	(0.1840)	(0.3062)	(0.3750)
$\dot{K}_t^{2001-05}$	−0.5010	−1.1060	−1.4109
	(0.1602)	(0.4146)	(0.5846)
$\dot{K}_{t-4}^{1997-01}$	0.4972	0.7216	0.9542
	(0.1602)	(0.2607)	(0.3813)
$\dot{K}_{t-8}^{1993-97}$	−0.3464	−0.4556	−0.1669
	(0.1607)	(0.3399)	(0.3062)
R^2	0.3411	0.2704	0.2439
Observations	30	30	30

Note: Standard errors are given in parentheses.

capital rather than producing marketable output. Theory also predicts that lagged ICT capital growth should be positively associated with TFP growth. As Table 1.2 clearly shows, we find that data from all the countries fit the theory. In fact, TFP growth is negatively correlated with contemporaneous ICT capital growth and positively associated with one-lag ICT capital growth.

U.S. TFP growth in the early 2000s: a case study

Alternative data treatment

The data treatment in the previous section followed Basu et al., but has its disadvantages. Those authors compressed their data into a single (differenced) observation for each industry, limiting the number of observations available. They also adopted a particular "lag structure" of ICT investment without presenting the reader with any exploratory regressions that could inform what the lag structure should be. The heart of the debate in this paragraph is centered on the nature of the industry fixed effect. In fact, if we think that γi is independent of all explanatory variables in all time periods, using a transformation to eliminate γi such as first-differencing or fixed effect, results in inefficient estimators.

In this section, we attempt to address these issues by returning to a levels specification, pooling our data across years and using the conventional Hausman test to compare three different treatments of the data: random effects (RE), fixed effect (FE), and pooled OLS (PO). The Hausman test fails to reject the null hypothesis of equivalence of RE and

FE for both the specifications of equations (13) and (14), which leads us to conclude that the RE estimators might be preferable in terms of efficiency to the FE ones. On the other hand, the Hausman test rejects the null hypothesis of equivalence of RE and PO and of equivalence of FE and PO for both the specifications of equations (13) and (14), which leads us to conclude that the RE estimators might be preferable in terms of efficiency to the PO ones. For the RE and FE estimation, we add year dummies to allow different intercepts across periods, which reflects the fact that we may have different distributions in different times, and with a larger number of observations, we do not need to exercise caution in using the RE and FE estimators any more, since they are now less sensitive to violations of the classical assumptions.

How many years do ICT investments need to become productive?

We estimate the following econometric model just for the USA, with random effect, fixed effect (at the industry level), and pooled OLS:

$$TFP_{it} = \beta_0 + \beta_1 ICT_{it} + \beta_2 ICT_{it-4} + \beta_3 ICT_{it-8} + \cdots + \gamma_i + \alpha_t + v_{it} \qquad (13)$$

where we regress TFP in 2001–05 on
- ICT capital in 2001–05, 1997–2001 and 1993–97;
- an industry-specific fixed effect (γi) and time dummies (αts);
- in i = 1, 2, ..., 30 industries in the dataset.

We also use this specification to explore the lag between ICT investment and its impact on productivity. Brynjolfsson and Hitt (2002), with an empirical study of 527 large US firms that covers the period 1987–94, find that computerization has a positive effect on productivity over long periods – that is, of about five to seven years. Basu et al. (2003) confirm these results of long-run effects of ICT on productivity during the 1990s, with a delay of about five years. Has this time lag become shorter in the 2000s? In fact, it is possible that it has changed. If sufficient organizational capital was accumulated in the 1990s, then it may be that a shorter period is now required to absorb new ICT investments in the productive process, since the base for the new investments has already been built. In particular, Anderson and Tushman (1986) argue that technology evolves through periods of incremental change punctuated by technological breakthroughs that either enhance or destroy the competences of firms in an industry. These effects decrease over successive discontinuities. Another theoretical reason to argue for shorter time lags is that ICT-literacy or human capital expertise in ICT is much more widespread in the 21st century in the USA than it was during the 1980–90s. We will address this question in the next section, where we explore the fundamental role of software engineers in the diffusion of information technologies across industries.

A quick look at Figure 1.4 supports the notion that a huge wave of ICT investments occurred during the 1990s and required a shift in the skills and knowledge base in order to operate the core technology. In the first years of the 21st century, we observe a much lower growth rate of ICT capital. Such incremental innovations substitute for older technologies, yet do not render obsolete skills required to master the old technologies. To explore these ideas more systematically, we run two fixed-effect OLS regressions, where the dependent variable is TFP in the period 2001–05. The independent variable is in both cases ICT capital lagged variable. In first case, the lag of reference is 1998–2002 while in the second case it is 1997–2001. Finally, we add ICT 1993–97 as a control in both regressions. The results are shown in Table 1.3: column (1) for the first regression and column (2) for the second. Notice that the signs of the coefficients are those predicted by the theory.

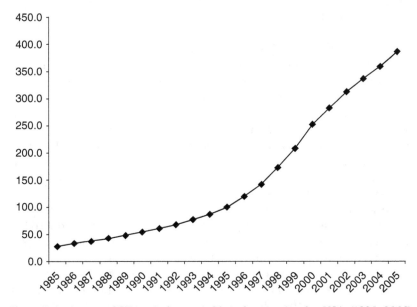

Figure 1.4 Average ICT capital across 30 industries in the USA (1985–2005) (1995=100), EU KLEMS

Source: EU KLEMS.

Table 1.3   Effect of ICT capital on TFP with different time lags

	(1) TFP 2001–05			(2) TFP 2001–05		
	RE	FE	PO	RE	FE	PO
ICT 2001–05	−0.0409	−0.0402	−0.0630	−0.0518	−0.0502	−0.0859
	(0.0109)	(0.0116)	(0.0176)	(0.0125)	(0.0131)	(0.0221)
ICT 1998–02				0.0909	0.0873	0.1626
				(0.0194)	(0.0197)	(0.0421)
ICT 1997–01	0.0919	0.0887	0.1657			
	(0.0198)	(0.0201)	(0.0453)			
ICT 1993–97	−0.0822	−0.0807	−0.1625	−0.0585	−0.0577	−0.1114
	(0.0419)	(0.0421)	(0.0857)	(0.0394)	(0.0396)	(0.0713)
R^2	0.3817	0.3818	0.1152	0.3827	0.3829	0.1239
Industry	30	30	30	30	30	30
Observations	150	150	150	150	150	150

Note: Standard errors are given in parentheses.

We view the results of Table 1.3 as providing some support for the notion that the lag between ICT investment and its impact on measured productivity has declined since 2000, coherently with the idea of a shorter time lag than the one observed by Brynjolfsson and Hitt (2002) for the economy of the USA during the 1980s and mid-1990s and by Basu et al. (2003) during the 1990s.

The fundamental role of software engineers

Basu et al. (2003) supply an interesting model of unmeasured complementary capital investment, but do not explain what complementary capital means. They argue that complementary capital accumulated by the firms in the economy is constituted by the resource cost of training workers and creating new business structures to take advantage of ICT; this concept is somewhat vague and open-ended. Bloom et al. (2008) offer a slightly different conceptualization of complementary capital that focuses on the decentralization of decision-making and adoption of labor market practices that enhance worker productivity.

While not denying the potential explanatory power of these views in helping us understand the impact of ICT investment on productivity, we offer a different and more narrowly technological view of complementary capital. We also argue that firms need costly co-investments in complementary capital to fully benefit from ICT investments as in Bresnahan et al. (2002), but we focus more on the customization process required in these ICT investments. Standardized ICT hardware and packaged software are widely available internationally. However, we posit that these standard components must be organized into customized or semicustomized networks designed to meet the needs of individual businesses. This process of customization is irreducibly labor intensive, requiring the engagement of professionals who both understand business processes and can design software systems to enable these processes. In fact, firms need the efforts of software engineers and computer scientists, in order to customize ICT investments to the specific needs of their firms. There is excellent reason to believe that the availability of workers with these skills varies widely across OECD economies. The USA trains and educates a larger number of skilled software professionals than any other OECD economy. But in addition to the "indigenously trained" software engineers that it generates, the US economy has also been able to import large numbers of software professionals from other countries (especially India) during periods in which demand for these skills was especially strong. In fact, in some years during the 1990s, the USA arguably imported more software professionals than it produced domestically. More recently, US firms have been able to outsource much of their software customization work to offshore suppliers of these services. Since the late 1990s, the USA has accounted for between 60 and 70 percent of Indian software exports; all of Europe accounts for 30 percent or less. Accounting for its indigenously trained engineers, its imported engineers and its offshore contingent software engineering labor force, it is likely that the USA has access to a much, much larger pool of human resources to tap for these software customization projects. This keeps the quality adjusted price of these services low for US firms, even small ones. Unfortunately, data limitations constrain our ability to undertake a direct comparison of available software labor resources across EU economies and beside the USA.

In principle, the European labor force survey coordinated by Eurostat (http://epp.eurostat.ec.europa.eu/statistics_explained/index.php/Employment_statistics) contains the information we would need to compare employment of software engineers across industries and countries, but we were unable to obtain access to these data. In principle, the Indian software industry association NASSCOM provides data on the regional and country breakdown of software exports that could be employed to estimate European access to offshore workers, but we have yet to acquire these data as well. However, if there is anything to our notion of software engineers playing a special role in creating this narrower concept of complementary capital, than that suggests a positive correlation in the data between TFP and the intensity of software engineering skills in the industrial labor force. So, the larger the share of software engineers in a particular industry, the greater the benefits of ICT capital on TFP in that industry. In order to test this hypothesis, we estimate the following econometric model for the USA, with fixed effect, random effect (at industry level), and pooled OLS:

$$\text{TFP}_{it} = \beta_0 + \beta_1 \text{ICT}_{it} + \beta_2 \text{ICT}_{it\text{-}4} + \beta_3 \text{ICT}_{it\text{-}8} + \beta_3 \text{ENG}_{it\text{-}4} + \gamma_i + \alpha_t \nu_{it} \qquad (14)$$

where we regress TFP in 2001–05 on
- ICT Capital in 2001–05, 1997–2001 and 1993–97;
- the ratio of computer scientists to total employment (ENG) in 1997–2001;
- an industry-specific fixed effect (γ_i) and time dummies (α_ts);
- in i = 1, 2, ..., 24 industries in the dataset.

In some specifications of the above model, we include also an interaction term between $\text{ICT}_{it\text{-}4}$ and $\text{ENG}_{it\text{-}4}$ to fully capture the effect of the work of software engineers on the diffusion of ICT capital in an industry. The results of the fixed effect regressions are shown in Table 1.4. First, notice the sign of the coefficients are those predicted by the theory. Column (1) of Table 1.4 is important because it shows a direct, positive, and statistically significant effect on TFP_{it} of the one-period-lagged share of computer scientists of total employment in industry i, when this term is introduced in Basu et al.'s (2003) model of unmeasured complementary capital. Column (2) is probably the most difficult to interpret,

Table 1. 4   Effect of ICT capital and of software engineers on TFP (fixed effect)

	1	2	3	4
ICT 2001–05	−0.0556	−0.0542	−0.0542	−0.0528
	(0.0118)	(0.0120)	(0.0120)	(0.0121)
ICT 1997–01	0.2096	0.2071	0.2107	0.2032
	(0.0277)	(0.0280)	(0.0278)	(0.0281)
ICT 1993–97	−0.2489	−0.2514	−0.2514	−0.2575
	(0.0478)	(0.0481)	(0.0481)	(0.0483)
S. Engineers 1997–01	1.3114	0.9515	1.1751	
	(0.3073)	(0.5963)	(0.3639)	
Interaction		0.0011		0.0032
		(0.0015)		(0.0008)
Normalized interaction			0.0011	
at ICT mean			(0.0015)	
R^2	0.5962	0.5985	0.5985	0.5867
Industries	24	24	24	24
Observations	120	120	120	120

since neither the coefficient on the share of computer scientists, nor the coefficient on the interaction term are significant.

To solve this problem, following the procedure in any textbook, we normalized the interaction term at the mean of ICT capital in the period 1997–2001. Column (3) shows this new specification. The new coefficient on ENG_{it-4} is the effect on TFP of the one-period-lagged share of computer scientists at the mean of ICT capital. This effect is positive and statistically significant. Finally, Column (4) is just a check to show that the statistically insignificant coefficient on the share of computer scientists in Column (2) is caused by a problem of multicollinearity, given by the high correlation between the coefficients. Indeed, when we replace the term ENG_{it-4} in the specification of model (13) with the interaction term, the latter becomes also significant. Tables 1.5 and 1.6 show the results of random effect and pooled OLS regressions, respectively.

The most important theoretical implication of Table 1.4 is that the coefficient on the share of software engineers, especially the one found in Column (3), is probably the best description of the complementary capital accumulation: at time 1, firms in a given industry invest in IT capital and accumulate complementary capital in the form of knowledge embedded in their employees and in software engineers, which customizes ICT investments. Over the next period, these investments are realized in the form of TFP growth.

Table 1.5 Effect of ICT capital and of software engineers on TFP (random effect)

	1	2	3	4
ICT 2001–05	−0.0563	−0.0539	−0.0539	−0.0530
	(0.0115)	(0.0123)	(0.0123)	(0.0117)
ICT 1997–01	0.2107	0.2056	0.2056	0.2031
	(0.0273)	(0.0292)	(0.0292)	(0.0276)
ICT 1993–97	−0.2489	−0.2518	−0.2518	−0.2558
	(0.0474)	(0.0506)	(0.0506)	(0.0477)
S. Engineers 1997–01	1.1249	0.4443	0.8883	
	(0.2621)	(0.4830)	(0.2747)	
Interaction		0.0021		0.0032
		(0.0015)		(0.0007)
Normalized interaction at ICT mean			0.0021	
			(0.0015)	
R^2	0.5946	0.5951	0.5951	0.5867
Industries	24	24	24	24
Observations	120	120	120	120

Table 1.6   Effect of ICT capital and of software engineers on TFP (pooled OLS)

	1	2	3	4
ICT 2001–05	−0.0564	−0.0452	−0.0452	−0.0511
	(0.0231)	(0.0220)	(0.0220)	(0.0227)
ICT 1997–01	0.2033	0.1478	0.1478	0.1865
	(0.0599)	(0.0586)	(0.0586)	(0.0590)
ICT 1993–97	−0.2306	−0.2431	−0.2431	−0.2311
	(0.1029)	(0.0975)	(0.0975)	(0.1007)
S. Engineers 1997–01	0.6410	−2.7119	0.7925	
	(0.2218)	(0.9133)	(0.2139)	
Interaction		0.0169		0.0039
		(0.0044)		(0.0010)
Normalized interaction at ICT mean			0.0169	
			(0.0044)	
R^2	0.1819	0.2727	0.2727	0.2165
Industries	24	24	24	24
Observations	120	120	120	120

In the next paragraph, we summarize our conclusions and we sketch some policy implications associated with the above predictions.

Conclusion

This chapter extends the previous literature in two separate ways. In the first section, we applied Basu et al.'s (2003) model of unmeasured complementary capital investment to the USA, Belgium, and France. Whereas Basu et al. find mixed evidence, at best, for the view that slow productivity growth in the UK can be explained by their model of complementary capital investment, we find much stronger evidence that relatively meager productivity growth in Belgium and France exhibit patterns consistent with the Basu et al. model. In particular, while Basu et al. argue that the acceleration of TFP growth in the USA during the period 1995–2000 was due to early investments in ICT and complementary capital during the 1980s and early 1990s, we can argue that the USA continued to invest in ICT and in complementary capital during the late 1990s and we trace the benefits of these investments on TFP growth during the first years of the 21st century. We also find that the USA continued these investments in ICT during the first years of the 2000s, the benefits of which should be realized in the next years. We fully recognize that Basu et al.'s parsimonious specification includes few controls and the limitations of the data allow for relatively little in the way of robustness checks. We treat this evidence as preliminary, and we hope to undertake further investigation with more disaggregated data over a larger sample of countries and years as the research project progresses.

In the second section, we began to investigate the concept of complementary capital that lies at the core of the Basu et al. model, and we began to search for empirical measures of different aspects of this capital concept. While it is likely that organizational restructuring and re-engineering is necessary in order to realize the full benefits of ICT investment, we also believe that ICT hardware and standardized software needs to be combined with custom programming, creating networks and systems designed to apply the power of the standardized components in a way that best meets the idiosyncratic needs of individual businesses. This debate is present also in the literature, where one school of thought focuses on the concept of "organizational capital," while the other focuses on the concept of "social capital."

The former relies on the organizational supremacy of US firms with respect to the rest of the world, while the latter argue that the environment in the USA per se gives an advantage in exploiting ICT investments, thanks to the access to a high-skilled job market. Organizational capital can be described as changes in business processes, organization structure, and innovations in customer and supplier relations. Brynjolfsson and Hitt (2000, p. 25) find that "total capital stock (including intangible assets) associated with the computerization of the economy may be understated by a factor of ten" and they also refer to Milgrom and Roberts (1990) arguing that "to be successful, firms need to adopt computers as part of a 'system' or 'cluster' of mutually reinforcing organizational changes". On the other hand, social capital can be described as changes in the relations among organizations in the forms of trust, information channels and norms. In this regard, Chandler (1977 cited in Basu et al. 2003, p. 21), focusing on the relevance of social capital in each nation, notes that "new technologies may be somewhat specific to a country's particular and institutional arrangements and Coleman (1988) shows that social capital has a major role in the creation of human capital. Software does not (yet) write itself; the customization process is irreducibly labor intensive and requires the engagement of skilled workers who understand both the needs of the adopting enterprise and the technical details of software customization. If our view is correct, then this necessary process of customization creates a role for human capital, in the form of highly skilled labor supply, to impact the process of ICT investment.

While we have not yet been able to access high-quality data that measures the numbers of software workers across industries, countries, and time, we find evidence strongly supporting the view that the USA has access to a much larger software workforce than any other OECD economy, even adjusting for the relatively large size of the economy of the USA. Institutional economists focus only on the third form of social capital and show that institutions facilitate the transfer of knowledge and information across firms, reducing uncertainty (Johnson, 1992). Thus, the firm is at the center of a cluster of clients, suppliers, financial and public institutions, and universities. In particular, Porter's Diamond of National Advantage puts factor conditions at the heart of this interaction and assigns to government the role of creating specialized factors (Porter, 1990). We cannot deny that, in the USA thanks to more market-oriented universities that fostered the advanced development of training programs for indigenous workers, thanks to public policies more oriented to the openness of labor markets to highly skilled immigrants and thanks to the ability of US firms to outsource software programming tasks to firms located offshore (especially in India) – the labor force available for software customization is quite large.

Our view suggests the existence of a correlation between lagged measures of software worker intensity in the labor force of an industry and TFP – a correlation that parallels that of the lagged ICT investment variable in timing. It is also possible that the level of software worker intensity could raise the productivity of ICT investment, suggesting an interaction term.

We present extremely preliminary regressions that validate the existence of a correlation between software intensity and TFP. We acknowledge that these findings are at best indicative, and plan to pursue this further with more disaggregated and complete data for multiple countries. The policy implications of our alternative view could differ from that of Basu et al. (2003). Basu and his co-authors suggest that, at least for the UK, the productivity impact of ICT investment could very well rise to US-like levels in the near future. The absence of this productivity surge to date is largely a consequence of the UK having begun its ICT investment a bit later. It is possible, though, that, if an economy's inability to access software labor constrains its returns on ICT investment, Europe may not realize a US-like productivity surge from its ICT investment until and unless it can muster more labor resources for the necessary process of customization. This raises a possible role for immigration, training, and "outsourcing promotion" policies in closing the transatlantic productivity divergence.

Appendix

Table A1.1 United States of America: total factor productivity growth by industry, 1990–2005

Industries	2001–2005	1996–2000	Acceleration	1996–2000	1990–1995	Acceleration
Agriculture, hunting, forestry, fishing	1.00	1.86	−0.86	1.86	1.25	0.62
Mining and quarrying	−3.56	1.26	−4.82	1.26	1.28	−0.02
Food, beverages, and tobacco	0.94	0.08	0.85	0.08	0.26	−0.18
Textiles, textile , leather, and footwear	1.46	1.85	−0.38	1.85	0.43	1.42
Wood and of wood and cork	0.48	0.11	0.37	0.11	−1.52	1.63
Pulp, paper, paper , printing, publishing	1.40	1.12	0.28	1.12	−0.95	2.07
Coke, refined petroleum, and nuclear fuel	−0.04	−3.00	2.96	−3.00	−0.06	−2.94
Chemicals and chemical products	0.72	0.52	0.20	0.52	−0.01	0.54
Rubber and plastics	1.36	1.40	−0.04	1.40	1.09	0.31
Other non-metallic mineral	1.45	0.99	0.46	0.99	0.40	0.59
Basic metals and fabricated metal	0.35	1.98	−1.64	1.98	0.77	1.22
Machinery, NEC	2.24	0.59	1.64	0.59	0.22	0.37
Electrical and optical equipment	4.23	7.97	−3.74	7.97	3.97	4.00
Transport equipment	2.11	0.75	1.36	0.75	0.12	0.63
Manufacturing nec; recycling	2.36	1.22	1.14	1.22	0.24	0.98
Electricity, gas and water supply	−0.22	1.84	−2.06	1.84	0.25	1.59
Construction	−0.59	−1.08	0.49	−1.08	−1.29	0.22
Sale, maintenance, and repair of motor vehicles	2.48	2.38	0.10	2.38	0.98	1.41
Wholesale trade and commission trade	0.60	0.11	0.49	0.11	0.83	−0.72
Retail trade	3.21	1.93	1.28	1.93	0.17	1.76
Hotels and restaurants	0.93	−0.66	1.59	−0.66	−0.12	−0.54
Transport and storage	1.50	−0.42	1.92	−0.42	0.43	−0.85
Post and telecommunications	4.44	−1.34	5.78	−1.34	0.05	−1.39
Financial intermediation	0.42	1.94	−1.53	1.94	0.23	1.71
Real estate activities	1.56	−0.31	1.86	−0.31	0.60	−0.91
Renting of M&EQ and other business activities	0.60	−1.47	2.08	−1.47	−0.81	−0.66
Public admin and defence	−0.31	−0.08	−0.23	−0.08	−0.14	0.07
Education	0.30	−0.53	0.83	−0.53	−0.25	−0.28
Health and social work	1.18	−0.27	1.45	−0.27	−1.06	0.79
Other services	0.30	−0.39	0.69	−0.39	−0.49	0.10
Average across industries	1.10	0.68	0.42	0.68	0.23	0.45

Source: EU KLEMS.

Table A1.2   France: total factor productivity growth by industry, 1990–2005

Industries	2001–2005	1996–2000	Acceleration	1996–2000	1990–1995	Acceleration
Agriculture, hunting, forestry, fishing	0.60	1.24	−0.64	1.24	2.71	−1.47
Mining and quarrying	0.43	−5.59	6.02	−5.59	2.37	−7.96
Food , beverages, and tobacco	0.23	−0.21	0.44	−0.21	−0.18	−0.03
Textiles, textile , leather, and footwear	0.91	0.84	0.07	0.84	0.18	0.65
Wood and of wood and cork	1.57	1.63	−0.06	1.63	1.02	0.61
Pulp, paper, paper , printing, publishing	0.37	0.30	0.07	0.30	−0.16	0.46
Coke, refined petroleum, and nuclear fuel	−0.16	2.19	−2.35	2.19	7.51	−5.32
Chemicals and chemical products	0.36	−0.21	0.57	−0.21	0.15	−0.36
Rubber and plastics	1.50	4.46	−2.96	4.46	4.90	−0.44
Other non-metallic mineral	−0.27	1.06	−1.33	1.06	0.39	0.68
Basic metals and fabricated metal	0.07	0.35	−0.29	0.35	−0.61	0.97
Machinery, nec	1.38	1.59	−0.22	1.59	0.96	0.63
Electrical and optical equipment	1.65	1.91	−0.27	1.91	1.88	0.03
Transport equipment	−0.03	1.28	−1.31	1.28	0.41	0.87
Manufacturing NEC; recycling	−0.54	1.45	−1.99	1.45	0.45	1.00
Electricity, gas, and water supply	2.30	1.53	0.76	1.53	1.01	0.52
Construction	−0.35	−0.17	−0.18	−0.17	0.28	−0.45
Sale, maintenance and repair of motor vehicles	−1.45	−1.12	−0.33	−1.12	−2.24	1.12
Wholesale trade and commission trade	0.13	1.30	−1.17	1.30	2.11	−0.81
Retail trade	−0.12	−0.36	0.24	−0.36	0.62	−0.97
Hotels and restaurants	−0.65	0.29	−0.94	0.29	−1.40	1.68
Transport and storage	−0.10	1.66	−1.76	1.66	0.99	0.67
Post and telecommunications	3.51	4.70	−1.18	4.70	2.15	2.54
Financial intermediation	−0.21	0.66	−0.87	0.66	−0.90	1.56
Real estate activities	0.48	1.60	−1.12	1.60	0.75	0.86
Renting of M&EQ and other business activities	−0.35	−0.91	0.56	−0.91	−1.60	0.69
Public admin and defence	0.58	0.43	0.15	0.43	−0.21	0.64
Education	−1.58	−1.60	0.02	−1.60	−0.68	−0.91
Health and social work	0.52	−0.99	1.50	−0.99	−0.27	−0.71
Other services	1.19	0.72	0.47	0.72	−0.64	1.36
Average across industries	0.40	0.67	−0.27	0.67	0.73	−0.06

Source: EU KLEMS.

Table A1.3 Belgium: total factor productivity growth by industry, 1990–2000

Industries	2001–05	1996–00	Acceleration	1996–00	1990–95	Acceleration
Agriculture, hunting, forestry, fishing	−0.47	1.48	−1.94	1.48	2.07	−0.59
Mining and quarrying	−0.16	−0.55	0.39	−0.55	0.09	−0.64
Food, beverages, and tobacco	0.35	−0.37	0.72	−0.37	−0.21	−0.15
Textiles, textile, leather, and footwear	0.41	0.80	−0.39	0.80	0.68	0.12
Wood and of wood and cork	0.77	0.64	0.13	0.64	−0.21	0.86
Pulp, paper, paper, printing, publishing	0.48	−0.58	1.07	−0.58	−0.55	−0.04
Coke, refined petroleum, and nuclear fuel	−0.04	−1.61	1.57	−1.61	−0.72	−0.89
Chemicals and chemical products	−0.26	0.03	−0.28	0.03	−0.14	0.16
Rubber and plastics	1.74	0.36	1.38	0.36	1.44	−1.08
Other non-metallic mineral	−0.07	−0.61	0.54	−0.61	0.43	−1.04
Basic metals and fabricated metal	−0.05	0.67	−0.72	0.67	−0.04	0.71
Machinery, NEC	−0.07	1.79	−1.85	1.79	−0.73	2.52
Electrical and optical equipment	−0.05	2.65	−2.70	2.65	−0.40	3.05
Transport equipment	0.41	0.47	−0.06	0.47	−0.33	0.80
Manufacturing NEC; recycling	−0.30	1.06	−1.36	1.06	−0.23	1.29
Electricity, gas, and water supply	−0.79	3.64	−4.43	3.64	−0.16	3.81
Construction	0.42	0.01	0.41	0.01	0.27	−0.26
Sale, maintenance, and repair of motor vehicles	−1.16	−0.72	−0.44	−0.72	−1.36	0.64
Wholesale trade and commission trade	0.40	−1.59	2.00	−1.59	−0.97	−0.62
Retail trade	−0.84	0.07	−0.92	0.07	−0.36	0.43
Hotels and restaurants	−0.63	−0.29	−0.34	−0.29	−0.61	0.33
Transport and storage	0.05	−0.78	0.83	−0.78	0.96	−1.74
Post and telecommunications	1.46	−1.55	3.01	−1.55	−1.31	−0.24
Financial intermediation	1.28	2.07	−0.79	2.07	3.24	−1.16
Real estate activities	−1.71	−1.50	−0.21	−1.50	−0.56	−0.94
Renting of M&EQ and other business activities	−0.06	−0.69	0.63	−0.69	−0.09	−0.59
Public admin and defence	−0.61	0.10	−0.71	0.10	0.89	−0.79
Education	−0.57	0.20	−0.77	0.20	−0.57	0.77
Health and social work	−0.43	−0.61	0.18	−0.61	−0.84	0.23
Other services	−0.76	−0.69	−0.07	−0.69	−0.13	−0.56
Average across industries	−0.04	0.13	−0.17	0.13	−0.02	0.15

Source: EU KLEMS.

Table A1.4   Macro performance: USA, France, and Belgium (annual percentage change)

	1980–85	1985–90	1990–95	1995–00	2000–05
GDP Growth					
USA	2.62	3.33	2.35	3.78	2.50
France	1.57	2.97	1.40	2.63	2.00
Belgium	1.50	2.80	1.83	2.65	1.95
Hours worked annual growth rate					
USA	1.23	2.00	1.12	1.97	0.15
France	−1.35	0.27	−0.50	0.45	0.23
Belgium	−0.92	0.68	−0.37	1.17	0.70
Labor Productivity growth rate (GDP per hour worked)					
USA	1.23	1.35	1.23	1.82	2.33
France	0.55	2.68	1.87	2.22	1.80
Belgium	0.92	2.12	2.22	1.43	1.23
Multi-Factor Productivity growth rate					
USA		0.80	0.70	1.20	1.65
France		2.00	1.10	1.40	1.07
Belgium		1.60	1.40	1.30	1.04*
Contribution of ICT Equipment to growth of total capital services					
USA		1.90	2.10	4.50	2.31
France		1.20	0.90	2.30	1.60
Belgium		1.90	1.40	2.40	1.98*
Contribution of NON-ICT Equipment to growth of total capital services					
USA		2.00	1.40	2.30	1.92
France		2.10	1.50	1.50	1.55
Belgium		1.90	1.50	0.90	1.54*

*Excludes 2005.

Source: OECD.

Table A1.5 List of industries and conversion table

Industries	European SIC code	Industries	American SIC code
Agriculture, hunting, forestry, fishing	AtB		
Mining and quarrying	C	Mining and quarrying	10,12t14
Food , beverages, and tobacco	15t16	Food and tobacco	20t21
Textiles, textile , leather, and footwear	17t19	Textile and leather	22t23,31
Wood and of wood and cork	20	Wood	24
Pulp, paper, paper , printing, publishing	21t22	Paper and publishing	26t27
Coke, refined petroleum and nuclear fuel	23	Petroleum	29
Chemicals and chemical products	24	Chemicals	28
Rubber and plastics	25	Rubber and plastics	30
Other non-metallic mineral	26		
Basic and fabricated metals	27t28	Basic and fabricated metals	33t34
Machinery, nec	29		
Electrical and optical equipment	30t33	Electrical and optical equipment	35t36, 38
Transport equipment	34t35	Transport equipment	37
Manufacturing NEC; recycling	36t37	Manufacturing nec	39
Electricity, gas, and water supply	E	Electricity, gas and water	49
Construction	F	Construction	15t17
Sale, maintenance, and repair of motor vehicles	50	Sale, maintenance, repair of motor vehicles	55,75
Wholesale trade and commission trade	51	Wholesale trade	50t51
Retail trade	52	Retail trade	52t54, 56t57, 59
Hotels and restaurants	H	Hotels and restaurants	58, 70
Transport and storage	60t63	Transport and storage	40t47
Post and telecommunications	64	Post and telecommunications	48
Financial intermediation	J	Financial intermediation	60t64, 67
Real estate activities	70	Real estate activities	65
Renting of M&EQ and other business activities	71t74		
Public admin and defence	L		
Education	M	Education	82
Health and social work	N	Health	80
Other services	O		

Notes

1. Throughout the chapter, we will refer to "investment in ICT hardware", but we consider purchases of packaged software to be part of this investment. In most datasets in OECD countries, purchases of packaged software are tracked with some degree of completeness; unfortunately, custom and "own account" software is not measured as comprehensively, and there are now good price indices with which one can deflate these purchases. These omissions of the data are important in our reinterpretation of the Basu et al. model, as explained later in the chapter.
2. This paradox was summed up in a quip attributed to Nobel Laureate Robert Solow, who noted, in the late 1980s, "We see computers everywhere except in the productivity statistics."
3. In the 1960s, the French government declared its intention to create "the great European city of science in the sun." The result was Sophia Antipolis. Located on the French Riviera between Nice and Cannes, Sophia Antipolis is about a quarter of the size of Paris and has been a slow-burning project, making steady progress over the years without grabbing the imagination (Des Dearlove, "The Cluster Effect: Can Europe Clone Silicon Valley?", *Strategy+Business*, Third Quarter, 2001).
4. For our theoretical model, we closely follow Basu et al. (2003). Bloom et al. (2008) and Bresnahan et al. (2002) also emphasize the notion of complementary capital in their own work on the impact of ICT on productivity.
5. Bresnahan et al. (2002) refer to how information technology is used in production as a process of organizational redesign and of substantial changes to product and service mix, not just as a process of plugging in computers and telecommunications equipment in order to achieve service quality or efficiency gains.
6. This dataset is available at http://www.euklems.org
7. This dataset is available at http://www.bls.gov/oes/
8. The difference in the occupational code across the years regards all the occupational codes in the database. It is part of a more general refocusing of the Bureau of Labor Statistics in order to better track all the new professions, but the specific category considered in this study is always labeled as "computer scientists" in each of the five years.
9. We have data about the ratio of computer scientists compared to total employment in 1997–2001 for 24 industries only. Thus, we have to decrease the number of industries from the original 30 of the European SIC code to the current 24 of the American SIC code. A list of industries and a 'conversion' table is given in the Appendix.

References

Altomonte, C. and M. Nava (2005) *Economics and Policies of an Enlarged Europe*, Cheltenham and Northampton: Edward Elgar.
Anderson, P. and M.L. Tushman (1986) "Technological Discontinuities and Organizational Environments", *Administrative Science Quarterly*, Vol. 31, No. 3, pp. 439–65.

Audretsch, D.B. and S. Klepper (2000) *Innovation, Evolution of Industry and Economic Growth*, Cheltenham and Northampton: Edward Elgar.

Basu, S., J.G. Fernald and M.D. Shapiro (2001) "Productivity Growth in the 1990s: Technology, Utilization, or Adjustment?", *Carnegie-Rochester Conference Series on Public Policy*, Vol. 55, No. 1, December, pp. 117–165.

Basu, S., J.G. Fernald, N. Oulton and S. Srinivasan (2003) "The Case of the Missing Productivity Growth: Or, Does Information Technology Explain Why Productivity Accelerated in the United States but Not the United Kingdom?", Federal Reserve Bank of Chicago, WP 2003–08.

Bloom, N., R. Sadun and J. Van Reenen (2008) "Americans Do IT Better: US Multinationals and the Productivity Miracle", NBER Working Paper 13085.

Bosworth, B.P. and J.E. Triplett (2002) "Baumol's Disease has been Cured: IT and Multifactor Productivity in US Services Industries", Brookings Workshop on Services Industry Productivity.

Bresnahan, T.F. and M. Trajtenberg (1995) "General Purpose Technologies: Engines of Growth", *Journal of Econometrics*, Vol. 65, No. 1, pp. 83–108.

Bresnahan, T.F., E. Brynjolfsson and L.M. Hitt (2002), "Information Technology, Workplace Organization and the Demand for Skilled Labor: Firm-level Evidence", *The Quarterly Journal of Economics*, Vol. 117, No. 1, pp. 339–76.

Brynjolfsson, E. and L.M. Hitt (2000) "Beyond Computation: Information Technology, Organizational Transformation and Business Performance", *Journal of Economic Perspectives*, Vol. 14, No. 4, pp. 24–48.

Brynjolfsson, E. and L.M. Hitt (2002) "Computing Productivity: Firm-Level Evidence", MIT Working Paper (4210–01).

Chandler Jr, A.D. (1977) The Visible Hand: The Managerial Revolution in American Business, Cambridge, MA: Harvard University Press.

Cohen, W. and D. Levinthal (1990) "Absorptive Capacity: A New Perspective on Learning and Innovation", *Administrative Science Quarterly*, Vol. 35, pp. 128–52.

Coleman, J.S. (1988) "Social Capital in the Creation of Human Capital", *American Journal of Sociology*, Vol. 94, pp. 95–120.

European Commission (2004) *The EU Economy: 2004 Review*, Directorate-General for Economic and Financial Affairs.

European Commission (2007) *The EU Economy: 2007 Review*, Directorate-General for Economic and Financial Affairs.

Greenwood, J. and M. Yorukoglu (1997) "1974", *Carnegie-Rochester Conference Series on Public Policy*, Vol. 46, pp. 49–95.

Gust, C. and J. Marquez (2004) "International Comparisons of Productivity Growth: The Role of Information Technology and Regulatory Practices", Labor Economics , Vol. 11, No. 1, *pp. 33*–58.

Inklaar, R., M.P. Timmer and B. van Ark (2007) "Mind the Gap! International Comparisons of Productivity in Services and Goods Production", *German Economic Review*, Oxford: Blackwell.

Johnson, A. (1992) "Functions in Innovation System Approaches" mimeo for Nelson and Winter Conference in Aalborg, June 12–15, 2001

Jorgenson, D.W. and K.J. Stiroh (1999) "Information Technology and Growth", *American Economic Review*, Vol. 89, No. 2, pp. 109–15.

Jorgenson, D.W. and K.J. Stiroh (2000) "U.S. Economic Growth at the Industry Level", *American Economic Review*, Vol. 90, No. 2, pp. 161–7.

McGrattan, E.R. and E.C. Prescott (2009) "Openness, Technology Capital and Development", *Journal of Economic Theory*, Vol. 144, No. 6, pp. 2454–76.

Milgrom, P. and J.M. Roberts (1990) "The Economics of Modern Manufacturing: Technology, Strategy and Organization", *American Economic Review*, Vol. 80, No. 3, pp. 511–28.

Nelson, R. (1993) *National Innovation Systems*, Oxford University Press.

Porter, M.E. (1990) "The Competitive Advantage of Nations", *Harvard Business Review*, Vol. 68, No. 2.

Stiroh, J.K. 2001. "Information technology and the U.S. productivity revival: what do the industry data say?," Staff Reports 115, Federal Reserve Bank of New York.

Van Ark, B., J. Melka, N. Mulder, M. Timmer and G. Ypma (2002) "ICT Investments and Growth Account for the European Union, 1980–2000", Final Report for the DG Economics and Finance of the European Commission.

2
Technical Efficiency and the Role of Information Technology: A Stochastic Production Frontier Study across OECD Countries

Sophia P. Dimelis and Sotiris K. Papaioannou

Introduction

Information and communication technology (ICT) is considered as the latest major technological breakthrough which is expected to have a significant impact on long-run economic growth. Now, it is almost certain that ICT had a significant impact on labor productivity growth in the USA and EU and accounts for a part of the faster productivity growth witnessed in USA during the late 1990s (van Ark et al., 2003). There is less consensus, however, among economists on its impact on technical progress and total factor productivity (TFP) growth (see Gordon, 2000).

According to the findings of Stiroh (2002), ICT is correlated with labor productivity growth but not correlated with TFP growth in US manufacturing industries. We wish to contribute to this direction by examining the impact of ICT capital (which constitutes a part of TFP) on the technical efficiency of OECD countries. The existing literature has concentrated more on the effects of ICT on growth or productivity and, although an essential relationship exists between efficiency and productivity (Grosskopf, 1993), the question of whether ICT affects the level of technical efficiency has been examined in few firm-level samples (Lee and Barua, 1999; Milana and Zeli, 2002; Becchetti et al., 2003) and recently in two cross-country studies (Thompson and Garbacz, 2007; Repkine, 2008). We contribute to the relevant literature in several ways. As compared to other cross-country studies, our study employs a much broader cluster of ICT inputs which includes hardware, software and communications.

We believe that the essential characteristic of ICT is the match of computers and chips with sophisticated software and communication networks. In this way we treat ICT as an entire cluster of interrelated assets, the impact of which we intend to test for technical efficiency. Second, this study does not treat ICT as a conventional type of input affecting output through traditional channels of capital deepening. Instead, we evaluate the ICT impact by explicitly assuming that ICT is a special type of technology and knowledge capital, the impact of which should be evaluated on TFP through the channel of technical efficiency.

Finally, and more importantly, we evaluate the percentage contribution of ICT in reducing cross-country inefficiencies by using a framework developed by Coelli et al. (1999). At the aggregate cross-country level, the measurement of technical efficiency might be quite important in identifying ways to promote economic growth. A low level of technical efficiency, for an individual country, would imply that higher economic development could be achieved by efficiently producing more output with the same level of inputs. On the other hand, a highly efficient country should rely more on technical progress in order to achieve a higher level of economic development.

We use stochastic frontier analysis to quantify the impact of ICT in cross-country technical efficiency. A stochastic production frontier approach is used which simultaneously estimates a stochastic production frontier with a technical inefficiency function (Battese and Coelli, 1995). We apply this approach by looking into the effects of ICT on technical inefficiency across a selection of 17 OECD countries (Australia, Austria, Belgium, Denmark, Finland, France, Germany, Greece, Ireland, Italy, Japan, Netherlands, Portugal, Spain, Sweden, United Kingdom, United States) in the period 1990–2005. Clear evidence is found for a significant ICT impact in the reduction of cross-country inefficiencies. In particular, the results show that, on average, ICT contributed by more than 5 percent to the increase of technical efficiency. The efficiency estimates indicate that the most efficient countries are Belgium and the Netherlands, followed by the USA.

The rest of this chapter is organized as follows. The next section summarizes the results of the relevant literature. The third section discusses the econometric specification of the model. In the fourth section the data are described and some descriptive statistics are presented, while the fifth section provides the empirical results. Finally, the fifth section concludes.

A survey of empirical literature

A number of papers have been developed in the economics and econometrics literature that use stochastic frontier analysis in order to measure and identify determinants of technical efficiency. In this section, we will focus on studies carried out at the aggregate cross-country level and on studies which examine the impact of ICT on technical efficiency (see Table 2.1 for a brief presentation of the relevant literature).

Fare et al. (1994) analyzed the productivity growth of 17 OECD countries for the period 1979–88. They used non-parametric methods and decomposed productivity into technical change and efficiency improvement. Their results showed that US productivity growth was based mainly on technical change, while Japan's productivity growth was based on efficiency change. Koop et al. (1999) used the same sample of countries during the same time period to analyze the components of output growth. However, they used a Bayesian stochastic frontier framework and showed that efficiency change was a significant component in explaining output growth of OECD countries.

Recent cross-country studies have focused on several factors related to technical efficiency. Adkins et al. (2002) used a broad set of 73 developed and developing countries during the period 1975–90 to simultaneously estimate a stochastic production function and the sources of cross-country inefficiencies. Their results showed that institutions that promote economic freedom in turn promote efficiency. Milner and Weyman-Jones (2003) analyzed the impact of trade openness and country size on aggregate national efficiency by using non-parametric methodologies in a group of 85 developing countries during the period 1980–89. After having estimated the efficiency levels of countries, the regression analysis showed that trade openness indeed has a positive and significant impact on country efficiency. With respect to the country size, the results indicate a negative but not always significant effect on national efficiency.

Jayasuriya and Wodon (2005) used a panel dataset to estimate a production frontier of 71 countries for the 1980–98 period. They also analyzed the impact of urbanization on productive efficiency and showed a positive and significant impact attributed to the presence of spillover effects and scale economies. Kneller and Stevens (2006) investigated whether human capital and R&D have any impact on productive efficiency. They used a dataset for nine industries in 12 OECD countries for the period 1973–91. The results are in favor of a positive and significant

Table 2.1 Summary of related literature

Study	Country sample	Time period	Variable of interest	Impact on efficiency
ICT Related Studies				
Lee and Barua (1999)	US manufacturing firms	1978–84	IT capital	Positive and significant
Milana and Zeli (2002)	Italian firms	1997	ICT investment	No evidence for insignificant effects
Becchetti et al. (2003)	Italian firms	1995–97	ICT investment	Positive and significant effect of software
Thompson and Garbacz (2007)	93 developed and developing countries	1995–2003	Diffusion of telecommunications	Positive and significant in developing countries, no effect in OECD countries
Repkine (2008)	50 developed and developing countries	1980–2004	Telecommunications' capital	Positive and significant in developing countries, no effect in developed countries
Other Cross Country Studies				
Fare et al. (1994)	17 OECD countries	1979–88		Significant contribution of efficiency change to Japan's productivity growth, significant effect of technical progress to US productivity growth
Koop et al. (1999)	17 OECD countries	1979–88		Significant contribution of efficiency change to output growth
Adkins et. al (2002)	73 developed and developing countries	1975–90	Institutions, freedom	Positive and significant
Milner and Weyman-Jones (2003)	85 developing countries	1980–89	Trade openness, country size	Positive and significant for trade openness
Jayasuriya and Wodon (2005)	71 developed and developing countries	1980–98	Urbanization	Positive and significant
Kneller and Stevens (2006)	Nine industries in 12 OECD countries	1973–91	Human capital, R&D	Positive and significant for human capital
Henry et al. (2009)	57 developing countries	1970–98	Trade, trade policy	Positive and significant for both variables

impact of human capital in reducing productive inefficiency. In contrast, the results are less robust with respect to R&D. The most recent cross-country study to examine technical efficiency is that of Henry et al. (2009). They used a sample of 57 developing countries during the period 1970–98 and their results indicate significant differences in efficiency levels across countries and over time. Furthermore, they show a significant influence of trade and trade policy in raising output through embodied technology improvements, as well as through efficiency improvements.

To our knowledge there exist at least five published studies which examine the impact of ICT or ICT components on technical efficiency. Three of them focus on the firm level; the other two analyze the impact of telecommunications on cross-country technical efficiency. With respect to the firm level studies, Lee and Barua (1999) examine the impact of information technology (IT) across a sample of manufacturing firms in 1978–84. The results indicate that the firm-level inefficiencies reduce with an increase in IT intensity. Milana and Zeli (2002) examined the impact of ICT on technical efficiency across a sample of Italian firms in 1997.

First, they used data envelopment analysis to measure technical efficiency of each individual firm. As a second step, they used regression analysis to examine the impact of ICT on technical efficiency and found that a positive relationship could not be rejected in the entire group of firms. Becchetti et al. (2003) examined the effects of ICT on technical efficiency of small and medium-sized Italian firms, during the period 1995–97. The results indicate a positive effect of software investment on technical efficiency of Italian firms.

At the aggregate cross-country level, on which this study focuses, Thompson and Garbacz (2007) used measures of telecommunication services to examine their impact on technical efficiency. They used a sample of 93 developed and developing countries during 1995–2003 and the effects were quite important for low-income countries that operate below the frontier. In contrast, these effects were insignificant for developed countries of the OECD. Repkine (2008) estimated the impact of telecommunications capital on technical efficiency of 50 developed and developing countries during the period 1980–2004. The results indicate that telecommunications capital positively affects technical efficiency of developing countries. In contrast such effects did not exist in developed countries, since any efficiency gains had been exhausted.

Econometric specification

Production frontier modeling

In this study, we will follow the one-stage stochastic frontier specification proposed by Battese and Coelli (1995). Therefore, we will incorporate a technical inefficiency model into a stochastic production frontier, we will simultaneously estimate at one stage the level of technical efficiency of each individual country and we will identify determinants of technical inefficiency.

One of the main assumptions in frontier analysis is that all producers share a common production structure and, therefore, face an identical production function. Given the high degree of economic integration and the liberalization of most OECD economies, we make the assumption that OECD countries have access to common production technologies and face the same production function:

$$Y_{it} = Ae^{\lambda t} \left(L_{it}\right)^{\alpha} \left(K_{it}\right)^{\beta} e^{(V_{it} - U_{it})} \tag{1}$$

The subscripts of i and t denote country and year, respectively, while Y measures GDP of each country. A is the level of technology to which all countries have identical access, λ is the rate of technical change and t is a time trend which captures technical progress over time. V_{it} is the random variable assumed to be independently and identically distributed $N(0, \sigma_v^2)$ and independent of U_{it}. The latter is the non-negative random error, associated with technical inefficiency of production. This error term is assumed to be independently distributed of V_{it} and has a half normal distribution equal to the upper half of the $N(0, \sigma_u^2)$ distribution.

In this study, we measure labor input (L) in hours worked, since the variable of the number of workers might hide changes in hours worked caused by part-time work or variations in overtime.

The parameters α and β are the output elasticities of labor (L) and physical capital (K). After taking a logarithmic transformation, output in each industry can be expressed as a function of labor and physical capital:

$$\ln\left(Y_{it}\right) = c + \lambda t + \alpha \ln\left(L_{it}\right) + \beta \ln\left(K_{it}\right) + V_{it} - U_{it} \tag{2}$$

Following Battese and Coelli (1995), the technical inefficiency effects are assumed to be a function of a set of explanatory variables z_{it} and can be defined as:

$$U_{it} = \delta \sum_{j=1}^{n} \delta_j z_{j,it} + W_{it} \tag{3}$$

where z_{it} is a vector of variables assumed to influence inefficiency and δ_js are parameters to be estimated. The random variable W_{it} is defined by the truncation of the normal distribution. The technical efficiency of country i at time t is estimated as:

$$TE_{it} = \exp(-U_{it}) \tag{4}$$

Furthermore, by estimating the parameters $\sigma^2 = \sigma_v^2 + \sigma_u^2$ and $\gamma = \sigma_u^2/\sigma_v^2 + \sigma_u^2$, we can test whether $\gamma=0$.[1] A rejection of the null hypothesis that $\gamma = 0$, against the alternative that γ is positive, implies that deviations from the frontier are due to inefficiency effects.

Inefficiency variables: the role of ICT

Modeling the impact of ICT might be a complex task. Our main concern in particular relates to whether ICT should be treated as a separate production input which affects output by the traditional channel of higher capital deepening, or whether it should be modeled in a way that affects technical progress or technical efficiency.

According to the theory of GPT, ICT is a technology that has broad applicability in all sectors, improves the flow of information, reduces transaction costs and finally raises TFP. Empirically, van Ark et al. (2003) have argued that higher TFP observed in the USA during the late 1990s is linked to intensive use of ICT in some service (wholesale and retail trade, financial securities) and manufacturing (ICT-producing) industries. Since the focus of the present study is on the impact of ICT on technological progress, ICT is not treated here as a conventional capital but, rather, as a special type of technology input that gives rise to the technical efficiency of countries. We wish to test this formally by estimating the technical inefficiency model of equation (3), in which ICT as a share of GDP is used as an explanatory variable. We will further include a variable to proxy human capital as another factor influencing technical efficiency. This variable is measured as the share of hours worked by highly skilled persons. We should note that there is some debate with respect to the role of human capital in economic growth. Mankiw et al. (1992) argue that human capital should enter the production function as a separate input. In contrast, Benhabib and Spiegel (1994) and Pritchett (2001) argue that human capital influences growth indirectly through TFP. Clearly, it is beyond the scope of this chapter to address this issue.

However, since our interest mainly lies in the determinants of technical efficiency, we will evaluate its impact on technical efficiency by assuming that human capital plays a significant role in the absorptive capacity and technology transfer across countries (Kneller and Stevens, 2006) and, therefore, in their level of technical efficiency. We also use the volume of international trade of each country as another explanatory variable in equation (3).

Higher trade volumes allow countries to specialize and gain comparative advantage which, in turn, lead to scale economies and higher efficiency. International trade is, also, considered as an important channel of technology transfer through imports of intermediate inputs and capital equipment (Feenstra et al., 1992). Furthermore, international trade is expected to affect the level of efficiency through higher competition and removal of rent-seeking activities (Bhagwati and Krueger, 1973). We expect that the impact of this variable on inefficiency will be negative. The parameters of the production function (2) as well as of the inefficiency function (3) are estimated simultaneously at one stage by maximum likelihood and by using the computer program FRONTIER 4.1, which is developed by Coelli (1996).

Data and descriptive statistics

This analysis is based on a selection of 17 OECD countries (Australia, Austria, Belgium, Denmark, Finland, France, Germany, Greece, Ireland, Italy, Japan, Netherlands, Portugal, Spain, Sweden, United Kingdom, United States) in the period 1990–2005.

Table 2.2 presents a detailed description of the data and their sources. The data concerning GDP, volume of international trade and the number

Table 2.2   Definitions and sources of variables

Variable name	Definition	Source
Y	GDP in constant ppp dollars	OECD factbook 2008: economic, environmental, and social statistics
t	Time trend	
K	Capital Stock	Initial Values from Penn World Tables; Figures of Gross Fixed Capital Formation from World Development Indicators
L	Hours Worked	OECD Factbook 2008: Economic, Environmental, and Social Statistics
H	Share of hours worked by high skilled persons	EU KLEMS Growth and Productivity Accounts
ICT	ICT Investment as a Share of GDP	ICT Investment Figures from OECD Factbook 2008: Economic, Environmental, and Social Statistics
OPEN	Volume of International Trade as a share of GDP	OECD Factbook 2008: Economic, Environmental, and Social Statistics

of hours worked were taken from OECD (2008), while the data regarding hours worked by highly skilled persons were provided by the EU KLEMS (2007) database. Initial data on capital stock were taken from *Penn World Tables* (Heston and Summers, 1991), while capital stock estimates for the subsequent years are calculated by adding for each year the gross fixed capital formation (World Bank, 2008) and subtracting capital depreciation (IMF, 2008). The ICT investment data are provided by OECD (2008). We should acknowledge that ICT investment assets are subject to rapid technological change and quality improvement. Thus, we need to have accurate price indices in order to correctly measure ICT investment series. These should be constant quality price indices that reflect price changes for a given set of characteristics of ICT (Schreyer et al., 2003). For this reason, we use harmonized price indices for ICT assets which are currently used in the computation of growth in capital services presented in the OECD productivity database.[2] Additionally, these harmonized deflators are purchasing power parity adjusted and this helps us to improve the international comparability of ICT investment across countries. Although no claim is made that the harmonized deflator is necessarily the correct price index for a given country, Schreyer et al. (2003) suggest that the possible error due to using a harmonized price index is smaller than the bias arising from using national deflators.[3] All the value variables are expressed in purchasing power parity in order to make the data compatible across countries. It should be made clear that the choice of countries and time period is dictated by the availability of data for all variables used in this empirical study.

With this in mind, first a description of the data is made and then follows the econometric analysis.

Table 2.3 contains some descriptive statistics for all variables that will be employed in our econometric analysis, while Table 2.4 displays the estimated GDP shares of ICT investment across individual countries for the period 1990–2005. It is worth mentioning the cases of Australia and the USA, being by far the most ICT-intensive countries (3.63 percent of GDP in Australia and 3.56 percent of GDP in USA) in 2005, followed by Sweden, the UK, Denmark and Japan. In contrast, Ireland, Portugal, Greece and Italy present very low rates of ICT investment.

Empirical results

Econometric results

Table 2.5 contains the maximum likelihood estimates of the stochastic production frontier for the selection of 17 OECD countries in the

Table 2.3   Descriptive statistics of variables

Variable*	Obs	Mean	Std. Dev.	Min	Max
Y**	272	27.08	1.29	24.84	30.15
K**	272	27.2	1.27	24.69	29.96
L**	272	23.53	1.25	21.59	26.28
ICT**	272	2.49	0.81	0.78	4.86
H	272	21.53	1.43	18.98	25.13
OPEN	272	34.13	18.65	8.1	92.2

* The countries included in the sample are Australia, Austria, Belgium, Denmark, Finland, France, Germany, Greece, Ireland, Italy, Japan, Netherlands, Portugal, Spain, Sweden, United Kingdom, United States.
** Variables in logs.

Table 2.4   ICT investment as a share of GDP (figures in %)

	1990	1995	2000	2005
Australia	2.57	3.17	4.03	3.63
Austria	1.74	1.75	2.33	1.90
Belgium	3.05	2.55	3.87	2.73
Denmark	2.77	2.85	3.07	3.32
Finland	2.37	2.56	2.73	2.82
France	1.75	1.71	2.66	2.35
Germany	2.35	1.88	2.55	1.85
Greece	0.84	1.05	1.86	1.73
Ireland	0.87	1.17	1.43	0.82
Italy	2.01	1.80	2.27	1.72
Japan	2.19	2.39	3.42	3.10
Netherlands	2.51	2.36	3.12	2.79
Portugal	1.60	1.66	2.17	1.64
Spain	2.60	2.01	2.66	1.98
Sweden	2.71	3.33	4.75	3.49
UK	2.59	3.12	4.30	3.29
USA	2.86	3.36	4.86	3.56

Source: OECD Factbook 2008: Economic, Environmental, and Social Statistics.

period 1990–2005. The proposed production function includes a time trend and the inputs of physical capital and labor, measured in hours worked.

The technical inefficiency equation is simultaneously estimated using as regressors the ratio of ICT investment to GDP, a proxy for human capital (measured as the share of hours worked by highly skilled persons) and the volume of international trade of each country as a share of GDP.

Table 2.5 Maximum likelihood estimates

	1		2		3	
	coef.	t-stat	coef.	t-stat	coef.	t-stat
Production Function						
c	2.06*	6.4	0.29*	3.09	1.97*	3.37
t†	0	–1.32	0	–1.26	–0.02*	–5.19
K	0.33*	11.82	0.33*	14.64	0.28*	10.85
L	0.70*	24.47	0.71*	19.73	0.62*	19.35
H			0.07*	4.28		
ICT					0.14*	5.42
Inefficiency Function						
c	3.43*	8.67	1.49*	10.45	2.63*	5.31
ICT	–0.06*	–4.8	–0.05*	–5.37	–0.04*	–2.59
H	–0.09*	–5.85			–0.06*	–3.05
OPEN	–0.33*	–11.2	–0.31*	–13.52	–0.30*	–11.32
σ^2	0.01*	9.93	0.01*	11.98	0.01*	8.94
γ	0.52**	1.87	0.1	0.2	0.03	0.09
Log likelihood	210.06		207.7		228.39	
Observations	272		272		272	

† See Table 2.3 for the definitions of variables.
* Significant at the 5 percent level of significance.
** Significant at the 10 percent level of significance.

As we can see from the baseline results reported in column (1), physical capital and labor have a significantly positive effect on output. The results are plausible and compare well with those provided by the empirical growth literature. The coefficient on time trend appears to be insignificantly negative and indicates that the time trend might not be a good proxy for technological progress.[4] To determine whether deviations from the estimated frontier are due to inefficiency effects, a test of the null hypothesis that $\gamma = 0$, against the alternative that γ is positive, is used. As it is evident, the parameter γ is significantly different from zero, and this implies that inefficiency effects are present and that we should proceed with the estimation of parameters related to the sources of inefficiency.

The technical inefficiency results indicate that a rise in the share of ICT in GDP contributes significantly to reducing inefficiencies among countries. In particular, the estimates of column (1) imply that doubling the share of ICT investment in GDP would, on average, reduce the inefficiency level of a country by 6 percent, ceteris paribus. With respect to the variables of human capital and the volume of international trade, we can distinguish a significantly negative, and quite sizeable in magnitude, association with technical inefficiency.

Although the arguments above were in favor of including ICT and human capital variables in the inefficiency function, we would prefer to check the robustness of our results across alternative specifications. For this reason, we re-estimate our model by considering human capital as directly affecting output through the production function (column (2)) and by allowing for additional effects of ICT as a traditional production input (column (3)). In this way we can test for additional direct effects of ICT and human capital through their inclusion into the production function. From the reported results in column (2), we can see that when human capital enters the production function, its direct effect on output is positive and significant.

We believe that this result (combined with its negative effect on technical inefficiency) complements those from previous studies which support either that human capital should be included as an input in the production function (Mankiw et al., 1992) or that human capital affects output indirectly through TFP (Benhabib and Spiegel, 1994; Pritchett, 2001).

Our study indicates that this indicator of human capital has direct, as well as indirect, effects on growth for the particular sample of countries and for this specific time period. The results with respect to the remaining variables do not change significantly. In column (3), we report estimates after having included ICT as a factor of production. Since ICT enters the production function directly, its measure should be denoted in physical capital terms.[5] As it is evident, the elasticity of ICT capital is highly positive and significant, implying a strong and positive association of ICT with output. Importantly, it seems that the ICT impact is quite sizeable, given that the share of ICT in total non-residential gross fixed capital formation was about 15–20 percent in most OECD countries during the period under investigation (OECD, 2008).

This result compares well with the growth accounting results obtained from Colecchia and Schreyer (2002) for a sample of OECD countries during the 1990s which show that the ICT contribution was about 15–20 percent of output growth. With respect to the impact of ICT on technical inefficiency, we can see that its impact remains significantly negative but lowers slightly in magnitude.

Efficiency scores across countries and over time: contribution of ICT to efficiency

Table 2.6 presents average efficiency measures for the 17 OECD countries, in 1990–95, 1995–2000, 2000–05 and the entire period

Table 2.6 Average efficiency scores

Country*	Rank	1990–1995	1995–2000	2000–2005	1990–2005
Belgium	1	0.89	0.93	0.96	0.92
Netherlands	2	0.88	0.93	0.95	0.92
USA	3	0.84	0.9	0.92	0.89
Ireland	4	0.74	0.89	0.95	0.86
UK	5	0.77	0.84	0.88	0.83
France	6	0.76	0.82	0.87	0.81
Sweden	7	0.73	0.8	0.86	0.8
Denmark	8	0.72	0.78	0.82	0.77
Austria	9	0.72	0.76	0.82	0.77
Germany	10	0.71	0.75	0.81	0.76
Spain	11	0.71	0.77	0.79	0.75
Australia	12	0.69	0.75	0.79	0.74
Italy	13	0.71	0.75	0.77	0.74
Finland	14	0.66	0.73	0.79	0.72
Greece	15	0.63	0.67	0.74	0.68
Japan	16	0.61	0.65	0.68	0.65
Portugal	17	0.6	0.63	0.65	0.63

* Countries are sorted in descending order according to their average efficiency scores.

1990–2005. The most efficient countries in the sample are Belgium and Netherlands followed by the USA and other north European economies. On the other hand, the least efficient countries in the sample are Greece, Japan and Portugal. The efficiency rankings, in general, show that the north European countries and the USA lead in terms of technical efficiency, while the south European countries are relatively less efficient. This sounds reasonable enough given the fact that the latter are comparatively less developed (in GDP per capita terms). In general, the efficiency ranks are in accordance with the negative linkage established between ICT and technical inefficiency, since the majority of the least ICT-intensive countries (Table 2.4) are also among the less efficient ones.

In general, all OECD countries have managed to increase their average level of technical efficiency between 1990 and 2005, with the majority of them moving from the level of 75 percent to levels close to or even above 85 percent.

It should be noted that no country included in this sample has witnessed a decrease in its level of technical efficiency. However, there exist significant disparities in the level of technical efficiencies across countries. Despite the significant increase in their efficiency levels, several south European countries (like Spain, Greece or Italy) have not yet achieved convergence with other OECD countries.

On the contrary, their levels of technical efficiency seem to be close to the initial efficiency levels (in the beginning of the 1990s) of several north European countries. As an extreme example, we should mention the case of Portugal, whose level of technical efficiency has only slightly improved from 60–4 percent. In this section, we will also evaluate the contribution of ICT on technical efficiency for each country and across time. According to the framework introduced by Coelli et al. (1999), we calculate the contribution of ICT to technical efficiency as the difference between gross efficiency and efficiency net of the impact of ICT.

According to Battese and Coelli (1993), technical efficiency of each country i is calculated as:

$$TE_{it} = E\left[\exp(-u_{it}) \mid \varepsilon_{it}\right] = \left\{\exp\left[-\mu_{it} + \frac{1}{2}\overline{\sigma}^{2}\right]\right\} \cdot \left\{\Phi\left[\frac{\mu_{it}}{\overline{\sigma}} - \overline{\sigma}\right] / \Phi\left[\frac{\mu_{it}}{\overline{\sigma}}\right]\right\} \qquad (5)$$

where Φ is the standard normal distribution function,

$$\varepsilon_{it} = V_{it} - U_{it}, \ \mu_{it} = (1-\gamma) \cdot \left[\delta + \sum_{j=1}^{n} \delta_j z_{j,it}\right] \quad \gamma\varepsilon_{it} \text{ and } \overline{\sigma}^{2} = \gamma(1-\gamma)\sigma^{2}$$

By replacing the unknown parameters in equation (5) with the maximum likelihood estimates we obtain estimates of technical efficiency of country *i* at time *t*. The obtained technical efficiencies in equation (5) are gross measures which include the impact of ICT. To obtain measures of net technical efficiency (net of ICT influences), we replace the term

$$\sum_{j=1}^{n} \delta_j z_{j,it}$$

in equation (5) with

$$Min\left[\sum_{j=1}^{n} \delta_j z_{j,it} - \delta_{ICT} ICT\right]$$

and recalculate efficiency predictions.

These predictions may be interpreted as net efficiency scores because they involve predictions of efficiency when all countries are assumed to face identical and the most favorable ICT effects (Coelli et al., 1999). The differences between net and gross efficiency scores represent the contribution of ICT to the efficiency of each country. The results reported in Table 2.7 show that ICT in general contributed significantly in the improvement of technical efficiencies across countries and over time. The highest contribution is observed for countries which operate some way below the frontier, such as Greece, Japan, Italy, etc. On the other hand, we observe a zero or even slightly negative contribution

Table 2.7 Contribution of ICT to efficiency

	Across countries				Across time		
	Net efficiency (%)	Gross efficiency (%)	Contribution of ICT (%)		Net efficiency (%)	Gross efficiency (%)	Contribution of ICT (%)
Greece*	77.32	67.71	9.61	1990	79.41	71.96	7.45
Japan	73.25	64.71	8.54	1991	79.68	72.02	7.67
Italy	81.57	73.90	7.67	1992	79.81	72.09	7.72
Australia	81.97	74.34	7.64	1993	79.79	72.15	7.65
Denmark	84.66	77.08	7.58	1994	80.55	73.60	6.95
Portugal	70.09	62.72	7.37	1995	81.17	75.12	6.05
France	87.51	81.36	6.16	1996	81.67	76.13	5.54
Austria	82.67	76.70	5.97	1997	82.43	77.86	4.57
Spain	80.96	75.35	5.61	1998	82.82	79.03	3.79
Finland	77.70	72.29	5.41	1999	83.51	80.36	3.16
Germany	79.09	75.56	3.53	2000	84.30	82.64	1.66
Ireland	88.72	85.80	2.93	2001	84.45	82.43	2.02
Sweden	82.55	79.67	2.88	2002	84.72	81.85	2.87
USA	91.16	88.48	2.68	2003	84.91	81.64	3.28
UK	83.70	82.99	0.71	2004	85.46	82.61	2.84
Netherlands	90.85	91.77	-0.92	2005	85.68	83.53	2.16
Belgium	89.13	92.39	-3.27				

* Countries are sorted in descending order according to the average contribution of ICT.

for countries close to the frontier, such as Belgium, the Netherlands, the UK and the USA. The policy implication of these findings is direct for countries some way below the world technology frontier wishing to achieve technological convergence with the most developed countries. The impact of ICT on the improvement of technical efficiency was positive across time, with the highest contribution observed in the early 1990s.

Discussion

Recent developments in ICT seem to have altered the global economic environment. Efficient collaboration and coordination, up-to-date and accurate information, as well as information availability and accuracy, are essential for economic success (Gholami et al., 2006). In this way, ICT seems to have facilitated efficiency by making many business processes and transactions more effective (Jorgenson, 2001). Moreover, ICT has offered the chance for countries to free themselves from the limitations of geography (Gholami et al., 2006), allowing the flow of information to the most remote economies and making knowledge accessible to anyone. Goods and services are now offered on the global market efficiently through the use of ICT, leading to substantial efficiency gains in production and distribution of goods and services. Overall, we expect that the direct impact of ICT on technical efficiency will be reflected in higher levels of economic development and higher growth rates in GDP.

The reported figures of Table 2.8 reveal a very high correlation coefficient between the level of efficiency of each country and its level of economic development (measured in GDP per capita terms).

The same holds for the association between efficiency change and GDP per capita growth (Table 2.9), which is indicative of the fact that, on average, the fastest-growing countries are those with the highest efficiency improvement.

Table 2.10 shows that efficiency change is significantly correlated with TFP growth in several OECD countries, such as Austria, Finland, France, etc. For other countries, however, there does not exist such a relationship. Nevertheless, it is not necessary for a country to be efficient and at the same time be a technological leader, in the sense that we may expect technological convergence in less developed countries but not always in countries which innovate and lead the world technology frontier (Bernard and Jones, 1996).

It should be noted that the evidence of this study partially departs from the results provided by two recently published cross-country

Table 2.8 GDP per capita – efficiency

	GDP per capita ($ ppp international)			Efficiency (in levels)			Corr.
	1990–95	1995–2000	2000–05	1990–95	1995–2000	2000–05	
Australia	23 562.92	26 761.00	30 195.42	0.69	0.75	0.79	0.97
Austria	27 050.14	29 908.86	32 715.32	0.72	0.76	0.82	0.99
Belgium	25 835.31	28 272.04	31 000.77	0.89	0.93	0.96	0.96
Denmark	26 505.39	29 826.36	32 199.33	0.72	0.78	0.82	1
Finland	21 711.08	24 647.81	28 947.87	0.66	0.73	0.79	0.92
France	25 341.62	27 263.10	29 890.99	0.76	0.82	0.87	0.98
Germany	26 999.34	28 998.94	30 961.24	0.71	0.75	0.81	0.99
Greece	17 684.24	19 021.45	22 784.66	0.63	0.67	0.74	0.96
Ireland	19 057.89	26 577.38	35 422.02	0.74	0.89	0.95	0.94
Italy	24 355.11	26 276.31	28 083.32	0.71	0.75	0.77	0.91
Japan	26 875.86	28 143.39	29 138.03	0.61	0.65	0.68	0.93
Netherlands	27 120.18	30 885.98	34 034.66	0.88	0.93	0.95	0.98
Portugal	16 441.08	18 688.03	20 559.36	0.6	0.63	0.65	0.93
Spain	20 307.41	22 842.04	26 259.86	0.71	0.77	0.79	0.89
Sweden	24 051.53	26 456.76	30 334.04	0.73	0.8	0.86	0.96
UK	23 924.74	27 112.96	30 693.32	0.77	0.84	0.88	0.95
USA	32 745.22	36 426.32	40 003.06	0.84	0.9	0.92	0.96

Table 2.9 GDP per capita growth – efficiency change

	GDP per capita growth (%)			Efficiency change (%)			Corr
	1990–95	1995–2000	2000–05	1990–95	1995–2000	2000–05	
Australia	1.14	3.13	1.85	1.13	2.01	0.62	0.4
Austria	1.55	2.79	0.90	0.41	1.90	0.82	0.75
Belgium	1.26	2.48	1.14	0.29	1.30	0.16	0.89
Denmark	2.01	2.43	0.97%	1.28	1.41	1.02	0.74
Finland	–1.1%	4.50	2.25	1.93	2.29	1.51	0.45
France	0.77	2.44	1.00	0.44	2.14	0.61	0.89
Germany	1.66	1.87	0.51	0.67	2.10	1.02	0.85
Greece	0.34	2.91	4.02	–0.06	2.45	1.65	0.56
Ireland	4.06	8.32	3.64	3.24	3.66	0.39	0.62
Italy	1.23	1.87	0.29	1.22	1.43	0.14	0.67
Japan	1.22	0.77	1.16	–0.12	1.76	1.63	0.69
Netherlands	1.62	3.43	0.72	0.68	1.15	0.12	0.81
Portugal	1.46	3.68	0.25	0.10	1.65	–0.07	0.81
Spain	1.23	3.65	1.73	0.44	1.84	0.00	0.61
Sweden	0.10	3.26	2.21	0.71	2.75	1.18	0.7
UK	1.40	2.91	2.00	1.60	1.89	0.57	0.56
USA	1.17	2.94	1.36	0.76	1.63	0.20	0.78

Table 2.10 TFP growth – efficiency change

	TFP growth (%)			Efficiency change (%)			Corr.
	1990–95	1995–2000	2000–05	1990–95	1995–2000	2000–05	
Australia	1.55	1.78	1.29	1.13	2.01	0.62	−0.16
Austria		1.63	0.45	0.41	1.90	0.82	0.75
Belgium	1.57	1.31	0.74	0.29	1.30	0.16	0.42
Denmark	1.80	0.44	0.23	1.28	1.41	1.02	0.59
Finland	1.41	2.56	1.66	1.93	2.29	1.51	0.76
France	1.10	1.44	0.90	0.44	2.14	0.61	0.62
Germany	1.45	1.28	0.67	0.67	2.10	1.02	0.51
Ireland	3.02	5.39	2.55	3.24	3.66	0.39	0.39
Italy	1.20	0.34	−0.62	1.22	1.43	0.14	0.59
Japan	0.97	0.83	1.47	−0.12	1.76	1.63	0.13
Netherlands	1.74	0.77	0.37	0.68	1.15	0.12	−0.46
Portugal		2.53	0.02	0.10	1.65	−0.07	0.59
Spain	0.74	−0.22	0.08	0.44	1.84	0.00	−0.2
Sweden	0.85	1.49	2.24	0.71	2.75	1.18	0.32
UK	1.39	1.25	1.17	1.60	1.89	0.57	0.22
USA	0.69	1.33	1.69	0.76	1.63	0.20	−0.33

studies (Thompson and Garbacz, 2007; Repkine, 2008). These studies indicate that no ICT effects exist in the technical efficiency of OECD countries, since they found that these countries operate close to the production frontier.

In contrast to these studies, the present work shows that there is considerable scope for improvement and that ICT has significantly reduced cross-country inefficiencies in OECD countries. The critical point that differentiates the present study from others is the fact that our sample is relatively homogeneous and it does not include countries that operate at different stages of economic development and under heterogeneous macroeconomic environments. Consequently, we have imposed a common production function in countries quite close to each other and in this way we believe that the findings of this study are closer to reality. The findings of several studies for firms operating both in the USA (Lee and Barua, 1999) and Italy (Milana and Zeli, 2002; Becchetti et al., 2003) confirm our results, since they have established a positive link between ICT and technical efficiency of production.

Conclusion

This chapter applies a production frontier approach to simultaneously estimate a technical inefficiency model within a production function framework. The main subject under investigation is the role of ICT in reducing inefficiencies across countries. A selection of 17 OECD countries in 1990–2005 is utilized for this purpose. Overall, the production frontier results, as well as the inefficiency estimates, provide strong evidence for a significant ICT impact in reducing country inefficiencies. At a comparative level, Belgium and the Netherlands were ranked as the most efficient countries in the sample, followed by the USA and other north European countries. Furthermore, it seems that several south European countries are relatively inefficient and have not yet converged with the efficiency levels of the most developed OECD countries.

The estimates generally indicate that the most developed OECD counties have already achieved a high level of technical efficiency. This implies their dependence on technological progress, in order to promote higher economic development. The policy implication for the less developed countries is that they should accelerate their adoption of information technologies, and technical advances in general, and should enhance their efficiency by aiming for more trade and competition and higher levels of human capital.

Notes

1. The parameter σ^2 is the overall variance of the error term, σ_v^2 is the variance of V_{it}, while σ_u^2 is the variance of the inefficiency term U_{it}.
2. We wish to thank the Productivity Department of OECD for kindly providing us with appropriate ICT deflators.
3. Large differences that have been observed between computer price indices in OECD countries are likely a reflection of differences in statistical methodology. In particular, those countries that employ hedonic methods to construct ICT deflators tend to register a larger drop in ICT prices than countries that do not.
4. Ideally, we should have included measures of R&D or innovative activity in order to account for technological progress. However such data are available for fewer countries and years and their use would lead to a severe reduction in the size of the sample.
5. Our estimates of ICT capital stock are based on ICT investment data provided by OECD (2008). In order to estimate initial ICT capital stock, we choose the steady state method, which is frequently used in several recent studies (e.g. Henry et al., 2009). Particularly, the initial value of capital stock is given by

$$ICT = \frac{1}{g + \Delta}$$

where I is investment in the initial period, g is the average annual growth rate of investment over the sample period and Δ is the depreciation rate. The depreciation rates for hardware, software and communications are reported by EU KLEMS and are equal to 0.315, 0.315 and 0.115, respectively. After having obtained I, g and Δ, we can proceed with the estimation of initial ICT capital stocks. The perpetual inventory method is used for the construction of ICT capital in subsequent years.

References

Adkins, L., R. Moomaw and A. Savvides (2002) 'Institutions, Freedom and Technical Efficiency', *Southern Economic Journal*, Vol. 69, pp. 92–108.

Battese, G. and T. Coelli (1993) 'A Stochastic Frontier Production Function Incorporating a Model for Technical Inefficiency Effects', Working Paper in Econometrics and Applied Statistics No. 69, Department of Econometrics, University of New England.

Battese, G. and T. Coelli (1995) 'A Model for Technical Inefficiency Effects in a Stochastic Frontier Production Function for Panel Data', *Empirical Economics*, Vol. 20, pp. 325–32.

Becchetti, L., D.A. Londono Bedoya and L. Paganetto (2003) 'ICT Investment, Productivity and Efficiency: Evidence at Firm Level Using a Stochastic Frontier Approach', *Journal of Productivity Analysis*, Vol. 20, pp. 143–67.

Benhabib, J. and M. Spiegel (1994) 'The Role of Human Capital in Economic Development: Evidence from Aggregate and Cross Country Data', *Journal of Monetary Economics*, Vol. 34, pp. 143–73.

Bernard, A.B. and C.I. Jones (1996) 'Technology and Convergence', *Economic Journal*, Vol. 106, pp. 1037–44.

Bhagwati, J. and A.O. Krueger (1973) 'Exchange Control, Liberalization and Economic Development', *American Economic Review*, Vol. 63, pp. 419–27.

Coelli, T. (1996) 'A Guide to FRONTIER 4.1: A Computer Program for Stochastic Frontier Production and Cost Estimation', Working Paper No. 96/07, Centre for Efficiency and Productivity Analysis, University of New England.

Coelli, T., S. Perelman and E. Romano (1999) 'Accounting for Environmental Influences in Stochastic Frontier Models: With Application to International Airlines', *Journal of Productivity Analysis*, Vol. 11, pp. 251–73.

A. Colecchia and P. Schreyer (2002) 'ICT Investment and Economic Growth in the 1990s: Is the United States a Unique Case? A Comparative Study of Nine OECD Countries', *Review of Economic Dynamics*, Vol. 5, pp. 408–42.

EU KLEMS (2007) *Growth and Productivity Accounts*, Groningen: University of Groningen.

Fare, R., S. Grosskopf, M. Norris and Z. Zhang (1994) 'Productivity Growth, Technical Progress and Efficiency Change in Industrialized Countries', *American Economic Review*, Vol. 84, pp. 66–83.

Feenstra, R., J.R. Markusen and W. Zeile (1992) 'Accounting for Growth with New Inputs: Theory and Evidence', *American Economic Review*, Vol. 82, pp. 415–21.

Gholami, R., S.Y. Lee and A. Heshmati (2006) 'The Causal Relationship Between Information and Communication Technology and Foreign Direct Investment', *World Economy*, Vol. 29, pp. 43–62.

Gordon, R. (2000) 'Does the New Economy Measure Up to the Great Inventions of the Past?', *Journal of Economic Perspectives*, Vol. 14, pp. 49–74.

Grosskopf, S. (1993) 'Efficiency and Productivity', in H. Fried, C. Lovell and S. Schmidt (eds), *The Measurement of Productive Efficiency: Techniques and Applications*, Oxford: Oxford University Press.

Henry, M., R. Kneller and C. Milner (2009) 'Trade, Technology Transfer and National Efficiency in Developing Countries', *European Economic Review*, Vol. 53, pp. 237–54.

Heston, A. and R. Summers (1991) 'The Penn World Table (Mark 5) Version 5,6: An Expanded Set of International Comparisons 1950–1988', *Quarterly Journal of Economics*, Vol. 106, pp. 327–68.

IMF (2008) *International Financial Statistics*, Washington DC: IMF.

Jayasuriya, R. and Q. Wodon (2005) 'Measuring and Explaining the Impact of Productive Efficiency on Economic Development', *World Bank Economic Review*, Vol. 19, pp. 121–40.

Jorgenson, D. (2001) 'Information Technology and the US Economy', *American Economic Review*, Vol. 91, pp. 1–32.

Kneller, R. and P. Stevens (2006) 'Frontier Technology and Absorptive Capacity: Evidence from OECD Manufacturing Industries', *Oxford Bulletin of Economics and Statistics*, Vol. 68, pp. 1–21.

Koop, G., J. Osiewalski and M.F.J. Steel (1999) 'The Components of Output Growth: A Stochastic Frontier Analysis', *Oxford Bulletin of Economics and Statistics*, Vol. 61, pp. 455–87.

Lee, B. and A. Barua (1999) 'An Integrated Assessment of Productivity and Efficiency Impacts of Information Technology Investments: Old Data, New Analysis and Evidence', *Journal of Productivity Analysis*, Vol. 12, pp. 21–43.

Mankiw, N.G., D. Romer and D.N. Weil (1992) 'A Contribution to the Empirics of Economic Growth', *Quarterly Journal of Economics*, Vol. 107, pp. 407–37.

Milana, C. and A. Zeli (2002) 'The Contribution of ICT to Production Efficiency in Italy: Firm Level Evidence Using Data Envelopment Analysis and Econometric Estimations', Working Paper No. 2002/13, OECD Science, Technology and Industry Department.

Milner, C.R. and T. Weyman-Jones (2003) 'Relative National Efficiency and Country Size: Evidence for Developing Countries', *Review of Development Economics*, Vol. 7, pp. 1–14.

OECD (2008) *Economic, Environmental and Social Statistics*, Paris: OECD.

Pritchett, L. (2001) 'Where Has All the Education Gone?', *World Bank Economic Review*, Vol. 15, pp. 367–91.

Repkine, A. (2008) 'ICT Penetration and Aggregate Production Efficiency: Empirical Evidence for a Cross Section of Fifty Countries', *Journal of Applied Economic Sciences*, Vol. 3, pp. 65–72.

Schreyer, P., P.E. Bignon and J. Dupont (2003) 'OECD Capital Services Estimates: Methodology and a First Set of Results', Working Paper No. 2003/6, OECD Statistics Department.

Stiroh, K. (2002) 'Are ICT Spillovers Driving the New Economy?', *Review of Income and Wealth*, Vol. 48, pp. 33–57.

Thompson, H. and C. Garbacz (2007) 'Mobile, Fixed Line and Internet Service Effects on Global Productive Efficiency', *Information Economics and Policy*, Vol. 19, pp. 189–214.

Van Ark, B., R. Inklaar and R. McGuckin (2003) 'ICT and Productivity in Europe and the United States: Where Do the Differences Come From?', *Cesifo Economic Studies*, Vol. 49, pp. 295–318.

World Bank (2008) *World Development Indicators*, Washington DC: World Bank.

3
Analyzing ICT Adoption across European Regions

María Rosalía Vicente and Ana Jesús López

Introduction

Information and communication technology (ICT) has been the driver of the major economic and social changes that have taken place in the last ten years. Hence, the European ICT sector accounts for 5 percent of gross domestic product, and contributes to productivity growth in a 20 percent (European Commission, 2010). Services are increasingly being delivered online. And for more and more people the internet has become a major component of their daily life. Over 250 million Europeans use the internet every day (European Commission, 2010). Within this context, the evaluation of the state of ICT in a territory has become key issue. In fact, there have been several calls for monitoring and benchmarking ICT at international, national and regional levels. Hence, the World Summit on the Information Society stated the need for international evaluation of information society developments. Likewise, successive European action plans for the information society (eEurope and i2010) have considered several measures and indicators to track ICT diffusion across the member states. Nevertheless, little is known about the regional spread of ICT. Most evidence has focused on American states (Atkinson and Andes, 2010), while the references to Europe are scarce (Billón et al., 2008, 2009; Vicente and López, 2010).

This chapter aims to gain further insight into ICT adoption across European regions. Therefore, we consider 216 regions in 30 countries – the 27 member states of the European Union, plus two candidate countries (Croatia and Iceland) and Norway – extending the area analyzed in previous studies (Billón et al., 2008, 2009; Vicente and López, 2010). On the basis of a set of five regional ICT indicators for the year 2010, we assess ICT adoption in each region, and identify groups of similar digital development. The next section describes the framework to measure ICT. Then, data details are presented, followed by the results of the analysis of ICT adoption by means of principal component and cluster techniques. The last section summarizes our principal findings.

Framework

From the very beginning of the diffusion of ICT, its role as an enabler of economic growth and competitiveness has underlined the importance of having appropriate indicators and measures of such phenomena in order to support and inform policy-making (Partnership on Measuring ICT for Development, 2008).

ICT spread has followed the typical S-curve of technological diffusion. This S-curve shows the existence of three phases in the diffusion process: a first phase in which the rate of adoption is very low, the technology is quite new so people decide to start using it little by little; once a critical mass of users is achieved, a second phase initiates and the diffusion speeds up so more and more people becomes users; and, finally, in a third phase, the rate of adoption slows down because most of potential users of the technology have already adopted it and, thus, the market for the technology reaches saturation point (Rogers, 2003). According to the OECD (2009) the S-curve should be used as the conceptual framework to analyze the changes driven by ICT. In this sense, the S-curve defines the following three stages in ICT diffusion:

- a first stage of 'readiness' in which the important elements are ICT infrastructure and ICT access;
- a second stage related to the 'intensity' of ICT usage, in which the focus turns to the extent to which ICT-related activities are carried out;
- a third stage reflecting the outcomes of successfully using ICT – that is, a stage related to 'impact'.

It is important to take into account that all these elements are strongly linked in the sense that there cannot be any use without access, and there will be no impact without any usage. In particular, impact depends on usage in three main ways: the numbers (i.e., more ICT users), the level of intensity (i.e., more texts being sent or more hours spent online) and the sophistication of use (i.e., teleworking, teleconferencing, online banking, or purchasing) (International Telecommunications Union,

2009). In addition, ICT skills are another critical element for impact. ICT will only make a difference to territories and people in terms of efficiency, competitiveness and welfare to the extent that their potential is fully utilized; and doing that requires the population to have the appropriate digital skills (International Telecommunications Union, 2009). In this sense, several authors have pointed out that the second layer shows up the digital divide, since there are important gaps in individuals' abilities regarding finding information online and critically reviewing it (Hargittai, 2002; OECD, 2007). Our framework of analysis considers three key elements to track ICT diffusion: access, use and skills. Only those territories performing well in these three dimensions will successfully reach of the impact stage. Therefore, indicators for these three elements will be indispensable inputs to properly assess the state of ICT across European regions.

Data

The data used in this study comes from Eurostat and, specifically, from its regional statistics on the information society for the year 2010 (Eurostat, 2010). The relevant geographical area is the 27 European Union member states, plus two candidate countries (Croatia and Iceland) and another European nation (Norway), making a total of 30 countries. The number of regions analyzed is 216, at NUTS1 or NUTS2 levels, depending on data availability. Such regional breakdowns correspond to the country itself in the following eight cases: Cyprus, Estonia, Iceland, Latvia, Lithuania, Luxembourg, Malta and Slovenia. Results regarding these territories should be thus interpreted with prudence, as there could be, in fact, internal inequalities that we are not able to catch.

Eurostat provides data on just five indicators related to the regional adoption on ICT, as shown in Table 3.1. Despite this low number of indicators, the five considered variables allow us to measure the three basic dimensions of ICT diffusion (access, use and skills), as stated in the previous section. Hence, the percentages of households connected to the internet and those with broadband can be considered as indicators of access; then, the percentages of individuals using the internet regularly, together with the rate of those buying online, would measure usage and intensity; and, finally, the percentage of individuals who have never used a computer would be an indicator of the need of digital skills.

The 2010 values for the variable related to home broadband connections (BB) were missing for both British and Dutch regions. Given

Table 3.1 Description of ICT indicators

Code	Variable	Dimension
HOMEC	Percentage of households with access to the Internet	Readiness
BB	Percentage of households with a broadband connection	Readiness
RU	Percentage of regular Internet users, those are, individuals who accessed the Internet, on average, at least once a week	Intensity
ECOM	Percentage of individuals who ordered goods or services online for private use	Intensity
NOPC	Percentage of individuals who have never used a computer	e-skills

that the 2009 values were known, and that the rates of home internet and home broadband (HOMEC and BB) are highly correlated (0.94), we applied the growth rate observed between 2009 and 2010 for home internet connections over 2009 broadband values. It should be noticed that all the information regarding ICT refers to households and individuals, while there is no data on enterprises. Nonetheless, a high correlation can be expected between the adoption among households/individuals and that of firms.

Therefore, our analysis might offer a fairly good picture of the regional situation, in spite of the lack of information for businesses.

Analysis of ICT adoption

As stated in previous sections, the comparative analysis of ICT development between territories (countries, regions or cities) requires the evaluation of three key facets: access, use and skills. Within this context, data can be analyzed along two main dimensions: individual indicators and territories (OECD and JCR, 2008). Hence, we will first analyze the structure of the ICT dataset by means of principal component analysis; and then, using cluster techniques, we will classify regions by ICT development. Multivariate techniques have been successfully employed by several authors in the analysis of ICT adoption and the digital divide across countries (Corrocher and Ordanini, 2002; Vicente and López, 2006; Trkman et al., 2008; Çilan et al. 2009). At the regional level, Vicente and López (2010) used factor analysis over the regions of the European Union but they did not combine it with cluster techniques.

Grouping ICT indicators

Principal component analysis is a multivariate technique that allows summarizing of the information contained in a dataset into a small number of variables, which are called principal components. Such components are linear combinations of the original variables, and retain as much information as possible from the original dataset (Hair et al., 1995).

This technique requires variables to be highly correlated with each other. As we can see in Table 3.2, our data clearly satisfies such condition. The correlation coefficients between the five considered indicators are all above 0.86.

Obtaining the principal components involves getting the eigenvalues of the covariance matrix of the dataset. Hence, Figure 3.1 shows

Table 3.2 Pearson correlation coefficients for the regional ICT indicators

	HOMEC	BB	RU	ECOM	NOPC
HOMEC	1	0.946	0.947	0.900	−0.932
BB	0.946	1	0.915	0.864	−0.909
RU	0.947	0.915	1.000	0.925	−0.977
ECOM	0.900	0.864	0.925	1	−0.928
NOPC	−0.932	−0.909	−0.977	−0.928	1

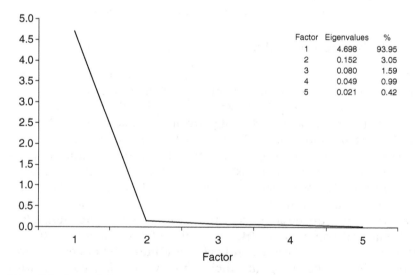

Factor	Eigenvalues	%
1	4.698	93.95
2	0.152	3.05
3	0.080	1.59
4	0.049	0.99
5	0.021	0.42

Figure 3.1 Scree plot

Table 3.3 Component loadings and communalities

	Component loadings	Communalities
RU	0.983	0.966
NOPC	−0.980	0.960
HOMEC	0.975	0.950
BB	0.956	0.914
ECOM	0.952	0.907

the scree plot which represents the graphical solution for principal component analysis. The X-axis shows the number of components and the Y-axis the corresponding eigenvalues arranged in descending order. We notice that the first component has an eigenvalue of 4.7, dropping sharply until 0.15 for the second component and stabilizing around 0.1 for the third, fourth and fifth ones. Literature suggests retaining all those components before the sharp decrease in eigenvalues stops. Such rule implies that just the first component will be considered in this case. The eingenvalue criterion leads to the same conclusion since the first component is the only one with a value over the unit. By dividing the eigenvalue of the first component by the total number of components (five), we get the percentage of the total variance explained by the component. Hence, the first component explains 94 percent of the total variance of the dataset (4.7/5). Therefore, the loss of information when going from the five initial variables to the new component is only 6 percent. Thus, the correlation coefficients between the retained component and the variables, the so-called component loadings, are very high, as shown in Table 3.3. Likewise, the retained component explains high percentages of the variance of each single indicator; in order words, communalities are high.

Taking the standardized values of each indicator in each region, we can compute component scores which will indicate to us the position occupied by each territory in ICT adoption, as well as the size of the digital gaps. Hence, Figure 3.2 shows a graphical representation of the size of such gaps across the 216 analyzed regions. The origin of the horizontal axis represents the European average in ICT. Each bar corresponds to the component score obtained by each region and indicates the extent to which that territory separates from the European ICT average. Thus, those regions on the positive side of the graph are above the European average, while those on the negative side are below

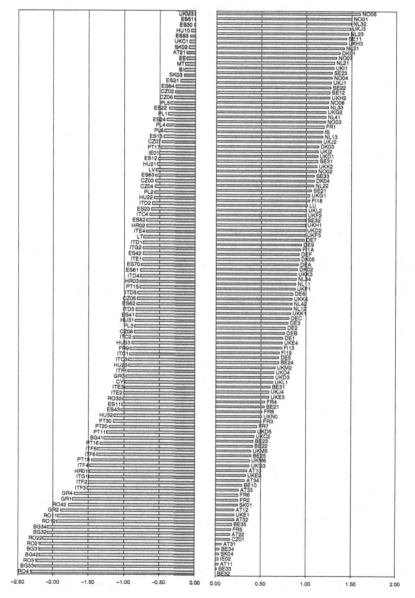

Figure 3.2   Size of ICT inequalities across 216 European regions (30 countries)

that threshold. In particular, out of the 216 analyzed territories, 101 regions have negative component scores and, therefore, are below the European average; 114 regions have positive scores and are over the average; there is one region whose situation coincides with the origin of the horizontal axis and therefore is on the average. The list of regions with their corresponding component score is shown in the Appendix in Table A 3.1.

We can see that the best-positioned region in ICT (a Norwegian region) gets a score over 1.5, while the worst-positioned regions get negative scores lower than –2. In fact, the Top-10 includes all Nordic regions (three Norwegian, one Danish, one Swedish and three Dutch regions), plus two British territories. In contrast, the Bottom-10 comprises Bulgarian and Romanian regions in equal numbers (five and five). If we consider the Top-20 and Bottom-20 regions, the situation changes little: the same countries in the Top-10 retain the Top-20, while Italian, Greek and Croatian regions are incorporated into the Bottom-20. Such results suggest that the European gaps in ICT adoption reflect mainly a north versus south-east divide. In order to get a bit more detail, Figure 3.3 shows the gaps between the Top-10 and Bottom-10 regions. For each ICT indicator we have reckoned the average of the ten best-positioned territories and that of the ten worst-positioned ones. We can see that gaps are huge and go from 50 percentage points for the proportion of population who has never used a computer to 72 percentage points for the proportion of population using

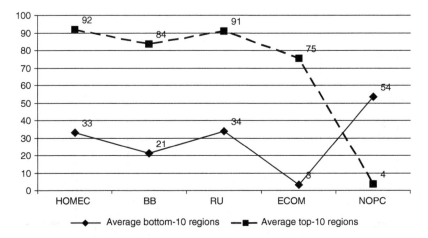

Figure 3.3 The ICT gaps between top-10 and bottom-10 regions

e-commerce. Moreover, it is striking to see that, in the year 2010, more than half of the population in the Bottom-10 regions have never used a computer.

Grouping regions

We have also run a cluster analysis in order to identify groups of regions which have similar ICT adoption levels. There are two main approaches in cluster analysis: hierarchical and non-hierarchical. The main difference between them is that in the former the number of groups to form is not known a priori, while in the latter such number is set by the researcher. The similarity (dissimilarity) between cases and groups are assessed by distance measures and linkage rules, respectively. In the case of analysis, we have used a hierarchical approach based on the squared Euclidean distance and Ward's linkage rule.

Figure 3.4 shows the dendogram; that is, the graphical representation of the cluster solution. It can be seen that two main groups of regions are formed, which then split into two each, and then into another two. A rule of thumb to know the number of clusters to be considered is to stop the analysis where there is a big break in the dendogram. In this case, we have considered the existence of five groups, which main characteristics are shown in Table 3.4 and which have been labeled according to their ICT performance. Hence, there is

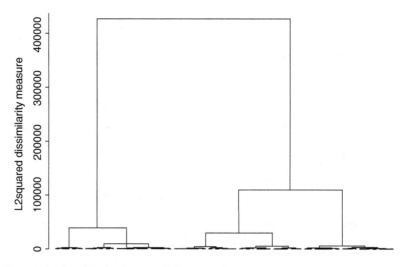

Figure 3.4   Graphical solution of cluster analysis

Table 3.4 Descriptive statistics of the ICT clusters across European regions

	Low performers (N = 15)		Medium-low performers (N = 56)		Average performers (N = 36)		Medium-high-performers (N = 41)		High-performers (N = 68)		Total (N = 216)	
	Mean	Std. Dev.	Mean	Std. Dev.	Mean	Std. Dev.	Mean	Std. Dev.	Mean	Std. Dev.	Mean	Std. Dev.
HOMEC	36.07	6.30	56.09	5.30	65.58	3.94	73.22	4.67	86.26	4.50	69.03	15.54
BB	24.53	6.63	48.79	5.81	59.14	5.70	65.88	6.22	77.59	5.42	61.14	16.03
RU	34.07	3.37	50.16	5.94	62.75	6.38	73.78	4.53	84.21	5.22	66.34	16.83
ECOM	4.73	3.20	16.07	4.78	30.58	4.99	51.78	9.17	67.07	7.05	40.54	23.46
NOPC	52.27	3.61	36.16	6.13	23.44	5.32	14.07	3.72	6.96	2.80	21.77	14.83

a first group of low performers integrated by 15 regions, whose main feature is that more than half of their population have never used a computer; then, a second group is composed of 56 medium–low performers whose broadband and internet penetration rates are about 50 percent; a third group is integrated by 36 regions, whose internet rates are over 60 percent; a fourth group consists of 41 regions in which half of the population are buying online; and, finally, a fifth group integrates 68 high-performing regions where 87 percent of households are connected to the internet and three-quarters connect through broadband, and 67 percent of individuals do e-commerce. It is interesting to notice that the distribution of clusters does not follow a normal distribution since the top-tail has a high frequency. This fact suggests that most regions are performing well in ICT, and just a minority are lagging behind and might have problems derived from such lag.

Conclusion

The spread of ICT has been accompanied by the need for proper measures and analysis of such phenomena at all levels: international, national, regional and local. However, efforts have focused mostly on carrying out cross-country comparisons, while the evidence on ICT adoption across regions is quite limited. Therefore, in this chapter, we have tried to remedy such deficiency by throwing some light on the adoption of ICT across Europe. Instead of focusing on just the members of European Union, we have widened the scope and incorporated into the analysis two candidate countries, as well as Norway. This has led to the inclusion of 216 regions.

To carry out our analysis, we have considered the five ICT indicators that Eurostat publishes in its regional statistics on the information society. Over this set of variables, we have run a principal component analysis in order to summarize such information in a smaller number of components, which allows for easier interpretation of the state of ICT. The results from the application of principal components show that regional differences are huge. Thus, the gap between top and bottom regions reaches the 50 percentage points. Furthermore, in the worst-performing ICT regions half of the population lack the basic digital skills and have never used a computer. Nonetheless, the cluster analysis reveals that only a minority of regions (16 out of the total of 216 – that is, 7 percent) are in such poor condition regarding ICT. In fact, there is a quite big group of regions performing extremely well in the use of these technologies (68 out of the total of 216 – that is, 31 percent), with figures of broadband penetration over 75 percent and almost 70 percent of the population using e-commerce. Such results suggest the need to implement urgent measures and actions to correct the situation of that minority of regions that are performing so poorly in ICT. In the year 2010, in a world that is becoming more and more digital and where services are increasingly being delivered online, the existence of territories where more than half of the population do not have access to the internet or have never used a computer is no longer tenable.

As ICT is becoming a major part of daily life for individuals and business, those territories lagging behind are very likely to end up excluded from the digital society and economy which is to be one of the pillars of the European growth strategy for the new decade. Nonetheless, there is a main drawback in our analysis that must be taken into account. The analysis of ICT adoption across European regions is based on just five indicators – those for which data is available. Although most ICT variables might be highly correlated, a proper analysis of the state of ICT in a territory might require the inclusion of other variables apart from the five considered. For instance, it would be interesting to know the percentage of population that accesses the internet wirelessly in each region and to have some indicator of individuals' digital skills (whether they find problems when searching for information on the internet; whether they feel confident in performing such activities) and on the activities they perform online besides e-commerce. Only when this information is available at regional level will a precise evaluation of ICT adoption be possible.

Appendix

Table A3.1 Descriptive statistics of the ICT clusters across European regions

Code	Name*	Size of ICT inequalities (Component score)	Cluster	Code	Name	Size of ICT inequalities (Component score)	Cluster
NO05	Vestlandet	1.60	5	AT31	Oberösterreich	0.07	3
NO01	Oslo og Akershus	1.50	5	BE34	Prov. Luxembourg	0.05	3
NL32	Noord-Holland	1.50	5	SK04	Východné Slovensko	0.04	3
UKJ3	Hampshire and Isle of Wight	1.49	5	IE02	Southern and Eastern	0.04	3
NL23	Flevoland	1.47	5	AT11	Burgenland	0.03	3
SE11	Stockholm	1.45	5	BE33	Prov. Liège	0.02	3
UKH3	Essex	1.44	5	BE32	Prov. Hainaut	0.00	3
NL31	Utrecht	1.42	5	UKM3	South Western Scotland	-0.01	4
DK01	Hovedstaden	1.37	5	ES51	Cataluña	-0.01	3
NO07	Nord-Norge	1.33	5	ES30	Comunidad de Madrid	-0.02	3
NL21	Overijssel	1.31	5	HU10	Közép-Magyarország	-0.06	3
UKI1	Inner London	1.30	5	ES53	Illes Balears	-0.08	3
SE23	Västsverige	1.29	5	UKC1	Tees Valley and Durham	-0.08	4
NO04	Agder og Rogaland	1.28	5	SK02	Západné Slovensko	-0.09	3
UKJ1	Berkshire. Buckinghamshire and Oxfordshire	1.28	5	AT21	Kärnten	-0.12	3
SE22	Sydsverige	1.27	5	EE	Estonia	-0.13	3
SE12	Östra Mellansverige	1.26	5	MT	Malta	-0.15	3

UKH2	Bedfordshire and Hertfordshire	1.26	5	SI	Slovenia	-0.15	3
NO06	Trøndelag	1.25	5	SK03	Stredné Slovensko	-0.16	3
NL33	Zuid-Holland	1.25	5	ES21	País Vasco	-0.21	3
UKG2	Shropshire and Staffordshire	1.22	5	ES64	Ciudad Autónoma de Melilla	-0.28	3
NL41	Noord-Brabant	1.22	5	CZ02	Strední Cechy	-0.29	3
NO03	Sør-Østlandet	1.21	5	CZ06	Jihovýchod	-0.30	3
FR1	Île de France	1.20	5	PL5	Region Poludniowo-Zachodni	-0.35	3
IS	Iceland	1.18	5	ES22	Comunidad Foral de Navarra	-0.37	3
NL13	Drenthe	1.18	5	PL1	Region Centralny	-0.38	3
UKJ2	Surrey, East and West Sussex	1.17	5	ES24	Aragón	-0.40	3
DK03	Syddanmark	1.14	5	PL4	Region Pólnocno-Zachodni	-0.41	3
UKI2	Outer London	1.13	5	PL6	Region Pólnocny	-0.43	3
UKD1	Cumbria	1.13	5	ES13	Cantabria	-0.44	3
SE31	Norra Mellansverige	1.13	5	CZ07	Strední Morava	-0.47	3
UKK2	Dorset and Somerset	1.12	5	PT17	Lisboa	-0.48	3
NO02	Hedmark og Oppland	1.11	5	IE01	Border. Midland and Western	-0.51	3
SE33	Övre Norrland	1.09	5	ES12	Principado de Asturias	-0.52	3
DK04	Midtjylland	1.09	5	HU21	Közép-Dunántúl	-0.54	2
NL22	Gelderland	1.08	5	LV	Latvia	-0.55	2
SE21	Småland med öarna	1.06	5	ES63	Ciudad Autónoma de Ceuta	-0.56	2

Continued

Table A 3.1 Continued

Code	Name*	Size of ICT inequalities (Component score)	Cluster	Code	Name	Size of ICT inequalities (Component score)	Cluster
UKG1	Herefordshire. Worcestershire and Warwickshire	1.04	5	CZ03	Jihozápad	-0.56	3
FI18	Etelä-Suomi	1.04	5	CZ04	Severozápad	-0.57	3
LU	Luxembourg	1.01	5	PL2	Region Poludniowy	-0.58	3
UKL2	East Wales	1.00	5	HU22	Nyugat-Dunántúl	-0.58	2
UKF2	Leicestershire. Rutland and Northamptonshire	1.00	5	ITD2	Provincia Autonoma Trento	-0.60	2
SE32	Mellersta Norrland	1.00	5	ES23	La Rioja	-0.62	2
UKH1	East Anglia	0.99	5	ITC4	Lombardia	-0.64	2
UKD2	Cheshire	0.99	5	ES52	Comunidad Valenciana	-0.69	2
UKF3	Lincolnshire	0.99	5	HR02	Sredisnja i Istocna (Panonska) Hrvatska	-0.69	2
DE7	Hessen	0.98	5	ITE4	Lazio	-0.69	2
DE9	Niedersachsen	0.95	5	LT	Lithuania	-0.73	2
FI1A	Pohjois-Suomi	0.94	5	ITD1	Provincia Autonoma Bolzano/Bozen	-0.74	2
DEF	Schleswig-Holstein	0.93	5	ITG2	Sardegna	-0.74	2
DK05	Nordjylland	0.92	5	ES42	Castilla-la Mancha	-0.74	2
DEA	Nordrhein-Westfalen	0.92	5	ITE1	Toscana	-0.74	2
DK02	Sjælland	0.91	5	ES70	Canarias	-0.76	2
UKK3	Cornwall and Isles of Scilly	0.90	5	ES61	Andalucía	-0.77	2

Code	Region		Score	Code	Region		Score
NL34	Zeeland	5	0.89	ITD4	Friuli-Venezia Giulia	5	−0.77
NL11	Groningen	5	0.89	HR03	Jadranska Hrvatska	5	−0.78
UKF1	Derbyshire and Nottinghamshire	5	0.88	PT15	Algarve	5	−0.78
DE6	Hamburg	5	0.86	ITD5	Emilia-Romagna	5	−0.81
UKK4	Devon	5	0.85	CZ05	Severovýchod	5	−0.82
NL42	Limburg	5	0.85	ES62	Región de Murcia	5	−0.82
NL12	Friesland	5	0.84	ITD3	Veneto	5	−0.83
UKK1	Gloucestershire. Wiltshire and Bristol/Bath area	5	0.83	ES41	Castilla y León	5	−0.84
DEC	Saarland	5	0.81	HU31	Észak-Magyarország	5	−0.85
DE3	Berlin	5	0.80	PL3	Region Wschodni	5	−0.85
DE2	Bayern	5	0.77	CZ08	Moravskoslezsko	5	−0.85
DEB	Rheinland-Pfalz	5	0.76	ITC2	Valle d'Aosta/Vallée d'Aoste	5	−0.87
DE1	Baden-Württemberg	5	0.75	HU33	Dél-Alföld	5	−0.89
UKE4	West Yorkshire	4	0.74	FR9	Départements d'outre-mer	4	−0.92
FI13	Itä-Suomi	4	0.74	ITC1	Piemonte	4	−0.92
FI19	Länsi-Suomi	4	0.70	ITC3	Liguria	4	−0.93
DE5	Bremen	4	0.70	HU23	Dél-Dunántúl	4	−0.94
BE24	Prov. Vlaams-Brabant	4	0.70	ITF1	Abruzzo	4	−0.95
UKM2	Eastern Scotland	5	0.66	GR3	Attiki	5	−0.97
UKD4	Lancashire	4	0.65	CY	Cyprus	4	−0.98
UKD3	Greater Manchester	4	0.64	ITE3	Marche	4	−0.99
UKL1	West Wales and The Valleys	4	0.63	ITE2	Umbria	4	−1.01
BE31	Prov. Brabant Wallon	4	0.61	RO32	Bucuresti - Ilfov	4	−1.02
UKJ4	Kent	4	0.59	ES11	Galicia	4	−1.03

Continued

Table A 3.1   Continued

Code	Name*	Size of ICT inequalities (Component score)	Cluster	Code	Name	Size of ICT inequalities (Component score)	Cluster
UKE3	South Yorkshire	0.59	4	ES43	Extremadura	-1.04	2
FR4	Est	0.55	4	HU32	Észak-Alföld	-1.14	2
BE21	Prov. Antwerpen	0.54	4	PT30	Região Autónoma da Madeira	-1.15	2
FR8	Méditerranée	0.52	4	PT20	Região Autónoma dos Açores	-1.21	2
UKN0	Northern Ireland	0.51	4	PT11	Norte	-1.24	2
FR3	Nord - Pas-de-Calais	0.51	4	BG41	Yugozapaden	-1.28	2
FR7	Centre-Est	0.46	4	PT16	Centro	-1.33	2
UKD5	Merseyside	0.44	4	ITF5	Basilicata	-1.38	2
UKC2	Northumberland and Tyne and Wear	0.43	4	ITF6	Calabria	-1.38	2
BE23	Prov. Oost-Vlaanderen	0.42	4	PT18	Alentejo	-1.46	2
BE22	Prov. Limburg	0.41	4	ITF4	Puglia	-1.49	2
UKM5	North Eastern Scotland	0.40	4	HR01	Sjeverozapadna Hrvatska	-1.49	2
BE25	Prov. West-Vlaanderen	0.39	4	ITG1	Sicilia	-1.50	2
UKM6	Highlands and Islands	0.38	4	ITF2	Molise	-1.50	2
UKG3	West Midlands	0.37	4	ITF3	Campania	-1.52	2
AT13	Wien	0.35	4	GR4	Nisia Aigaiou. Kriti	-1.70	1
UKE2	North Yorkshire	0.34	4	GR1	Voreia Ellada	-1.73	1

AT34	Vorarlberg	0.32	4	RO42	Vest	-1.78	1
BE10	Région de Bruxelles-Capitale / Brussels Hoofdstedelijk Gewest	0.30	4	GR2	Kentriki Ellada	-1.89	1
AT33	Tirol	0.26	4	RO11	Nord-Vest	-1.94	1
FR6	Sud-Ouest	0.25	4	RO12	Centru	-1.95	1
FR2	Bassin Parisien	0.25	4	BG34	Yugoiztochen	-2.08	1
SK01	Bratislavský kraj	0.25	4	BG32	Severen tsentralen	-2.08	1
AT12	Niederösterreich	0.21	4	RO22	Sud-Est	-2.14	1
UKE1	East Yorkshire and Northern Lincolnshire	0.21	4	RO21	Nord-Est	-2.18	1
AT32	Salzburg	0.21	4	BG31	Severozapaden	-2.19	1
BE35	Prov. Namur	0.18	4	BG42	Yuzhen tsentralen	-2.20	1
FR5	Ouest	0.17	4	RO31	Sud - Muntenia	-2.23	1
AT22	Steiermark	0.16	4	BG33	Severoiztochen	-2.26	1
CZ01	Praha	0.16	3	RO41	Sud-Vest Oltenia	-2.31	1

* Regions have been ordered according to the component score. Top-10 and Bottom-10 regions have been highlighted.

References

Atkinson, R.D. and S.M. Andes (2010) *The 2010 State New Economy Index*, Washington DC: Information Technology and Innovation Foundation.

Billón, M., R. Ezcurra and F. Lera-López (2008) 'The Spatial Distribution of the Internet in the European Union: Does Geographical Proximity Matter?', *European Planning Studies*, Vol. 16, No. 1, pp. 119–42.

Billón, M., R. Ezcurra and F. Lera-López (2009) 'Spatial Effects in Website Adoption by Firms in European Regions', *Growth and Change*, Vol. 40, No. 1, pp. 54–84.

Çilan, Ç. A., B.A. Bolat and E. Coşkun (2009) 'Analyzing the Digital Divide within and between Member and Candidate Countries of European Union', *Government Information Quarterly*, Vol. 26, pp. 98–105.

Corrocher, N. and A. Ordanini (2002) 'Measuring the Digital Divide: A Framework for the Analysis of Cross-country Differences', *Journal of Information Technology*, Vol. 17, 9–19.

European Commission (2010) *A Digital Agenda for Europe*, Brussels: European Commission.

Eurostat (2010) *Regional Information Society Statistics*, http://www.ec.europa.eu/eurostat (home page), last accessed 30 November 2010.

Hair Jr, J.F., R.E. Anderson, R.L. Tatham and W.C. Black (1995) *Multivariate Data Analysis with Readings*, London: Prentice Hall International.

Hargittai, E. (2002) 'Second-Level Digital Divide: Differences in People's Online Skills', *First Monday*, Vol. 7, No. 4-1, http://www.firstmonday.org (home page), last accessed 15 May 2005.

International Telecommunications Union (2009) *Measuring the Information Society: The ICT Development Index 2009*, Geneva: International Telecommunications Union.

OECD (2007) *Broadband and ICT Access and use by Households and Individuals*, Paris: OECD.

OECD (2009) *Guide for Measuring the Information Society*, Paris: OECD.

OECD and JRC (2008) *Handbook on Composite Indicators*, Paris: OECD.

Partnership on Measuring ICT for Development (2008) *The Global Information Society: A Statistical View*, Santiago de Chile: United Nations.

Rogers, E.M. (2003) *Diffusion of Innovations*, New York: Free Press.

P. Trkman, B.J. Blazic and T. Turk (2008) 'Factors of Broadband Development and the Design of a Strategic Policy Framework', *Telecommunications Policy*, Vol. 32, pp. 101–15.

Vicente, M.R. and A.J. López (2006) 'A Multivariate Framework for the Analysis of the Digital Divide: Evidence for the European Union-15', *Information & Management*, Vol. 43, pp. 756–66.

Vicente, M.R. and A.J. López (2010) 'Assessing the Regional Digital Divide across the European Union-27', *Telecommunications Policy* (in press).

Part II
Determinants of Demand for ICT

4
Determinants of Usages and Access to the Internet Services in Côte d'Ivoire

Auguste K. Kouakou

Introduction

The development of information and communication technologies (ICT) is strongly dependent on the dynamism of the telecommunications sector, which is the major infrastructure. For nearly a decade, the sector has been undergoing reforms aimed at opening it to competition anywhere in the world, and Africa in particular. With the technological advances (mobile telephony, Internet, copper cable, optical fiber, wireless local loop, ADSL, etc.), the convergence of voice-data-image and regulation tools, the impact of the telecommunication sector or the digital industries on the real economy has uncovered the concept of 'a new economy', wherein we take into consideration the effects of ICT on the economic growth and development.

The link between ICT and development is taken into account by the international community through the United Nations agencies such as the World Trade Organization (WTO), the International Telecommunication Union (ITU), the United Nations Development Programme (UNDP) through Millennium Development Goals (MDGs) and the United Nations Conference on Trade and Development (UNCTAD) annual report on information economy. Specifically, the WTO launched a reference paper, signed by Côte d'Ivoire, containing guidelines for the liberalization process and the introduction of competition in the telecommunication sector for the country members; ITU. The members of ITU made the commitment, during the World Summit on Information Society (WSIS) 2003 and 2005, to provide access to ICT to half of the world population by 2015. The MDGs comprise the objectives of telephone penetration with both wireline and wireless from 2000 to 2015 and they are driven by UNDP, the UN agency devoted to the problem of economic development. Recently UNCTAD's report on information economy in 2007 focused on the state of advances of ICT and its effect on economic development. Thus, the different reform processes being implemented in the developing countries address the answer to some sectoral, local, and international imperatives. Based on the Internet world statistics (2006), Africa, which represents 14.1 percent of the world's population, had a penetration rate of only 1.6 percent. In Côte d'Ivoire, the reform initiated by the Telecommunications Code of 1995, authorized the entry into the market of several players in the different segments of fixed line, mobile, Internet, and value-added services. Thus, the choice was clearly made by promoting the industry with the attraction of private capital. Apart from the operator of fixed line (the incumbent), in which the government owns 49 percent of the capital, the remaining market segments are wholly owned by private operators. Mobile phone operators are even progressing faster than fixed lines and Internet providers. This option has produced mixed results. While mobile telephony experienced an explosion and generated excitement, with more than 20 percent penetration rate in a decade, technologies such as wireline telephone and other newer products' (such as the Internet penetration experienced a slowdown. By the end of 2006, the penetration rate of the Internet in Côte d'Ivoire was about 6 percent of the total population, with a strong majority in Abidjan, the main economic city. It may be noted that the policy of universal service implemented at the beginning had not explicitly taken into account the development of the Internet service. Thus, it had not benefited from specific measures like the fixed lines operator. The National Telecommunications Fund set up in 1998 was not operational and this was to the detriment of the extension of the network in the whole country. Therefore, the development and dissemination of Internet service in Côte d'Ivoire has not been supported by a public policy, although the government has chosen to develop the market.

From Navas-savater et al. (2002), we notice that two issues prevented the spread of Internet service with the market development option. On one hand was the ineffectiveness of the market to promote access of the majority of the population in commercial areas covered by Internet providers and, on the other hand, the deficit in the coverage of the territory that hindered the connection to the Internet service. In the first aspect, the physical network is present but not affordable, while in the second one the capabilities of the network does not cover the entire country, including rural areas. The digital divide persists and deserves special attention. So the issue of the extension of the service and the reduction of the digital divide remain.

The main issue discussed in this study regards determining the factors that will foster access to the Internet in Côte d'Ivoire. Does the development of Internet service have to follow the path of the old technologies – the fixed and mobile telephone? This analysis should help to identify factors influencing distribution of the service in order to identify the relevant levers capable of contributing to the narrowing of the digital divide in the country. This study will particularly highlight the socio-demographic factors influencing the Internet access and elaborate whether there is a geographical divide; finally, it will present the effect of social capital.

Literature review

The digital divide, which is the gap between those who have access to ICT and those who do not have access, is still perceptible in the world. Using the aggregated data or survey data, different authors have highlighted the inequality of the access to Internet services (see Fink and Kenny, 2003; Hunter, 2002; Kiiski and Pohjola, 2002; OECD, 2001; Crandall, 2001).

In Africa, Conte (2001a) shows that there is a deep digital divide that is diminishing over time. The reduction of this unequal access requires a better understanding of the determinants of the choice at the individual and collective level. Based on an econometric analysis with aggregated data, it shows that variables such as education and training level, urbanization, standard of living, economic activity, equipment, access costs and Internet offers are the main determinants involved in the network access assessment (Conte, 2000). The unequal access to the network in African countries was also discussed by recent articles written by Fuchs C. and E. Horak (2006); see also Fuchs (2005). They show that liberalization and competition are not enough to bridge the digital divide, based on the facts and cases of Ghana and South Africa. They conclude that the reduction of the digital divide must be based not only on technological solutions but also on important changes in African societies, particularly in the production system, the organization of powers and the cultural aspects. The digital divide has a social (age, gender, marital status, language, rural/urban, ethnic origin), economic (income) and political (power, social relations) dimension, as well as some cultural aspects (competence, talent). Global strategies need to be considered when dealing with the digital divide issue.

This view is also shared by van Dijk (2006), Norris (2001), Castells (2002) and Wilson (2006). They take into account the geographical and location effect of the digital divide. These results are tested by Oyelaran-

Oyeyinka and Kaushalesh (2005) using a simultaneous equation model with African data. They highlight the relevance of macroeconomic, socio-demographic and technological variables. Sciadas (2002) analyses the digital divide in Canada with data from a household survey on the use of ICT. Many variables such as income, age, education level and geographic location or marital status play an important role in the penetration of the Internet in particular. It shows that the rate of adoption of the Internet in Canada is higher among low-income households than among those with higher incomes, a typical situation of a catch-up effect. Using qualitative models, Noce and McKeown (2007) analyze the determinants of Internet usage in Canada with data from a household survey of 2005. Their analysis highlights the socio-economic determinants of the use of the service and the geographical divide.

In the USA, recent studies from household surveys (Chaudhuri et al., 2005; Flammand Chaudhuri, 2007; Rappoport et al., 2002; Calabrese and Jung, 1992) take into account, in addition to the socio-economic determinants, residential access costs and regional specificities as an explanation of the access of households to high- or low-speed Internet connections. Similarly, they show that the level of income and education produce a greater impact on the likelihood of subscribing to the Internet at home, as well as marital status. In addition to socio-economic, geographic and technological factors, other authors raise the issue of the effects of learning and social capital on the likelihood of using the network (Le Guel et al. 2005; Lethiais Poussing, 2004; Lethiais et al., 2003; Oxendine et al., 2003; Horrigan, 2001; Moschella and Atkinson, 1998). They identify two types of divide: one relating to access and the other to utilization. Their work shows that the determinants of these two types of digital gap are different: while the access gap is linked to geographical barriers and socio-demographic characteristics, the utilization gap depends on the intellectual capability or individuals' cognitive ability and social capital. It depends on both the experience and social neighborhood of the user. Lethiais Poussing (2004) make a comparative analysis of the determinants using a survey from Brittany, in France, and Luxembourg. Their study yields two major findings: while Internet usage at work positively impacts the adoption of Internet at home in the two areas, it produces a substitution effect between usage in the office and at home, including online purchase, in Brittany.

Determination of the factors that guide adoption of the Internet in Côte d'Ivoire will take place in the light of this literature, using qualitative econometric methods with survey data on telecommunications in 2007.

Methodological framework

Dataset and variables

Datasets used in this study were taken from a survey conducted on behalf of the Telecommunications Agency of Côte d'Ivoire (ATCI) by the Ivorian Centre for Economic and Social Research (CIRES). For the survey, 1,500 households were drawn under a two-stage sample selection, with stratification of primary units and secondary units. At the first stage, the choice of 100 census districts (called DR) was made taking in ten strata. At the second stage, 15 households were chosen among each DR and thereafter a three-section questionnaire was developed based on fixed-line telephony, mobile phone and Internet service. The variables of the model are described in Table 4.1. In the database, the proportion of people who had access to the Internet was 44.6 percent compared to 55.4 percent who had no access, this out of a total of 1,495 respondents. The age of the respondent is an important dimension, as shown in previous studies. In our sample, age distribution shows a majority of young people under the age of 30 (57.72 percent) and 69.4 percent of them has access to the Internet regardless of the place of connection (an overall figure of 91 percent under 50 years old). Figure 4.1 shows that our sample is predominantly composed of young people, whose average age is between 20 and 30 years old. The sample is composed of 64.9 percent male and 35.1 percent women. Among those who have access to the Internet, 70 percent of them are male (respectively, 30 percent female) and 75 percent are not married.

With regard to education, more educated people (38 percent of our sample) have greater access to the Internet (55 percent) compared to poorly educated people (less than 9 percent). Independent professionals, representing 58.7 percent in the database, have a higher access level (64.6 percent) compared to other professions. In the sample, 75 percent of individuals have incomes less than 150,000 francs. Among those with access to the network, 66 percent are low-income individuals, while among those without access to the network, this category accounts for 80 percent. In other words, among individuals with income less than 50,000 francs and between 50,000 and 150,000 francs, access rates are 39 percent and 27 percent, respectively. It follows that people with low income have a high access rate to the Internet. We notice also that a higher proportion of people dwell in a decent house (62 percent) with a higher access rate (72 percent). The social capital variable was revealed by the membership of various types of associations, such as cultural, sports, politics, neighborhood or religious associations (see Putnam,

Table 4.1   Description of variables, sample frequencies according to Internet access

Variables	Description	Sample	Access to Internet	Non Access to Internet
			Proportion (%)	
Frequency of access			44.6	55.4
Sex				
Male	Male	64.86	70	60.63
Female	Female	35.14	30	39.37
Age				
[15–30]	If age between 15–30 years old	57.72	69.42	48.43
[30–50]	If age between 30 and 50	33.33	26.69	38.65
[50,+]	If age above 50 years old	8.95	3.9%	12.92
Marital status				
Married	Get married	35.60	24.74	44.44
Not married	Single, divorced, widow, never married	64.40	75.26	55.56
Religion				
Christian	Christian	61.99	66.12	58.57
Muslim	Muslim	30.93	26.54	34.54
Animist	Animist and others	7.08	7.35	6.88
Education				
None	No education level	10.29	2.55	16.55
Primary	Primary Education	14.50	6.15	21.14
Secondary	Colleges	37.07	35.38	38.41
High school	University and high schools	38.14	55.92	23.91
Professional activity				
Civil servant	Work in a public office	8.08	11.39	5.43%
Clerk, employee	Qualified employee	4.88	5.7	4.11
Unskilled worker	Non qualified employee	4.28	1.2	6.76
Professional	Individuals	24.05	17.09	29.59
Others	Retiree, non workers and other workers	58.72	64.62	54.11
Revenue				
[0–50]	under 50 000 frs CFA	47.98	39.27	52.74
[50–150]	between 50 and 150 000 frs	27.26	27.19	27.40
[150, +]	Above 150 000 frs CFA	24.75	33.53	19.86
Accommodation				
House-flat	House-flat	62.26	72.11	54.23
Precarious house	Precarious house	37.74	27.89	45.77
Member of an association				
yes	Member of an association	58.72	64.17	54.31
No	Not member	41.28	35.83	45.69

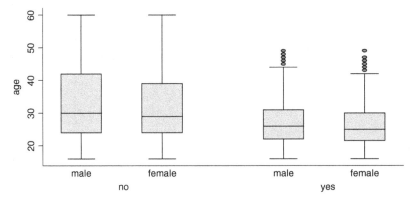

Figure 4.1   Boxplot of the age group by sex and over access to the Internet

1993). The main idea is that the network and its effect create value for memberships.

According to Putnam, participation in civic organization, levels of trust and charitable giving are different types of social capital. Thus, it appears that 59 percent of the individuals in the sample are members of associations, from whom 64 percent have access to the Internet. In the sample, the majority of people have an average use of the Internet (40.2 percent), followed by regular users (37.2 percent) and a low proportion of non-regular users (22.6 percent). For both men and women, the dominant mode is the average use (47 percent and 36 percent respectively). According to different modes (non-regular, medium and regular), men appear as a high proportion in each case (63 percent, 77 percent and 74 percent respectively).

The test of independence between gender and usage shows no relation using Pearson chi square (chi2 (2) = 0.4753, Pr = 0788). Young people have a high average use (49 percent, representing 79 percent of average users) and encompass a strong association between variables from Pearson chi square (chi2 (4) = 15.1858, Pr = 0.004). Most of the people among users have reached at least secondary education. The majority of them have an average use of the network.

Regarding professional activity, qualified employees, unskilled workers and professionals have also an average use with high frequency. Being network members, such as of professional or cultural associations, leads to a medium and regular use. However, the two variables are independent, according to Pearson chi square test (chi2 (2) = 2.1784; Pr = 0336). Table 4.2 summarizes these statistics.

Table 4.2 Statistics on the Internet usage (figures in %)

Variables	Usage (a)			Usage (b)			
	Non regular (90 days)	Average (7 days)	Regular	Non regular	Average	Regular	Total
Frequency usage	22.6	40.2	37.2	22.6	40.2	37.2	100
Sex							
Male	62.8	77.1	73.6	22.0	47.0	31.0	100
female	37.2		26.4	34.2	36.6	29.2	100
total	100	100	100				
Age							
[15–30]	67.6	79.1	63.5	24.0	48.9	27.1	100
[30–50]	27.7	17.8	33.2	28.1	31.5	40.4	100
[50,+]	4.7	3.1	3.4	33.3	38.1	28.6	100
total	100	100	100				
Marital status							
Married	21.6	15.1	32.6	24.8	30.2	45.0	100
Not married		84.9	67.4	25.5	48.1	26.3	100
total	100	100	100				
Religion							
Christian	69	65.5	71.3	25.6	42.5	31.9	100
Muslim	20.9	27.9	22.5	21.7	50.3	28.0	100
Animist	10.1	6.6	6.2	34.8	39.5	25.6	100
total	100	100	100				
Education							
None	0.7	0.8	2.2	14.3	28.6	57.1	100
Primary	7.4	3.5	3.4	42.3	34.6	23.1	100
Secondary	37.2	36.8	28.1	27.5	47.5	25.0	100
High school	54.7	58.9	66.3	23.1	43.3	33.6	100
total	100	100	100				
Professional activity							
Civil servant	19.2	30.8	33.3	14.7	42.6	42.7	100
Clerk, employee	13.5	16	13.8	20.6	44.1	35.3	100
Unskilled worker	1.9	4.3	2.3	14.3	57.1	28.6	100
Professional	44.2	39.4	35.6	25.3	40.6	34.1	100
Others	21.1	9.6	14.9	33.3	27.3	39.4	100
total	100	100	100				
Revenue							
[0-50]	52.9	41.9	36.5	27.8	40.2	32.0	100
[50-150]	9.8	27.9	23.6	9.8	51.0	39.2	100
[150, +]	37.3	30.1	40.0	23.4	34.6	42.0	100
total	100	100	100				
Accommodation							
House-flat	77.7	67.1	79.2	26.8	40.3	32.9	100
Precarious house	22.3	32.9	20.8	21.3	54.8	23.9	100
total	100	100	100				
Member of an association							
yes	61.5	66.3	60.7	24.6	46.2	29.2	100
No	38.5	33.7	39.3	26.6	40.6	32.7	100
total	100	100	100				

Model specification

Modeling access to the network: simple Logit model

The search for the factors behind the decision to adopt the Internet will be made from qualitative models. The model used is the simple logit model. For example, consider the random dichotomous variable, which takes the value 1 if the individual has access to the Internet and 0 otherwise:

$$y_i = \begin{cases} 1 \text{ if access to internet} \\ 0 \text{ if not access} \end{cases} \tag{1}$$

When an individual adopts the Internet network, he obtains a satisfaction which depends on its own characteristics and the economic environment. The model can be rewritten as follows:

$$y_i = \begin{cases} 1 \text{ if } y_i^* = x_i'\beta + \varepsilon_i \\ 0 \text{ otherwise} \end{cases} \text{ or } y_i = \begin{cases} x_i'\beta + \varepsilon_i & \text{if } y_i^* > 0 \\ 0 & \text{if } y_i^* \leq 0 \end{cases} \tag{2}$$

where y_i is the dependent variable capturing access to the Internet or not, with i = 1, 2,..., n, where n is the number of observations; x_i refers to the vector of k characteristics of the individual i influencing the access decision; ε_i is the random disturbance associated with the ith observation following a logistic distribution; y_i^* is the latent variable.

Given that:

$$E(y_i) = x_i'\beta \text{ and } P(y = 1/x_i) = P(y^* > 0 \mid x)$$
$$= P(x_i'\beta + \varepsilon_i > 0 \mid x) = F(x_i'\beta) = p_i \tag{3}$$

where p_i is the probability of Internet access.

Thus, using logistic cumulative function, the probability of having access to the Internet, given the individual characteristics, is:

$$P(y = 1/ x_i) = F(x_i'\beta) = \frac{\exp(x_i'\beta)}{1 + \exp(x_i'\beta)} \tag{4}$$

The probability of not having access to the network is given by:

$$1 - P(y = 1/x) = F(-x_i'\beta) = \frac{\exp(-x_i'\beta)}{1 + \exp(-x_i'\beta)} = \frac{1}{1 + \exp(x_i'\beta)} \tag{5}$$

To constrain the predictions to the range 0 to 1, we transform the probability into odds given by:

$$OR = \frac{p_i}{1 - P_i} = \frac{P(y = 1 \mid x)}{P(y = 0 \mid x)} = \frac{P(y = 1 \mid x)}{1 - P(y = 1 \mid x)}$$

which indicate how often something happens ($y_i = 1$) relative to how often it does not happen ($y_i = 0$), and range from 0 when $P(y = 1|x) = 0$ to ∞ when $P(y = 1|x) = 1$. The log of the odds, or logit, ranges from $-\infty$ to $+\infty$. This range suggests a model that is linear in the logit and takes the following form depending on the individual k characteristics:

$$\ln\left(\frac{p_i}{1-p_i}\right) = x_i' \beta \tag{6}$$

Thus the probability that $y_i = 1$ is an increasing function of the linear combination $x_i\beta$. The estimate of the model is based on maximizing the function of log-likelihood, which is written:

$$L(y,x,\beta) = \prod_{i=1}^{n}\left[\frac{1}{1+\exp(x_i'\beta)}\right]^{1-y_i}\left[\frac{\exp(x_i'\beta)}{1+\exp(x_i'\beta)}\right]^{y_i} \tag{7}$$

Modeling usage: ordered logit model

It will be also interesting to consider the frequency of usage after having access to the network. To do so, we create a variable named usage. It captures the frequency of use of the web whatever the place of use (office, home, school, cybercafé, etc.).

The 'usage' variable has an ordered form and yields three categories: category (1) when you have used the net at least once in the last three months (i.e., 90 days), category (2) for at least once in the past week and category (3) when you use Internet every day.

Initially, considering that this variable was ordinally scaled, we decide to use an ordered logit model that estimates the relationship between an ordinal dependent variable and a set of independent variables. It is specified as follows:

$$y_i = \begin{cases} 1 = 1/90 \ days & if & y_i^* < \alpha_1 \\ 2 = 1/7 \ days & if & \alpha_1 \le y_i^* < \alpha_2 \\ 3 = 1/1 \ days & if & y_i^* \ge \alpha_2 \end{cases} \tag{8}$$

The probability of observing $y_i = m$ for given values of the independent variables corresponds to the region of the distribution where y^* falls between α_{m-1} and α_m:

$$P(y_i = m \mid x) = P(\alpha_{m-1} \le y_i^* < \alpha_m \mid x) \tag{9}$$

Substituting $x\beta + \varepsilon$ for y^* leads to the standard formula for the predicted probability in the ordered regression model:

$$P(y_i = m \mid x) = F(\alpha_m - x_i' \beta) - F(\alpha_{m-1} - x_i' \beta) \tag{10}$$

The ordered logit model (OLM) will simultaneously estimate multiple equations whose number equals the number of categories minus one. In our case, because we have three possibilities, the model will estimate two equations: the first equation comparing category 1 to 2 and 3 and the second equation comparing 1 and 2 to category 3. Each equation models the odds of being in the one category mentioned as opposed to the other categories. This method estimates the independent variable effect on the frequency or intensity of usage falling above or below a given cut-point. Each cut-point or threshold is defined as a separation of two contiguous categories. The most commonly used version of the ordered logit model assumes that the impact of each variable is the same for all cut-points. This is known as the assumption of parallel regression or proportional odds – that is, that the effects of the explanatory variables on the cumulative response probabilities are constant across all categories. In other words, factors explaining the shift from the first to the second category (1 to 2) should not be different from the factors explaining the shift from the second to the third (2 to 3).

If no particular reason guides to such stability in factors explaining the usage frequency, we will use a variant of ordered logit regression named the generalized ordered logit model (Fu, 1998; Cameron and Trivedi, 2005; Williams, 2006). This less restrictive method is similar to ordered logit regression, but relaxes the proportional odds assumption on the data. In contrast to the OLM, our generalized ordered logit model (GOLM) produces two sets of estimates that correspond to each cut-point. The econometric results are analyzed in the following section.

Empirical findings

We check for collinearity and drop from the model variables that are strongly correlated. Thus, we drop the revenue, diploma and type of city variables. After analyzing the residuals, we use the logistic functional form to fit the model. We run the likelihood-ratio test, the Wald test and the proportion of correctly classified. For the OLM, we assess the proportional odds assumption using an approximate likelihood-ratio test of whether the coefficients are equal across categories. A significant test statistic provides evidence that the parallel regression assumption has been violated (see Table 4.4 for the parallel regression test). Then, we estimate the model using the GOLM.

Access to the Internet

We have tested two kinds of logit models in Table 4.3: the first one uses socio-demographic and economic variables, and the second takes into account a social capital variable.

The first logit model yields several results. Compared to being a woman, which is the basis, from the variable related to gender, it can be said that males are more likely to access the network than women. Thus, we can conclude that the digital divide is gender-oriented, against females.

Belonging to the age group above 30 years negatively affects the probability of accessing the network as compared to the reference age group between 15 and 30 years. As age increases, one's chances of accessing the Internet reduce drastically. Hence, it can be concluded that the Internet is a youth phenomenon. Study findings also show that unskilled individuals and professionals are less likely to access the Internet in comparison to a civil servant. In other words, being an executive, a public servant or an office clerk increases the chance to access the network compared to others. Related to housing, the fact of living in precarious housing reduces the probability to access the network as opposed to individuals resident in satisfactory accommodation.

This type of low-grade/temporary housing and district are not fully covered by the network so there is both a commercial and an access gap. This situation is strongly correlated with the question of geographical divide. The more educated an individual is, the more likely he/she is to access the network. Moreover, the effect is more significant as education level increases from primary to tertiary, looking at the odds ratios. There appears to be a digital divide in access between educated and non-educated individuals. Education level is an important factor which influences the ability of individuals to join the network. In a nutshell, this raises the question of a cognitive digital divide. However, access cannot be explained by variables such as marital status and religion. In the second model, we introduce social capital through the variable 'membership of an association'. By introducing social capital, we get the results of the second logit model. Social network effects are taken into account by measuring the membership of associative networks of all types (promotional, professional, district, village, generational, etc.). These opportunities promote social links, using ICTs to stay in contact.

Table 4.3 Model of access to the Internet: logit (1) and logit (2)

Variables[a]	Model logit(1)			Model logit(2)		
	Coefficients[b]	dy/dx[c]	Odds ratio[d]	Coefficients	dy/dx	Odds ratio
Gender[e]						
Male	0.497 (2.94)***	0.116 (3.04)**	1.644 (2.94)**	0.459 (2.71)**	0.107 (2.78)**	1.583 (2.71)**
Age[f]						
[30–50]	−0.820 (3.90)***	−0.187 (4.14)***	0.440 (−3.90)***	−0.884 (4.20)***	−0.201 (−4.49)***	0.413 (−4.20)***
[50,+]	−1.825 (5.36)***	−0.325 (8.11)***	0.161 (−5.36)***	−1.840 (5.37)***	−0.327 (−8.14)***	0.159 (−5.37)***
Marital status[g]						
Not married	0.282 (1.37)	0.067 (1.39)	1.326 (1.37)	0.347 (1.70)	0.082 (1.73)	1.415 (1.70)*
Education level[h]						
Primary	1.401 (1.77)*	0.336 (1.97)*	4.061 (1.77)*	1.360 (1.72)	0.327 (1.89)	3.895 (1.72)*
Secondary	3.087	0.648	21.910	3.067	0.645	21.467
	(4.21)***	(6.11)***	(4.21)***	(4.18)**	(6.03)***	(4.18)***
High school	4.095 (5.56)***	0.769 (10.28)***	60.036 (5.56)***	4.021 (5.46)**	0.761 (9.89)***	55.759 (5.46)***
Accommodation[i]						
Precarious type	−0.488 (2.83)***	−0.114 (2.88)**	0.614 (−2.83)**	−0.488 (2.81)**	−0.114 (2.87)**	0.614 (−2.81)**

Continued

Table 4.3 Continued

Variables[a]	Model logit(1)			Model logit(2)		
	Coefficients [b]	dy/dx [c]	Odds ratio [d]	Coefficients	dy/dx	Odds ratio
Religion[j]						
Muslim	0.125	0.030	1.133	0.137	0.033	1.147
	(0.70)	(0.69)	(0.70)	(0.75)	(0.74)	(0.75)
Animist	0.097	0.023	1.101	0.093	0.022	1.098
	(0.33)	(0.32)	(0.33)	(0.31)	(0.31)	(0.31)
Professional activity[k]						
Employee	0.080	0.019	1.084	0.031	0.007	1.038
	(0.20)	(0.20)	(0.20)	(0.08)	(0.08)	(0.08)
Unskilled worker	-1.936	-0.321	0.144	-1.806	-0.309	0.164
	(2.76)***	(-5.19)***	(-2.76)**	(2.53)*	(-4.49)***	(-2.53)*
Professionals	-0.797	-0.178	0.451	-0.820	-0.183	0.440
	(2.62)***	(-2.89)**	(-2.62)**	(2.67)**	(-2.96)**	(-2.67)**
Others	-0.657	-0.158	0.518	-0.649	-0.156	0.522
	(2.37)**	(-2.39)*	(-2.37)*	(2.34)*	(-2.36)*	(-2.34)*
Association member				0.639	0.152	1.894
				(4.08)**	(4.13)***	(4.08)***
Constant	-2.819			-3.097		
	(3.55)***			(3.89)**		
Observations	1020			1020		
Correctly classified	74.41%			74.02%		

Notes: Robust z statistics in parentheses.(a) variables; (b) coefficients and robust z statistics in parenthesis, * significant at 10%, ** significant at 5%, *** significant at 1%;(c) marginal effects; (d) Odds ratio; (e) base= female; (f) base= [15–30[years old; (g) base= married; (h) base= none; (i) base= house-flat; (j) base=Christian; (k) base=civil servant.

Source: Our results with STATA 10.

It appears that being a member of these associations has a positive effect on the probability of access to the Internet.

So an individual with an important social capital network has almost twice to the probability of getting connected to the Internet, according to odds ratios. Maintaining this level of relationship requires social networking and sending email, and may explain the positive effect highlighted in the regression. Several organizations have been established since the outbreak of political conflict in the country.

Frequency of the Internet usage

If a significant test statistic provides evidence that the parallel regression assumption has been violated, then the generalized logit model is used (Table 4.4). Table 4.5 presents the results of the ordered model. Results are given only when dependent variables take modalities 1 and 2. However, the analysis is done by considering the combinations of alternatives: the second column shows the analysis of category 1 against category 2 and 3, and then the last column provides the analysis of category 1 and 2 against alternative 3. It appears that the intensity of usage is also gender-oriented whereby females are less likely to have frequent use of the Internet than men. Being a woman increases the probability of being less connected to the Internet regularly. The likelihood of being in a category of regular user decreases as age increases. Being a retiree or an inactive person reduces likely frequency of use still further. Compared to the first column, we notice in the second one that age, gender and type of professional activity cannot discriminate the explained variable. Regarding marital status, being unmarried is not a factor that encourages regular use of the Internet. It should be noted also that, as education level increases, the chances of it having a positive effect on usage increase similarly. In other words, the more educated you are the more likely to use the network. The impact of social network is significant and negative, suggesting that efforts should be made to yield a reverse effect on the usage as in the access model.

Conclusion

The reduction of the divide in the adoption of information technology and communications, the Internet in particular, is promoted by a better understanding of factors behind the spread of the service in the population. This study was designed to investigate the determinants of adoption of the Internet in Côte d'Ivoire, based on a household survey. It shows that variables such as age, location, type of employment,

Table 4.4 Test of proportional ratio using Omodel Logit

Variable	Coefficients
Female	−0.381
	(2.15)**
[30–50]	−0.180
	(0.75)
[50, +]	−1.332
	(2.80)***
Not married	−0.523
	(2.12)**
Primary	−0.737
	(1.21)
Secondary	−0.724
	(1.30)
High school	−0.402
	(0.72)
Precarious house	−0.117
	(0.66)
Muslim	−0.055
	(0.30)
Animist	−0.285
	(0.96)
Employee	−0.475
	(1.18)
Unskilled worker	−0.382
	(0.51)
Professionals	−0.489
	(1.55)
Others	−0.705
	(2.38)**
Membre d'une association	−0.177
	(1.09)
Observations	611

Approximate likelihood-ratio test of proportionality of odds across response categories: $chi2(15) = 31.77$ (Prob $> chi2 = 0.0069$) A significant test statistic provides evidence that the parallel regression assumption has been violated.

education and social capital are important factors in the decision to adopt the Internet network. In particular, a younger person is likely to access to the Internet. Having a job or an income-generating activity is a condition that enables one to access the network; the reverse of which is also true. Similarly, location has a non-negligible effect on

Table 4.5 Model of usage using generalized ordered Logit Model

Variables	1 fois/90 jours		1 fois/7 jours	
	Coefficients	Odds ratio	Coefficients	Odds ratio
Gender				
Female	−0.459	0.63	−0.261	0.77
	(2.17)**		(1.22)	
Age				
[30–50]	−0.654	0.52	0.158	1.17
	(2.19)**		(0.57)	
[50, +]	−1.672	0.19	−0.823	0.44
	(3.17)***		(1.55)	
Marital status				
Not married	−0.197	0.82	−0.711	0.49
	(0.66)		(2.55)**	
Education level				
Primary	−0.034	0.97	−1.280	0.28
	(0.04)		(1.83)*	
Secondary	−0.303	0.74	−1.056	0.35
	(0.42)		(1.72)*	
High school	−0.016	0.98	−0.672	0.51
	(0.02)		(1.10)	
Accommodation				
Precarious house	0.197	1.22	−0.427	0.65
	(0.85)		(1.92)*	
Religion				
Muslim	0.080	1.08	−0.152	0.86
	(0.35)		(0.67)	
Animist	−0.226	0.80	−0.254	0.78
	(0.64)		(0.71)	
Professional activity				
Employee	−0.915	0.40	−0.121	0.89
	(1.68)*		(0.28)	
Unskilled worker	−0.294	0.75	−0.326	0.72
	(0.27)		(0.33)	
Professionals	−0.693	0.50	−0.324	0.72
	(1.51)		(0.90)	
Others	−1.271	0.28	−0.300	0.74
	(2.96)***		(0.90)	
Association member	0.112	1.12	−0.392	0.67
	(0.56)		(2.06)**	
Constant	2.634		1.220	
	(2.91)***		(1.63)	

Observations = 611 – Log pseudo likelihood = −621.19915 – Wald chi2(30) = 64.13 (Prob > chi2 = 0.0003) – Robust z statistics in parentheses – * significant at 10%; ** significant at 5%; *** significant at 1%.

the dissemination of the service. The importance of level of education produces a positive effect on the network connection. Finally, it appears that social capital is a key incentive for individuals to join the network. The variable on the place of residence highlights the existence of a geographical divide, even in a big city like Abidjan. The digital divide is also cognitive. It may be noted that the digital divide is gender-related, which reveals that we have to encourage network access for females. Income, religion and marital status are not significant, suggesting that we cannot describe access using these variables. We notice also that many people have an average use of the network. To promote usage, gender, age and activity are key factors.

Finally, this study may provide a basis for policies promoting access to the network and usage for the majority of individuals, with an emphasis on increasing education and training levels, improving accommodation and promoting social activity policies. To harness benefit of Internet access, public policies have to tackle universal access problems, focusing on incentives to invest and encourage both access and usage for targeted citizens and areas in the country.

References

Calabrese, A. and D. Jung (1992) 'Broadband Telecommunications in Rural America', *Telecommunications Policy*, Vol. 16, No. 3, pp. 225–36.

Cameron, A.C. and P. Trivedi (2005) *Microeconometrics: Methods and Applications*, Cambridge, MA: Cambridge University Press.

Castells, M. (2002) The Internet Galaxy: Reflexions on the Internet, Business and Society, Oxford: Oxford University Press.

Chaudhuri, A., K. Flamm and J. Horrigan (2005) 'An Analysis of the Determinants of Internet Access', *Telecommunications Policy*, Vol. 29, pp. 731–55.

Collier, P. (1998) 'Social Capital and Poverty, Social Capital Initiative', Working Paper No. 4, The World Bank, November, http://siteresources.worldbank.org

Conte, B. (2000) 'Les déterminants de la diffusion d'Internet en Afrique', DT/48/2000, CED, Université Montesquieu-Bordeaux IV,http://conte.u-bordeaux4.fr/ (home page)

Conte, B. (2001a) 'La fracture numérique en Afrique', Centre d'économie du développement (CED), Université Montesquieu-Bordeaux IV, http://conte.u-bordeaux4.fr (home page)

Conte, B. (2001b) 'La diffusion d'Internet en Afrique: ce que disent les chiffres', *Canadian Journal of Development Studies*, Vol. XXII, No. 3.

Crandall, R. (2001) 'The Digital Divide: Bridging the Divide Naturally', *The Brookings Review*, Vol. 19, No. 1, pp. 38–43.

Fink, C. and C. J. Kenny (2003) *W(h)ither the Digital Divide?*, Washington DC: World Bank.

Flamm, K.S. and A. Chaudhuri (2007) 'An Analysis of the Determinants of the Broadband Access', *Telecommunication Policy*, Vol. 31, pp. 312–26.

Fu, V.K. (1998) 'Estimating Generalized Ordered Logit Models', *Stata Technical Bulletin*, Vol. 8, pp. 160–4.

Fuchs, C. (2005) 'The Internet as a Self Organizing Socio-technological System', *Cybernetics and Human Knowing*, Vol. 12, No. 3, pp. 37–81.

Fuchs, C. and E. Horak (2006) 'Africa and the Digital Divide', *Telematics and Informatics*, Vol. 25, pp. 99–116.

Horrigan, J. (2001) 'On Line Communities: Networks that Nurture Long-distance Relationships and Local Ties', *Pew Internet and American Life Study*, http://www.pewInternet.org (home page).

Hunter, W.R. (2002) 'Bridging the Digital Divide: New Route to Development or New Form of Democracy?', *Global Governance*, Vol. 8, pp. 443–66.

International Telecommunications Union (2005) *ITU Telecommunications Indicators Data Base*, Geneva: ITU.

Kiiski, S. and M. Pohjola (2002) 'Cross-country Diffusion of the Internet', *Information Economics and Policy*, Vol. 14, No. 2, pp. 297–310.

Le Guel, F., T. Penard and R. Suire (2005) 'Adoption et usage de l'Internet: une étude économétrique sur données Bretonnes', *Economie et prévision*, Vol. 167 , pp. 67–84.

Le Guel, F. and T. Penard (2004) 'Internet et les ménages Luxembourgeois: peut-on encore parler de fracture numérique dans le grand-Duché?', *Economie et entreprise*, Vol. 3, December, CEPS/INSTEAD.

Lethiais, V. and N. Poussing (2004) 'Adoption, usage d'Internet et apprentissage: une comparaison Bretagne/Luxembourg', *Cahier de recherche*, Vol. 0-2004, http://www.marsouin.org/IMG/pdf/Lethiais-Poussing_0-2004.pdf

Lethiais V., A. Rallet, J. Vicente (2003) 'TIC et réorganisation spatiale des activités économiques: introduction', *Géographie, Economie, Société*, Vol. 5, No. 3–4, pp. 275–85.

Moschella, D. and R. D Atkinson (1998) *The Internet and Society: Universal Access, Not Universal Service*, Washington DC: Progressive Policy Institute.

Navas-Savater, J., A. Dymond and N. Junutumen (2002) 'Telecommunications and Information Services for the Poor: Toward a Strategy for Universal Access', The World Bank Group, World Bank Discussion Paper No. 432, Washington DC.

Noce, A.A. and L. McKeown (2007) 'A New Benchmark for Internet Use: A Logistic Modelling of Factors influencing Internet Use in Canada', *Government Information Quarterly*, Vol. 25, No. 3, pp. 462–76.

Norris, P. (2001) *Digital Divide: Civic Engagement, Information, Poverty and the Internet Worldwide*, Cambridge, MA: Cambridge University Press.

OECD (2001) *Understanding the Digital Divide*, Paris: OECD.

Oxendine, A., E. Borgida , J.L. Sullivan and M.S. Jackson (2003) 'The Importance of Trust and Community in Developing and Maintaining a Community Electronic Network', *International Journal of Human–Computer Studies*, Vol. 58, No. 6, pp. 671–96.

Oyelaran-Oyeyinka, B. and L. Kaushalesh (2005) 'Internet Diffusion in Subsaharan Africa: A Cross Country Analysis', *Telecommunications Policy*, Vol. 29, pp. 507–27.

Putnam, R.D. (1993) 'The Prosperous Community: Social Capital and Public Life', *The American Prospect*, Vol. 13.

Rappoport, P., D. J. Kridel, L. D. Taylor and J. Alleman (2002) 'Residential Demand for Access to the Internet', http://www.colorado.edu/engineering/alleman /print_files/Forcasting_ the_Demand_for_Internet_Services.PDF

Sciadas, G. (2002) 'Découvrir la fracture numérique', *statistique canada*, Cat. No. 56F0004MIF.

Van Dijk, J. (2006) *The Internet Society: Social Aspects of New Media*, 2nd edn, London: Sage.

Williams, R. (2006) 'Generalized Ordered Logit/Partial Proportional Odds Models for Ordinal Dependent Variables', *Stata Journal*, Vol. 6, No. 1, pp. 58–82.

Wilson, E.J. (2006) *The Information Revolution and Developing Countries*, Cambridge, MA: MIT Press.

World Bank (2006) *World Bank Development Indicators Data Base 2005*, Washington DC: World Bank.

5

Difference between Adoption and Access Frequency to Internet and Consumer Surplus

Walid Hadhri, Mohamed Ayadi, and Adel Ben Youssef

Introduction

New products and services have significantly affected how households live, consume and allocate their time between different activities. Their adoption has grown rapidly last decade. These new goods and services have a significant impact on consumer welfare. Many studies have tried to quantify these economic impacts by measuring consumer surplus (Nevo 2001; Petrin, 2002, Goolsbee and Petrin, 2001; Greenwood and Kopecky, 2007).[1]

The Internet is a new service whose adoption and access frequencies are growing rapidly. Modeling the Internet demand function and quantifying its impacts on consumer welfare is an important analytical and empirical challenge (Hausman, 2002; Brynjolfsson et al., 2003; Gentzkow, 2006; Goolsbee and Klenow, 2006). Goolsbee and Klenow (2006) (henceforward G and K) have estimated this Internet contribution to the consumer surplus during 2005 and they found that it ranges between US$2,500 and US$2,800 in the USA. They use a specific two arguments utility function modeling a link between the time opportunity cost of time dedicated to Internet and income. Since this initial work, as far as we are aware, few empirical findings were developed in order to compare their results and methodologies within other countries.

The aims of this chapter are twofold: first, we estimate a demand function and a consumer surplus of Internet for French households using the same methodology that G and K applied on the French household survey data for 2005. Second, we challenge this methodology by considering a more realistic hypothesis. We suppose a concave demand function for Internet instead of the GandK's linear demand function. We also assume that the intensity of Internet use could be affected by some specific households' characteristics and some other activities like TV watching or computer gaming. We use Heckman methodology, estimating Internet adoption and access intensity patterns separately to resolve the selection bias problem.

Many households, for various reasons, do not use the Internet. Perhaps they cannot afford access, or they are not aware of Internet services. They may reject Internet use or simply be unable to use it (this is the case for poorly educated or disabled people). There are significant differences in Internet adoption decision and access. Adoption alone is not necessarily the only measure to evaluate Internet usage effect on consumer welfare. Heckman has developed a two-step method to correct selection bias (identifying factors contributing to the selection bias). The Heckman method attempts to control for the effect of non-random selection by incorporating both the observed and unobserved factors that affect non-response.

Our results show that French households have found the Internet to be a valuable addition to their welfare levels. In 2005, the French consumer surplus ranged between $1,240 and $3,126, if we use the GandK methodology; between $1,679 and $3,126 if we use our concave demand function; but between $2,107 and $2,651 if we use our two-stage estimation method.

This chapter is organized as follows. The first section discusses the econometric specifications for the basic Internet demand function. The second section depicts Internet adoption and frequency differentiation for Internet demand analysis. The third section presents the data and the variables used. The fourth section discusses the econometric results. The final section concludes.

Econometric specification of the Internet demand function

Goolsbee and Klenow (2006) identify a link between the opportunity cost of time (time devoted to other uses compared to time devoted to Internet) and the wage rate. They consider that Internet users maximize the following separable utility function:

$$U = \theta(C_I^{\alpha_I} L_I^{1-\alpha_I})^{1-\frac{1}{\sigma}} + (1-\theta)(C_O^{\alpha_O} L_O^{1-\alpha_O})^{1-\frac{1}{\sigma}} \tag{1}$$

Where (L_I) and (L_O) are fraction of time spent using Internet services and on other goods and services, respectively. (C_I) and (C_O) are, respectively, the consumption time devoted to Internet services and the consumption of other goods and services. θ is a weight allocated to Internet sub utility. Finally, $(1 - \alpha_I)$ and $(1 - \alpha_O)$ are time intensities of Internet and other goods and services, respectively. Starting from a standard model of leisure/work trade-off, Internet users have to consider the following budget constraint:

$$P_I C_I + F_I + P_O C_O = W(1 - L_I - L_O) \tag{2}$$

P_I and P_O are prices of Internet services and of other goods, respectively. F_I is the fixed cost of Internet access. P_I is the marginal cost of using Internet services. We consider that the marginal cost is zero because Internet access is priced as a flat monthly fee. W is the average monthly wage.

The combined Cobb-Douglas bundles are denoted as:

$$U_I = C_I^{\alpha_I} L_I^{1-\alpha_I} \text{ and } U_O = C_O^{\alpha_O} L_O^{1-\alpha_O}.$$

ρ_I and ρ_O are the weighted average of the market price and the price of time (i.e., the wage). This allows us to write the following prices:

$$\rho_I = \left(\frac{P_I}{\alpha_I}\right)^{\alpha_I} \left(\frac{W}{1-\alpha_I}\right)^{1-\alpha_I} \text{ and } \rho_O = \left(\frac{P_O}{\alpha_O}\right)^{\alpha_A} \left(\frac{W}{1-\alpha_O}\right)^{1-\alpha_O}$$

Then, the optimal choices for the bundles become:

$$U_I = \frac{W - F_I}{\rho_I(1+\Delta)} \qquad U_O = \frac{W - F_I}{\rho_O(1+\Delta)}$$

where,

$$\Delta = \left(\frac{\rho_I}{\rho_O}\right)^{\sigma-1} \left(\frac{1-\theta}{\theta}\right)^{\sigma}$$

The optimal choices for the bundles in terms of their consumption and time counterparts are:

$$C_I = \frac{\alpha_I \rho_I U_I}{P_I} \qquad C_O = \frac{\alpha_O \rho_O U_O}{P_O}$$

$$L_I = \frac{(1-\alpha_I)\rho_I U_I}{W} \qquad L_A = \frac{(1-\alpha_O)\rho_O U_O}{W}$$

Using these optimal choices we can get the following expression for Δ:

$$\Delta = \frac{(1-\alpha_I)\left(1 - \dfrac{F_I}{W}\right) - L_I}{L_I}$$

The fixed cost FI is typically very small relative to full income (0.3 percent for our sample). Internet access costs are small flat fees so that $F_I/W = 0$. Consequently, we adopt the assumption that there is no marginal use pricing. This allows us to write $\alpha_I = 0$. Thus, the above expression of Δ becomes approximately equal to the time spent on other activities $(1 - L_I)$ relative to the time spent on Internet activities.

$$\Delta = \frac{1 - L_I}{L_I}$$

Using the prices ρ_I and ρ_O, the following expression can be rewritten δ (according to the wages) as follows:

$$\Delta = AW^{(\alpha_O - \alpha_I)(\sigma - 1)}\left(\frac{1 - \theta}{\theta}\right)^\sigma$$

where

$$A = \left[\frac{(P_I/\alpha_I)^{\alpha_I}(1 - \alpha_O)^{1 - \alpha_O}}{(P_O/\alpha_O)^{\alpha_O}(1 - \alpha_I)^{1 - \alpha_I}}\right]^{(\sigma - 1)}$$

A consumer maximizes a utility function (1) subject to his budget constraint (2). Given the fact that the G and K Internet demand function has two arguments – time opportunity cost (time devoted to other uses compared to time devoted to Internet) and wage rate[2] – we can write the expression (3) as follows:

$$In\left[\frac{1 - L_I}{L_1}\right] = \ln(A) + (\alpha_A - \alpha_I)(\sigma - 1)\ln(W) + \sigma\ln\left(\frac{1 - \theta}{\theta}\right) \tag{3}$$

The left-hand side of equation (3) is the log of ratio of time spent on non-Internet activities $(1 - L_1)$ relative to time spent on the Internet L_I. $\ln(A)$ is a constant term across consumers. $(\alpha_O - \alpha_I)$ measures the difference between time intensity of the Internet and other goods. σ is the substitution elasticity between the two bundles. As θ may change from one Internet user to another, G and K consider $\sigma\ln\left(\frac{1 - \theta}{\theta}\right)$ as an error term, which will be denoted by ε in the following equations.

In order to compare our results to those obtained by G and K we consider the same specification defined by G and K applied for the French household survey data. Second, we consider alternative specifications, adding two more realistic components (concavity of wage effect and non-income variables). Blundell et al. (1993) consider that consumer demand patterns typically found in micro data sets vary considerably across households, with different household characteristics and different levels of income. We model this variability by allowing for non-linear $\ln(W)$ terms. To describe individual household preferences, we first abstract from all explanatory variables except income and write our demand function as follows:

$$\ln\left[\frac{1-L_I}{L_I}\right] = \alpha + \sum_{j=1}^{L} \beta_j g_j(\ln(W))$$

$g_j(\ln(W))$ are known polynomials in W.

This form is sufficiently general to cover many of the popular forms for Engel curves. To illustrate these points more explicitly, we consider a quadratic extension of our demand equation. In this model L=2 and the g_js are simply polynomial logarithmic terms, so that our demand equation may be written as

$$\ln\left[\frac{1-L_I}{L_I}\right] = \alpha + \beta_1 \ln(W) + \beta_2 [\ln(W)]^2 \tag{4}$$

The Internet demand function may increase when wage increases; however, over a certain level of wage the impact seems to be smaller and people do not increase their connection time at the same level. We have some kind of concavity of Internet demand function. Young people and well-educated persons use the Internet more intensively than older people. Seniority (i.e., Internet experience) modifies Internet preferences. On the other hand, Internet is considered to be in competition with other activities, like playing computer games. Those two sets of variables must be added to the Internet demand function as non-income variables (NINC). We can write the expression (4) as the following:

$$\ln\left[\frac{1-L_I}{L_I}\right] = \alpha + \beta_1 \ln(W) + \beta_2 [\ln(W)]^2 + \gamma \text{NINC} + \varepsilon \tag{5}$$

Internet adoption and access frequency differentiation for Internet usage analyses

In our sample, data are censored. Indeed, we will be able to identify factors underlying access frequency (or Internet demand) only if Internet access frequency is higher than zero. Internet demand function of Internet user does not, in general afford a reliable estimate of what non-users would demand if they became users. Internet demand function, estimated for selected samples, does not, in general, estimate population demand functions. Comparisons of Internet demand of present users with demands of non-users result in a biased estimate of the effect of the random treatment of users.

Characterization of the selection bias problem (Heckman, 1979)

Consider a random sample of I observations. Equations for individual i are as follows:

$$Y_{1i} = X_{1i}\beta_1 + U_{1i} \tag{6a}$$

$$Y_{2i} = X_{2i}\beta_2 + U_{2i}$$
$$i = 1,\ldots I, \tag{6b}$$

where X_{1i} is a vector of exogenous $1 \times K_j$ regressors, β_j is a $K_j \times 1$ vector of parameters,
and

$$E(U_{ji}) = 0, \qquad E(U_{ji}U_{j'i''}) = \sigma_{jj'} \quad if \ \ i = i''$$
$$= 0 \quad if \ \ i \neq i''$$

The final assumption is a consequence of a random sampling scheme. The joint density of U_{1i}, U_{2i} is $h(U_{1i}, U_{2i})$. Suppose that one seeks to estimate equation (6a) but that data are missing on Y_1 for certain observations. The population regression function for equation (6a) may be written as

$$E(Y_{1i}|X_{1i}) = X_{1i}\beta_1$$

However, the regression function for the subsample of available data is

$$E(Y_{1i}|X_{1i}, sample\ selection\ rule) = X_{1i}\beta_1 + E(U_{1i}\ |\ sample\ selection\ rule)$$

If the conditional expectation of U_{1i} is zero, the regression function for the selected subsample is the same as the population regression function. Least squares estimators may be used to estimate β_1 on the selected subsample. The only cost of having an incomplete sample is a loss in efficiency. However, in the general case, the sample selection rule that determines the availability of data has more serious consequences.

Suppose that data are available on Y_{1i} if $Y_{2i} > 0$, while if $Y_{2i} < 0$, there are no observations on Y_{1i}. In the general case

$$E(U_{1i} \mid sample\ selection\ rule) = E(U_{1i} \mid X_{1i}, Y_{2i} \geq 0)$$
$$= E(U_{1i} \mid X_{1i}, Y_{2i} \geq -X_{2i}\beta_2)$$

In the case of independence between U_{1i} and U_{2i}, so that the data on Y_{1i} are missing randomly, the conditional mean of U_{1i} is zero.

However, in the general case, it is non-zero and the subsample regression function is

$$E(Y_{1i} \mid X_{1i}, Y_{2i} \geq 0) = X_{1i}\beta_1 + E(U_{1i} \mid U_{2i} \geq -X_{2i}\beta_2) \tag{7}$$

The selected sample regression function depends on X_{1i} and X_{2i}.

Regression estimators of the parameters of equation (1a) fit on the selected sample omit the final term of equation (7) as a regressor, so that the bias that results from using non-randomly selected samples to estimate behavioral relationships is seen to arise from the ordinary problem of omitted variables.

Heckman's estimator and its properties

Assume that $h(U_{1i}, U_{2i})$ is a bivariate normal density. Using well known results of Johnson and Kotz (1972):

$$E(U_{1i} \mid U_{2i} \geq -X_{2i}\beta_2) = \frac{\sigma_{12}}{(\sigma_{12})^{1/2}} \lambda_i$$

$$E(U_{2i} \mid U_{2i} \geq -X_{2i}\beta_2) = \frac{\sigma_{22}}{(\sigma_{22})^{1/2}} \lambda_i$$

Where

$$\lambda_i = \frac{(Z_i)}{1 - \Phi(Z_i)} = \frac{(Z_i)}{\Phi(-Z_i)}$$

where ϕ and Φ are the density and distribution function for a standard normal variable, respectively. 'λ_i' is the inverse of the Mills ratio, which is a monotone decreasing function of the probability that an observation is selected for the sample, $\Phi(-Z_i)$ $(= 1 - \Phi(Z_i))$, where

$$Z_i = -\frac{X_{2i}\beta_2}{(\sigma_{22})^{1/2}}$$

The full statistical model for normal population disturbances can now be developed. The conditional regression function for selected samples may be written as

$$E(Y_{1i} \mid X_{1i}, Y_{2i} \geq 0) = X_{1i}\beta_1 + \frac{\sigma_{22}}{(\sigma_{22})^{1/2}}\lambda_i,$$

$$Y_{1i} = E(U_{1i} \mid X_{1i}, Y_{2i} \geq 0) + V_{1i} \tag{8}$$

where

$$E(V_{1i} \mid X_{1i}, \lambda_i, U_{2i} \geq -X_{2i}, \beta_2) = 0$$
$$E(V_{1i}^2 \mid X_{1i}, (\lambda_i, U_{2i} \geq -X_{2i}, \beta_2) = \sigma_{11}((1-\rho^2) + \rho^2(1+Z_i\lambda_i - \lambda_i^2))$$

where

$$\rho^2 = \frac{\sigma_{12}^2}{\sigma_{11}\sigma_{22}}$$

and

$$0 \leq 1 + \lambda_i Z_i - \lambda_i^2 \leq 1$$

If one knew Z_i and hence λ_i, one could enter λ_i as a regressor in equation (8) and estimate that equation by ordinary least squares. The least squares estimators of β_1 and $\sigma_{12}/(\sigma_{22})^{1/2}$ are unbiased but inefficient. In practice, one does not know λ_i. But in the case of a censored sample, in which one does not have information on Y_{1i} if $Y_{2i} < 0$, but one does know X_{2i} for observations with $Y_{2i} < 0$, one can estimate λ_i by the following procedure (Heckman, 1979):

1. Estimate the parameters of the probability that $Y_2 > 0$ (i.e., $\beta_2/(\sigma_{22})^{1/2}$) using *probit* analysis for the full sample.
2. From this estimator of $\beta_2/(\sigma_{22})^{1/2} = \beta_2^*$ one can estimate Z_i and hence λ_i. All of these estimators are consistent.
3. The estimated value of λ_i may be used as a regressor in equation (8) fit on the selected subsample.

Regression estimators of equation (8) are consistent for β_1 and $\sigma_{12}/(\sigma_{22})^{1/2}$ (coefficients of X_{1i} and λ_i, respectively).

Internet demand function with censored sample

We define a variable *Adopt_i* such that:

adop_i = 1 if individual i adopts Internet;
adop_i = 0 if individual i does not adopt Internet.

We note Y_{1i}, the log of ratio of time spent on non-Internet activities $(1-L_i)$ relative to time spent on the Internet L_i.

However,

$$Y_{1i} = \alpha + \beta_1 \ln(W) + \beta_2 [\ln(W)]^2 + \gamma\,NINC \qquad \text{if } adop_i = 1$$

$$Y_{1i} \qquad \text{(unobserved)} \qquad\qquad\qquad \text{if } adop_i = 0$$

Using Heckman's two-step selection method we will consider two separate equations: a selection equation, estimating the probability of Internet adoption, which help us to evaluate inverse of the Mills ratio, and the Internet demand equation adjusted for selection bias, used to estimate the determinants of Internet access frequency.

(1): Selection equation: probability of Internet adoption

We consider a latent variable

$$Y_{2i} = X_{2i}\beta_2 + \varepsilon_{2i} \tag{9a}$$

where X_{2i} is a vector of individual-level controls, including demographics and wages; we suppose ε_{2i} has normal distribution $N(0; \sigma_2)$. We suppose that

$$Adopt_i = 1 \text{ if } Y_{2i} > 0; \tag{9b}$$

(2): Internet demand equation adjusted for selection bias

Internet access frequency is observed only if individuals adopt Internet. From equation 9, we can write:

$$adop_i = 1 \text{ if } \varepsilon_{2i} > (-X_{2i}\beta_2)$$
$$adop_i = 0 \text{ if not}$$

According to Heckman (1979), we can write the equation of access frequency:

$$E\left(Y_{1i}/W_i, NINC_i, adopt_i = 1\right) = \alpha + \gamma NINC_i\beta_2 + \beta_1 W + \beta_2 W^2$$
$$+ E\left(\varepsilon_{2i}/adopt_i = 1\right)$$

Thus, the access frequency equation on the selected sample depends at the same time on X_{2i}, W_i and $NINC_i$.

$$E\left(Y_{1i}/W_i, NINC_i, adopt_i = 1\right) = \alpha + \gamma VSD_i + \beta_1 W + \beta_2 W^2 + E\left(\varepsilon_{2i} > -X_{2i}\beta_2\right)$$

Indeed,

$$E\left(Y_{1i}/W_i, NINC_i, adopt_i = 1\right) = \alpha + \gamma VSD_i + \beta_1 W + \beta_2 W^2 + E\left(\varepsilon_{2i} > -X_{2i}\beta_2\right) \quad (10)$$

where, ρ is the coefficient of correlation of the errors terms ε_{1i} and ε_{2i}. ϕ and Φ are, respectively, the density and distribution function for a standard normal $N(0; \sigma_2)$.

We follow the Heckman two-stage estimate procedure, giving consistent estimators for the parameters of our model.

At the first stage: we estimate the parameter $\dfrac{\beta_2}{\sigma_2} \equiv \beta_2$ (where $\sigma_2 = 1$) using maximum likelihood for probit model (9a, 9b). At the second stage: we apply the ordinary least squares (OLS) to the access frequency equation under the assumption of normality of the residuals:

$$E\left(Y_{1i}/adopt_i = 1\right) = \alpha + \gamma NINC_i + \beta_1 W + \beta_2 W^2 + \rho\sigma_2\hat{\lambda}_i + v_i \quad (11)$$

Where $\hat{\lambda}_i = \dfrac{(X_{1i}\hat{\beta}_1)}{\Phi(X_{1i}\hat{\beta}_1)}$ is a consistent estimator of the inverse of Mills ratio:

$$\lambda_i = \frac{(X_{2i}\beta_2)}{\Phi(X_{2i}\beta_2)}$$

Data and variables definitions

Data

In order to estimate the parameters of Internet demand function, we have used the French household survey data of October 2005. Questions about Internet preferences and consumption patterns were put to 5,603 representative households.

In order to carry out the approximation of the intensity of Internet use (the dependent variable of our model), we consider the number of days of connection per individual. Thus, following Goolsbee and Klenow's (2006) assumptions, we compute the frequency of access in the form of classes and we approximate each variable by its average as Table 5.1 shows.

On average, in 2005, each French person was connected to Internet for 4.64 hours per week (IDATE, 2005) against 7.7 hours per week in the USA during the same period, which corresponds to 4.1 percent of his/her non-sleeping time.[3] The monthly Internet subscription cost in France is €25 for DSL connection and €9.46 for low broadband (IDATE, 2005). In our sample, 71 percent individuals access to DSL connection against 29 percent who access low-level connections. Thus, the average

Table 5.1   Access time to Internet

Number of times per month	Type of frequency	Day average numbers per stage	Percentage of population (%)
All days or almost	Strong	30	26
At least four times per month	Average	15	13
From one to three times per month	Very weak	2	8
Not user	Null	0	53

cost of connection (FI) is €20.49 per month, which represents 0.38 percent of average income.[4]

Variables

There are a number of determinants affecting households' adoption and Internet use such as: demographic factors, geographic location and housing, main location of Internet access, types of application or service used, level of education, Internet and computer skills and lifestyle.

The following aspects of claimed Internet adoption and frequency access behavior were measured.

Demographic factors

Traditionally, demographic variables have always been examined as the initial predictors of Internet adoption and use. We control demographic factors such as level of income, age, number of children at home, marital status of respondent (married or not) and owning or not owning housing. Consistent with reasoning from our theoretical model and the literature, we develop four hypotheses for empirical tests.

Income (**ln(W)**) is a very strong determinant of household Internet adoption and access. It is expected to have significant and positive impact related to the intention to adopt Internet, and a significant and negative impact on how time is spent individually online. The variable age (Age) is expected to have the same effect (negative) on Internet adoption and frequency access – that is, younger Internet users spend more time online. For a larger number of studies, number of children in a household also becomes a significant factor of Internet adoption and Internet frequency access. We enlarge our analysis beyond the effect of the usual demographics and geographic location on Internet frequency access to include the effect of location of Internet access and reasons for using the Internet.

Main location of Internet access

An Internet user is defined as someone who has had access to the Internet in the last month. On an INSEE survey respondents were required to indicate their present access location to the Internet from a list of possible locations. The survey asked individuals about usage of Internet at the houses of friends or other family members (Internet Friends/Family), at cybercafés (Internet Café) and at school and university (Interne University/School). Furthermore we analyze also the effect of access to Internet on a laptop (Internet Laptop). These variables are expected to have positive effect on Internet frequency access. These five variables are also dummy variables.

Internet services used

There are now thousands of Internet 'home pages' which serve as information sources for individuals, institutions and organizations. Most administrations, banks, universities, public and private organizations provide information over the Internet. It is possible to access information on personal banking, play games, listen to music and so on. The World Wide Web also provides very easy access to some government documents and legislative materials.

Respondents who have access to the Internet were asked to indicate their specific uses of it. We analyze the effect of many Internet services used on the time spent online. More specifically, the use of the Internet for home banking (Home Banking), playing games online (Playing Games), listening and downloading music (Music Online), accessing administrative information (Administrative Information) and to online shopping (Online Shopping). These services are used generally by active users.

These five variables were measured as a dummy variable relative to 1 if respondent uses each of these Internet services and 0 if not. The correlation between decision to adopt Internet and education, ICT skills and lifestyle is well established in the literature. One of our aims is to analyze the relation between these three factors and the Internet adoption decision.

Level of education

In many publications researchers consider education as another major factor affecting the Internet adoption decision. They find that people with a high level of education are more likely to adopt Internet. For education variables, we make the distinction between two levels: high school diploma (High School Graduate) and university graduate (University/College Graduate).

Computer and Internet skills

Our study examines the role of computer skills (Computer Skills) and Internet skills (Internet Skills) on Internet adoption. Skills were considered as an individual's ability to use the computer and the Internet efficiently and effectively.

Many studies raise the fact that the question of Internet adoption inequalities does not relate to income, education, age, location, but it is more related to ICT skills. People with higher levels of e-skills are more likely to adopt the Internet. Responders were asked to answer questions on seven computer skills – such as, whether they could: copy or delete a file, use the copy/delete tool to move information in a document, install/uninstall software, install new equipment (printer, modem, etc.), use basic arithmetic formulas in a spreadsheet software (Excel, Quattro, Lotus, etc.), compress or decompress files (by using Winzip, Winrar, Winace, for example) and write a computer program by using a specific data-processing language (e.g., visual BASIC, FORTRAN, java, C++) – and five Internet skills, such as whether they could: use a search engine (Yahoo, Google, etc.), send emails with attached files (document, photograph), visualize the history of the visited pages, remove temporary files and cookies and create or update a website. These answers are summed on two scores (Computer Skills score and Internet Skills score). Lifestyle ICT equipment, such as mobile phone (Mobile Phone), laptop (Laptop), DVD (DVD) and digital camera (Digital Camera), influences positively the probability of Internet adoption. They exhibit the individual's propensity toward such technologies. These variables were measured by dummy variables which took 1 if a household owned each of these ICT tools and 0 if not.

Econometric results

We estimated, first, the decision or the probability of Internet adoption. This analysis consists of a simple porbit model in which the dependant variable is probability of the Internet adoption decision. It's a dummy variable that is equal to 1 for the adopters and 0 for the non-adopters. The independent variables are various factors which would have an effect on this probability, such as age, educational level, income and number of children in the family. Second, we estimated Internet use, based on the time that the individual spends online. The dependant variable represents the number of hours per week that the individual spends connected to the Internet. Several explanatory variables are the observed factors that are supposed to have an influence on the results, such as income, age, Internet connection type (low or high band) and location of Internet use. The variable for the correction of selection problem (inverse Mills ratio) is obtained in the first stage. It was necessary to control for bias due to heteroscedasticity problems involved by correction of the selection problem.

Stata uses the Huber-White estimator to control for the bias due to clustering. This technique deflates the standard errors of the parameter estimates, in this case the coefficients, correcting the inference statistics. The output from this estimation is displayed in Table 5.2.

Estimated elasticity was computed. Table 5.2 reports the basic G and K model, Internet access frequency models (without and with non-income variables) and an Internet adoption equation estimated by probit model. Table 5.2 estimation results indicate a statistical significance of all the covariates. One can conclude that all the signs of our coefficients, expected in theory, are verified.

Internet adoption model

By observing all the explanatory variables of the Internet adoption model, it can be outlined that almost all variables have a statistically significant effect on Internet adoption and our results confirm most of the theoretical expected effects. First, we found a strong relationship between Internet use and income level. Higher income means greater affordability and higher usage levels of Internet and, thus, we would expect a positive association between higher income and higher probability of Internet usage. Our results confirm that higher-income people have a higher probability of adopting Internet (Table 5.2, column 8 and column 9). Furthermore, income is a statistically significant factor that increases the probability of Internet adoption. On the other hand, many studies have found that younger people are more able to use the Internet. Our results confirm this assertion. Age seems to be one of the most important determinants of Internet adoption. The older the individuals, the lower the Internet usage. For instance, a 1 percent increase in the individual's age yields a significant decrease of around 0.8 points of percentage of probability of Internet adoption.

Higher levels of income and younger people are more willing to use Internet

Household size and type is an important determinant in Internet adoption. This can be seen using both the measure of household type and the presence of children. Big families (families with children) have higher probability of Internet adoption.

Our results confirm that households comprising a single family have a higher probability of adopting the Internet. This result confirms that

Table 5.2 Internet adoption and Heckman access frequency

| | | | Heckman Access Frequency Model | | | | | | |
| | Basic Model | | Basic Regression | | Model with NINC | | Internet Adoption Model | | |
Variables	Coef.	T-stat	Coef.	T-stat	Coef.	T-stat	Coef.	T-stat	
Socio-Economic Factors									
ln(W)	0.2064 ***	4.92	0.1502 ***	3.91	0.0777 **	2.12	0.0466 ***	7.71	
$[\ln(W)]^2$	−0.0288 ***	−5.20	−0.0195 ***	−3.92	−0.0106 **	−2.26	—	—	
Age	—	—	—	—	−0.0030 *	−1.87	−0.0087 ***	−5.10	
# Children in household	—	—	—	—	0.0251	1.46	0.0380 *	1.91	
Married	—	—	—	—	0.0733 *	1.84	0.0797 *	1.87	
Owner of housing	—	—	—	—	−0.0012	−0.03	0.0915 **	2.13	
Main Location of use									
Internet Friends/Family	—	—	—	—	0.1564 ***	4.05	—		
Internet café	—	—	—	—	0.1126 *	1.78	—		
Internet University/School	—	—	—	—	−0.1302 **	−2.02	—		
Internet Laptop	—	—	—	—	−0.1035 ***	−2.92	—		
Services used									
Home Banking	—	—	—	—	−0.2422 ***	−6.97	—		
Playing Games	—	—	—	—	−0.1331 ***	−3.27	—		
Music Online	—	—	—	—	−0.1092 ***	−2.92	—		
Administrative information	—	—	—	—	−0.1460 ***	−3.93	—		
Online shopping	—	—	—	—	***	−6.74	—		

(Continued)

Table 5.2 Continued

| | Heckman Access Frequency Model | | | | | | | | | | |
| Variables | Basic Model | | Basic Regression | | Model with NINC | | Internet Adoption Model | | | |
	Coef.	T-stat	Coef.	T-stat	Coef.	T-stat	Coef.		T-stat	
Level of Education										
High school graduate	–	–	–	–	–	–	0.1744	***	3.85	
University/college graduate	–	–	–	–	–	–	0.6159	***	11.96	
Skills										
Computer Skills	–	–	–	–	–	–	0.0369	***	2.89	
Internet Skills	–	–	–	–	–	–	0.6401	***	43.20	
Lifestyle										
Mobile Phone	–	–	–	–	–	–	0.0369	*	1.80	
Laptop	–	–	–	–	–	–	0.4416	***	8.22	
DVD	–	–	–	–	–	–	0.2370	***	5.01	
Numerical Camera	–	–	–	–	–	–	0.1892	***	4.84	
Constant	3.7142 ***	113.80	3.4824 ***	104.04	4.1028 ***	41.42	-1.7783	***	-13.90	
P			0.6512		0.4774					
Σ			0.9594		0.8585					
λ (Mills)			0.6247 ***		0.4099 ***					
# obs	2 462		5 603		5 603		2 462			

younger people often ask for Internet access, in particular for communication uses (chat, forum, email, etc.) or P2P. We have found significant and positive coefficients of the variables 'Married' and 'Children in Household'. Our econometric results, reported in Table 5.2, show that housing status has a significant and positive effect on Internet adoption. Our results demonstrate that households owning a house have a higher probability of using the Internet, compared to households renting their house. There is a strong link between education and the use of Internet services. Our results confirm earlier findings that a higher level of education is associated with a higher level of household Internet use. Indeed, we have a correlation between higher school or university graduate and the probability of adopting the Internet. The greater the level of education, the greater the probability of Internet use. Our results related to income and education effect confirm the assertion of Chaudhuri et al. (2005), according to which income and level of education have a significant positive effect on Internet adoption.

In order to explain the usage differences of the Internet, many studies show that the level of ICT skills appears to be one of the most important factors. Internet adoption is positively correlated with computer and Internet skills. Our econometric estimation demonstrates that computer and Internet skills increase the probability of Internet access or adoption. The coefficients of the variables 'Computer Skills' and 'Internet Skills' are positively and statistically significant. This confirms the idea that skilled people have a higher probability of adopting the Internet.

Finally, we obtain an interesting result in the weak link between ICT equipment and uses and the probability of Internet adoption. Our results confirm that a lifestyle that indicates ICT and electronic tool use positively correlates with Internet use. All the other variables have a positive and statistically significant coefficient. Indeed, using an ICT or electronic tool (such as a mobile phone, laptop, DVD or digital camera) influences positively the probability of adoption of the Internet. We are in the presence of 'technophile households', those with a 'wired lifestyle' (Hoffman et al., 1998). Our findings confirm the fact that higher education level, computer and Internet skills and lifestyle have a positive effect on Internet adoption.

Heckman access frequency model

As we have seen, the estimates generally have the expected sign and are statistically significant. Many studies have found that Internet usage frequency is directly related to various socio-economic factors such as age, income and marital status.

Our purpose is to add interesting factors affecting this frequency, such as location of use, which take into account whether the Internet is used alone or with other people and the kind of Internet services used. The Mills ratio is significant, and indicates that the two-stage estimation procedure is appropriate. As wages increase, time devoted to Internet access decreases. This result, already found by Goolsbee and Klenow (2006), confirms the seminal Becker (1964) theory on time allocation. We desire more leisure activities as income increases. High-income groups have more disposable income to spend on these technologies than lower-income groups. The opportunity cost of time is more important for high-income groups, and thus as income increases we spend less time on the Internet (Goldfarb and Prince, 2008). Moreover, if wages rise, time-intensive activities, such as the Internet, become more expensive; wage rises will lead to a shift in consumption.

However, the relation between wage and Internet use is nonlinear, as the effect of ln(W) on Internet use increases but remains less than proportional. The estimation results confirm this nonlinearity as the sign of $[ln(w)]^2$ is negative and statistically significant. We conclude that Internet intensity may be an increasing but concave function. The econometric estimation shows that the coefficient of regression between the logarithm of wages and time devoted to the Internet is positive and is equal to 0.07.

According to this value, we can conclude that the more affluent the person, the less he/she surfs on the web; the more significant the income, the more the time of connection decreases. This result is primarily related to the opportunity cost of time. Indeed, income lost during one hour is more important to a rich person than to a poor one; individuals on a low level of income can spend more time on such leisure, as their cost of time is low. Moreover, the Internet can be used as a utility – that is, individuals on a low level of income can find services to which they do not have access elsewhere. From this perspective, it could be said that the leisure time of individuals on a low level of income is more important than for others. All non-income variables (NINC) have the expected signs. The age of the household head (Age) has a positive effect – that is, the older the household head, the higher is his intensity of Internet use. This variable demonstrates the seniority effect. Thus, persons having greater experience of Internet use may use the facility more intensely and spend more time in order to access various services (such as, email, home banking, information and so on). Furthermore, as the Internet is a network technology, perhaps, at this stage of diffusion (2005), the offline network is still the socially dominant network. In fact, seniority has a positive impact on building social networks. Household income level has a negative effect on time devoted to Internet connection. However age has a positive effect on time spent online.

The coefficient for marital status of respondent (Married) is positive and significant at the 10 percent level of significance. Our results suggest a negative and significant relationship between marital status and time spent online. One argument is that the individual's time devoted to the family reduces time devoted to Internet connection. Thus, married people may be disposed to spend less time online. The presence of children and home ownership do not have an effect over time connected to the Internet. Coefficients of these two variables are statistically insignificant.

The number of Internet users has increased strongly. Indeed, location of Internet use outside home increased. Our results show that location of use is a strong predictor of time spent online. Access to Internet at friends' or other family members' homes (Internet Friends/Family) and at a cybercafés (Internet Café) has significant and negative effect on time devoted to Internet connection. However, access to Internet at school and university (Interne University/School) is correlated positively with Internet frequency use. This result can be explained by the offline network. Types of Internet connection and access to Internet on a laptop are a positive correlation with time devoted to Internet connection. Finally, our econometric results, reported in Table 5.2 (column 6 and column 7), show that the purpose of Internet use has a positive effect on Internet frequency use. The coefficient for home banking (Home Banking), playing games online (Playing Games), listening and downloading music (Music Online), accessing administrative information (Administrative Information) and online shopping (Online Shopping) are all positives and significant at the 1 percent level of significance. Use of these services gives us an indication of the effect of the experience in the use of Internet. Different activities reflect the needs, personality characteristics and tastes of Internet users. Home banking, playing games online, listening to and downloading music, accessing administrative information and online shopping have positive and significant effects on time spent online.

Difference between Internet adoption and access frequency

In our econometric estimations we note a difference between the effects of different variables on the adoption and the frequency of access to Internet – for example, income level, age and marital status. Also, we note differences in the statistical significance in other variables, such as presence of children and home ownership. Thus, our empirical results are consistent with our hypotheses.

- *Difference in household income effect*: income level has a positive effect on Internet adoption. However, conditional on adoption, it has negative effect on time spent online.
- *Difference in household age effect*: age has a negative effect on Internet adoption. However, conditional on adoption, it has positive effect on time spent online.
- *Location of Internet access* has a significant impact on the time spent on line.
- *Purpose of Internet use* has a positive and significant effect on time spent online.
- *Higher education and skills levels* of head of household corresponds to a higher chance of Internet adoption.
- *Lifestyle* has positive effect on Internet adoption.

Internet consumer surplus

In order to approximate the consumer surplus we use the equivalent variation value (EV) associated to our Internet demand function. This approach was developed and used first by Hausman (1981, 1997, 1999) and Hausman and Newey (1995). They consider the formula (12) as an estimation of the equivalent variation value.

$$EV = 0.5 \times L_I \Big/ \left[\sigma \left(1 - L_I \left(\frac{1 - F_1}{W} \right) \right) \right] \tag{10}$$

where F_I is the average cost of Internet connection, L_I is time spent on Internet activities and σ is the price elasticity. Results reported in Table 5.3 show that, on average, the consumer surplus obtained in the USA is higher than that obtained in France for the same period for all our estimates. This consumer surplus gap may be associated to three complementary explanations. On the one hand, in 2005, diffusion delays regarding Internet connection were still an issue in France, but less so in the USA. Internet adoption and usage were less significant in France

Table 5.3   Internet consumer's surplus comparison between the United States and France

Variables	United States	France1	France2	France3
Time of connection (hours/week)	7.7	4.64	4.64	4.64
Time devoted to the Internet	6.9%	4.1%	4.1%	4.1%
Part of the budget devoted to the Internet	0.33%	0.38%	0.38%	0.38%
Part of the budget by associating the leisure cost	0.12%	0.14%	0.14%	0.14%
Surplus fraction in the income	2.9%	2.6%	2.6%	2.07%
Elasticity	1.32	0.40	0.62	0.78
Consumer's surplus ($)	$2500–3800	$1786	$2651	$2107

A: France1: Basic Model.
B: France2: Heckman Access Frequency Model (Basic regression).
C: France3: Heckman Access Frequency Model (Model with NINC variables).

than in the USA. Also, the time devoted to Internet in the USA (7.7 hours per week) was higher than that in France (4.64 hours per week). This delay is narrowing nowadays; the consumer surplus gap will be reduced. The consumer surplus gap may be affected also by income differences between the USA and France. GDP per capita in France is lower by 23.68 percent than in the USA. Finally, the surplus gap could be explained by cultural differences, which act on collective consumer preferences, as the Internet demand elasticity between the two countries differs slightly. However, one can see the difference between our specification and that of Goolsbee and Klenow. Our estimation, taking into account the concavity of the demand function of Internet demand, leads to a lower level of consumer surplus. It seems, for us, more appropriate to take into account these facts and to consider this relationship, in order to compare the results obtained in the USA.

Conclusion

The objective of this chapter was to measure, in a simple way, the consumer surplus when service consumption has a strong component in terms of time devoted to use. From this point of view, the Internet is illustrative of these new services. We carried out calculations of the opportunity cost of this activity in France by setting realistic assumptions, starting from statistics provided by the survey of INSEE 2005 and the available statistics at the IDATE and the ARCEP. To solve the problem of selection, we based our work on the method of estimate using two stages, pioneered by James Heckman (1979). We noted differences between the effects of various variables on the adoption and the frequency of access to Internet. Our estimation shows that, on average, the French have a surplus which varies between \$2,107 and \$2,651. This estimation was made under a strong hypothesis that needs to be relaxed. We suppose that leisure time is evaluated at the same rate as working time and that the labor market is able to provide the necessary working hours.

We suppose, in addition, that time spent on the Internet is leisure time, but this is not always the case. The dividends in terms of business opportunities, transactions, work, training, better information to enable better actions are not considered here, while they are a fundamental motivation of Internet navigation nowadays. Third, the estimation of intensity of use is based upon the frequency of access. A better measurement of intensity of usage allows us to have a more realistic demand function and, thus, consumer surplus estimation.

Notes

1. Nevo (2001) has calculated consumer gains from the introduction of the ready-to-eat cereal industry. Petrin (2002) finds large consumer effects from the introduction of the minivan. Goolsbee and Petrin (2001) have calculated the gains from direct broadcast satellites and competition with cable television. Greenwood and Kopecky (2007) measure the welfare gains from personal computers in Canada. Another way of studying these impacts is to consider the price index.
2. For more details see Goolsbee and Klenow (2006).
3. We consider that a person may sleep about eight hours per day. Thus, the non-sleeping available time may be 112 hours per week. This time is allocated between Internet connection (4.1 percent), other leisure (60.2 percent) and work (35.7 percent).
4. For the USA, Goolsbee and Klenow (2006) obtain 0.33 percent.

References

ARCEP (Autorité de Régulation des Communications Electroniques et des Postes) (2005) 'Rapport d'activité de l'Autorité de Régulation des Communications Electroniques et Postales 2005', ARCEP.

Becker, G.S. (1964) *Human Capital: A Theoretical and Empirical Analysis with Special Reference to Education*, Chicago: University of Chicago Press.

Blundell, R., P. Pashardes and G. Weber (1993) 'What do We Learn about Consumer Demand Patterns from Micro-Data?', *American Economic Review*, Vol. 83, No. 3, pp. 570–97.

Bresnahan, T.S. and R.J. Gordon (1997) *The Economics of New Goods*, Chicago: University of Chicago Press.

Brynjolfsson, E., M. D. Smith and Y. J. Hu (2003) 'Consumer Surplus in the Digital Economy: Estimating the Value of Increased Product Variety at Online

Booksellers', Working Papers 4305-03, Massachusetts Institute of Technology (MIT), Sloan School of Management.

Chaudhuri, K., A. K. Flamm and J. Horigan (2005) 'An Analysis of the Determinants of Internet Access', *Telecommunications Policy*, Vol. 9, No. 10, October.

Gentzkow, M. (2006) 'Valuing New Goods in a Model with Complementarities: Online Newspapers', NBER Working Papers Series No. 12562, October.

Goldfarb, A. and J. Prince (2008) 'Internet Adoption and Usage Patterns are Different: Implications for the Digital Divide', *Information Economics and Policy*, Vol. 20, No. 1, pp. 2–15.

Goolsbee, A. and P. J. Klenow (2006), 'Valuing Consumer Products By the Time Spent Using Them: An Application to the Internet', *American Economic Review*, Vol. 96, No. 2, pp. 108–13.

Goolsbee, A. and A. Petrin (2001) 'The Consumer Gains from Direct Broadcast Satellites and the Competition with Cable Television', National Bureau of Economic Research Working Paper, W8317, Cambridge, MA.

Greenwood, J. and K.A. Kopecky (2007) 'Measuring the Welfare Gain from Personal Computers', *Economie d'Avant Garde Research Reports*, Vol. 15.

Hausman, J. (1981) 'Exact Consumer Surplus and Deadweight Loss', *American Economic Review*, Vol. 71, pp. 662–76.

Hausman, J. (1997) 'Valuing of New Goods Under Perfect and Imperfect Competition', in T. Bresnahan and R. Gordon (eds), *The Economics of New Goods*, Chicago: University of Chicago Press.

Hausman, J. (1999) 'Cellular Telephone, New Products and the CPI', *Journal of Business and Economic Statistics*, Vol. 17, No. 2, pp. 188–94.

Hausman, J. (2002) 'Sources of Bias and Solutions to Bias in the CPI', NBER Working Paper No. 9298.

Hausman, J. and G. Leonard (2002) 'The Competitive Effects of a New Product Introduction: A Case Study', *Journal of Industrial Economics*, Vol. 50.

Hausman, J. and W.K. Newey (1995) 'Nonparametric Estimation of Exact Consumers Surplus and Deadweight Loss', *Econometrica*, Vol. 63, No. 6, pp. 1445–76.

Heckman, J.J. (1976) 'The Common Structure of Statistical Models of Truncation, Sample Selection and Limited Dependent Variables and a Simple Estimator for Such Models', *Annals of Economic and Social Measurement*, Vol. 5, pp. 475–92.

Heckman, J.J. (1979) 'Sample Selection Bias as a Specification Error', *Econometrica*, Vol. 47, pp. 153–61.

Hoffmann, M.P. (1998) 'Developing Sustainable Management Tactics for Cucumber Beetles in Cucurbits', SARE (Sustainable Agriculture Research and Education Program) 1998 Annual Report.

IDATE (Institut de l'Audovisuel et des Telecommunications en Europe) (2005) 'Use-IT: qui consomme quoi en 2015?', IDATE.

Johnson, N.L. and S. Kotz (1972) *Distribution in Statistics: Continuous Multivariate Distributions*, New York: Wiley.

Nevo, A. (2001) 'New Products, Quality Changes, and Welfare Measures Computed from Estimated Demand Systems', NBER Working Paper No. W8425.

Petrin, A. (2002) 'Quantifying the Benefits of New Products: The Case of the Minivan', *Journal of Political Economy*, Vol. 110, No. 4, pp. 705–29.

6
Valuing Time-Intensive Goods: An Application to Wireless and Wired Internet

Ergin Bayrak

Introduction

Economic theory has a range of techniques for estimating the value derived from an economic activity. In the case of valuing a public resource, calculating the cost of recycling or the net present value of exploiting the resource are popular methods. In the case of the consumption of existing or introduction of new goods and services, estimating the price elasticities from expenditure data and inferring the consumer surplus is typical.

However, not all public resources or goods and services permit the application of these techniques. Some resources go into the production of numerous goods and services the (present) value of which are hard to quantify and aggregate. For some goods and services, on the other hand, expenditure data is either not available or does not represent the true cost of consumption, especially when consumption is highly time intensive. The conventional method of estimating the elasticity from expenditure data could be misleading in the case of highly time-intensive goods, since the market price constitutes a minuscule part of the total cost of consumption compared to the opportunity cost of time spent using the good. An alternative to the traditional method in the case of time-intensive goods is to estimate the elasticity and welfare from the variation in the opportunity cost of time.

The Internet is an important example of a time-intensive good for which the market expenditure is minuscule compared to the opportunity cost of the time spend in consumption. According to national income and product accounts, out of the $8.7 trillion that went to personal consumption expenditures in 2005, only $18 billion went to Internet service providers, which amounts to (scaling up for the

37 percent non-subscribers) 0.33 percent of the total expenditure; consumers report to be spending around 10 percent of their non-sleep time on the Internet. The time share of the Internet is about 30 times higher than the expenditure share, which illustrates the highly time-intensive nature of Internet consumption. Observing this peculiarity, Goolsbee and Klenow (2006) provide a simple utility model that includes consumption in the form of market expenditures and time. The model allows a more concrete estimation of the welfare gains from the Internet that takes into account the time-intensive nature of consumption.

In this chapter, as we look at the welfare derived from the use of wireless and wired Internet, we highlight the importance of this new approach to estimating welfare from the consumption of time-intensive goods as introduced by Goolsbee and Klenow (2006). Taking data on wages as the opportunity cost of time, and Internet time use data, we estimate the elasticity in a more accurate way that takes into account the time-intensive characteristic of the Internet. Furthermore, we restrict the attention to consumers with home networks and highlight the different demand characteristics and welfare attainments of consumers who connect to the Internet through wireless networks from those who connect through other (wired) types of networks. The incremental consumer surplus from using wireless networks relates to another important problem: the valuation of unlicensed radio spectrum.

The problem of valuing radio spectrum has difficulties that lie in the intersection of the two types of difficulties mentioned above. As a public resource, it is used by numerous devices for providing numerous services. Radio and TV broadcasting, mobile communications and data networking are few notable examples, besides garage door openers, baby monitors, microwave ovens, police radars – the list goes on. There are an estimated 15 million TVs using over-the-air broadcast, 800 million mobile phones, over 250 million Wi-Fi devices, and about 1 billion Bluetooth devices in the market, and the value derived from the consumption of these devices – which, in turn, is partly due to the ability of these devices to use radio spectrum – is quite challenging. On the other hand, as an intermediate good, estimating the demand for and the price elasticity of radio spectrum itself is also difficult because of the high heterogeneity with respect to the characteristics of different frequencies and the lack of an established market where spectrum is traded in large volumes from which variation in expenditure data can be observed to estimate elasticities.

Attaching a value to radio spectrum or the welfare derived from the use of it has gained importance recently because of the increased attention to *white spaces* – that is, the unused frequencies in the digital television broadcast bands. The gradual completion of the transition from analogue to digital broadcast, which will leave even more unused spectrum, raises the question of how and to what type of uses the white spaces should be allocated. First of the three approaches to managing spectrum, command and control (whereby the allocation of spectrum is done by a regulatory authority based on comparative hearings and pre-engineered technical rules), is unanimously regarded as inefficient and almost completely abandoned. Most of the debate on white spaces is centered around the other two regimes that came to be called 'licensing' and 'commons'.

Licensing is the approach to spectrum management whereby the spectrum is divided into spectral frequency bands and the exclusive rights to operate in a band at a certain geographical area is licensed to an entity, with the licenses being sold at auctions. In most of the recent allocations, licenses are flexible – meaning that the licensee has flexibility on the choice of end use offered and the technology employed.

Commercial Mobile Radio Services (CMRS) bands around 0.8, 0.9 and 1.9 GHz, Advanced Wireless Service (AWS) bands around 1.7 and 2.1 GHz are examples of exclusively licensed bands for flexible use by the licensee. Most notable uses of these bands consist of cellular voice and data communications services. Commons, on the other hand does not limit the right to operate to a number of licensees. An unlimited number of users share spectrum subject to some maximum power restrictions to counter interference. Industrial, Scientific and Medical (ISM) bands around 2.4 and 5.8 GHz are examples of Commons spectrum, with the most notable uses being the Wi-Fi and Bluetooth wireless networking devices. There have been studies that try to estimate the value of licensed spectrum bands and promote a licensing regime for further allocations. Hazlett (2005) has estimated the consumer surplus from the CMRS bands in 2003 to be $81 billion or around $500 per subscriber. Hausman (1997), on the other hand, has estimated that the introduction of cellular communications resulted in $30 to $50 billion consumer surplus per year. However, to our knowledge, there has not been a study that estimates the welfare gains from unlicensed spectrum bands. In this chapter, we take on the task of estimating part of the welfare gains associated with the use of unlicensed spectrum, keeping in mind the difficulties that prevent the application of the typical methods. Realizing that it is difficult to calculate and aggregate the welfare gains from all the goods and services that use unlicensed spectrum, we take wireless networking (for it is one of the most popular uses of unlicensed spectrum) as a first attempt to calculate a lower bound on the welfare gains from goods and services that use unlicensed spectrum. We look at the consumer surplus derived from Internet consumption and we restrict our attention to those consumers who report having some type of home network. We estimate the incremental consumer surplus of the consumers who connect to the Internet through wireless networks, over those who connect via wired Ethernet, powerline or HomePNA networks. We find as a very conservative estimate, that the consumers who connect to the Internet through wireless networks obtain $824 more consumer surplus per year than those consumers who use wired networks. The chapter is organized as follows. In the next section we present the model as introduced by Goolsbee and Klenow (2006). In the third section we talk about the data and the estimation of elasticities. The fourth section presents welfare calculations. The fifth section concludes.

Model

Consumers maximize the following utility function, which incorporates the time-intensive nature of the Internet as a consumption good.

$$U = \theta(C_i^{\alpha}L_i^{1-\alpha})^{\frac{\sigma-1}{\sigma}} + (1-\theta)(C_o^{\beta}L_o^{1-\beta})^{\frac{\sigma-1}{\sigma}}$$

where C_i is the consumption of Internet services and L_i is the time spent using the Internet. All other goods and services consumed form the composite good C_o with the time spent on the composite good being L_o. θ represents the utility weight of the Internet bundle compared to that of the composite bundle. Finally $(1-\alpha)$ and $(1-\beta)$ represent the time intensities of the Internet and the composite bundles, respectively.

The following is the budget that constrains consumers in their utility maximization.

$$P_iC_i + F + P_oC_o = W(1 - L_i - L_o)$$

where W is the wage, P_i and P_o are the prices of the Internet service and the composite bundle, respectively. F is the fixed cost of access to the Internet, including the network setup. P_i can be interpreted as the price of marginal consumption which is zero in practice since Internet access is usually priced as a flat monthly fee.

The combined Cobb-Douglas bundles are denoted as $Y_i = C_i^\alpha L_i^{1-\alpha}$ and $Y_o = C_o^\beta L_o^{1-\beta}$ Letting the price on the bundles ρ_i and ρ_o be the weighted average of the market price and the price of time (i.e., the wage), we have

$$\rho_i = \left(\frac{P_i}{\alpha}\right)^\alpha \left(\frac{W}{1-\alpha}\right)^{1-\alpha} \text{ and } \rho_o = \left(\frac{P_o}{\beta}\right)^\beta \left(\frac{W}{1-\beta}\right)^{1-\beta}$$

Then, the optimal choices for the bundles become

$$Y_i = \frac{W-F}{\rho_i(1+\Delta)} \text{ and } Y_o = \frac{W-F}{\rho_o(1+1/\Delta)}$$

where

$$\Delta = \left(\frac{\rho_i}{\rho_o}\right)^{\sigma-1}\left(\frac{1-\theta}{\theta}\right)^\sigma$$

Breaking down the bundles into their consumption and time counterparts gives the optimal choices as

$$C_i = \frac{\alpha \rho_i Y_i}{P_i} \quad C_o = \frac{\beta \rho_o Y_o}{P_o}$$

$$L_i = \frac{(1-\alpha)\rho_i Y_i}{W} \quad L_o = \frac{(1-\beta)\rho_o Y_o}{W}$$

Using the optimal choices on the Internet bundle and the time spent on Internet, we can get the following expression for Δ:

$$\Delta = \frac{(1-\alpha)(1-\frac{F}{W})-L_i}{L_i}$$

Observing that the cost of the access to the Internet is a small flat fee ($F/W \approx 0$), with no marginal use pricing ($\alpha = 0$), the above expression becomes approximately equal to the time spent on activities other than Internet relative to the time spent on the Internet.

$$\Delta \approx \frac{1-L_i}{L_i}$$

Using the prices of the bundles and rearranging, we get another expression for Δ in terms of the wage

$$\Delta = AW^{(\beta-\alpha)(\sigma-1)}\left(\frac{1-\theta}{\theta}\right)^\sigma$$

where

$$A = \left[\frac{(P_i/\alpha)^\alpha (1-\beta)^\beta}{(P_o/\beta)^\beta (1-\alpha)^\alpha} \right]^{\sigma-1}$$

Equating the two expressions and taking the natural logarithm gives

$$\ln\left(\frac{1-L_i}{L_i}\right) \approx \ln(A) + (\beta-\alpha)(\sigma-1)\ln(W) + \sigma \ln\left(\frac{1-\theta}{\theta}\right)$$

The left-hand side of the equation is the log of time spent on non-Internet activities relative to time spent on the Internet, which can be found in the data. ln(A) is a constant across consumers. ln(W) is the log of the wage and can be found in the data as well. The difference between the time intensities of the two bundles $(\beta-\alpha)$ can also be measured from the data. So, from the estimation of this equation, assuming that the error term arises from the individual variation in the utility weight parameter θ the coefficient of the wage can be translated into an estimate of the elasticity of substitution between the two bundles, which in turn can be used to calculate the consumer surplus.

Data and estimation

We use the *North American Consumer Technographics* data from Forrester Research. The data comes from a survey conducted with a nationally representative sample of 60,000 households. The survey includes various questions on ownership and use of various goods and services, with a focus on telecommunications. Demographic, attitudinal and behavioral variables are present as well. We take the sample of 4,865 respondents who report having some type of home network and are online at least monthly. Of the 4,865 respondents, 2,991 have a wireless network and the remaining 1,874 have other types of networks. We use data on the hours per week spent by the respondents on the Internet for personal reasons, income of the respondent and ownership and type of home networking devices. We also use data on the time spent on the Internet for work-related reasons to contrast the implications of the model. We include some demographic controls to refine the results in some of the regressions. In the survey, answers to the questions regarding Internet time use are grouped as one to four hours, five to nine hours and so on. For a conservative estimate we take the lower bounds of these intervals for our main results in the text but present the results taking the mid-points as well. The respondents with wireless networks spend an average of 10.66 hours per week on the Internet for personal reasons.

This corresponds to 9.5 percent of the respondents' non-sleep time of 112 hours, assuming eight hours of sleep per day. For respondents with wired networks, time spent on the Internet for personal reasons is 11.04 hours on average or 9.8 percent of non-sleep time. The numbers in the case where we use midpoints for time use calculations become 12.54 hours (11.1 percent) for wireless network owners and 12.92 hours (11.5 percent) for wired network owners.

The time intensities of the two bundles can be calculated as one minus the ratio of market expenditures on the bundle to market expenditures plus time expenditures

$$(1-\alpha) = 1 - \frac{P_iC_i}{P_iC_i + WL_i} \quad \text{and} \quad (1-\beta) = 1 - \frac{P_oC_o}{P_oC_o + WL_o}$$

Dividing the numerator and the denominator by $W(1 - L_i - L_o)$ and letting the expenditure shares of the Internet and the composite bundle be E_i and E_o respectively gives

$$(1-\alpha) = 1 - \frac{E_i}{E_i + \dfrac{L_i}{1 - L_i - L_o}} \quad \text{and} \quad (1-\beta) = 1 - \frac{E_o}{E_o + \dfrac{L_o}{1 - L_i - L_o}}$$

We substitute 0.0033 for the expenditure share of the Internet (E_i), 0.9967 for the expenditure share of the composite (E_o) and 0.3570 for the share of work time in the non-sleep time of the consumer ($1 - L_i - L_o$). The consumers with wireless networks spend 0.0951 of their time on the Internet and the remaining 0.5476 on leisure activities other than the Internet. These yield time intensities of $(1-\alpha) = 0.9877$ for the Internet and $(1-\beta) = 0.6060$ for the composite in the case of wireless network owners. Owners of wired networks spend 0.0986 of their time on the Internet and 0.5442 of their time on other leisure activities. These yield time intensities of 0.9881 for the Internet and 0.6045 for the composite in the case of wired network owners.

These statistics, along with their counterparts in the case where we take midpoints for time use calculations, are presented in Table 6.1. We use the time intensities in the calculation of the elasticities from the coefficient on the log of wage. The results of the regressions are reported in Table 6.2. The positive coefficients show that the respondents with higher incomes report spending less time on the Internet. Wireless network owners are more responsive to changes in the opportunity cost of time with an elasticity of 1.6381. Wired network owners, on the other hand, have an elasticity of 1.5222.

Table 6.1   Summary statistics

	Mean Internet Use	(1–α)	(1–β)	Mean full income*
Wireless Network Owners	10.66 hrs(9.5 %)	0.9877	0.6060	$239295
Wired Network Owners	11.04 hrs(9.8 %)	0.9881	0.6045	$190280
Wireless Network Owners (mp)	12.54 hrs(11.1 %)	0.9895	0.5986	$234904
Wired Network Owners (mp)	12.92 hrs(11.5 %)	0.9898	0.5970	$186762

(mp): taking midpoints for time use calculations, *: work and leisure time valued at wage.

Table 6.2   Regression of $\ln((1-L_i)/L_i)$ on $\ln(W)$

	Coefficient	Standard Error	R^2	Implied Elasticity σ
Wireless Network Owners	0.2436	0.0327	0.0182	1.6381
Wired Network Owners	0.2003	0.0404	0.0129	1.5222
Internet for Work	−0.1507	0.0334	0.0055	N/A
Wireless Network Owners (c)	0.3131	0.0452	0.1219	1.8190
Wired Network Owners (c)	0.2558	0.0568	0.1439	1.6685
Wireless Network Owners (mp)	0.1893	0.0246	0.0194	1.4841
Wired Network Owners (mp)	0.1626	0.0305	0.0149	1.4139
Internet for Work (mp)	−0.1152	0.0253	0.0056	N/A
Wireless Network Owners (c) (mp)	0.2408	0.0340	0.1275	1.6150
Wired Network Owners (c) (mp)	0.1985	0.0428	0.1511	1.5066

(mp) mid points.

(c): controlling for value of assets, education and time spent on the Internet for work related reasons.

As a contrast, in rows (3) and (8) of Table 6.1, we replicate the regression taking the time spent on the Internet for work-related reasons as the independent variable. It can be assumed that respondents have little or no control of the time spent on the Internet for work-related reasons, thus the coefficient need not be consistent with the models prediction for personal Internet use. As indicated by the negative coefficient, people report to spend more time on the Internet for work-related reasons as wages increase, but in this scenario it is not natural to think of the wage as the opportunity cost of the time spent on the Internet for work-related reasons.

These results are consistent with the findings of Goolsbee and Klenow (2006) that, as the opportunity cost of time increases, people spend less time on the Internet for personal reasons, but this is not true for the time spent on the Internet for work-related reasons. However, conditional on having some type of network, we find the elasticities to be higher than those found in Goolsbee and Klenow (2006). Our benchmark regressions give estimates of the elasticity of 1.68 and 1.52, whereas Goolsbee and Klenow's larger sample of all respondents who are online at least monthly gives an elasticity of 1.32, which is not surprising since the larger sample includes respondents who rarely go online.

As a second attempt to refine the estimates, we include some control variables. We include education level of the respondent, number of hours spent on the Internet for work-related reasons and the combined value of owned assets of the respondent. The implied elasticities go up slightly. The regression including the wireless network owners posits an elasticity of 1.8190 compared to 1.6685 for wired network owners. Furthermore, in the last five rows we report the results of the regressions where we use midpoints for time use calculations. Elasticities go down slightly but the effect on welfare estimates is quite pronounced as we will illustrate in the next section.

Welfare

The consumer surplus can be approximated by equivalent variation. We use the expenditure function

$$E(P_o, P_i, F, W, u \mid Y_i > 0) = F + \frac{P_o}{(1 + 1/\varDelta)^{(1/(1-\sigma))}} \left(\frac{u}{1-\theta}\right)^{\frac{\sigma}{\sigma-1}}$$

and its counterpart in the case when Internet consumption is not available

$$E(P_o, W, u \mid Y_i = 0) = P_o \left(\frac{u}{1-\theta}\right)^{\frac{\sigma}{\sigma-1}}$$

to calculate the equivalent variation as a percentage of full income

$$\frac{EV}{W} = \frac{E(P_o, W, u(P_o, P_i, F, W \mid Y_i > 0) \mid y_i = 0)}{W} = \left[\left(1 + \frac{1}{\varDelta}\right)^{\frac{1}{\sigma-1}}\left(1 - \frac{F}{W}\right) - 1\right]$$

The consumer surplus naturally depends on the elasticity of substitution σ between the Internet bundle and the composite bundle. Revoking the assumption that the Internet has a small flat subscription fee ($F/W \approx 0$) and no price for marginal consumption ($\alpha = 0$), the equivalent variation becomes

$$\frac{EV}{W} = (1 - L_i)^{\frac{-1}{\sigma-1}} - 1$$

Using the elasticity estimates we can calculate the equivalent variation relative to income. In Table 6.3 we present the results of these calculations. For respondents with wireless networks, the consumer surplus turns out to be 16 percent of full income (wage income plus the value of leisure). For those respondents with other wired types of networks the consumer surplus is 22 percent of full income.

However, since the utility of consumption of the first unit is very high, with a log demand, the above calculations tend to overestimate the consumer surplus. To counter this effect and get a conservative estimate of the consumer surplus, we linearize the demand, as in Hausman (1999), and use the fact that consumer surplus relative to full income is equal to the expenditure share divided by twice the elasticity, which is equal to $0.5 * L_i / \sigma (1 - L_i(1 - F/W))$ in our model.

The calculations yield a consumer surplus of 3.2 percent of full income for wireless network owners. This is corresponds to $6,755 per year for the wireless network owner with the median full income in the sample. On average, wireless network owners realize a consumer surplus of $7,648.

The median income consumer with a wired network realizes $6,009 of consumer surplus per year, which is 3.5 percent of the full income and, on average, wired network owners realize $6,840 consumer surplus per year. The difference in the average consumer surplus is $844 per year in the case without controls. Controlling for the value of assets, time spent on the Internet for work and education slightly decreases the welfare estimates. The average consumer surplus of wireless network owners goes down to $7,285 per year. The average consumer surplus of consumers with a wired network goes down to $6,461 per year. The incremental consumer surplus realized by wireless network

Table 6.3   Consumer surplus as a percentage of full income

	σ	EV/W (%)	EV/W (l) (%)	EV/W at median income	EV/W at average income	Difference
Wireless Owners	1.6381	16	3.2	$6755	$7684	
Wired Owners	1.5222	22	3.5	$6009	$6840	$844
(c)						
Wireless Owners	1.8190	13	2.9	$6342	$7285	
Wired Owners	1.6685	16	3.2	$5723	$6461	$824
(mp)						
Wireless Owners	1.4841	27	4.2	$8762	$9980	
Wired Owners	1.4139	34	4.6	$7570	$8618	$1362
(c) (mp)						
Wireless Owners	1.6150	21	3.9	$8404	$9642	
Wired Owners	1.5066	26	4.2	$7415	$8399	$1242

(mp): linearized, (c):controlling for value of assets, education and Internet time use for work related reasons.

owners on average goes down to $824 per year with the controls. The welfare estimates go up across the board in the case where midpoints are used in the calculation of time use. The Incremental consumer surplus that the wireless networks owners realize goes up to $1,362 in the benchmark case and is slightly lower at $1,242 when controlling for assets, education and Internet time use for work-related reasons. It is important to point out that these estimates, although taking into account the time intensities in a more accurate way, still have to be viewed with caution.

The first reason to be cautious is that all of the non-sleep time for the consumer is valued at the wage. If consumers value their leisure time less than the wage, then we would be overestimating the welfare gains. We also do not take into account other time-intensive substitutes to the Internet except the composite. Taking into account other time-intensive substitutes like watching TV or gym membership would increase elasticities and would reduce the welfare estimates.

Conclusion

High time intensity of use for a good or service is one of the reasons that makes traditional approaches estimating elasticities difficult to apply. However, if there is enough variation in the time use data, and the opportunity cost of time, elasticities can be estimated from data on time use and wage instead of market prices. In the case of highly time-intensive goods, the true cost of consumption includes the opportunity cost of time besides the minuscule market expenditures. Using the variation in time use and wage data is likely to give more accurate estimates of elasticities and welfare than using market price and consumption data. We use a simple utility model proposed by Goolsbee and Klenow (2006) and estimate the welfare gains from using the Internet for consumers with different types of home networks. We find that the consumer surplus from the Internet is around $7,000. With the most conservative estimate, consumers with wireless networks are found to be realizing, on average, $824 more consumer surplus from the use of the Internet compared to wired network owners. However, we note that these estimates, although taking into account the time intensity explicitly, have to be viewed with caution since all leisure is valued at the wage in the model and no other time-intensive substitutes to the Internet are considered.

References

Goolsbee, A. and P. J. Klenow (2006), 'Valuing Consumer Products By the Time Spent Using Them: An Application to the Internet', *American Economic Review*, Vol. 96, No. 2, pp. 108–13.

Hausman, J. (1997) 'Valuing of New Goods Under Perfect and Imperfect Competition', in T. Bresnahan and R. Gordon (eds), *The Economics of New Goods*, Chicago: University of Chicago Press.

Hausman, J. (1999) 'Cellular Telephone, New Products and the CPI', *Journal of Business and Economic Statistics*, Vol. 17, No. 2, pp. 188–94.

Hazlett, T. (2005) 'Spectrum Tragedies - Avoiding a Tragedy of the Telecommons: Finding the Right Property Rights Regime for Telecommunications', *Yale Journal on Regulation*, Vol. 22, Summer.

7
Contingent Valuation of Digital Identification Card and Electronic Signature Service in Luxembourg

Alex Durand

Introduction

This chapter refers to the concept of willingness to pay (WTP), defined as what an individual will agree to pay for a benefit (service, equipment, prevention program) funded entirely or in part by the community (Godfroid I., 1996). The concept may be illustrated using a method, the contingent valuation method (CVM) (Mitchell and Carson, 1989). The method relies on a conceptual framework based on the random utility model (RUM) (Haneman, 1984). It is generally limited to the fields of the environment (Loomis et al., 2000) and health (Chanel et al., 2004), and is little used in the field of innovation (Le Gal-Ely, 2003). One objective of the chapter is to show that it is possible to apply CVM in the field of innovation in information and communication technologies (ICT). The innovation this study focuses on is a digital identification card and electronic signature service (www.luxtrust.lu/solutions/choix/choix) and its adoption by individuals aged 16 to 74 years residing in Luxembourg. The service would safeguard electronic exchanges (purchases of books and DVDs, sales, bank transactions or exchanges of information with public services), first, by identifying merchants, suppliers and public services on the Internet and, second, by allowing the individual using the service to electronically sign for all transactions made online. Thus, the risk of dispute and contesting of transactions is reduced if the transaction does not go as planned. The chapter has four sections. In the first section the WTP model used to estimate the value of the service is outlined. It is divided into three steps. The first step attempts to show that it is possible to model the interest in the service expressed by the respondent using a PLS logistic regression. The second step shows that the ability to calibrate such a model can be used to classify every respondent in a level of interest band from the lowest to the highest, with the highest band having the dual objective of defining consistent profiles of potential users identifying 'early adopters' as well as those who might be characterized as '*late* adopters'. Finally, the third step is devoted to estimating the average annual willingness to pay that can be differentiated according to the user's profile, as well as defining the overall annual economic value and the different values of the service. The three other sections of the chapter describe results associated with these steps.

Theoretical model

The contingent valuation was performed *a posteriori*, with a three-step procedure to establish an economic value of the service that could be derived in the near future from the digital identification card and electronic signature for residents aged 16 to 74.

Step 1

The expression of interest in a digital identification card and electronic signature (y_i) of a respondent i, $\forall i = 1,...,N$ is the result of his evaluation of how much he thinks he benefits from using the service. This benefit cannot be directly measured. It reflects the difference (Δu_i) between the utility that he associates with the adoption of the service and that which he associates with the status quo, characterized by not adopting the service. If the difference in utility is positive or null (and respectively negative), the benefit perceived is positive or none (and respectively negative), the respondent indicates that he is interested, either $y_i = 1$ (and respectively not interested, or $y_i = 0$) in the service. Finally, $y = f(\Delta u)$ as in

$$
\begin{cases}
y_i = 0 & \Delta u_i < 0 \\
y_i = 1 & 0 \leq \Delta u_i
\end{cases}
\qquad
\begin{aligned}
&(1a) \\
&(1b)
\end{aligned}
$$

The function u_i designating the utility function that characterizes the preferences of respondent *i*, theoretically (Hanneman, 1984) consists of two additive and separable parts, one which is observable v_i, the other e_i not observable and unpredictable. It can be expressed as follows

$$u_i = v_i + e_i \tag{2}$$

Assuming a logistic distribution of the error term ($\varepsilon_i = \Delta e_i$), the specified model is a logit, which is estimated using the maximum likelihood, taking into account the following probabilities:

$$\begin{cases} P(y_i = 0) = 1 - F(a_0 + x_{0i}\beta) \\ P(y_i = 1) = F(a_0 + x_{0i}\beta) \end{cases}$$

(3a)
(3b)

where F indicates the logistic distribution function ($F(.)=\exp(.)/(1+\exp(.))$), where x_{0i} is the row vector of the k variables explaining x_{oij} with characteristics, habits and behaviors relative to respondent i's use of the computer and Internet, and where ($x_{0i}\beta$) results from the difference (Δv_i) provided that v_i is linear. Wherever the predictors x_{oj} are very dependent on each other, it is useful to refer to the logistic regression PLS.

Doing this will avoid the situation where certain predictors are ultimately declared not significant, and others appear with a coefficient with a sign opposite to what is expected. The PLS algorithm that was used is that described by Tenenhaus in the logistic regression used to estimate the quality of Bordeaux wines (1998, 2005). This algorithm studies the linear combinations of X orthogonal components t_h such as

$$t_h = Xw_h^*$$

(4)

where X is the matrix illustrating reduced, centered k variables x_j and where w_h* is the column vector formed by w_{hj}, to then create the logistic regression of y on its components, or

$$\log[(\pi_i/1 - \pi_i)] = \sum_{h=1}^{H} c_h t_{h,l} + a$$

(5)

where π_i is the probability of the event (y=1) for an individual having the characteristics of the individual i and where (a,c_h) are the parameters to estimate.

The choice of the number of components t_h is determined by the value of statistic Q_h^2. The number 'h' component is introduced if Q_h^2 has a value greater than or equal to 0.0975. The statistic Q_h^2 is calculated as follows:

$$Q_h^2 = 1 - (\chi^2 \text{ cross validation, step } h)/(\chi^2 \text{ substitution, step } h-1) \quad (6)$$

with $\chi^2 = \sum_{i=1}^{n}((y_i - \pi_i)^2/\pi_i(1 - \pi_i))$, χ^2 Pearson's calculated in step h first by substitution replacing π_i with the estimate using logistic regression for components t_1 through t_h and then with cross-validation by estimating π_i without using observation i.

Step 2

Once the (a, c_h) parameters have been estimated, a palatability score is derived for each respondent i. This score is the estimated score of probability $\hat{\pi}_i$ that he will be interested in the service, or

$$\hat{\pi}_i = e^{\sum\limits_{h=1}^{H} \hat{c}_h t_{h,i} + \hat{a}} \bigg/ 1 + e^{\sum\limits_{h=1}^{H} \hat{c}_h t_{hii} + \hat{a}} \qquad (7)$$

From the distribution of scores, the ability to calibrate the model is further used to derive an indicator for differentiating the level of interest (S_m) $\forall m = 1,...,M$, which is a single respondent profile, as it becomes possible to form couples $(\hat{\pi}_i; S_m)$.

Step 3

The distribution of palatability scores is then used to estimate WTP in the relationship $cap = g(\hat{\pi})$. A priori, the higher the level of interest, whether evaluated in terms of probability $\hat{\pi}$ or profile S_m, the greater the WTP. Since the payment card is the method used for questioning that was chosen to reveal the WTP in this study, the option of ordinal regression may be considered[1] such as

$$\log\left[(\pi_{il}/1 - \pi_{il})\right] = \alpha_l + d\hat{\pi}_i \qquad (8)$$

where $\pi_{il} = P(cap_i \leq l)$ $\forall l = 1,...,L-1$ is the probability that the i respondent's WTP is less than or equal to the value l, whilst $\hat{\pi}_i$ is the estimated probability that respondent i is interested in the service in question, and (α_l, d) the parameters estimate.

After deriving the estimators (α_l, d), the model is used to create the probability distribution for willingness to pay for each respondent i, such that

$$\sum_{l=1}^{L} \hat{\theta}_{il} = 1 \qquad (9)$$

where $\hat{\theta}_{il} = \hat{\pi}_{il}$, where $\hat{\theta}_{il} = \hat{\pi}_{il+1} - \hat{\pi}_{il}$ $\forall 2 \leq l < L$ and where $\hat{\theta}_{iL} = 1 - \hat{\pi}_{iL-1}$ for $l = L$.

This individualized distribution may be used to calculate expected WTP per individual. Simply total the different products of the multiplication of the estimated probability that the willingness is included between l and $l + 1$ the corresponding category centre c_l, so that

$$M_i^* = \sum_{l=1}^{L} \hat{\theta}_{il} c_l \tag{10}$$

M_i^* represents the average WTP for an individual whose characteristics are those of respondent i. From this measurement, four indicators may be derived: $M_{S_m}^* = \overline{M}_{i,S_m}^*$ and $M^* = \overline{M}_i^*$ which represent, respectively, the average annual WTP for an individual with the profile S_m and that for an individual taken from the resident population aged 16 to 74 years, $V_{S_m} = P_{S_m} M_{S_m}^*$ and $V_G = PM^*$, which is the annual economic value attached to the service intended for the entire population with profile S_m, and of size P_{S_m}, respectively, to that intended for the entire resident population aged 16 to 74 years, of size P.

Empirical estimate of interest

After a brief description of the benefits of the service for all 1,509 Luxembourg residents aged 16 to 74 years, it was possible to observe their positive (y = 1) or negative (y = 0) response to the following simple question: 'Would you be interested in a digital identification card and electronic signature?' Observing the distribution of responses shows that 616 respondents state an interest (40.51 percent),[2] while 893 state that they have no interest (59.49 percent).

In order to select discriminant variables, the variable (y) was cross-validated with the 146 variables which make up the group of potential predictors taken from the 'TIC-ménages' (household) survey conducted by the TNS-ILRES market research institute on behalf of Luxembourg's national statistics institute (STATEC). Regarding 127 binary variables, of which 118 are responses to 15 multiple choice questions, and five polytomous nominal variables, the statistics and tests selected are Khi2 and its p-value as well as Cramer's V.

As for the remaining eight ordinal variables and six discrete variables, the statistics and tests associated with Wilcoxon/Kruskal-Wallis, Median, Savage and Kendall's Tau were used. The interpretation of these two batteries of tests and statistics led to the selection of 28 binary variables of which some were obtained after combining their methodology – for example, where the variable characterizing the response to the question 'Where have you used your computer during the last three months?' was concerned. In addition, two nominal polytomous variables were also selected – for example, the one referring back to the profession of the respondent. Finally, 11 of the discrete or ordinal variables were retained, although some were altered – for example the one concerning the respondent's age. The illustration of 41 preselected predictors using a full disjunctive table reveals 99 variables which have been centered and reduced to be used to estimate the binary interest response (y) in a logistic regression PLS. The results of this regression estimate as a function of the three PLS components selected, $t_h = Xw_h^* \ \forall h = 1,2,3$ (see Appendix A 7.1) are presented in Table 7.1.

From the third step of the PLS algorithm, the Q_3^2 statistic has a value strictly less than 0.0975 (see Table 7.2). Thus, one to two components are enough to sum up the relationship between the predictors as well as the predictors with the interest variable.

However, three PLS components have been chosen. The ability to calibrate the resulting logistic regression is actually greater than that of a model that has one component or two. On the one hand, the partition table associated with the calculation of the Hosmer and Lemeshow (H and L) test shows that the rate of participants interested in the service is increasing at any point of predicted risk, which is not the case with the other models. On the other hand, compared with the two other models, the statistic of the H and L test, or 4.119, is closest to null value and the threshold associated with the test, 0.846, is closest to unity.

Table 7.1   Estimate log $[(\pi/1-\pi)] = \sum_{h-1}^{3} C_h t_h + a$

Illustration of the PLS logistic regression coefficients as a function of selected PLS

Target: y
1 if the respondent states an interest in the service
  (40.51%)
0 if he states that he is not interested in the service
  (59.49%)

Parameters	Regression coefficient	Wald
t1 Component PLS 1	4.016 (0.018)	>4*
t2 Component PLS 2	4.909 (0.042)	>4*
t3 Component PLS 3	4.484 (0.057)	>4*
a Constant	−0.652 (0.005)	>4*

* Significant at a 1% threshold / Overall significance: LR(3) = 133,941.288 (p_value < 1%); Quality of fit: Hosmer & Lemeshow (S(8) = 4.119; p_value = 0.846).
Discrimination: Index C = 0.838.

Table 7.2   Selection of the number of PLS components for h = 1 to 4

Significant contribution of component th in step h if Qh2 > 0.0975			
Step h	1	2	3	4
Q_h^2		0.1329	−0.0438	−0.0780

An individualized examination of the properties of the model chosen confirms that it has definite explanatory power, additional proof that a relationship exists between the items describing the respondent and the interest he has in the service.

The results of the LR test with three degrees of independence shows that, at the threshold of 1 percent, the null hypothesis of overall independence of the model from the observations may indeed be rejected. of the three PLS components, perfectly independent of the other, also contributes in a statistically significant way to explaining the interest in the service at a threshold level below 1 percent. They also have a Wald statistic value exceeding four.

Finally, from the examination of the discriminant power of the model it can be observed that, with a C index of 0.838, discrimination may be characterized as good. The value of this index is 1.676 times greater than that of a random model, which would establish the C index at 0.5.

Interest profile

The model previously estimated is used to calculate a palatability score for each respondent i. This score is the estimated probability $\hat{\pi}_i$ that he will be interested in the digital identification card and electronic signature service. From observing the graph illustrating the rate of respondents declaring a positive interest not just in deciles (HandL test), but in score percentiles, it is possible to segment all respondents (see Figure A 7.1). Six interest segments result: 'not interested', 'slightly interested', 'medium minus interested', 'medium plus interested', 'highly interested' and 'very highly interested'. Table 7.3 illustrates this segmentation.

Table 7.3　Segmentation

Segment	Probability (Minimum threshold in %)	Average rate of respondents interested (%)	Respondents included (number)	Population involved (%)
No interest	0	1.448	181	12.261
Slight interest	4.325	11.238	302	19.962
Medium minus interest	20.285	28.762	226	15.151
Medium plus interest	36.015	45.938	302	19.732
High interest	58.512	68.003	302	20.315
Very high interest	80.294	86.795	196	12.578

In each segment is a profile in terms of predictors which helps explain interest (Table A 7.2).[3] The use of the Cramer V indicator to express the intensity of the causal relationship between each of the predictors and each of the segments precisely identifies the predictors that distinguish the segments. For example, a respondent identified as 'very highly interested' in the service will tend to have the following profile. He states that the last time he ordered or purchased products or services online for personal use using email was less than one year ago (100 percent). He states that he has used online services and activities for personal use in the last three months, which include banking transactions (96 percent), arranging travel and lodging (96 percent), downloading official forms (92 percent) and obtaining information from the websites of public authorities (90 percent). He states that he has ordered products and services over the Internet during the last 12 months for personal use, including books, magazines, newspapers and e-learning materials (91 percent), travel and lodging (86 percent) and tickets for entertainment (81 percent). This type of respondent represents 196 individuals taken from the sample, or 12.6 percent of the total population involved. Some 86.8 percent of these respondents answered that they were interested in the service. Each has a palatability score greater than or equal to 80.3 percent. This category is characterized as 'early adopters'. The opposite of the 'early adopter' is the respondent who is not interested in the digital identification card and electronic signature. He is associated with the following profile. He states that he belongs to the socio-professional category of the unemployed or pensioners (73 percent). He states that he is over 49 years old (85 percent). He states that he has a maximum level of education of 'secondary school – first cycle' (94 percent). He states that no member of his household has Internet access at home (83 percent). He states that the last time he used a computer and the Internet was three months ago or even longer (100 percent and 99 percent, respectively). (The responses to questions B2 and C2 are 100 percent and 99 percent respectively in the case of response 'not specified or other'.) He states that he has not taken a course (of at least three hours) on how to use a computer (100 percent). This type of respondent represents 181 individuals taken from the sample, or 12.3 percent of the total population involved. Of these, 1.5 percent responded that they were interested in the service. Each has a palatability score strictly less than 4.3 percent. This category is characterized as 'late adopters'.

Estimate of willingness to pay

To estimate the willingness to pay for the service $cap = g(\hat{\pi})$, the option of asking questions about using payment cards distributed 'afterwards' for between €0 and €100 per year per person was selected. Table 7.4 illustrates the distribution of responses using this card method.

To establish the relationship between responses supplied about the payment card with palatability scores, the ordinal regression option was selected. Table 7.5 illustrates the results of the estimate of this regression. The analysis of the estimate results shows that, with a threshold of 1 percent, there is a positive causal relationship between willingness to pay and estimated probability $\hat{\pi}$ that the respondent is interested. In other words, a respondent who is that much more interested will be prepared to pay more to take advantage of the digital identification card and the electronic signature. Then, the predictions generated by the model allow for the creation of a probability distribution of willingness to pay for each respondent of the sample. It has been used to calculate an expectation of WTP per person, and derives four indicators of WTP. They are illustrated in Table 7.6.

To receive the service, the respective annual fixed rate $M_{S_m}^*$ capped at €3.2/year, €4.3/year, €6.4/year, €10.3/year, €17.3/year and €23.6/year could be reasonably proposed to the potential user whose profile is that of a respondent classified respectively as 'not interested', 'slightly interested', 'medium minus interested', 'medium plus interested', 'highly interested' and 'very highly interested'. Thus, each profile may be associated with a single rate band. The analysis that this makes possible confirms, in terms of segmentation, the analysis previously carried out in terms of probability, that is to say that willingness is an increasing function of estimated probability $\hat{\pi}$ as well as of the respondent's interest profile S_m.

If the option of distributing the service targeting 'early adopters' is chosen, the economic value of the service V_{S6} represents in the order of €1 million /year. If, conversely, no discriminant strategy is adopted, it is an annual fixed rate M* capped at €10.7/year, which would be proposed to any potential user taken from the resident population aged 16 to 74 years. Given the scale of the targeted population, the annual economic value of the service V_G would be on the order of €3.8 million.

Conclusion

This chapter concludes the third experiment conducted by the Public Research Centre Henri Tudor on the subject of contingent valuation

Table 7.4 Distribution of responses using the payment card method

*C	Don't know	0	5	10	15	20	25	30	35	40	45	50	100	TOT
l	12	11	10	9	8	7	6	5	4	3	3	2	1	
c_i	0	0	7.5	12.5	17.5	22.5	27.5	32.5	37.5	45	45	52.5	100	
P_l	23.89	36.64	5.39	7.14	4.61	7.09	3.53	1.77	1.76	0.36	1.00	4.74	2.08	100

* C: methods possible with the payment card in euros/year.
l: numbering of categories.
c_i: centre of category.
P_l: weighted percentage of responses per category.

Table 7.5   Results of the estimate

Target CAP ≤ l for l = 1 through 12

Parameters	Regression coefficient	Wald
Constant 1	−5.510 (0.014)	>4*
Constant 2	−4.263 (0.010)	>4*
Constant 3	−4.066 (0.009)	>4*
Constant 4	−3.849 (0.009)	>4*
Constant 5	−3.662 (0.008)	>4*
Constant 6	−3.344 (0.008)	>4*
Constant 7	−2.831 (0.007)	>4*
Constant 8	−2.553 (0.007)	>4*
Constant 9	−2.158 (0.007)	>4*
Constant 10	−1.873 (0.007)	>4*
Constant 11	0.060 (0.006)	>4*
Probability $\hat{\pi}$ (average 0.405)	+3.196 (0.012)	>4*

* Significant at a threshold of 1%.
Overall significance: LR(1) = 81,410.1543 (p_value<1%);
Discrimination: Index C = 0.697.

Table 7.6   Willingness to pay for the benefits of the digital identification card and electronic signature in Luxembourg

Segment (S_m)	Number of individuals (thousands and %) per segment (P_{S_m})	Average willingness to pay (euros) per person and per segment $(M^{*}_{S_m})$	Economic value (thousands of euros) per segment $(V_{S_m} = P_{S_m} M^{*}_{S_m})$
No i	43,183.000	3.232	139,580.702
Slight i	70,307.000	4.262	299,679.440
Medium minus i	53,361.000	6.360	339,360.554
Medium plus i	69,497.000	10.302	715,951.917
High i	71,549.000	17.269	1235,600.732
Very high i	44,301.000	23.599	1045,445.117
	Total population (P) 352,198	Average annual willingness to pay (M*) 10.720	Overall annual economic value $(V_G = PM^{*})$ 3,775,618

applied to the field of innovation in ICT. The first study concerned the economic evaluation of a service that could be provided in the near future to the Luxembourg mobile telephone subscriber who has near field communication (NFC) technology. The second study considered the possibility of applying radio frequency identification (RFId) to libraries and its impact in terms of operational benefits, as well as necessary financial considerations. This last study considers the evaluation of the willingness of the resident aged 16 to 74 years to pay in order to take advantage of a digital identity card and electronic signature that serve to safeguard online exchanges.

This study generated three results of interest. The first is the segmentation that was defined. It assigns each representative of the targeted population a level of interest in the service expressed on a six-point scale ranging from 'not interested' to 'very highly interested' as a function of his characteristics, habits and behaviors concerning computer and Internet use. Such a result may be used to improve the rate of return on promotional campaigns, for example, by avoiding bothering certain segments with poorly targeted campaigns, or reaching the same number of receptive individuals but reducing the number of individuals contacted, for example, by only soliciting respondents considered to be 'interested in the service in question' (see Appendix A7.2) who belong mostly to interest categories 'highly interested' and 'very highly interested'. Further, the first result may be used to implement an incentive program for those who might be characterized as 'late adopters' – for example, by creating training on how to use a computer and the Internet that specifically targets members of the public 'over 49 years old and retirees'. The second result of interest is the fee proposal, on average between €10 and €11/year per person, which can be tailored as it is potentially adjustable according to the category of interest the resident belongs to. For example, a resident identified as an 'early adopter', that is to say 'very highly interested', could be offered access to the service for a financial consideration of an amount equal to about €23.6/year. Conversely, as concerns 'late adopters', an incentive program could be established with a reduced fee for the unemployed on the order of €3.2/year. With regard to the marketing policy implemented by the Luxtrust[4] company to distribute the service for a flat rate of €57.50 all taxes included (€50 without VAT), including a Smartcard for personal use, valid for three years,[5] members of the public targeted should consist of a majority of individuals assessed as 'highly interested' and 'very highly interested', which represents a maximum rate of penetration of the resident population aged 16 to 74 years in the order of 32.9 percent. Finally, the third result of interest in this study is the creation of an economic measurement of overall value of the service for the 352,000 residents aged 16 to 74 years. That value comes to approximately €3.8 million/year. The public decision criteria considered for WTP include the following: if the total value of individual WTP is greater than the cost of the project under consideration, the project will be undertaken; that total, or €3.8 million/year, may serve as an upper limit on the investment decision as concerns the choice of the amount to devote to distribution, improvement and promotion of a digital identification card and electronic signature service in Luxembourg.

The result set generated by this study is information that is imperfect and incomplete by default, warrants discussion and should be discussed, but is a solid resource for decision-making. In fact, it offers an opportunity to evaluate the demand side, to give an outline before implementation and, thus, the possibility for the decision-maker to create or align his market strategy wherever there is a question of distributing a new service in the territory of Luxembourg. Also, contingent evaluation is an instrument of interest for *ex ante* evaluation which should certainly be used cautiously, but more systematically in the field of innovation.

Appendix

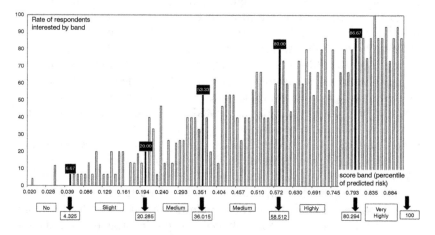

Figure A7.1 Segmentation

Table A 7.1 Illustration of components

Illustration of components t_h as function of X: $t_h = Xw_h{}^*\forall h=1,2,3$

Questions	Parameters	$w_1{}^*$	$w_2{}^*$	$w_3{}^*$
	Student/self-employed	0.0016	-0.0462	-0.0208
	Employed	0.0588	0.0603	-0.0106
Profession of the respondent	Unemployed, retired, or other	-0.0694	-0.0173	0.0402
	Under 18 years	-0.0177	-0.0605	-0.0133
	Between 18 and 49 years	0.0670	0.0801	0.0599
Age of the respondent	Over 49 years	-0.0616	-0.0490	-0.0541
	Primary	-0.0875	-0.1276	-0.1108
	Secondary 1st cycle	-0.0336	0.0031	0.0859
	Secondary 2nd cycle	0.0307	0.0362	0.0319
Q121 Can you tell me which school levels you have successfully completed?	Higher education (secondary+1 through secondary+3, IST, ISERP, IEES,...)/university (secondary+4 or more)	0.0522	0.0153	-0.0799
Q24-2 Has/does not have children aged 12 through 16	Does not have/has	-0.0146	-0.0129	-0.0299
		0.0146	0.0129	0.0299
Q24-3 Has/does not have children under the age of 12 – mind the code	Does not have/has	-0.0321	-0.0578	-0.0586
		0.0321	0.0578	0.0586
Q24-1 – Size of household – total number of individuals in the household	2 members in the household	-0.0204	-0.0144	-0.0256
	3 members in the household	-0.0004	-0.0198	-0.0227
	Between 4 and 8 members in the household	0.0221	0.0344	0.0481
A2. Does a member of your household have Internet access at home (even if the access is not used)?	Yes	0.1113	-0.0078	-0.0279
	No	-0.1113	0.0078	0.0279
	The day before	0.1467	-0.1646	0.0469
B1. When was the first time you used a computer?	In the last seven days up to 15 days	-0.0273	0.1232	0.1529
	During the last 3 months	-0.1736	-0.0529	-0.2817

Continued

Table A7.1 Continued

Illustration of components t_h as function of X: $t_h = Xw_h^* \forall h=1,2,3$

Questions	Parameters	w_1^*	w_2^*	w_3^*
	Every day or almost every day	0.1200	0.0286	-0.0602
	At least once a week (but not every day) to at			
B2. On average, how often have you used a	least once a month	-0.0346	-0.0351	0.0446
computer during the last three months?	Not specified or other	-0.1467	0.1646	-0.0469
B3. Where have you used a computer during	At home	0.1226	-0.0702	-0.0111
the last three months?	Away from home	0.1226	-0.0702	-0.0111
	Yesterday	0.1471	-0.2285	0.1418
	The last 7 days	-0.0069	0.0386	0.0498
C1. When was the last time you used the	During the last 15 days	-0.0146	0.0394	0.0476
Internet?	During the last 3 months	-0.1543	0.1563	-0.1648
	Every day or almost every day	0.1089	-0.0166	-0.1470
	At least once a week (but not every day) to at			
	least once a month	-0.0054	-0.0053	0.0559
	At least once a month (but not every week)/less			
C2. On average, how often have you used	than once a month	-0.0262	-0.0036	0.0797
the Internet during the last three months?	Not specified or other	-0.1471	0.2285	-0.1418
C3. Where have you used the Internet		0.1153	-0.0926	-0.0499
during the last three months? (by computer				
or other)	At home/away from home	-0.1153	0.0926	0.0499

Banking transactions (e-banking): yes/no	0.1326	0.1937	0.1446
	-0.1326	-0.1937	-0.1446
Download official forms: yes/no	0.1212	0.1699	0.1105
	-0.1212	-0.1699	-0.1105
Send and receive e-mails: yes/no	0.1417	-0.1325	-0.1554
	-0.1417	0.1325	0.1554
Search information on products and services: yes/no	0.1249	-0.0012	-0.0503
	-0.1249	0.0012	0.0503
Obtain information from public authorities: yes/no	0.1071	0.0746	-0.0617
	-0.1071	-0.0746	0.0617
Use services for travel and lodging; yes/no	0.1073	0.0743	0.0030
	-0.1073	-0.0743	-0.0030
Search for other information or online services: yes/no	0.1089	0.0221	-0.0401
	-0.1089	-0.0221	0.0401
Read – download newspapers – online information magazines: yes/no	0.0901	0.0428	-0.0449
	-0.0901	-0.0428	0.0449
C5. What online services and activities have you used for personal purposes in the last three months? Download programs: yes/no	0.0916	0.0211	-0.0936
	-0.0916	-0.0211	0.0936
Consult the Internet to learn: yes/no	0.0938	0.0491	-0.0319
	-0.0938	-0.0491	0.0319
C11. How often do you make backup copies or files (documents, images, and so on) from your computer on a diskette, cd, or on an Internet server? Always or almost always	0.0574	0.0523	0.0376
From time to time	0.0330	-0.0381	-0.0984
Never or almost never/does not apply (because I don't keep files on a computer)	0.0091	-0.0007	0.0623
Not specified or other	-0.1471	0.2285	-0.1418
D1. When was the last time you ordered or purchased products Less than a year	0.1424	0.2051	0.1132
More than a year	-0.0567	-0.1551	-0.0556

Table A 7.2 Profile of extreme segments

			Extreme segments							
			1. Not interested				6. Very highly interested			
					Extreme values				Extreme values	
Average percentage of respondents interested			1.52				0.87			
Estimate of interest			0***				1***			
Average probability of being considered			2.79				0.85			
Questions	Parameters	Average in population	Average	VC	´=0	1	Average	VC	´=0	1
			12.26				12.58			
Profession of the respondent	Student/self-employed	0.14	0.03				0.11			
	Employed	0.555	0.24				0.81			
	Unemployed, retired, or other	0.291	0.73	*			0.08			
Age of the respondent	Under 18 years	0.048	0.00				0.00			
	Between 18 and 49 years	0.619	0.14	*			0.86			
	Over 49 years	0.333	0.85	*			0.14			
Q121 Can you tell me which school levels you have successfully completed?	Primary	0.116	0.46	*			0.01			
	Secondary 1st cycle	0.389	0.48				0.18			
	Secondary 2nd cycle	0.212	0.04				0.31			
	Higher education (secondary+1 through secondary+3 IST, ISERP, IEES…)/university (secondary+4 or more)	0.283	0.03				0.51			

Q24-2 Has/does not have children aged 12 through 16	Does not have/has	0.780		0.93	0.69
		0.220		0.07	0.31
Q24-3 Has/does not have children under the age of 12 – mind the code	Does not have/has	0.719		0.95	0.57
		0.281		0.05	0.43
Q24-1 - Size of household – total number of individuals in the household	2 members in the household	0.425		0.66	0.36
	3 members in the household	0.277		0.22	0.25
	Between 4 and 8 members in the household	0.299		0.11	0.38
A2. Does a member of your household have Internet access at home (even if the access is not used)?	Yes	0.771	**	0.17	0.98
	No	0.229	**	0.83	0.02
B1 – When was the last time you used a computer?	Yesterday	0.804	**	0.00	1.00
	In the last 7 to 15 days	0.039		0.00	0.00
	During the last 3 months	0.157	**	1.00	0.00
B2. On average, how often have you used a computer during the last three months?	Every day or almost every day	0.615	*	0.00	0.96
	At least once a week (but not every day) to at least once a month	0.189		0.00	0.04
	Not specified or other	0.196	**	1.00	0.00

Continued

Table A7.2 Continued

Questions	Parameters	Average in population	Average 12.26	VC	Extreme values =0	1	Average 12.58	VC	Extreme values =0	1
B3. Where have you used a computer during the last three months?		0.754	0.00	**			0.96			
	At home/away from home	0.246	1.00				0.04			
C1. When was the last time you used the Internet?	Yesterday	0.781	0.01	**			1.00			
	The last 7 days	0.008	0.00	**			0.00			
	During the last 15 days	0.010	0.00				0.00			
	During the last 3 months	0.201	0.99	**			0.00			
C2. On average, how often have you used the Internet during the last three months? day)	Every day or almost every day	0.563	0.00	*			0.92			
	At least once a week (but not every	0.157	0.00				0.08			
	At least once a month (but not every week)/less than once a month	0.062	0.1				0.00			
	Not specified or other	0.219	0.99	**			0.00			
C3. Where have you used the Internet during the last three months? (by computer or other)		0.719	0.01	**			0.95			
	At home/away from home	0.281	0.99	**			0.05			

C5. What online services and activities have you used for personal purposes in the last three months?					
Banking transactions (e-banking): yes	0.456	0.00	*	0.96	*
no	0.544	1.00	*	0.04	*
Download official forms: yes	0.376	0.00		0.92	*
no	0.624	1.00		0.08	*
Send and receive e-mails: yes	0.712	0.01	**	1.00	
no	0.288	0.99	**	0.00	
Search information on products and services: yes	0.677	0.01	**	0.97	
no	0.323	0.99	**	0.03	*
Obtain information from public authorities: yes	0.442	0.00	*	0.90	*
no	0.558	1.00	*	0.10	*
Use services for travel and lodging: yes	0.553	0.00	*	0.96	*
no	0.447	1.00	*	0.04	*
Search for other information or online services: yes	0.597	0.00	*	0.93	*
no	0.403	1.00	*	0.07	
Read – download newspapers – online information, magazines: yes	0.420	0.00	*	0.80	
no	0.580	1.00	*	0.20	
Download programs: yes	0.371	0.00		0.74	
no	0.629	1.00		0.26	
Consult the Internet for learning: yes	0.465	0.00	*	0.85	
no	0.535	1.00	*	0.15	

Continued

Table A7.2 Continued

Questions	Parameters	Average in population	Average 12.26	VC	Extreme values =0	1	Average 12.58	VC	Extreme values ´=0	1
C11. How often do you make backup copies of files (documents, images, and so on) from your computer on a diskette, cd, or on an Internet server?	Always or almost always	0.201	0.00				0.42			
	From time to time	0.266	0.00				0.31			
	Never or almost never/does not apply (because I don't keep files on a computer?	0.315	0.01				0.27			
	Not specified or other	**0.219**	**0.99**	**			**0.00**			
D1. When was the last time you ordered or purchased products or services online and not by means of e-mail?	Less than a year	0.508	0.00	*			1.00			
	More than a year	0.508	0.00	*			1.00			
	Not specified or other	0.201	0.99	**			0.00	*		
D2. What types of products and services have you ordered or purchased for personal purposes on the Internet during the last 12 months?	Books, magazines, newspapers, e-learning materials: yes/no	0.282	0.00				0.91	**		
		0.718	1.00				0.09	**		
		0.240	0.00				0.86	**		
		0.760	1.00				0.14	**		
	Travel and lodging: yes/no	0.184	0.00				0.81	**		
	Tickets for entertainment: yes/no	0.816	1.00				0.19	**		

Question	Response				
E1. When was the last time you took a course of any kind (of at least three hours) on using the computer?	During the last 3 months	0.76	0.00		0.09
	Between 3 months and 3 years	0.168	0.00		0.37
	More than 3 years	0.237	0.00		0.30
	Never took one	0.362	0.00		0.25
E3. For which of the following have you used a computer?	Not specified or other	0.157	1.00	**	0.00
	Copy or move a file or folder: yes/no	0.727	0.00	**	0.98
		0.273	1.00	**	0.02
	Use the copy or cut and paste tools to make a duplicate or transfer information in a document: yes/no	0.703	0.00	**	0.99
		0.297	1.00	**	0.01
	Use basic arithmetic formulas to add, subtract, or divide numbers in document: yes/no	0.540	0.00	*	0.90
		0.460	1.00	*	0.10
	Connect and install new equipment or devices, for example a printer or modem: yes/no	0.594	0.00	*	0.87
		0.406	1.00	*	0.13
	Identity and resolve computer problems (for example a computer that is slow): yes/no	0.431	0.00	*	0.73
		0.569	1.00	*	0.27
E4. For which of the following activities have you used the Internet?	Send e-mail with attached file, photos, etc.: yes/no	0.702	0.01	**	0.99
		0.298	0.99	**	0.01
	Use a search engine to find information: yes/no	0.753	0.01	**	1.00
		0.247	0.99	**	0.00
	Find, download, and install software: yes/no	0.483	0.00	*	0.85
		0.517	1.00	*	0.15
	Protect the computer against viruses, spyware, and advertising (adware): yes/no	0.595	0.00	*	0.88
		0.405	1.00	*	0.12

Continued

Table A7.2 Continued

Questions	Parameters	Average in population	Average	VC	Extreme values		Average	VC	Extreme values	
			12.26		′=0	1	12.58		′=0	1
E5. Where, or how did you learn to carry out these activities?		0.662	0.01	**			0.99			1
	Self-taught by "trial and error": yes/no	0.338	0.99	**			0.01		′=0	
E6. Do you think your computer skills are adequate if you were looking for a new job or if you'd like to change jobs in less than a year?	Not specified or other	0.137	0.50	*			0.04			
	Yes	0.497	0.00	*			0.81			
	No	0.319	0.37				0.14			
	Does not apply	0.047	0.12				0.01			

* Value of cramer's v coefficient (cv) ≥ 0.3.
** Cramer's v ≥ 0.6.
*** A priori the closest threshold to the ideal threshold (that which completely separates the positives from the negatives, without false positives or false negatives) associated with a statistic c with a unitary value (c = 1), is not easy to determine. it is situated between 0.340 and 0.594 for an individual rate correctly calculated, distributed around 75 percent. to be rid of false negatives, as for this kind of study it is preferable to incorrectly estimate a respondent as interested rather than to incorrectly estimate him as not interested, a low-level threshold has been chosen, that being 0.400. thus a respondent whose score is greater than 0.40 is estimated to be "interested" in contrast to an individual whose score is less than that limit. in regard to the threshold, 75.22 percent of respondents are correctly estimated for an error rate of 27.78 percent, which implies 27.21 percent false positives and 21.27 percent false negatives.

Notes

1. Terra (2005) specifies the use of a regression interval in this context.
2. Weighted percentage as a function of the weighting of respondents in the population.
3. In order to reduce the size of the working paper, Appendix A7.2 only presents the extreme segments. The profile of intermediate segments has thus not been integrated. It can be provided by email upon request.
4. Certification authority established in 2005 for the Luxembourg government and major participants in the private sector, particularly in the financial sector.
5. www.luxtrust.lu/solutions/tarifs/tarifs

References

Chanel, O., S. Luchini, A. Paraponaris, C. Protiere and J.-C. Vergnaud (2004) 'Les consentements à payer pour des programmes de prévention sanitaire incluent-ils de l'altruisme? Enseignements d'une enquête concernant la fièvre Q', *Revue Economique*, Vol. 55, No. 5, pp. 923–46.

Droesbeke, J.J., M. Lejeune and G. Saporta (2005) 'Méthodes statistiques pour données qualitatives', –in M. Tenenhaus (ed.), *Régression logistique*, Paris: Technip, p. 276.

Durand, A. (2008) 'Evaluation ex-ante du service offert par le RFId à la bibliothèque', La revue de l'innovation: La Revue de l'innovation dans le secteur public, Vol. 14(2), 2009, article 10, p. 25.

Durand, A. and A.-L. Mention (2007) 'Quel marché pour la téléphonie mobile NFC à Luxembourg', MIWIS: Montpellier International Workshop on Information Systems, 'SI et création de valeur: déterminants, apports et mesures', p. 24.

Godfroid, P., L. Eeckhoudt and M. Marchand (1996) 'Le consentement à payer', excerpt from the thesis, 'Risque de santé, médecine préventive et médecine curative'.

Hanemann, M.W. (1984) 'Welfare Evaluations in Contingent Valuation Experiments with Discrete Responses', *American Journal of Agricultural Econometrics*, Vol. 67, No. 3, pp. 332–41.

Le Gall-Ely, M. (2003) 'Un test de validité de l'analyse conjointe et de l'évaluation contingente dans le cadre de l'évaluation d'un service sans référent de marché', Laboratoire d'Economie et Sciences Sociales de Rennes (LESSOR), Université de Rennes II – Haute-Bretagne, Séminaire Méthodes quasi-expérimentales de l'IREIMAR, 18 November, p. 27.

Loomis, J., P. Kent, L. Strange, K. Fausch and A. Covich (2000) 'Measuring the Total Economic Value of Restoring Ecosystem Services in an Impaired River Basin: Result from a Contingent Valuation Survey', Department of Agricultural and Resource Economics, Colorado State University, Fort Collins, in Ecological Economics, No. 33, Boston: Boston University, pp. 103–17.

Mitchell, R.C. and R.T. Carson (1989) *Using Surveys to Value Public Goods: The Contingent Valuation Method, Resources for the Future*, Washington DC: RFF Press.

Tenenhaus M. (1998) *La régression PLS : théorie et pratique,* Paris: Technip.

Tenenhaus, M. (ed.) (2005) *Régression logistique,* Paris: Technip.

Terra, S. (2005) 'Guide de bonnes pratiques pour la mise en oeuvre de la méthode d'évaluation contingente', Direction des études économiques et de l'évaluation environnementale, Série Méthode (http://www.ecologie.gouv.fr), 05-M04, p. 77.

8

Blogs and the Economics of Reciprocal Attention

Alexia Gaudeul, Chiara Peroni, and Laurence Mathieu

Introduction

This chapter offers a model of blogging activity in which members of blogging communities derive utility from their blog being read as well as from reading others' blogs. We argue that, in this context, an inverse relation between content produced and attention devoted to others occurs naturally as a result of a competitive equilibrium in an economy where the currency is mutual attention. Such an inverse relation is expressed as follows: in a network, an agent that offers little content compared to others will need to compensate for this by devoting more attention to others in order to maintain her place in the network; conversely, an agent that offers a lot of content compared to others will devote less attention to others. We are able to check the model's predictions by using a number of measures of activity and involvement in social relations from data gathered on the activity of 2,767 bloggers drawn randomly from http://www.livejournal.comLiveJournal. We argue that the empirical patterns of mutual attention in that sample are broadly consistent with our model.

Context

In recent years, blogs have established themselves as an important way to produce, promote and read content on the Internet, and also as a tool for social networking. Although statistics on blogs and bloggers are notoriously fickle (Bialik, 2005), a number of statistics suggest the importance of the blogging phenomenon. Henning (2005) estimated the number of blogs at 53 million by the end of 2005 (see Figure A 8.1 in Appendix). A previous report by Perseus Development Corporation

(2004) estimated that about one third of them were active. Technorati, which ranks blogs by popularity, claimed to track about 113 million blogs in May 2008. A seller of search-targeted advertising, Chitika, estimated from its own data that the top 50,000 blogs in terms of Technorati ranking generated a total of $500 million in ad revenues in 2006, with the top 5,000 getting 80 percent of those revenues.[1] A survey by eMarketer estimated advertising on social networking sites at $1.2 billion in 2008.[2] A number of companies are involved in the development of blogging software and the management of blogging platforms. Among those are Google's Blogger, Six Apart's Typepad, SUP's LiveJournal, Wordpress, Facebook and News Corp's MySpace. Beyond those companies directly involved in blogging, the influence of blogs is wide ranging – for example, in news reporting,[3] but also in a range of other economic activities, such as tourism (see Wenger, 2008).

The empirical part of this chapter relies on a novel dataset from LiveJournal (henceforward LJ), a web-based community where Internet users can maintain their blog. This study focuses on LiveJournal because it provides more detailed and easily accessible information on users' activity than other blog hosts. Information on LJ users is accessible on their public profile, the content of which is described in Appendix. Some data is provided by default and cannot be hidden by the user: user name, account number, date of creation, status of the account (i.e., early adopter, permanent, paid, free, sponsored), name and number of friends and readers, number of posts made, number of comments made and received, etc. Other data, such as the blogger's date of birth, location, list of interests, and any additional information, is provided on a voluntary basis.[4] LJ is essentially an aggregation tool with lock-in effect: it provides an environment in which bloggers can read each other's public and private entries, exchange comments, participate in communities, and thus develop relations with other LJ users that are not replicable on any other blogging tool. Blogs on LiveJournal tend to belong to a specific genre in blogging –online diaries (Krishnamurty, 2002). Online diaries are blogs that focus on the personal issues of the individual maintaining them. This category accounts for the vast majority of existing blogs (Herring et al., 2004). Our data and our analysis does not, therefore, necessarily apply to other types of blogs, such as topic-oriented or group blogs, as those tend to be independently hosted or hosted on other blogging platforms. Our analysis is meant to model the networking, communal and sharing aspects of blogging. It is not meant as a 'general theory' of blogging in all its diverse aspects.

Created in 1999 by Brad Fitzpatrick, LJ is based on open-source code and was initially maintained by a community of volunteers. LJ was purchased in January 2005 by Six Apart, the owners of Typepad – another popular blog host. The profit-making aspect of LJ then became more important: sponsored (advertising-bearing) accounts were introduced and the discrepancy between services offered to free versus paying users widened. In December 2007, Six Apart sold LJ to SUP, a Russian company that was already managing LJ in Russia, and which removed, in March 2008, the option to create free accounts. Widespread protests by users led to the option being reinstated in August 2008.[5]

In February 2009, the number of blogs on LJ totaled more than 18 million, of which 1.2 million (7 percent) had been updated in the previous 30 days. Of the top 15 countries, 63 percent of users were located in the USA, 13 percent in the Russian Federation, 6 percent in Canada and 5 percent in the UK.[6] The average age of bloggers on LJ was 25, the median was 22 and the mode was 20. Bloggers do not have to display their age publicly, but their birth date must be provided to LJ for legal reasons. Of the 72 percent of users who chose to reveal their gender to LJ on registration, two-thirds were female. (Data on individual bloggers' gender is not available publicly but is collected by LJ for internal statistical purposes, with an option for the user not to disclose gender on registration.) This is more than on many other blogging platforms and may be a reflection of the popularity of LJ among online diarists and teen bloggers, who tend to be female (Herring et al., 2004).

Much of the analysis in this chapter focuses on the lists of friends and on the act of friending. Those words have a range of different meanings on LJ (Raynes-Goldie and Fono, 2006). At a technical level, a friend is a blog the user subscribes to, so its updates appear on the user's 'friends' page', a page where the entries made by the blogger's friends appear in reverse chronological order. Listing someone as a friend is what is referred to as friending. While some LJ friendships reflect 'real-world' friendships, many are exclusive to LJ. Those are formed and maintained by reading and posting comments on each other's blogs.

Friending is a meaningful act. Friending someone means they are able to read one' 'friends-only' entries – that is, those entries that are not accessible unless one is logged in LJ and one is listed as a friend. Not all users choose to make such 'filtered' entries, but a large proportion restrict access to at least some of their posts. Friending is a public act, since other users can observe who is friends with whom via the friend list on the blogger's public profile. Finally, friending is a costly act, as it commits the blogger to at least browse through and comment on their friends' entries – otherwise, friendships may be withdrawn ('unfriending').[7] Friendships are generally established with the expectation of reciprocity. This means that a user usually expects a friend to read her back in return; it also means that an user may be reluctant to friend someone who is unlikely to reciprocate the friendship, and may drop from her friend list those who do not reciprocate her friendship after a while. (For more on the social dynamics of LJ, see Raynes-Goldie, 2004, and Marwick, 2009.) While some users have an instrumental view of their list of friends and attempt to gain status by engaging in 'popularity contests' within LJ,[8] most LJ users attach real significance to the act of friending and of dropping someone off their friend list. Many users do not welcome unsolicited friendships – that is, users who list another as friend when that user does not wish to reciprocate.[9] All this explains why the list of friends and 'friend of' (that is, the list of bloggers who list one as friend, from now on, 'readers') is a variable of great interest in our study.

Related literature

Drezner and Farrell (2008, p. 13) note that blogs are 'a major topic for research', and offer an 'extraordinarily fertile terrain for the social sciences'. A number of views have been expressed about the role, value and future of blogs and bloggers, in the media, in politics, or as a tool for collaboration and information sharing. Ribstein (2005, 2006) and Lassica (2001) consider blogs as a newly emergent media form, while Lemann (2006) questions their value to journalism. Drezner and Farrell (2008) evaluate blogs as a tool of political influence, while Sunstein (2008) worries that blogs may contribute to a fracture in the political discourse. Schmidt (2007) considers blogging networks as communities of shared practices, with their own rules in selecting blogs to read, interacting with other bloggers and choosing what to publish. Huck (2008) is interested in how blogs help consumer choice and affect firms' reputations. Quiggin (2006) argues that blogs are part of the 'creative commons', along with Wikis and open-source software.

More closely related to this chapter are qualitative studies of bloggers' motivations and quantitative studies of the relation between their activity and the structure of their network of relations. Raynes-Goldie (2004) and Raynes-Goldie and Fono (2006) find that bloggers are interested in producing their own content and broadcasting their opinions on current events, interacting with other bloggers and engaging in debate with them, as well as in joining communities of shared interests. Nardi (2004, p. 10) underlines the social aspects and dynamics of online diaries, and speculates, as we do, that 'blogging is as much about reading as writing, as much about listening as talking'. Bar-Ilan (2005) shows that bloggers act as information hubs with links to a number of topical web sources. Furukawa et al. (2006) find that blog entries are primarily read-through links from other blogs. Backstrom et al. (2006) observe that links between bloggers can be partly explained through common membership in communities on LJ. Lento et al. (2006) explain that continued activity within blogging networks is positively related to the number of relations established with other bloggers. Mishne and Glance (2006) evidence a relationship between the popularity of a weblog and the number of comments it attracts. Bachnik et al. (2005) establish that blog networks are only weakly connected, that they have small worlds properties and that large blogging networks have clique properties (i.e., have few relations with other networks). Paolillo et al. (2005) determine that LJ users' interests and their network of friends are largely uncorrelated. On the other hand, Kumar et al. (2004) note that a combination of age, location and interests explains a large part of cross-linking patterns between users of LJ.

This chapter contributes to the above literature with a network structural perspective. This approach, inspired by insights from sociology (Granovetter, 1973), is motivated by the growing importance of networks to economics (Gui and Sugden, 2005).

We present a model of formation of links among individuals along the lines of Watts (2001), Jackson (2003) and Newman (2003). We differ from those papers in that we are interested in gaining insights on the structure of directed networks (see, for example, Caffarelli, 2004). We focus on what drives links' reciprocation, and in the related issue of the strength of relationships in a network. (This area of study has been explored only recently; one can see Brueckner, 2006.)

The main contribution of this chapter is to exploit measures of the structural characteristics of bloggers' networks, along with measures of the type and extent of their activities. We consider not only the structure of links that an agent maintains, but also their direction, their intensity and the intensity of the activity of the agent. We study the activity – content production and attention devoted to others – of each node (agent) in a context where money plays no role and there is no exchange currency – an agent cannot 'pay' attention she receives from someone with the attention she devotes to another agent. Our study allows us to develop insights into the motivations of bloggers and how those determine their interactions and relations with others: we show that bloggers' posting activity depends on their audience – which would not happen if they only cared about expressing themselves. We also develop insights into blogging norms: a widespread expectation of reciprocity in individual relations between bloggers means that the attention a blogger receives will be proportional to how much attention she devotes to other bloggers. However, we show that an agent may exchange attention received with content produced: bloggers are ready to get less attention from a blogger if that blogger provides sufficient content, up to some limit. Indeed, we show that large deviations from a pattern of reciprocal friendship are sanctioned. This chapter thus contributes along the lines of Dohmen (2009) or Gu et al. (2009) to the literature on how reciprocal behavior influences the structure of human activity by showing how reciprocity matters empirically in an online setting.

The third section presents the model on which we ground our working hypotheses. Those are then tested empirically in the fifth section using data described in the fourth section.

A model of reciprocal (in)attention

In the following, we consider a model in which agents derive utility from being paid attention to, and from reading the content of others. In a competitive equilibrium, each individual relation that an agent maintains must give her the same utility. This means that an agent that provides more content than others has to be 'paid' more attention. More content is thus reciprocated with more attention, and vice-versa. The model thus introduces a more general form of reciprocity than if agents were to link only with agents that have the same number of friends as they have, or only link with agents that display their same level of overall blogging activity, or exchange one comment for one comment. The model fits the case of blogging, where, indeed, a typical blogger's reading list will include a variety of more and of less popular blogs, and of blogs that vary in their level of activity,[10] so that the terms of trade will vary from blog to blog. We define a blogger's utility as a function of the number of other bloggers she is linked to, of the strength of those links and of the bloggers' activity. Consider thus representative agent i who is part of a network of N agents who produce their own content and read content generated by others. $e=(e_1,e_2,...,e_N)$ denotes the vector of content produced by agents in the set $N = \{1,2,...,N\}$ consisting of all agents in the network. $n = (n_{ij})_{i,j \in N, j \neq i}$ denotes the vector of attentions – for example, agent i devotes attention n_{ij} to the content produced by $j \neq i$. Denote

$n_i = (n_{ji})_{j \in N, j \neq i}$ and define $N_i = card(j \in N | n_{ji} > 0)$ the cardinality of the subset of N consisting of agents in N who read content produced by i. We assume free entry and perfect information, which implies that new agents may enter at no cost and all agents know N,e and n.

A simple additive form[11] for the total utility of a representative agent i is

$$U_i(n, e) = \underbrace{\lambda_i \sum_{j \neq i} n_{ji} e_i}_{\text{Utility from being read}} + \underbrace{\sum_{j \neq i} n_{ij} e_j}_{\text{Utility from reading others}} - \underbrace{C(e_i)}_{\text{Cost of production}} \tag{1}$$

subject to $\sum_{j \neq i} n_{ij} \leq T_i$. $\lambda_i \geq 0$ measures the propensity to enjoy being read, while the propensity to enjoy reading others is normalized to 1. $C(.)$ is the cost of content production, increasing and convex in the content produced. T_i is the attention budget of agent i – that is, the total attention that she can devote to her friends. We could also define T_i as the total time budget available for blogging, including both content production and attention.[12]

Choice of effort

To begin with, consider the choice of effort by representative agent i, taking the vector of attention n as given. Maximizing $U_i(n,e)$ with respect to e_i, we find that at the optimum, given the concavity of the maximization problem, one obtains $C'(e_i) = \lambda_i \sum_{j \neq i} n_{ji}$. As the cost function is convex, this means that the higher the sum of attention devoted to agent i, the more the agent will devote effort to his blog. In order to draw further implications, from this, we will make the following assumption:

1 *The sum of attention devoted to i,* $\sum_{j \neq i} n_{ji}$, increases in the number of her readers, $N_{\cdot i}$.

If the above assumption is verified, then i's effort will be increasing in the number of his readers, which may be tested rather easily using the data available. Is this assumption reasonable, however? That is, will an agent with more readers necessarily be receiving more attention in the aggregate? This depends on how elements in the vector of attention $n_{\cdot i}$ vary with $N_{\cdot i}$. Suppose, for example, that the distribution of the elements of $n_{\cdot i}$ is independent of i's number of readers. Then, the higher one's number of readers, the higher the attention one receives and the higher one's effort level. However, this independence assumption will not be verified if, for example, agents link exclusively with agents that have the same number of readers, or the same quality or quantity of content as they have. Suppose, for example, blog networks were perfect cliques – that is, all agents within the network were linked with each other, and none have links outside the clique. Assume also all agents in the network devote the same time budget T to blogging and devote equal attention to each of their friends. Then $n_{ji} = T/N$ for any j in the clique. We then have $C'(e_i) = \lambda_i T$ and, therefore, effort in a clique is unrelated to the number of members of that clique.

Note, however, that, in reality, blogging networks have 'small-world' properties, whereby a core of heavily interlinked individuals have a few links with a periphery of individuals who themselves belong to the core of other networks (Bachnik et al., 2005). There may be other reasons why the sum of attention devoted to i would not increase with her number of readers. Some readers may, for example, devote less attention to more popular blogs and more attention to obscure blogs – out of a form of snobbery because those are perceived as more 'exclusive', or because those offer better chances of getting attention reciprocated. Subject to the above caveats, we will, therefore, express hypothesis H1, according to which one should observe a positive relation between content produced and number of readers:

> *Hypothesis H1 (network size): Bloggers with more readers display higher levels of content production and general blogging activity.*

Note that H1 could also be derived from a model of audience whereby readers are attracted to bloggers who produce more and better content. However, such a model would not, in our opinion, adequately reflect the dynamics of blogging. For example, such a model would neglect relevant issues that make the expression of H1 non-trivial, such as the issue of how elements in $n_{.i}$ vary with $N_{.i}$. Furthermore, such a model would not allow us to derive further implications as below.

Mutual attention

Consider now the intensity of relations between agents. Consider entrant i who has the choice between establishing a link with agent j or agent k. Suppose i takes his own effort and the effort of j and k as given – that is, i neglects how his choice whom to read affects their effort, as well as how their choice to reciprocate attention or not will affect his own effort. Alternatively, one may assume less realistically that agent i is able to predict the result of a whole chain of reaction and counter-reaction to the establishment of this new friendship, and thus knows how e and n come out after she establishes the link.[13] Agent i prefers establishing the link with j if the gain in utility from doing so, $\lambda_i n_{ji} e_i + n_{ij} e_j$ (the first part is what is gained from being read by j, the second is what is gained by reading j), is more than the gain in utility from establishing a link with k, $\lambda_i n_{ki} e_i + n_{ik} e_k$ With free entry and perfect information about the attention and effort exerted by all agents in the network, the surplus gained from creating a link should be the same across all agents. If that was not the case, then any agent who offered greater surplus would keep on gaining friends at the expense of others. Therefore, it must be that the surplus obtained from j and from k is equal, so that $\lambda_i n_{ji} e_i + n_{ij} e_j = \lambda_i n_{ki} e_i + n_{ik} e_k$ which can be rewritten as

$$\lambda_i(n_{ki} - n_{ji})e_i = n_{ij}e_j - n_{ik}e_k \tag{2}$$

Note that while this relation holds at the margin ('marginal' friend), it also determines the relation between number of friends, readers and activity in the aggregate. In order to draw some implications from this expression, we will make the following assumption:

2 For any i and j, $n_{ij}e_j$ is non-decreasing in e_j.

This assumption simply states that the utility derived by i from reading the content produced by j does not decrease as j puts more effort into his blog. Note that this does not necessarily mean that n_{ij}, the attention devoted by i to j, will increase in e_j, only that their product will increase in e_j. Note also that a higher e_j does not necessarily mean making more posts or more comments – in which case, beyond a certain point, saturation would set in and i would stop actively following j – but rather exerting more effort into producing better, more interesting (not necessarily longer) posts, or more perceptive and helpful comments. From this point of view, it is hard to argue against this assumption.

Suppose, therefore, that this assumption is verified, and consider the case where $e_j > e_k$ (agent j offers more or better content or interactions). Then, from formula (2), I must have $n_{ki} > n_{ji}$. This means that agent k, who produces less content than agent j, must devote more attention to i than agent j does in order to provide the same utility and thus be kept as a friend by i. Conversely, agent k, who devotes more attention to i than agent j does, need not produce as much content as agent j in order to be kept as a friend by i. Note that this relation also holds in the extreme case in which $n_{ij} = 0$ (j does not reciprocate i's friendship). In that case, the non-reciprocating j should be observed to produce more or better content than an otherwise similar but reciprocating agent. One should thus observe the following inverse relation between content produced and attention devoted to others: agents that offer comparatively little content for others to read will devote more attention to their friends than those agents that offer more content do. Such an inverse relation occurs naturally as the outcome of competition in a market where mutual attention is being exchanged. Agents do not build or sustain links if they are not balanced in terms of attention received and content provided. Note, however, that this inverse relation may also emerge simply out of a sense of fairness, whereby each blogger is required to contribute equally, though in different ways, to the maintenance of the network of relations they belong to.

What we observe is how many bloggers follow a blogger versus how many that blogger follows. The number of blogs one follows is only an imperfect signal of how much attention is devoted to each blogger on one's reading list, but it is reasonable to expect, everything else being equal, that a blogger with many friends will not be able to devote as much time to each of them as a blogger with fewer friends. Furthermore, a blogger who maintains a balance between readers and friends is also more likely to be reciprocating the attention of his friends than an agent with more readers than friends. Consider two agents, i and j, similar in all respects except that, while both have N friends, i has M readers while j has $M+1$. This means that j reciprocates the readership of at least one less reader than i does. Therefore, everything else being equal, fewer reciprocations at the individual level are reflected in an increase in the number of readers versus the number of friends at the aggregate level. We can thus spell out hypothesis H2 as follows:

Hypothesis H2 (aggregate reciprocity): Bloggers with a high ratio of readers to friends will be observed to produce more content than otherwise identical bloggers with a lower ratio.

Note that we do not attempt to explain why some agents would produce more content than others. It might be that some agents are more proficient at it or have more of an inclination to do so. As hypothesized in H1, this gains them a bigger audience. For various reasons, a bigger audience may tend to be less reciprocated than a smaller audience – because of limits on the attention a blogger can devote to other bloggers, for example. What H2 states is quite different from this, however: we say that bloggers who have more readers than friends will produce more than those with a balanced friend list irrespective of how many readers or friends they have. That is, a blogger with ten friends and 15 readers will produce more than a blogger with ten friends and ten readers, in exactly the same way as a blogger with 100 friends and 150 readers will produce more than a blogger with 100 friends and 100 readers. (Indeed, we will see that both the ratio of readers over friends – 1.5 in both cases – and the difference between readers and friends – five in the first case, 50 in the second – are related to content production.) This means that H2 is not merely a consequence of H1, but is rather a separate consequence of our model.

In what follows, we identify relations between network size, structure and content production in a sample of users of LJ, and check whether hypotheses H1 and H2 are verified. We consider whether there is a relation between how many readers a blogger has and how much content she produces, and between the level of aggregate reciprocity within an agent's network and how much content is produced by that agent.

The data

The data used in this study are observations on the list of friends, readers and posting activity of 2,767 bloggers on LJ. This sample was selected using a script that chooses bloggers at random.[14]

This chapter uses regression techniques to study the relationship between network size, bloggers' activity and reciprocity. Network size is measured by one bloggers' friends and subscribers (readers). Measures of bloggers' activity are as follows:

1. Commitment, as measured by the length of time the blog has been active (*duration*).
2. Content production, as measured by the number of posts per day (*entries per day*).
3. Intensity of interactions, as measured by:
   a) How many comments are received (per post).
   b) How many comments are posted (per friend).
   c) How many communities the blogger belongs to.

In the analysis, posting activity is normalized by length of activity (entries per day). This allows us to distinguish the genuine 'intensity' of the posting activity from the mere effect of a blog's duration. (For example, a blog that is active for a long time may accumulate a high number of posts, even though the posting activity is low, whereas a blog that has been updated for a shorter amount of time may post more actively but total a much lower number of entries.)[15] Among measures of the intensity of interactions, one should note that the number of communities one belongs to may have an ambiguous effect on one's capacity to establish relations with other bloggers. Indeed, communities may draw attention away from reading individual blogs, but may also provide a way to gain access to bloggers with interests in common.

To filter out mechanical agents, we restricted attention to those blogs with a duration of at least ten days, which post less than 20 journal entries per day. The descriptive statistics of the variables used in the analysis are given below. Appendix describes the variables in the dataset in greater detail and compares the sample's characteristics with those of all accounts created on LJ since its beginning.

Two noticeable features of the data are skewness and large standard deviations. In what follows, the 'typical' user is therefore described using median values. The median offers a better description of the centre of a distribution than the mean when data are skewed, because it is robust to extreme values. Our blogger lists 41 friends (i.e., she reads the blogs of 41 LJ users) and, in turn, she is subscribed to by 39 bloggers (readers), which highlights a considerable level of aggregate reciprocity. The number of comments posted/received is also remarkably balanced.

The blogger follows, and is a member of, 14 communities. She created 390 entries (posts) since the blog's inception. The duration, a measure of the blog's lifetime, is the length of time between the creation of the blog and its last update. Duration is about 1,165 days (i.e., more than three years).

A new entry is typically added every two days (entries per day). Individual posts receive two comments (comments received per post), whereas the blogger makes about 20 comments on the journals of each of her friends (comments made per friend). This data evidences bloggers'

Table 8.1   Summary statistics

Variables	Mean	Median	St. dev	Min	Max	obs
Friends	95	41	175	0	1944	2340
Readers	124	39	350	1	7855	2092
Number of entries	871	390	1596	0	24094	2340
Comments received	4041	705	10910	1	239564	2340
Comments posted	3855	1022	7624	0	106505	2337
Member	27	14	39	1	506	1463
Entries per day	1.42	0.45	2.74	0	19.90	2340
Comments received per post	3.65	2	5.57	0	75	2336
Comments made per friend	44.21	20.70	98.03	0	3109	2296
Duration	1198	1165	818	10	3185	2336

considerable commitment, although the frequency of updating and the posting activity varies greatly among users. In view of their skewness, data were transformed on the logarithm scale for performing regression analysis. Computations were carried out using the econometrics and statistical software Stata and S-Plus.

Empirical analysis

This section analyses bloggers' network properties, and verifies implications of the theoretical model presented in the third section, namely hypothesis H1 and H2, which we recall below. Bloggers who display higher levels of content production and general blogging activity have more readers. Bloggers with relatively more friends than readers produce less content than other bloggers; conversely, bloggers with relatively fewer friends than readers produce more content than others.

To verify these hypotheses, we estimate a set of activity equations in which the number of readers and the ratio of readers to friends are regressed on measures of bloggers' effort, such as commitments to one's blog, content production and intensity of interaction with other bloggers. We also consider the role of measures of reciprocal attention and network symmetry. Figure 8.1 presents a scatter plot of the number of friends against the number of readers. This graph offers a preliminary idea of the structure of the network, and helps to motivate the analysis. The relation between the two variables is very strong, with the observation points concentrated on a virtually 45-degree line. A fitted simple regression line is also reported.

The simple regression coefficient on ln(readers) equals 0.94, which is highly significant with a t-statistic of 161.63. Most bloggers thus have a similar number of friends and readers, which we can interpret as evidence of reciprocal attention in the aggregate. We also note that, close to zero, observations are more dispersed and that there are more values of readers associated to a specific value of friend than conversely. The graph highlights several data points (denoted by the letters A, B, C, D) which correspond to agents whose relative location motivates the following analysis.

From hypothesis 1, agent B, with more readers than agent A, should be more active than agent A. From hypothesis 2, agent C, with the same number of readers but less aggregate reciprocation (fewer friends) than agent D, should be more active than agent D.

The following investigates the determinants of a blogger's network size – that is, their position on the regression line; it also investigates

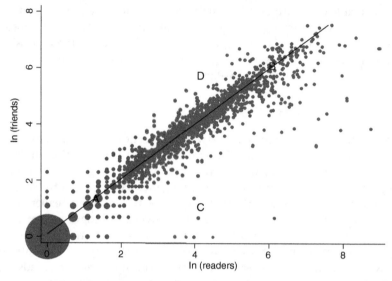

Figure 8.1   Scatter plot of friends vs. readers in a sample of users of LiveJournal

exceptions from the reciprocity of attention, and checks whether such departures can be accounted for by content production.

Testing the first hypothesis

In what follows, we regress the numbers of readers on several indicators of bloggers' activity, to check whether higher levels of content production and activity increase the network size (H1).

The model is as follows:

$$ln(readers) = \lambda + \beta_1 \, ln(member) + \beta_2 \, ln(entries) + \\ + \beta_3 \, ln(comm.\ received) + \beta_4 \, ln(comm.\ posted) + \beta_5 \, ln(duration) + \varepsilon; \tag{3}$$

Here, member denotes the number of communities one is a member of, entries the number of entries per day, comments received the number of received comments (per post), comments posted the number of comments posted (per friend) and duration the duration in days; ε is an iid error term. A preliminary analysis of residuals and leverage revealed several outliers, which we removed. The removal of outliers follows the procedure proposed by Belsley (1980), which identifies highly influential observations as those characterized by either a high leverage or a high residual. The first column of Table 8.2 presents results for the regression of equation (3).

Measures of goodness-of-fit suggest the model is quite successful at describing the data: the R^2 shows that the equation explains a great proportion of the variation in readers, and the F statistic (F stat) for the overall significance of the regression rejects the null that the slope coefficients are jointly zero at any conventional level of significance. The analysis of regression errors reveals certain degrees of non-normality and heteroskedasticity in the data, which is confirmed by the Breusch-Pagan (BP) test statistic. To correct for the potential loss of efficiency, we compute coefficients' t-statistics using White's robust covariance matrix estimator.

One can see that all coefficients are significant. The largest coefficients are associated with number of comments per post and duration: a 1 percent increase in these variables leads, respectively, to about a 0.8 percent and a 0.6 percent increase in the number of readers, ceteris paribus. The smallest effect is that of the number of communities the blogger belongs to. This seems to confirm the ambiguous effect of com-

Table 8.2   Multiple regressions with measure of reciprocity

Dependent variable:	ln(readers)		ln(readers)		reciprocity	
ln(member)	0.153	***	0.170	***	−0.035	***
	(−15.80)		(−18.16)		(−4.20)	
ln(entries)	0.585	***	0.580	***	0.012	
	(−42.21)		(−44.45)		(−1.05)	
ln(comments received)	0.776	***	0.742	***	0.720	***
	(−56.42)		(−57.73)		(−4.98)	
ln(comments posted)	−0.466	***	−0.526	***	0.130	***
	(−30.18)		(−36.91)		(−9.56)	
ln(duration)	0.597	***	0.600	***	−0.007	
	(−30.20)		(−31.25)		(−0.40)	
reciprocity			0.474	***		
			(−14.64)			
constant	0.830	***	0.975	***	−0.305	***
	(−6.72)		(−8.07)		(−2.57)	
obs	1321		1321		1321	
R^2_{adj}	0.88		0.9		0.23	
F stat	1493	0.00	1621	0.00	46.70	0.00
BP	29.56	0.00	70.46	0.00	29.70	0.28
	4.81	0.00	5.40	0.00	6.25	0.43

Robust t-statistics are in parentheses; p-values for F, BP and RESET statistics in parentheses.

munity membership on the intensity of interaction, which was noted in the previous section.

Bloggers with more readers write more entries per day (more active), write fewer comments per friend (reduction in attention given), showing that, indeed, as posited, bloggers who are more popular can devote less attention on average to each of their friends than other bloggers can do[16] but receive more comments per post (increase in attention received). The signs of the coefficients are thus consistent with intuition and the prediction of H1: an important characteristic of one blogger's network size – that is, the number of subscribers, or readers – is positively related to content production and activity.

The norm of reciprocity

Before estimating the second activity equation, we consider whether adherence to the norm of reciprocity affects a blogger's number of readers. Bloggers who do not reciprocate readership may have fewer readers because bloggers expect readership to be reciprocated and do not, therefore, maintain unreciprocated relations, or because bloggers are deterred from subscribing to those blogs which have more readers than friends as this means that chances of reciprocation are low. We therefore estimate a version of the activity equation (3) which includes a measure of reciprocal attention, reciprocity. This is computed by taking the logarithm of the ratio of readers to friends, as follows:

$$reciprocity = \ln(readers/friends) \qquad (4)$$

One can see that reciprocity is zero when the number of friends equals the number of readers. Furthermore, increases in reciprocity indicate that the number of readers increases relative to the number of friends.

The second column of Table 8.2 reports estimates of the activity equation (3) with the added variable. Reciprocity has a positive coefficient, suggesting that lower aggregate reciprocation does not negatively affect network sizes. Sign, size and significance of other variables' coefficients are not substantially altered by the inclusion of the new variable. This suggests that the information contained in reciprocity is incremental to that provided by other regressors. Controlling for its effect slightly improves the goodness-of-fit of the model. The value of the BP test statistic, however, increases considerably, and the analysis of partial residuals casts doubt on the explanatory power of the added variable. It is possible, from this estimate, to deduce the effect of activity measures and reciprocity on the number of friends. This is done as follows. Consider again the estimated activity equation (3) with reciprocity:

$$ln(readers) = \hat{\alpha} + \hat{\beta}X + \hat{\gamma}(reciprocity),$$

where X is the set of regressors other than reciprocity. Interestingly, the equation above implies

$$ln(friends) = \hat{\alpha} + \hat{\beta}X + (\hat{\gamma} - 1)(reciprocity) \tag{5}$$

This means that, while reciprocity has a positive and statistically significant effect on the number of readers, its effect on the number of friends is negative (0.474–1=–0.526).

Testing the second hypothesis

To examine the second hypothesis (H2), which relates content production and ratio of readers to friends, we estimate a second activity equation, in which reciprocity is regressed on the various activity measures listed in the fourth section. The model is as follows:

$$reciprocity = \alpha + \beta_1\, ln(member) + \beta_2\, ln(entries) + \beta_3\, ln(comm.\, received) \\ + \beta_4\, ln(comm.\, posted) + \beta_5\, ln(duration) + \varepsilon; \tag{6}$$

Explanatory variables are as in the model of equation (3). Estimation results are given in the last column of Table 8.2. Compared to the regression of readers over activity, coefficients are smaller in size, and number of posts and duration are not significant. Interestingly, however, measures of posting activity and number of entries (albeit the latter not significant) are positively related with reciprocity, as predicted by H2. In particular, the coefficient of comments posted, which displays the most significant and largest effect on reciprocity, enters the estimated equation with a positive sign. We note that this variable is mostly related to the level of a blog's interactivity, in that it measures the activity of the blogger in other users' blogs, as opposed to indicators of activity in her own blog (such as, for example, entries posted). This can be interpreted as evidence that willingness to interact does affect network patterns, and increases the number of readers relative to number of friends. Duration and community membership have negative coefficients, but those are small and, for duration, insignificant. The regression explains about 27 percent of the variation in the dependent variable, which is perhaps disappointing.

The F test statistic for the regression decisively rejects the null of joint lack of significance of the regressors. Notably, the BP test does not reject its null of constant variance. In summary, results from this analysis show that there exists a positive and statistically significant relation between level of activity and number of readers, confirming hypothesis (*H*1). The evidence in favor of hypothesis (*H*2) is less favorable, but offers some interesting insights. Noticeably, measures of posting activity and number of entries (albeit the latter not significant) are positively related with reciprocity, as predicted by H2. One problem with the analysis of this section is that network structures are characterized by a large degree of endogeneity (Bramoullé, 2009; Mihaly, 2007; Weinberg, 2007). For example, the estimation of the first activity equation shows that a norm of reciprocity may affect friending patterns. In turn, this variable, by definition, depends on readership and friendship. This circularity may lead to biased estimates. To investigate the possible endogenous effect of reciprocity, and handle the endogeneity bias, the following uses instrumental variable techniques.

Instrumental variable estimation

This section applies a version of the instrumental variable technique to the estimation of the first activity equation (3). This allows us to test for the endogeneity of the reciprocity measure, and to treat it as an exogenous variable in the model of the number of readers. Results are shown in Table A 8.2, in the Appendix, along with OLS estimates for comparison. The OLS model given in Table A 8.2 does not include the variable 'comments posted', so that OLS results are comparable to IV results. However, this leads to the exclusion of a relevant variable, therefore to biased results. In interpreting IV results, one should consider that the bias in OLS estimates is induced not only by the endogeneity, but also by the exclusion of comments posted. This is due to the limited choice of instruments available in the dataset. Results evidence that endogeneity is a concern in this dataset.[17] IV coefficients are consistently higher than those produced by OLS estimation, although the sign of the activity measures' coefficients does not change. The most striking result refers to reciprocity: not only does its effect turn positive, but it also enters the activity equation with a large elasticity of about 3.5. Hausman's test statistics rejects its null of exogeneity of reciprocity at every significance level, which supports the adequacy of the IV procedure.

Interestingly, the above results are consistent with bloggers attaching a 'stigma' to failing to reciprocate. Indeed, the negative sign of reciprocity implies that, when the number of readers increases relative to the number of bloggers who are befriended, then the number of readers (and of friends) is lower than that which measures of activity would predict. It may be, as conjectured previously, that bloggers do not want to friend bloggers who do not adhere to the norm of reciprocity and thus appear unlikely to reciprocate. However, it may also be that a blogger with many readers may reach a limit on how many readers she can add back as friends and reasonably follow, and thus be less likely to reciprocate beyond that limit. It could also be that those bloggers who do not adhere to the norm do not care about how many readers they get, which is why they get less of them than their activity would otherwise predict. In the following, we consider a different indicator of network structure to check the robustness of our results: we examine whether imbalances in the bloggers' networks may explain more than aggregate reciprocity. It may indeed be that networks that are balanced are more attractive, while imbalances in any direction are stigmatized.

The effect of imbalances

This section explores how imbalances in friendships relates to blogging activity's measures and network size. Reciprocity measured the number of readers relative to the number of friends. It did not tell us, however, whether the network became more or less asymmetric. As a result, the interpretation of the effect of reciprocity in the activity equations was ambiguous. Quite apart from the relative number of friends versus readers, bloggers may react to whether a fellow blogger maintains a balance between friends and readers or not. For example, a blogger who friends too many bloggers relative to how many read her back in return could be seen as too eager, or indifferent to the act of reciprocation, and thus get fewer readers than her activity would suggest.

We therefore consider the effect of a measure of network imbalances, called asymmetry, and defined as follows:

$$reciprocity = \alpha + \beta_1 \ln(member) + \beta_2 \ln(entries) + \beta_3 \ln(comm.\,received) \\ + \beta_4 \ln(comm.\,posted) + \beta_5 \ln(duration) + \varepsilon; \tag{7}$$

Here, one can see that any departure from zero signals an increase in the asymmetry of the network. Using the measure of imbalance given above, we re-estimated the activity equations of previous sections. Table A 8.2 in the Appendix presents results from this estimation.

One can see that results for the first activity equation are comparable with those reported in Table 8.2, except that the coefficient on asymmetry is lower than the coefficient on reciprocity.[18] In contrast, results for the second activity equations differ substantially when the different measure is considered. When considering asymmetries, effects of activity measures are sizeable and all significant. One can see that the coefficient on comments posted is now negative, indicating that its positive effect on reciprocity was not a robust result.

In summary, the above results shows that the degree of asymmetry in a blogger's network is positively related to his posting activity, and negatively related to the number of comments he posted on other bloggers' entries. Therefore, the more a blogger posts comments, the less his network is asymmetric, which seems reasonable since making more comments means one has closer, and thus likely reciprocal, relations with others. It is not clear, however, why other measures of activity and interaction enter the equation with a positive sign. A possible explanation is that some bloggers are extroverts who combine higher levels of activity with a higher propensity to friend others, who then reciprocate only with a lag or not at all. This could be checked with a panel dataset, and is left for future research.

Conclusion

This chapter analyzed patterns of relationship and content production among bloggers from a theoretical and empirical perspective. The analysis has identified statistically significant positive relations between the size of and degree of reciprocity within a blogger's network of relations, and her blog's durability, intensity of activity and degree of interactivity. Main results are as follows:

- posting activity and intensity of interaction are positive determinants of network size;
- departures from aggregate reciprocity can be accounted for by content production;
- failure to reciprocate attention is sanctioned with a lower popularity than other measures of activity might normally warrant.

These results suggest that bloggers who produce more content devote less attention to others. Furthermore, bloggers sanction deviations from the norm of reciprocity, which occur when a blogger does not return friendship as expected.

This analysis has several limitations. First, because it is not possible to observe the entire network, the empirical analysis relies on a random sample, albeit representative of the wider community. Second, stylized facts summarized above describe aggregate behavior. In addition to aggregate data, the availability of individual data would help in assessing the predictions of the theoretical model concerning reciprocal attention. For example, one could verify directly whether blogs' subscriptions are indeed reciprocal. Another problem is to determine the direction of causality between number of readers, or network size, and content production. This can be addressed through the estimation of panel regressions, and is left for future research. Furthermore, more research is needed on what determines the reciprocation of relationships in the network.

Future work will rely on the collection of data over several periods, as well as on gathering of further quantitative and qualitative information, such as blogs' rankings on search engines and differences in bloggers' attitudes and objectives. This will hopefully enable us to address these difficulties.

Appendix

Data description

Original data

- User: User name (pseudonym).
- Location: Region and/or country where the blogger is based.
- Friends: Number and list of weblogs read by the blogger. Limited to other blogs on LJ.
- Readers (or 'friends of' in LJ terminology): List of those bloggers with an account on LJ who read one's weblog. This can be divided between:
  - Mutual friends: A subgroup of readers; number and list of those bloggers whose friendship is reciprocated. This statistic is not provided as a default and must be activated by the user.
  - Also friend of: A subgroup of 'readers'; number and list of those bloggers whose friendship is not reciprocated. Again, this statistic is not provided as a default and must be activated by the user.
- Communities: Number and list of communities the blogger reads. Communities are blogs with a specific theme to which all members can contribute posts and comments.
- Member of: Number and list of the communities one is member of. Differs from communities in that one can read a community without being a member of it (but one generally cannot contribute if one is not a member).
- Posting access: Differs from member of in that one can be a member of a community but not have access to posting there.
- Feeds: Number and list of those weblogs not on LJ that are read by the blogger via LJ. Those can be read via their RSS feed and appear on the blogger's 'friends' page' (list of entries by friends).

- Account type: Accounts, can be free, sponsored, paid; permanent or belong to early adopters. Early adopters are the first few members of LJ. Paid accounts give access to the full range of LJ's services and do not display any advertising. Permanent accounts are accounts that are paid for life. Sponsored accounts display advertising. Free accounts display less advertising than sponsored accounts but have reduced functionality.
- Date created: Date on which the weblog was created.
- Date updated: Last date on which the weblog was updated (i.e., when an entry was last posted).
- Journal entries: Number of posts written since the weblog was created.
- Comments posted: Number of comments made on entries in other weblogs or communities.
- Comments received: Number of comments made by other bloggers on one's own entries, and own comments in reply to those.

Processed data
- Days since creation: Difference between date of data collection and date of creation of the blog (in days).
- Days since update: Difference between date of data collection and date of the last update (days).
- Duration: Difference between date of creation and date of last update (days).
- Active: 1 if weblog was updated less than eight weeks ago, 0 otherwise.
- Entries per day: Number of journal entries divided by duration
- Comments per post: Comments received divided by number of posts
- Comments per friends: Comments made divided by number of friends.
- Reciprocity: Readers divided by friends, expressed in logarithm.

Representativity of the sample
Table A 8.1 compares features of the randomly selected bloggers to those of LJ, for an informal check of the representativeness of the sample.

One can see that the stock of bloggers on LJ is young and predominantly located in the USA. The random sample is essentially a representation of active bloggers on LJ. This is because the random script provided by LJ is designed to select active blogs in order to spare the user having to sift through inactive blogs.

Table A 8.1   Comparison table

	Random sample	LiveJournal
Updated last month	100%	7%
Updated last week	100%	3%
Updated on the day	61%	1%
Countries	US: 38%, Russia: 31%, Ukraine: 8%, Canada: 3%, UK:3%.	US: 63%, Russia: 13%, Canada: 6%, UK: 5%.
Age (in years)	Average: 30, Median: 27, Mode: 24.	Average: 25, Median: 22, Mode: 20.

Source: http://www.livejournal.com/stats.bml.

The distribution of nationality thus reflects countries in which LJ is presently popular (Russia and Ukraine), rather than LJ's country of origin (the USA), where competition from http://www.bebo.com/Bebo and http://www.facebook.com/Facebook dented LJ's popularity among high school and college students, respectively. This is also why the average age of bloggers in our sample is higher than in LJ's stock.

Figure A 8.1 represents the evolution of the number of hosted weblogs from 2000–05 (in logarithmic scale).

Instrumental variable estimation of number of readers

Table A 8.2 shows the result of the instrumental variable estimation of the number of readers.

The effect of network imbalances

Table A 8.3 shows the results of the estimation of the activity equations using the asymmetry measure.

Blogs and the Economics of Reciprocal Attention. The version of the chapter included in this book was presented at the conference Internet Use and Impact, held in Marseille, 5–6 November 2009. Earlier versions were presented at the Second FLOSS Workshop in Rennes in June 2008, at the fifth bi-annual conference on the Economics of the Software and Internet Industries, in Toulouse in January 2009, and at the Annual Conference of the Royal Economic Society, in Guilford in April 2009. A later version of this chapter was published in the Economics Bulletin, Vol. 30, No. 3. We are grateful to conferences' participants and to Adelina Gschwandtner, Peter Moffatt, and Paul Seabright for useful discussion. The support of the ESRC is gratefully acknowledged. The opinions and views expressed in this chapter are those of the authors and do not reflect those of the CRP Henri Tudor, STATEC and Observatoire de la Compétitivité.

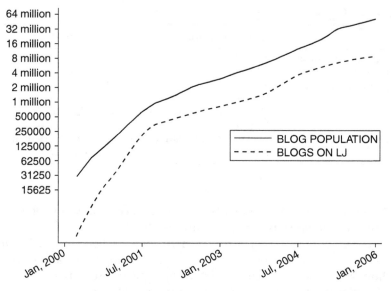

Figure A8.1   Number of hosted weblogs from 2000 to 2005 (in logarithmic scale)

Source: Henning 2005 and LJ statistics (http://www.livejournal.com/stats/stats.txt http://www.livejournal.com/stats/stats.txt), both accessed February 20, 2009.

Table A8.2   IV regression of first activity equation: model estimates and comparison with OLS regression

ln(readers)	IV		OLS	
ln(member)	0.024		0.190	***
	(−0.62)		(−12.99)	
ln(entries)	0.630	***	0.390	***
	(−13.20)		−(21.41)	
ln(comments received)	1.040	***	0.607	***
	(−17.53)		−(27.89)	
ln(comments posted)	(instrument)			
ln(duration)	0.570	***	0.236	***
	(−7.71)		(−8.97)	
reciprocity	−3.680	***	0.060	
	(−10.40)		(1.12)	
constant	−0.293		1.8	***
	(−0.56)		(9.38)	
obs	1321.0		1321.0	
Hausman test	113.8	***		

Robust (for IV estimation) and ratios in parentheses.

Table A8.3 Multiple regressions with measure of asymmetry

Dependent variable:	ln(readers)		ln(readers)		asymmetry	
ln(member)	0.153	***	0.12	***	0.193	***
	(15.80)		(13.64)		(7.53)	
ln(entries)	0.585	***	0.49	***	0.499	***
	(42.21)		(36.32)		(14.9)	
ln(comments received)	0.776	***	0.672	***	0.6	***
	(56.42)		(49.60)		(16.75)	
ln(comments posted)	−0.466	***	−0.375	***	−0.526	***
	(−30.18)		(−27.80)		(−14.70)	
ln(duration)	0.597	***	0.515	***	0.472	***
	(30.20)		(28.00)		(8.99)	
asymmetry			0.174	***		
			(18.56)			
constant	0.83	***	0.78	***	0.291	
	(6.72)		(6.90)		(0.88)	
obs	1321		1321		1321	
	0.88		0.908		0.403	
F stat	1493	***	2055	***	156	***
BP	29.56	***	23	***	58.83	***
RESET	4.81	***	4.7	***	5.75	***

Robust t-statistics are in parentheses; p-values for F, BP and RESET statistics in parentheses.

Notes

1. http://www.scribd.com/doc/219285/Blogging-Revenue-Study, accessed 21 February 2009.
2. http://www.emarketer.com/Article.aspx?id=1006799, accessed 21 February 2009.
3. Mainstream news coverage has controversially relied on (micro)bloggers in its coverage of the Mumbai terrorist attacks or of the Green Revolution in Iran. A May 2008 survey by Brodeur, a unit of Omnicom Group, found that journalists made use of blogs for their news report, felt that blogs influenced the focus and brought diversity to news, but also felt that they lowered the quality and accuracy of news reports, as well as the tone of the coverage (http://www.brodeurmediasurvey.com, accessed 25 February 2009).
4. Users can provide additional information in the 'bio', a space where bloggers present themselves.
5. More information on LJ and its history can be found in its Wikipedia entry (http://en.wikipedia.org/wiki/livejournal, accessed 21 February 2009).
6. Source: http://www.livejournal.com/stats.bml, accessed 9 February 2009.
7. Lack of explanation and due care often leads to 'drama' on LJ! 'Friendship' on LJ, therefore, acquires a meaning that is not present to the same extent in other blog networks or with RSS readers; it is a public show of confidence, a commitment and a sign of readiness for closer intimacy.

8. Other forms of status are associated with the length of time one has been on LJ, to the design of one's LJ, to the identity of one's friends, to the popularity of the communities one maintains and, occasionally, to the quality of one's entries! Status may also be imported from the 'real world'.

9. A number of tools are available on LJ to prevent unwanted interaction – for example, making one's entries friends only, preventing or screening comments by people other than friends, listing unwanted (unreciprocated) friends in a separate list, banning unwanted friends from commenting in one's journal, etc.

10. This, at least, is the pattern we observed on LiveJournal (data not reported here for lack of space).

11. More general utility representations could be adopted and would generate the same set of insights.

12. We would then express the cost of production in terms of time spent producing and write:

$$\sum_{j \neq i} n_{ij} + C(e_i) \leq T_i$$.

This is of no consequence in the subsequent analysis, however.

13. The later expressions of net surplus from a new relation would, thus, take account of the fact that additional attention by a new friend *i* may lead a blogger to increase his or her own activity and modify the attention she gives to other agents in the network.

14. http://www.livejournal.com/random.bml. The data was then collected using Screen-Scraper, a software that extracts content from websites and adds it to a database (http://www.screen-scraper.com).

15. When considering the effect of a blog's lifetime, one should also note that a blogger who has been updating for a long time is likely to accumulate many friends, irrespective of his or her level of activity. This is because there is some inertia in the friending process on LiveJournal: LJers tend to keep a blogger on their list even after that blogger has stopped updating and as long as that blogger does not drop them. Indeed, some bloggers like to inflate their list of friends and readers and thus may maintain reciprocal links long after they cease being active.

16. This partially settles a common proposition according to which some bloggers are more popular and active than others merely because they devote more time to blogging than others do, or because they are better able to maintain relations with many people at the same time (through faster typing, for example!).

17. The model is estimated using two-stage least squares procedure. Identification is achieved by excluding comments posted from the IV regression, as this variable is highly correlated with the reciprocity measure. More details on this estimation method can be found in Greene (1980), chapter 5.

18. One should note that the measure of asymmetry enters the readers' equation with a positive sign, even when estimation uses the instrumental variable method. Results for IV regressions are not reported for lack of space. They are available from the authors on request.

References

Bachnik,W., S. Szymczyk, P. Leszczynski, R. Podsiadlo, E. Rymszewicz, L. Kurylo, D. Makowiec, and B. Bykowska (2005). Quantitative and sociological analysis of blog networks. *Acta Physica Polonica* B 36(10), 3179–91.

Backstrom, L., D. Huttenlocher, J. Kleinberg, and X. Lan (2006). Group formation in large social networks: Membership, growth and evolution. In *Proceedings of the 12th ACM SIGKDD international conference on knowledge discovery and data mining*, pp. 44–54. ACM:New York, NY, USA.

Bar-Ilan, J. (2005). Information hub blogs. *Journal of Information Science* 31(4), 297–307.

Belsley, D. (1980). *Conditioning diagnostics: collinearity and weak data in regression.* Wiley.

Bialik, C. (2005). Measuring the impact of blogs requires more than counting. *The Wall Street Journal.* May 26, http://tinyurl.com/7luge.

Bramoullé, Y. and B. Fortin (2009). The econometrics of social networks. CIRPEE Working Paper.

Brueckner, J. (2006). Friendship networks. *Journal of Regional Science* 46(5), 847–65.

Caffarelli, F. (2004). Non-cooperative network formation with network mainte-nance costs. Working Paper ECO 2004/18, European University Institute.

Dohmen, T., A. Falk, D. Huffman, and U. Sunde (2009). Homo Reciprocans: Survey evidence of behavioural outcomes. *The Economic Journal* 119, 592–612.

Drezner, D. and H. Farrell (2008). Introduction: Blogs, politics and power: a spe-cial issue of Public Choice. *Public Choice* 134, 1–13.

Furukawa, T., T. Matsuzawa, Y. Matsuo, K. Uchiyama, and M. Takeda (2006). Analysis of user relations and reading activity in weblogs. *Electronics and Communications in Japan* (Part 1: Communications) 89(12), 88–96.

Granovetter, M. (1973). The strength of weak ties. *American Journal of Sociology* 78(6), 1360–80.

Greene, W. (1980). *Econometric Analysis.* Prentice Hall.

Gu, B., Y. Huang, W. Duan, and A. B. Whinston (2009). Indirect reciprocity in online social networks – a longitudinal analysis of individual contributions and peer enforcement in a peer-to-peer music sharing network. McCombs Research Paper Series No. IROM-06-09.

Gui, B. and R. Sugden (2005). Why interpersonal relations matter for econom-ics. In B. Gui and R. Sugden (Eds.), *Economics and Social Interactions*, pp. 1–22. Cambridge University Press: Cambridge, UK.

Henning, J. (2005). The blogging geyser. Newsletter of the Web Marketing Association. April 8, http://www.webmarketingassociation.org/wma_news letter05_05_iceberg.htm.

Herring, S., L. Scheidt, S. Bonus, and E. Wright (2004). Bridging the gap: A genre analysis of weblogs. In *Proceedings of the 37th Annual Hawaii International Conference on System Sciences*, pp. 101–11.

Huck, S., G. Lünser, and J.-R. Tyran (2010). Consumer networks and firm reputa-tion: A first experimental investigation. *Economics Letters* 108(2), 242–44.

Jackson, M. O. (2003). A survey of models of network formation: Stability and efficiency. In G. Demange and M. Wooders (Eds.), *Group Formation in Economics: Networks, Clubs, and Coalitions.* Cambridge University Press: Cambridge.

Krishnamurty, S. (2002). The multidimensionality of blog conversations: The virtual enactment of September 11. In AOIR Internet Research 3.0.

Kumar, R., J. Novak, P. Raghavan, and A. Tomkins (2004). Structure and evolution of blogspace. *Communications of the ACM* 47(12), 35–39.

Lassica, J. (2001). Blogging as a form of journalism. *Online Journalism Review.* May 24, http://www.ojr.org/ojr/workplace/1017958873.php.

Lemann, N. (2006). Journalism without journalists. *The New Yorker.* August 7, http://www.newyorker.com/archive/2006/08/07/060807fa_fact1.

Lento, T., H. Welser, L. Gu, and M. Smith (2006). The ties that blog: Examining the relationship between social ties and continued participation in the Wallop weblogging system. In 3rd Annual Workshop on the Weblogging Ecosystem.

Marwick, A. (2009). LiveJournal users: Passionate, prolific and private. December 19, http://www.livejournalinc.com/press_releases/20081219.php.

Mihaly, K. (2007). Too popular for school? Friendship formation and academic achievement. Department of Economics, Duke University Working Paper NC27708.

Mishne, G. and N. Glance (2006). Leave a reply: An analysis of weblog comments. In 3rd Annual Workshop on the Weblogging Ecosystem.

Nardi, B. A., D. J. Schiano, and M. Gumbrecht (2004). Blogging as social activity, or, Would you let 900 million people read your diary? In *Proceedings of the 2004 ACM conference on Computer Supported Cooperative Work*, pp. 222–31. ACM Press.

Newman, M. E. J. (2003). The structure and function of complex networks. *SIAM Review* 45, 167.

Paolillo, J., S. Mercure, and E. Wright (2005). The social semantics of LiveJournal FOAF: Structure and change from 2004 to 2005. In G. Stumme, B. Hoser, C. Schmitz, and H. Alani (Eds.), *Proceedings of the ISWC 2005 Workshop on Semantic Network Analysis.*

Perseus Development Corporation (2003). The blogging iceberg. October 6, http://tinyurl.com/ceepn4.

Quiggin, J. (2006). Blogs, wikis and creative innovation. *International Journal of Cultural Studies* 9(4), 481–96.

Raynes-Goldie, K. (2004). Pulling sense out of today's informational chaos: LiveJournal as a site of knowledge creation and sharing. *First Monday* 9(12). http://firstmonday.org/htbin/cgiwrap/bin/ojs/index.php/fm/article/view/1194/1114.

Raynes-Goldie, K. and D. Fono (2006). Hyperfriends and beyond: Friendship and social norms on LiveJournal. In M. Consalvo and C. Haythornthwaite (Eds.), Internet Research Annual Volume 4: Selected Papers from the Association of Internet Researchers Conference. Peter Lang: New York, USA.

Ribstein, L. E. (2005). Initial reflections on the law and economics of blogging. University of Illinois, http://law.bepress.com/uiuclwps/papers/art25/.

Ribstein, L. E. (2006). From bricks to pajamas: The law and economics of amateur journalism. *William & Mary Law Review* 48, 185–249.

Schmidt, J. (2007). Blogging practices: An analytical framework. *Journal of Computer-Mediated Communication* 12, 1409–27.

Sunstein, C. (2008). Neither Hayek nor Habermas. *Public Choice* 134(1–2), 87–95.

Watts, A. (2001). A dynamic model of network formation. *Games and Economic Behavior* 34, 331–34.

Weinberg, B. (2007). Social interactions with endogenous association. NBER Working Paper 13038.

Wenger, A. (2008). Analysis of travel bloggers' characteristics and their communication about Austria as a tourism destination. *Journal of Vacation Marketing* 14(2), 169–76.

Part III
New Organizational Frontiers

9
File Sharing and Its Impact on Business Models in Music

Joost Poort and Paul Rutten

Introduction

Industries involved in creating, producing, commercializing and distributing content find themselves facing major change because of digitization. These include the music and film sectors, and for over a decade now also the games sector. Digitization is changing the face of the content industry, with new types of distribution emerging and the boundaries between the different industries blurring. New opportunities are arising while challenges to existing ways of operating require reinvention as digitization enables consumers to access music, films and games in new ways. File sharing – the uploading and downloading of music, films and games – has become a reality, even if experience shows that online sharing often occurs without the explicit agreement of the right holders, who thus do not receive any payment. Companies producing content worry about the damage to revenues for which file sharing is said to be to blame.

The impact of file sharing on the content industry's various sectors and the industry at large has been the subject of great debate. Its detractors believe that file sharing is causing untold damage to the content industry and is even putting its economic viability at stake. They warn that this might diminish the range of culture on offer and reduce opportunities for nurturing talent, and that, with investment resources drying up, cultural production practices will, over time, no longer meet society's need for a wide variety of content. This scenario typically crops up in discussions on the impact of file sharing on the music industry, which frequently also suggest that the film and games industries are heading down the same route as soon as file sharing really takes hold there, too. Others reject these arguments and feel that unlicensed digital distribution is the outcome of the content industry's failure to innovate and that the digital highway opens up new ways of leveraging; market players could tap into new value-creating opportunities. Instead of flagging inevitable cultural or social damage, they see opportunities to achieve cultural, social and economic value by new means. To this end, the content industry should reinvent itself by capitalizing on the value of content in different ways and at different times, directly through its end-users or indirectly through collaboration with other economic players, if need be outside the content industry itself. They believe content industry players should invest more time and resources in creating new business models to equip themselves for survival in the digital era.

This debate is not just about the content industry, it affects society as a whole. It is not merely the future of an industry that is at stake here, we are talking cultural diversity, opportunities for talented people to develop their creativity and turn it into content, and access to culture for the general public. This being so, the debate borders on several government policy areas.

This issue is of particular interest to those involved in cultural policy-making, as governments look to promoting the creation of and access to a wide range of high-quality cultural products. Likewise, it is relevant to a country's aim to develop a robust creative industry that is a key contributor to the economy, and thus also has a bearing on government policy to promote innovation and competitiveness in trade and industry. And, of course, the subject also involves the law, particularly in terms of intellectual property.

Against this backdrop, the primary purpose of this chapter is to identify the broader social, cultural and economic implications of file sharing for the music, film and games industries. The main focus will be on the music industry, which appears to have been affected most by file sharing, looking, in particular, at the situation in the Netherlands.

'File sharing' is the catch-all term for uploading and downloading, and encompasses a range of technologies. File sharing logically breaks down into downloading and uploading, with the latter particularly relevant in terms of the law, as any online offering of copyrighted content is not allowed under Dutch law without the prior consent of the right holder. By contrast, downloading copyrighted material is typically permitted, provided it is for the downloader's own use and meets certain requirements – regardless of whether the content comes from an 'illegal source'. Note that these rules do not apply to games, which are considered computer programs and are therefore governed by different laws. To gauge the economic and cultural implications of file sharing, this study will review the scale and consequences of licensed and unlicensed downloading for the content industries as these currently exist. With the aid of an examination of the scale of, background to and motives for 'free' downloading and the supposed link to content buying, this study identifies the broader social implications of unlawful uploads of copyrighted content. This chapter addresses the following questions. What are the key characteristics of and trends in the three industries – film, games and music – and their respective markets? To what extent are identified trends attributable to file sharing? What are the most important developments in the business models of the sectors of the entertainment industry investigated? What are people's key motives and considerations in file sharing? Are there any differences in file sharing between films, games and music? How much file sharing can be estimated to go on in the Netherlands? What are the possible implications of file sharing for consumer behavior in other markets in which this content is sold? What are the most important welfare effects in the short and longer terms? How are these created and what, to date, have been the roles of the content industry, distribution network operators, the government and consumers? What are the expected effects on cultural diversity and the accessibility of culture? The answers to the questions posed in this chapter are based on a mix of research methods and tools. To find answers to some of our questions we have consulted the relevant literature at various stages of our research and drawn on a range of secondary – particularly statistical – sources. To investigate the background to, motives for and practice of file sharing, we have talked to active uploaders and downloaders and commissioned a survey of a representative group of 1,500 internet users, conducted by research agency Synovate.

In addition, we have sounded out representatives of the different industry sectors about the effects of file sharing within companies in the entertainment industry and about the new content leveraging opportunities that the digital era offers.

Developments in the entertainment industry

This section provides a brief overview of the specific nature of the entertainment industry, and recent developments therein. In particular, the impact of the digital era on the industry is highlighted. Key trends in the entertainment market are also taken on board, with a focus on the music industry as manifesting the most important and far-reaching changes.

Experience goods and public goods

The film, games and music industries generate the bulk of their revenues by marketing their products directly to consumers. We are talking here about the release of films on DVD, music on CD and games on consoles, and not so much about the generation of royalties. This is the market in culture, information and entertainment, whose products appeal to consumers primarily for their symbolism, representing a world and evoking an experience. Their value is in the experience that consumers can typically only rate after consumption – which is why these are also known as 'experience goods'. To an important degree, marketing and promotion in these industries involve managing expectations – by selectively releasing parts of the product, for instance, a phenomenon known as sampling. In fact, the music industry is known for sharing its products with potential customers by releasing them for radio broadcasts and by producing music videos to promote them on TV. Experience has shown that consumers will then want to own their own copies of the music and thus have access at self-chosen times and frequencies. In the film and gaming industries, by contrast, broadcasting the whole product through mass media is unusual, as this is not expected to generate turnover the way it does in the music business. Broadcasting films on television is a way of generating revenues for film producers and distributors in itself, and is certainly not aimed at promoting DVD sales, even if this is often its effect – for example, television series whose DVD appeal lies in the fact that they have been previously broadcast. In this way, then, the music industry is significantly different from the film and games industries.

Although most entertainment industry products are in physical format – in the shape of DVDs, CDs and games – their value is primarily non-physical: it is in the experience, the story, the information. With all of these products essentially involving information, developments in information technology typically have major implications for the way in which the entertainment industry is able to operate or commercialize its products – the digital revolution being a case in point. Another typical feature of these experience goods is that their consumption by one consumer does not happen at the expense of other consumers' ability to use them. If someone buys and eats a loaf of bread, nobody else will be able to eat it, but this is not the case when someone watches a film on DVD or plays a computer game. The latter type of goods are called 'non-rival'. If it is possible to prevent a person from accessing goods, these are excludable and called 'club' goods, whereas if their access is non-excludable they are known as 'public' goods. Because of their non-excludable and non-rival nature, public goods often depend on public finance.

Traditional examples of public goods include street lighting and defence. The traditional way to finance public goods has been from public means. Another possible way to finance public goods is to introduce a cross subsidy. This is an obvious course of action when the provision of a public good increases the demand for other products or services that are excludable. A classic example here would be a lighthouse paid for from port dues levied at a nearby port. At this juncture, it is hard to find examples from the entertainment industry that match this model. A future scenario might envisage free access to music recordings, financed by revenues from concerts, promotional merchandise and advertising contracts signed by the artists involved. Discussions about new models for the music industry, which will be discussed later, often anticipate such a future. The physical formats carrying music, films and games are rival goods, but the information or files themselves is not. This enables consumers to share the music or films they own and make them accessible to others, in return gaining access to creative content that others have filed on their computers in digital format. Mutual advantage occurs, but the holder of the rights is kept out of the loop. With entertainment industry products essentially being information and digitally transmittable, the emergence of this type of file sharing was only to be expected as soon as technology made it possible. In the days before the digital revolution, consumers shared music by lending out LPs to others to make analogue tape recordings. This type of file sharing *avant la lettre* was circumscribed by technology only, but that did not stop the music industry from campaigning against the phenomenon under the slogan 'Home Taping is Killing Music'. The advent and ongoing development of digital technology has sharply reduced technological limitations, although entertainment industry companies, drawing on that same technology, are reintroducing these in the shape of copying restrictions and digital rights management (DRM). Such measures would all appear to be attempts to keep control of the spread of goods and to thus continue to be able to market these as club goods. Meanwhile, some content providers have had a change of heart because of the heavy resistance they have run into from consumers, who feel restricted in their use of the music they have actually bought.

High fixed costs of production

Production in the entertainment industry is often a collective process marked by a far-reaching division of labor that frequently even transcends companies. The film industry is a good example, as it brings together people and companies for each production and disbands them after the project is completed – a real 'project industry'. Games are similarly designed and produced by different companies at different locations around the world, turning out titles that the big global distributors will subsequently release on the console market through state-of-the-art digital networks that link locations and operations. Game production budgets are easily as large as those for major Hollywood movies. The music industry is not usually known for its massive scale and complex output, but even here production tends to involve large numbers of people and multiple companies. The entertainment industry typically spends large amounts on production compared with low distribution costs.

Also, production involves sunk costs that can only be recouped by leveraging recorded and released creative content, staging live performances – in the case of music – and marketing merchandise. If a music recording, film or game fails to catch on and the market for related live performances and merchandise does not materialize, these costs have to be written off in their entirety. This is different from most other industries, where fixed assets can usually be sold on to others and a proportion of spending thus recouped. Not so for the entertainment industry: there is simply no market for a dud film or an unpopular game. The sunk costs are truly sunk. By contrast, marginal costs – that is, the costs per extra unit of production, which in this industry typically relate to distribution – are relatively low and have even got close to zero in this digital age. After all, the costs of digital distribution are very limited, particularly as compared with production costs. This is what makes large-scale operations so profitable for the media industry: once it has recouped its high initial sunk costs, profits can shoot up as marginal costs are very low indeed.

Piracy and file sharing

This combination of high fixed costs and low marginal costs, together with the fact that entertainment goods are so easy to distribute, make this sector highly sensitive to illegal commercial activity. Some hijack creative content without the consent of its right holders and sell copies in the market. These pirates, as they are sometimes called, make relatively quick money as the costs of distribution – that is, the physical cost of copying data files or the cost or unlawful digital distribution – are very low indeed. They are also not burdened by high production costs, nor do they pay for any rights. Meanwhile, piracy interferes with the right holders' lawful marketing of their products, causing them to incur losses. To a lesser or greater degree, all sectors covered in this report face such commercially motivated infringements of their rights. The key features of entertainment products as described earlier have also made it relatively easy for the public at large to share digital music files, with the advent of P2P networks in the past decade – starting with Napster in 1999 – playing a pivotal role. These P2P networks differ from commercial piracy in a number of ways, as consumers downloading music – and, knowingly or unknowingly, making their own music libraries available to others – typically have other motives than commercial pirates who consciously infringe the rights of producers, artists and actors to line their own pockets. This is not to say that commercial considerations might not play a role in P2P networks, not necessarily because these networks are out to make money from music sharing as such but because they reach certain socio-demographic groups that might be attractive to advertisers. Obviously, there is a value to keeping these networks online, a motive that carried more weight in the early days of P2P networks, when Napster was sold to Bertelsmann. Later generations of P2P networks have been less driven by specific companies able to directly or indirectly generate revenues from the value of the network. Kazaa, for example, sold adware that made it possible to collect information about users that was then sold on to others – Microsoft, Netflix and DirectTV among them. When users protested, Kazaa launched a paid ad-free service alongside its free ad-supported one (Vaccaro and Cohn, 2004). P2P practices might be damaging to the industries we are investigating in this report, although the precise extent of the damage is very difficult to ascertain without intimate knowledge of consumers' motives and considerations. After all, downloading music may be argued to be a kind of sampling, a way of getting to know a piece of music that is comparable to listening to the radio or going to record shops and listening there before deciding whether or not to buy. The analogue age's counter-argument that not every home-taped recording implied one less vinyl LP sold would also seem to hold for the digital era: not every downloaded track implies a loss of revenue for the music industry. The discussion of a consumer survey in the next section and the review of the international literature in the fourth section delve deeper into the issues at stake.

To ensure that right holders enjoy the fruits of their labors, the law upholds copyright and related rights and right holders have a legal right to take action against the unlawful distribution of their work.

Under pressure

Today's still-dominant business model of key players in the entertainment industry is predicated on leveraging access to creative content on a large scale. Content is typically created under the auspices of companies in the music, film and games industries, which pick up the tab for production costs and sell the products on the consumer markets in physical formats (e.g., music on CD, film on DVD, games for consoles), screen them in cinemas (film) or grant performing rights for special use. And, of course, content can now also be distributed and marketed online, and on a scale previously undreamed of via the traditional channels. However, if the industry loses control of its products, it is currently very vulnerable indeed, seeing club goods turn into public goods with the inherent problem of recouping costs. As the entertainment industry is in the business of experience goods, it has a tough time predicting success: a large number of productions never break even and huge hits have to make up for flop-related losses. And those massive hits also have to prove that these companies can achieve financial performances that will please their shareholders. Both the music industry and, to a lesser degree, the film industry stress that file sharing hits them really hard. Rejecting the oft-heard argument that things cannot be all that bad, as their top hits account for huge sales, these industries point out that they need the revenues from such mega-sales to invest in new and unproven productions, many of which will never be successful. In other words, if the froth goes out of major productions, film, games and music companies will no longer be able to offer their current wide range of products. With the actual market for many Dutch entertainment industry products being, by definition, circumscribed, Dutch companies benefit a great deal less from economies of scale than their American counterparts. Add to this the high initial costs faced by national entertainment industries and we see a Dutch film industry that does not recoup its costs on the large majority of films. As a result, the industry fundamentally relies on public funding – as is the case in many other European countries – and film financing reflects a mixture of economic and cultural considerations. Music industry production budgets may not be as large, but here too the size of the national market is invariably a key budgetary consideration that warrants restraint. In the Dutch music business, recording companies typically have to make their own way in the market, while venues hosting bands that have yet to make it to the top tend to rely on government money.

The games industry is dominated by international repertoire. Entertainment games target worldwide markets and virtually none are made for specific countries or language areas. Games producers take an industry view of the national versus international issue, while governments try to get and keep them operating within their borders: games companies operate in growth markets and often provide a stimulus to a country's entertainment, and information industries. The games industry benefits indirectly from public funding – for instance, in terms of research and development – but this applies to industries outside entertainment as well.

The entertainment industry draws on information and communication technology to produce, market and distribute its products and services. And it is precisely because these products are in the information category – in the widest sense of the word – and are often distributed through information networks, that digital distribution's new features and possibilities have ushered in major changes, as we have noted. In fact, the games industry as we know it today is itself the brainchild of digital technology. Ironically, with its possibilities for endless reproduction and distribution and consequent massive increase in scale, digital technology at the same time also facilitates copyright breaches – a phenomenon that has been described as the 'digital paradox' (Rutten and van Bockxmeer, 2003). The music industry initially proved very reluctant to use digital opportunities for this very reason, but that has not prevented the widespread unauthorized distribution of creative content. Some industry watchers claim that this caution in distributing music, films and games online has, in fact, promoted unlawful distribution – and still does. This very trend is forcing the various players to take a close look at their current business models and, when finding that digitization is pushing them towards obsolescence, to develop new ones.

Digitization and digital distribution

Of course, the entertainment industry has itself been one of the first beneficiaries of digital breakthroughs. The digitization of physical formats ushered in a massive market, with consumers replacing some or all of their vinyl collections with CD recordings. The advent of the DVD was a major quality improvement in the film and video industries and proved a big boost to the video-buying market. The industry has benefited enormously from the digital formatting of films and other video material and it would seem that, even aside from the substitution effect, digital formats have themselves been a tremendous boon to turnover. With the launch of the Blu-ray disc the market now offers an even higher-quality format, in keeping with the trend for quality improvements within existing models of film formats. At this juncture, it is unclear what part Blu-ray will play in the development of the film and video industry. The introduction of digital formats has not fundamentally changed the value chains in the film and music industries; and, incidentally, neither have internet stores such as amazon.com. Granted, there have been changes in the individual links of the creation, production, release, distribution and consumption chain, and the traditional shops are now also up against e-tailers, but at this stage of digitization there is – as yet – no sign of entirely new links or the disappearance of players in the music industry value chain. This state of affairs is perhaps even more evident when it comes to online distribution. The digitization of information and communication networks has facilitated electronic distribution of, first, music and, later, also video. Despite the tremendous potential of this development, the entertainment industry has been very slow to respond, with fear of the unlawful distribution of digitized products being the rather questionable hold-up. The industry has long held on to a specific way of thinking and operating and has thus offered little room for the necessary radical innovations, with the music business not fast enough on its feet to move with the new situation. And time is also running out for the film and video industry. Skilful consumers mastering information and communication technology have combined with the development of network capacity to increasingly squeeze the entertainment industry's traditional business model. Digital consumers, wise to technological possibilities and new applications in the digital arena, are now making demands of products and services – demands that the entertainment industry, stuck in its traditional practices, has failed to meet sufficiently over the past few years. With the aid of ICT and innovative entrepreneurs who refuse to be held back by current intellectual property laws in their concepts and services design, consumers have had a taste of attractive products and services, which the entertainment industry has been slow, or failed, to develop. Established entertainment industry players have proved singularly unable to meet these consumers' needs, as Vaccaro and Cohn describe in their assessment of the music industry:

> Traditional firms have been accused of lacking the cultural capital to make a successful transition to a new business model in the information age, and it has been suggested that the record labels need to change their interaction from lawsuits to a marketing and promotional orientation. (Vaccaro and Cohn, 2004, p. 56)

The message is clear: the music industry should focus more on consumer wishes as to how music should be offered instead of seeking refuge in any established business fortress. Aside from the lawsuits that Vaccaro and Cohn mention, the entertainment industry has also tried to restrict consumer access to paid-for applications via digital rights management (DRM). However, the drawbacks of DRM have proved so many and so negative that operators are increasingly choosing to ignore this route altogether. For one thing, DRM-protected CDs often did not work on computers, restricting consumers in their freedom to play their music where they want and when they want. At the end of the day, it would seem that the music industry has done itself a grave disservice by its caution in offering music online and by bringing to bear the heavy guns of the law and DRM: file sharing has spread while turnover and profits in the record industry have declined. 1999 proved a watershed year for the content industry, particularly in music. It was the year that Napster set up business and the phenomenon of P2P networks become popular. Napster enabled consumers to share music via the internet and brought extensive music libraries within their reach, with right holders missing out. It would be possible to describe the history of P2P services and practices as a legal cat-and-mouse game involving the content industry, its interest groups, P2P designers, consumers, the law and law-and rule-making government as the main players.

The current state of play is one of still extensive traffic in copyright-protected information shared via P2P networks. This mainly involves music files, but the signs are that film and video files are gaining ground, which is made possible by these networks' increasing capacity. The music industry is now offering a growing supply of licensed downloads, the market for which is also expanding, but in hardly any country can it make up for the ongoing decline in CD sales. Note that attempts by major record companies to jointly develop the market for paid-for downloads through an integrated service have failed. Investments by several major music industry players in joint music services such as MusicNet and PressPlay have not been the hoped-for success nor brought the desired market positions. An OECD report notes that concerted efforts were dogged by difficulties in clearing rights and arguments about the nature, conditions and set-up of a joint platform in the face of a burgeoning P2P trade providing 'free' access to their music libraries. It also points out the lack of user-friendliness of the music industry's digital offering in the shape of complicated user interfaces and high up-front costs imposed by monthly subscription fees. But one of the most decisive factors, the OECD believes, was the lack of comprehensive and integrated music catalogues that consumers could buy from a single supplier, plus the fact that consumers were unable to get all the music they wanted. In 2005 the OECD counted over 200 licensed online offerings in OECD countries (OECD, 2005, p. 46). The market for licensed digital downloads was finally tapped in 2004 by Apple, serving consumers with its smart mobile iPod devices. Through its iTunes, Apple has since grown into the world's main online music seller, with a clear offering and pricing structure.

Market developments

Drawing on a range of data sources, we have collated the developments in the various market segments in the media industry in the Netherlands so as to facilitate comparison. The data involve music recordings (on CD and as licensed downloads), DVD sales, DVD rentals, cinema turnover based on average weekly takings and games software. For the sake of comparison, we have indexed turnover for each of these industries, with 1999 as the baseline (turnover in 1999 = 100). 1999 is not just the title of the memorable Prince song, but also saw Napster go online and sow the seeds of file sharing.

As the chart clearly shows, films on DVD and games software are the big growth markets. The cinema market has been stable for a fair number of years, barring a minor dip in 2005. By contrast, the markets for DVD rentals and music recordings are fading, with the latter the

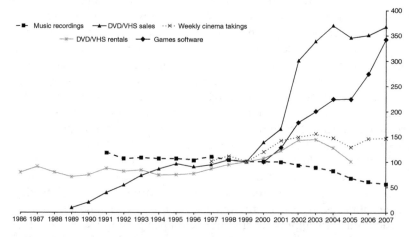

Figure 9.1   Turnover in market segments of the film and video, music, and games industries (1986–2007, indexed, 1999 = 100)

biggest loser. The turnover and sales data in the music industry show that market growth in licensed downloads has failed to make up for the downslide in the physical format market. This is not to say that file sharing is wholly to blame for the music industry's shrinking market: there is a real possibility that the industry's offering has become less tempting in recent years in the face of the numerous leisure spending alternatives – another possible explanation for the music business losing ground.

There are a number of reasons why the music industry has been the first to feel the pinch of the advent and rise of digital networks. For one thing, digital music uses relatively little bandwidth and even the first generation of networks had enough capacity to bring music to consumers' homes within an acceptable time frame. In terms of sound quality, downloaded music proved an acceptable substitute for CD-recorded music, and consumers were able to copy their music from physical format or directly from the internet onto a digital mobile player that was smaller, easier and more multifunctional than the portable CD player. Meanwhile, massive numbers of consumers put their CD collections online by participating in P2P networks such as Napster and, later, Kazaa, gaining access to a vast range of recordings in return for their own uploads – and all circumventing the established music industry.

The film industry could benefit from the music industry's cautionary tale. Instead, much like the music business in the early years of file sharing, it has spent the past few years honing its strategy of lawsuits and DRM. While sharing of filmed content would seem to have been on a swift upward trend, experiments with licensed film downloads remain few and far between. Lulled, perhaps, by the ongoing rise in DVD sales and cinema visits, the film industry is studying reinvention of its business model less assiduously than the music industry is now forced to do.

New business models: a short review

Many a review of the future of the entertainment industry advocates investment in new business models. However, there is no unequivocal definition of what a business model is, let alone any consensus on the road the entertainment industry should travel to find its new model. Discussions and contributions on new business models in the entertainment industry – which, incidentally, focus almost exclusively on the music industry – tend to have different emphases. Some zoom in on the *method of delivery and payment* for products and services – for example, selling CDs, games or DVDs online or offering content as downloads for consumers to pay for. Others focus on the potential implications of digitization in the *value chain*, and in particular on players that add too little value and are likely to fall victim to disintermediation, the most obvious threat being e-commerce cutting out the middle man that is the music shop, or record companies becoming obsolete as artists reach their audiences directly. Still others prefer a much more integrated approach and look at real-life existing models, or, more sweepingly, no longer link business models to industries or specific value chains, but to networks of companies that jointly market products or services in relatively loose configurations. An example would be an alliance of a music producer with a soft drinks maker, offering downloadable music on the latter's site to help promote sales of the drink. In this scenario, players normally operating in different industries create joint value by collaborating outside the box of traditional value chains. Digital networks and their potential uses across different sectors offer a range of possibilities for new connections through value networks that would typically be temporary, unlike familiar business models, unexpected and mostly innovative. The whole concept of the business model would give way to the value network, offering significantly less rigid relationships than those in the value chain of a fully fledged industry or specific company.

The OECD (2005) identifies four new online music business models that emphasize distribution and transaction of products and services rather than the structure of the industry:

- *Digital download (à la carte)*: music is sold directly per download (iTunes), is stored on the users' own devices and becomes their property.
- *Streaming subscriptions*: instead of paying per download, users pay a fixed monthly fee to stream an unlimited number of music files, but will not get to own them.
- *Portable subscriptions*: users can download large collections of music for a fixed monthly fee, with ownership cancelled if they stop paying their subscriptions.
- *Streaming radio:* listeners pay a monthly subscription fee for access to online radio.

Premkumar (2003) prefers 'digital distribution strategies' to business models and identifies no less than six actors in the value chain, with strategy variation mainly reflecting the degree to which one or more actors become redundant to the chain because they add insufficient value (disintermediation – a concept central to virtually all reviews of the impact of digital trends on business models).

- *Record company–retailer–customer*: the traditional chain remains in place. Customers go to their local music shops to make their own CD compilations on-site.
- *Record company–customer*: record companies sell digital files directly to customers and cut out retailers.
- *Record company–intermediary–customer*: record companies sell their digital files through online intermediaries, who work with many if not all providers of online music. Currently the dominant online model, this is a direct digital transposition of the traditional bricks-and-mortar shopping concept.
- *Artist–customer*: artists sell their own music to customers online, dis-intermediating record company and shop.
- *Artist–intermediary–customer*: artists sell their music to consumers through online retailers, cutting out the record companies.
- *Audio-on-demand*: customers pay a fixed amount to receive custom-ized playlists from a service provider.

In his analysis of the added value of the various agents in the music business's digital value chain, Frost (2007) concludes that the record companies have had their day. Advocating an overhaul of the music business, he finds that the value that this actor claims does not match the value it adds. He feels that cutting out the record companies offers the benefits of lowering prices to consumers and increasing revenues to artists. He also sees such lower prices as the key instrument to fight online piracy, and estimates that a bundle of songs such as the number currently sold on CDs should be priced at around $3. In their study of the evolution of business models and marketing strategies in the music industry, Vaccaro and Cohn (2004) define a business model as the way companies build and use their resources to offer more value for money to their customers than their rivals and thus make money. Three existing models come in for close scrutiny:

1. Traditional business models based on mass production and distribu-tion of physical formats.
2. Revolutionary models based on unauthorized P2P file sharing, ena-bled by software-providing companies and allowing consumers to share music without any payment to their right holders.
3. New business models under which consumers pay to download music from authorized providers.

Vaccaro and Cohn predict that the models that will survive are those that are able to deliver sufficient scale to turn the slim profit margins on individual downloads into solid earnings, particularly if they manage to combine this with add-on products and services such as hardware, subscriptions to online music magazines or concert tickets. Implicitly, the authors are saying that the new business model in its current set-up might not be fully viable on its own – a supposition corroborated by the fact that iTunes was at least partially designed to be a driver of iPod sales.

In response to this analysis, Frost would probably say that the record companies' takings in the existing download models are too high and that this is why they will never be a runaway success. Record companies in his perception simply take too much for what they deliver, and he feels disintermediation of the record companies is therefore inevitable. Whether or not record companies are indeed appropriating too big a cut from existing music downloads is a subject that merits further study. The striking thing about this limited review of academic research into the subject of potential new business models in the music industry is the rather narrow view the research takes. All the talk of new models aside, most analyses hardly venture beyond the commercialization of music recordings, with many of them also focusing mainly on the sale of these recordings – for example, through music and video streaming subscriptions to consumers. None of this addresses the observation, made in early in the second section, that music in the MP3 format is non-excludable and non-rival. To all intents and purposes, it meets the definition of a public good and there is, therefore, an inherent difficulty in recouping its cost. As long as file sharing remains a fact of life, its licensed counterpart will have to compete with 'free' in terms of price and ease of use.

An altogether different route, virtually ignored in the analyses we have briefly reviewed, would be to focus on alternative sources of revenue that do still guarantee excludability. One obvious choice would be to link recordings to live concerts, ringtones, merchandise and other types of income-generating activities for authors, artists, publishers and producers. Music could be brought into audiovisual productions – from commercials to music games for consoles – or be coupled to completely different types of product, ranging from cars and soft drinks to energy and clothes, with these products' marketing budgets paying for a chunk or all of the music recording costs.

An innovation that *has* taken the music industry by storm is what is known as the '360-degree contract', under which bands and artists sign over to a record company or investor a share in everything directly or indirectly related to their recordings, from merchandise and live performances to downloads and sponsorship revenues. The introduction of these contracts is a clear recognition of the link between the various sources of income from the different markets – think of the lighthouse paid for by port duties as an obvious analogy here. After all, in one way or another all this turnover is generated by music. Some artists sign 360-degree contracts with record companies and others with concert promoters, the most prominent among them being Live Nation. All this goes to show that business model innovation in the music industry is often more complex and wide-ranging than mere marketing and distribution of downloads. Focusing on new business models, Jacobs (2007) identifies a typical combination of product, process and transaction innovation. He draws on Margetta (2002), who argues that business models really break down into two separate parts, one involving everything to do with the making of something – that is, design, purchase of resources or commodities, and production – with the second part comprising all the activities involved in selling something: finding and reaching consumers, selling, distributing or offering a service. Jacobs pinpoints product and process innovation at the first stage and transaction innovation at the second stage of the model. If we combine Jacobs's approach with the concept of value networks that Ballon (2007), among others, has introduced into the discussion of business models, a broad playing field emerges that may well include just the new models the music industry is looking for.

The value network context, for instance, makes sense of the alliance between Universal Music and mobile operator Vodafone for music access via mobile phones. Ballon suggests that 'value' and 'control' take centre stage in research into and development of new models in the value network context, which would make for a better understanding of business model innovation in the music industry, and, at the end of the day, the wider entertainment industry also. What is more, these are precisely the terms within which the industry will have to operate if it is to stay in business.

File sharing: key funding of a Dutch survey

To gain a better grasp of consumers' file-sharing activity and its impact on the media industries, a representative survey of a sample of the Dutch population was conducted. The purpose of the survey was to find answers to the following questions. What are people's key motives and considerations in file sharing? Are there any differences in file sharing between films, games and music? How much file sharing can be estimated to go on in the Netherlands? What are the possible implications of file sharing for consumer behavior in other markets in which this content is sold? A questionnaire was first tested on a number of consumers. Following adjustments, research agency Synovate put the questionnaire to their online panel between 2 and 8 April. A total of 1,464 respondents completed questions about music (98 percent of the sample), 1,405 about films (94 percent) and 778 about games (53 percent). The sample is broadly representative of the Dutch internet population aged 15 upwards in terms of its socio-demographic characteristics and internet usage – with minor deviations. One such deviation was a slight over-representation of heavy internet users, prompting a weighting of the survey outcomes to arrive at a representative picture. Another point worth noting is that the Dutch internet population does not precisely coincide with the Dutch population because not everyone in the country has internet access. This chapter will sometimes extrapolate survey findings to the entire Dutch population, expressly noting this in the relevant instances and, if applicable, discussing the validity of any such observations. A key challenge in designing any questionnaire is that respondents may tend to give answers that they see as socially desirable.

We have attempted to prevent social desirability bias in various ways, one being that the questionnaire's introduction emphasizes both the anonymity of the information at all times and the fact that it is the government that commissioned the study. Furthermore, the survey was not introduced as being about file sharing or online piracy: the questions were said to be feeding into research on how consumers feel about films, music and games.

File sharers

Free downloading or file sharing is a very common phenomenon across virtually all socio-demographic groups of the Dutch population. Forty-four percent of those with internet access – that is, the Dutch internet population over the age of 15 – admit to file sharing on one or more occasions in the previous 12 months, which works out at around 4.7 million people. Most Dutch file sharers download music (40 percent of those who have internet access), followed at some distance by films (13 percent) and games (9 percent). Extrapolated to the Dutch population over the age of 15, we are talking an estimated:

- 4.3 million music sharers;
- 1.4 million film sharers;
- 1.0 million game sharers.

The young are particularly keen file sharers, with the 15–24-year age bracket strongly over-represented. Over 60 percent of them download music, around 20 percent films and games. File sharers are also relatively often male, particularly when it comes to films (74 percent) and games (61 percent) – a difference that is not explained by differences in film and game consumption. Regional differences are negligible and differences in education levels tend to be age-related, implying that respondents have not yet finished their studies.

A notable finding is that a large number of file sharers are unable to say what method or technology they use for downloading (e.g., P2P, Usenet, newsgroups, FTP address). Women and the over-35s often have no idea of the methods they themselves are using. Eighteen percent of music sharers sometimes download promotional site offerings, while all users of promotional sites were found to download from other – unlawful – sources. Most file sharers said they only engaged in downloading and did not upload. This would seem improbable as most P2P programs upload automatically. It seems quite likely that many file sharers are simply unaware that they are uploading. A mere one in 20 file sharers admits to adding new uploads themselves (e.g. recently bought music, films or games). The Dutch do much less paid-for downloading than they file share. Strikingly, the percentage of the population who have paid to download at some point in the past is significantly higher than the number of paying downloaders over the past 12 months. It would seem that paid-for downloads have not been attractive enough for people to keep doing it. As Figure 9.2 shows, most consumers see no difference between paying or not paying for downloads in terms of ease of use (57 percent), availability (54 percent) or quality (60 percent).

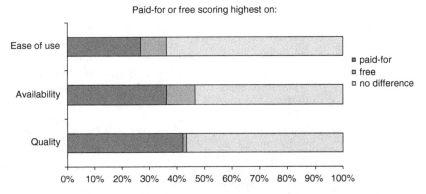

Figure 9.2 Perceptions of paid-for vs. free downloading (N = 1,500)

Those who do see a difference rate paying for downloads as the better option.

File sharing versus buying behavior

Buyers still outnumber file sharers by a wide margin. This is true for music, films and games, with **84** percent of the Dutch population over the age of 15 having bought – or paid to download – a CD, DVD or game in the past year. In fact, buying and file sharing often go hand in hand.

Music sharers are no less or more likely to be buyers of music than other people: 68 percent of downloaders also purchase music. And file sharers who buy music do not buy any more or less of it than non-file sharers, although they buy more merchandise and go to concerts significantly more often. As for films, file sharers turn out to buy DVDs no less or more often than anyone else: 61 percent of film sharers also buy DVDs. But if they buy, they buy significantly more DVDs than non-file sharers. On average, file sharers and non-file sharers go to the cinema equally often. Game sharers also buy games, and significantly more frequently too: 67 percent of file sharers are buyers as well. And if they buy, they buy significantly more games than non-file sharers. These results are summarized in Table 9.1.

Table 9.1   Differences in purchasing behavior between file sharers and non-file sharers

	Music	Films	Games
Buyers in the past 12 months: Yes/No	No difference	No difference	File sharers buy more often (61% vs 57%)
If a buyer in previous 12 months: number	No difference	File sharers buy more (12.0 vs 8.0 films)	File sharers buy more (4.2 vs 2.7 games)
Related products	File sharers typically visit concerts more often and buy more merchandise	No difference in cinema visits	No difference in buying merchandise
Total	No differences in buying music, but file sharers typically visit concerts more often and buy more merchandise	File sharers buy more DVDs	File sharers buy more games

Among file sharers, 63 percent of music downloaders might yet buy the music they first got for free online (see Table 9.2). Their main reasons for buying are loving the music – a key motive for over 80 percent – or wishing to support the artist (over 50 percent). Owning the CD sleeve and booklet are mentioned by a third of eventual buyers, as well as the higher quality of the CD.

Forty-eight percent of film sharers will buy a previously downloaded film at a later date, citing such reasons as liking it a lot or wanting the extra features the DVD offers. Between 50 percent and 60 percent say they download to discover new genres and directors/actors.

Game sharers also report sometimes buying a previously downloaded game at a later date; 63 percent of them do this. Their main reasons include thinking it a really good game. Wanting to own the original box and game were also frequently mentioned.

The fact that file sharing and buying are not mutually exclusive (and can even occur for the same title) is an interesting finding, but does not resolve all cause-and-effect issues: after all, aficionados of music, games or films will typically buy more, get into related products more but also download more. And so this finding does not give the definitive answer to what consumers would do if file sharing did not exist or became impossible. When asked point blank, the majority of consumers say they would *not* change their purchasing habits. Respondents claiming they would buy more and those saying they would buy less are roughly balanced, even if a slightly larger group feel they would buy *less music and fewer DVDs*, while the sale of *games* and visits to the *cinema* would go *up* according to the response of a slightly larger group. One possible explanation could be that discovering new music, films and games is a key driving force behind file sharing, as is meeting demand driven by lack of purchasing power.

Table 9.2   File sharers buying content after having previously downloaded (frequency and percentage)

Frequency (Number of times a year)	Music sharers	Film sharers	Game sharers
0	37%	52%	37%
1–2 times	30%	28%	39%
3–6 times	21%	10%	21%
6–12 times	7%	8%	2%
> 12 times	5%	2%	1%
Total	100%	100%	100%

Willingness to pay

The survey asked file sharers what they would consider a reasonable price for a CD, film or game they would really like to own. Please note that this is more than what they would be willing to pay on average for the products they are downloading and that this provides a better indication of the turnover producers might be missing out on due to file sharing. Figure 9.3 reveals what percentage of file sharers considers particular prices to be reasonable. Three-quarters of music sharers are willing to pay at least €8 for a CD (see also Table 9.4). The average 'reasonable price' for music is higher than for DVDs, at €5.

If willingness to pay (WTP) is defined by the highest average price mentioned, however, CDs prove the most appreciated and DVDs the least, a rather remarkable outcome in view of the current pricing structure in the market. If we look at the outcomes as presented in Table 9.3, another picture emerges: prices for CDs are fairly consistent and the differences between the top quartile and the 75 percentile relatively

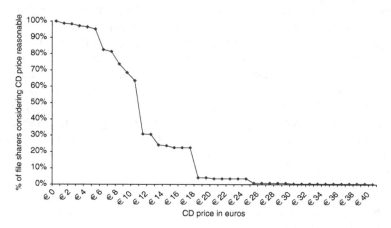

Figure 9.3   Music sharers find a reasonable price for a much-wanted CD

Table 9.3   Reasonable price according to file sharers

	Music	Films	Games
75 percentile	€8	€5	€7
Median	€9	€9	€19
Top quartile	€12	€11	€24

small – a result of little price differentiation in the market. Films are a rather different story, and the gap is extreme for games. These various perceptions would seem to reflect market differentiation as it currently exists. The games market breaks down into two categories – PC games and console games – that are known for their wide range in prices. This explains the large differences in the games category.

Motives and perceived effects

File-sharing sites are more than an alternative to buying. For one thing, file sharing offers an easy way to sample new genres, bands/artists, actors and games (Table 9.4). Many consumers download music, films or games that they would never have bought because of unfamiliarity.

Such sampling does not detract from physical format sales and might, in fact, create extra demand if consumers decide they wish to own music, a film or game after sampling it. In cases such as these, file-sharing websites might, in fact, increase the diversity of supply – or at the very least the perceived supply or the diversity of the supply these consumers have access to. Also, file-sharing sites have a social function for over 10 per cent of file sharers, a unique feature of this channel that is not shared by physical formats – nor by websites where one pays for downloads.

Respondents feel that the possibility of free downloading has a *positive effect on the accessibility* and diversity of music, films and games. File sharers, in particular, rate the positive effect highly.

File sharers and non-file sharers alike agree that free downloading is *negative* for *music artists, actors and game designers as well as record companies and film and game producers*. The effect on the *quality* of supply is *neutral*, especially according to file sharers.

Effects on industry turnover and welfare

This section places the findings of the consumer survey in a broader perspective by comparing them with other research conducted in the

Table 9.4 Functions of file-sharing sites: percentages of file sharers listing function

	Music	Film	Games
Discovering new genres	69	61	67
Discovering new bands, artists, actors, games	69	56	85
Making social contacts	13	13	14

Netherlands and elsewhere. It also presents estimates of the total number of files downloaded from unauthorized sources every year and critically discussed the international scientific literature about the impact of file sharing on the purchase of music, films and games, focusing primarily on recent studies (mainly 2006 and 2007) conducted independently of any direct stakeholders and whose publication was subject to editorial peer review.

Downloaders and downloads

Downloading from unauthorized sources is a widespread and growing global phenomenon. The number of people in the Netherlands who download music, films or games without paying is relatively large because of the high broadband penetration in the country, yet well in line with British and American figures. Across the board internationally, music downloading is by far the most common form of file sharing, followed at some distance by films and games.

Whereas estimates of the volume of unauthorized download traffic vary strongly, it is clear that it accounts for many billions of files per year worldwide and makes up a substantial share of international internet traffic. Based on a compilation of various sources, estimates for the Dutch market have been put at 1.5–2 billion music downloads per year, or 7.5 downloads for each track sold in the Netherlands. Note, however, that these are highly tentative calculations based on several – at times contradictory – sources.

How file sharing relates to sales

The literature describes various mechanisms through which file sharing results in an increase or, conversely, a decrease in digital media sales, or has no impact on sales whatsoever. These mechanisms are summarized in Table 9.5. The most prominent positive effect is the sampling effect: consumers are introduced to new music and this creates new demand.

When downloading serves consumers whose demand is driven by a lack of purchasing power, the effect on sales is neutral. File sharing has a negative impact on buying when it replaces paid-for consumption. The specific characteristics of music, films and games explain both the relationship between file sharing and buying and why download volumes differ greatly between these genres. The findings of empirical studies into the causal or other relationships between downloading and buying music vary widely, ranging from positive to neutral to negative. The studies are methodologically complex and some criticism can be

Table 9.5   Possible effects of file sharing on the purchase of CDs, films, games, and related products

Positive +	1. File sharing introduces consumers to music, films and games (and to artists and genres), thus creating demand. This is known as the sampling effect (Shapiro and Varian, 1999; Liebowitz, 2006) 2. File sharing allows consumers to pool their demand, resulting in increased demand* 3. File sharing enhances willingness to pay and demand for concerts and related products (complementary demand). 4. File sharing enhances the popularity of products, boosting demand driven by a lack of purchasing power (network effect)**
Neutral =	5. File sharing meets the demand of consumers who are not, or not sufficiently willing to pay and subsequently are not served by the manufacturer. 6. File sharing meets a demand for products that are not offered by manufacturers (e.g. film files for iPods).
Negative –	7. File sharing substitutes for the purchase of music, DVDs or games or cinema visits (substitution). 8. File sharing results in the deferred purchase of music, DVDs or games, at a lower price than the price at launch. 9. Sampling results in sales displacement as a result of fewer bad buys.***

Notes:

*This applies in particular to the exchange of media with friends rather than to the anonymous exchange through P2P networks.

**This applies in particular to the use of software for which network effects are clear. A (modest) network effect may also be found for lifestyle products such as music, films and games. Unauthorized use can also, under certain circumstances, have a positive effect on profits and investments without network effects as it can weaken competition between products. See: Jain (2008).

***Rob and Waldfogel (2006) show that on average people's appreciation of music is lower after it has been bought or downloaded than prior to the purchase.

raised about many of them. All in all, files sharing seems to have only a moderate effect on physical audio format sales. This is in line with the observed global downturn in sales. That said, there does not appear to be a direct relationship between the decline in sales and file sharing. The state of play in the film industry has been less researched to date, but available findings unanimously suggest a negative relationship. In the games industry download volumes are low and the implications unknown. Due to the empirical subtlety of the relationship between file sharing and sales and the diverse underlying mechanisms, it is very difficult to determine the relationship on a title by title basis. Measuring the possible harmful effect of a specific uploader's content is even more difficult, if not downright impossible.

Static analysis of welfare effects of downloading music

One clear conclusion that can be drawn from the deliberations above is that every file downloaded does not result in one less CD, DVD or game sold. The degree of substitution is difficult to determine and controversial, yet we can state with certainty that there is no one-on-one correlation between file sharing and sales. Below we seek to describe the economic scope of file sharing and its short-term effects. The analytical framework used is a welfare-theoretical approach. Rob and Waldfogel (2006) used a similar approach to calculate the welfare gains and losses for the music industry based on the relationship found between downloading and purchasing music. The premises of this approach are illustrated in the stylized Figure 9.4, where the diagonal line represents the demand (D) for CDs in relation to price. In a situation where there is no file-sharing activity, a Q_0 number of CDs will be sold at price P_{cd}, resulting in a turnover of $P_{cd} \times Q_0$ (the lightly shaded rectangle 'TURNOVER'). Given the high fixed costs and the low marginal costs that are so characteristic of the entertainment industry, in this particular case the gains for the producer – the producer surplus – roughly equal turnover.[1] Consumers may also benefit in that some would have been prepared to pay a higher price for a CD than they actually paid. Taken

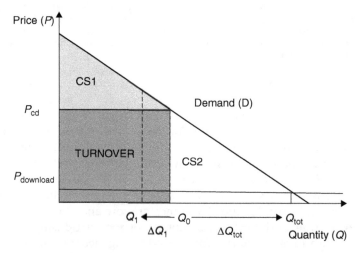

Figure 9.4   Media demand and wealth effects of file sharing

together, these amounts constitute the consumer surplus, represented by the darkly shaded triangle (CS1) in the graph. The creation of welfare in the economy is defined as the consumer surplus plus the producer surplus.[2]

Now assume that consumers have the opportunity of downloading the product. The horizontal line $P_{download}$ represents the costs (in terms of effort and time) of file sharing. Far more consumers (Q_{tot}) are interested in the CD at this lower price and consumption of the CD increases by ΔQ_{tot} because consumers who initially were not prepared to pay the higher price now buy the product (Table 9.5, effect 5). At the same time, however, some of the consumers who used to buy the CD may now download the music, resulting in a reduction in demand for the CD by ΔQ_1 (substitution: Table 9.5, effect 7). In this stylized example this would amount to a total of $\Delta Q_1 + \Delta Q_{tot}$ consumers downloading the CD, resulting in turn in lost revenues for producers (in this case this is equated with a lower producer surplus) of $\Delta Q_1 \times P_{cd}$. This wealth is not lost but goes directly into the pockets of consumers who choose to download rather than to buy, thus creating additional consumer surplus. Even more consumer surplus is created and represented in the graph as the triangle between demand D, the initial vertical line Q_0 and the download costs $P_{download}$. This is a new surplus compared with the initial situation and constitutes welfare gains to society.

In summary, we saw that in this stylized static analysis substitution resulted in a redistribution of welfare (producer surplus becoming consumer surplus) without a net effect. Meeting demand that is not driven by purchasing power creates welfare gains for society. The positive impact of file sharing on sales, mainly attributable to sampling, results in a lower degree of substitution.[3] If the sampling effect or other positive effects were to dominate, demand would even increase on balance and both the consumer and the producer surplus would rise. The above effects can be quantified with the aid of:

- the number of downloads of music, films and games ($\Delta Q_1 + \Delta Q_{tot}$);
- the number of file sharers who would buy music if downloading were not possible (ΔQ_1);
- file sharers' (average) valuations or WTP.

Above we emphasized the diversity and controversiality of the estimated effects. Figures for the number of downloads per day showed considerable variation and consumers themselves found it hard to reliably quantify the amount of material they had downloaded. Based on the available material, we put the number of music downloads in the Netherlands ($\Delta Q_1 + \Delta Q_{tot}$) at *1.5–2 billion per year*. The market value for all these downloads amounts to the same volume in euros. Note, however, that this may not be equated with lost revenues.

The next step is to determine the extent of substitution. Based on the number of downloads given above, a substitution ratio of 20 percent, as used by Rob and Waldfogel (2006), would seem unrealistically high as this would imply that 300–400 million fewer tracks are sold as a result of file sharing, which is equivalent to 1.5–2 times the downturn in sales reported for the Dutch music industry since 1999. Taking Peitz and Waelbroek's (2004) estimate as an upper limit, namely that a 20 percent decline in total sales may be attributed to file sharing, which is still relatively high, this would result in lost revenues of, at most, €100 million in the Netherlands. This, in turn, is equivalent to a *substitution ratio of at most 5–7 percent*, or one track less sold for every 15–20 downloads.

The third step is to determine the value of downloads that do not result in substitution, known as the additional consumer surplus. We have pointed out that every file downloaded may not be assumed to lead to one less track sold; similarly, it would not be correct to assume that the value of free downloads – the additional consumer surplus – equals the retail value of the downloads. This is expressed in the stylized Figure 9.4: in addition to substitution, the real rise in demand as a result of file sharing may be attributed to demand that is driven by a lack of purchasing power. As shown in the graph, the welfare gains would be more or less equal to half the retail value of the downloads. Rob and Waldfogel (2006) found that, on average, students' valuation of downloaded music was one-third to half lower than that for purchased music.

The additional consumer surplus can be estimated using data about file sharers' WTP. These data were collected in the consumer survey and were depicted in Figure 9.3. The area under the curve in Figure 9.3 is equal to the weighted average 'reasonable price' given by the file sharers, namely €10.67 for a CD. Multiplying this reasonable price by the 69 percent of respondents who said they would 'probably' or 'most probably' buy the CD for this price, puts the average actual WTP for a much-wanted downloaded CD at €7.36. This is 40 percent lower than the average price of a CD sold in 2007 (€12.31) and is well in line with the 33–50 percent lower valuation found by Rob and Waldfogel and the estimate of half the price that can be derived from Figure 9.4.[4] Figure 9.3 also shows that about one quarter of file sharers felt that a price that was higher than the average retail price of €12.31 would still be reasonable. Again, adjusting this for the likelihood that consumers will actually buy the CD for that price means that roughly 17 percent of all file sharers would be willing to buy the CD for the retail price if downloading were not possible. This percentage is slightly lower than the 20 percent found by Rob and Waldfogel, but much higher than the 5–7 percent derived from the estimates made by Peitz and Waelbroeck. An important difference, however, is that this substitution ratio does not relate to all downloads, but to highly valued downloads only.[5]

In order to calculate the additional consumer surplus, one cannot simply multiply the WTP for *highly valued music* by the total download volume of 1.5–2 billion tracks a year. Much-wanted downloads tend to be the downloads that file sharers keep. Young consumers keep the equivalent of an average of 8–16 months of downloaded material on their computers or players. Based on this calculation, the consumer surplus represented by file sharers' built-up download collections amounts to about 60 percent of the retail value. English research shows that the music collections of young people (under the age of 25) equals about 1,000 MP3s, suggesting an additional consumer surplus of around €600. For the 25-plus age bracket, the average download collection totaled 200 MP3s per person, which is equivalent to a surplus of around €120. Downloaded music files for all music sharers taken together represent a value of €1–1.5 billion.

This value has been built up over a period of several years, in some cases even from as early as the launch of Napster in 1999. The *consumer surplus* created by music sharing in the Netherlands would then amount to an estimated minimum of *€200 million per year.* Based on the above assumptions, this is a conservative estimate (collections have been estimated to have been built up over a long period of time, namely an average of five to eight years, and the surplus for deleted downloads has been set at zero). At most half this amount is generated at the expense of the producer surplus and therefore constitutes a transfer of welfare. The remainder constitutes welfare gains. Needless to say, these calculations are necessarily based on assumptions and contain many uncertainties. Many of the underlying data are not precisely known. That said, it is clear that the direction and magnitude of the amounts calculated are plausible. An annual surplus of €200 million for 1.5–2 billion downloaded tracks gives an average value of 10–13 cents per track, about one eighth to one tenth of the cost of tracks (€0.99) on iTunes and other sites.

The consumer survey referred to earlier showed that not all music genres are equally popular among file sharers. Whereas classical music is downloaded relatively infrequently, file sharing of genres such as soul/urban, experimental, rock, dance and pop is all the more frequent. This is in line with the fact that the younger age brackets are fervent file sharers.[6] Sales of these popular youth genres are therefore likely to be more heavily impacted by file sharing. That said, a one-on-one relationship has not been found. The consumer survey revealed that experimental and avant-garde music are frequently downloaded even though few respondents actually stated a preference for these genres. In this light it is worth taking a closer look at Blackburn's (2004) findings, which showed that while popular music artists are negatively impacted by file sharing, lesser known artists benefit. In principle, this development favorably affects the diversity of supply, yet a decline in income from popular artists can put pressure on investments in talent development.

Contrary to Zentner's (2006) observation that international repertoire is more popular among young, frequent file sharers, and that national repertoire, which tends to be more readily appreciated by older generations, suffers less from file sharing, there is no evidence for the Netherlands showing that Dutch music is downloaded any less, or more, than other music genres. Conversely, according to figures provided by the Dutch association for producers and importers of image and sound carriers (NVPI), the market share of classical CD sales has dropped from a stable 10 percent up until 2002 to 5 percent in 2005.

These examples underline once again that the relationship between the drop in CD sales and file sharing is an ambiguous one: the frequency of downloading does not always correspond to the popularity of a particular music genre, and the shift in sales figures and market shares of different genres cannot be directly related to download frequency.

Price trends

Figure 9.5 shows price trends for an average CD, DVD, game or cinema visit. As discussed, turnover from sales of music recordings has plummeted. As average nominal prices have remained more or less stable, average prices have dropped in real terms. By comparison, prices of purchased and rented DVDs/VHSs have also remained virtually stable over the years. The price of cinema tickets has risen in line with general inflation (which averaged 2.2 percent per year). The average price of games has fluctuated strongly over time, presumably in part

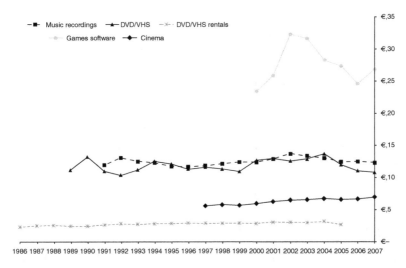

Figure 9.5 Nominal price trends in market segments of the entertainment industry

as a result of the large price difference between PC games and console games.

Combining Figure 9.1 and Figure 9.5 would reveal that turnover of the three segments taken together (cinemas, DVD/VHS rentals and sales) has risen from around €306 million in 1999 to €571 million in 2005 (even reaching €642 million in 2004). No figures are available for DVD rentals for the years after 2005, but the upturn in cinema takings and DVD sales following the dip in 2005 is expected to have positively impacted DVD rentals as well.

Conclusions and policy recommendation

The degree to which the decline in music sales may be attributed to file sharing is under discussion, as was emphasized in the fourth section of this chapter. Overall static welfare effects of file sharing, however, are highly positive due to the fact that most file sharing is no substitute for buying music and hence creates additional welfare. Only an estimated 1 in 20 downloaded tracks leads to a track less sold. The question remains how file sharing and digitization affect the music industry in the long term. Are the welfare effects still positive from a dynamic perspective? And how do business models in music respond?

The second section dealt at length with developments relating to new business models in the entertainment industry. It presented a number of explanations for the fact that the music industry was the first to suffer the effects of the rise and workings of file sharing. Whereas the music industry long failed to respond to the changing needs of consumers, file sharing has succeeded in meeting these needs. Online and mobile music sales are showing impressive growth, yet have so far failed to make good the losses suffered by the record industry. The consumer survey also showed that many consumers who have on occasion downloaded from paid-for sites have stopped doing so, suggesting that the initial content offered did not meet their expectations. A disappointed customer is not likely to come back.

As music is steadily acquiring the characteristics of a public good, the industry is now focusing on other sources of income that derive value from music's broad accessibility. Live concerts constitute an ever-growing source of income. In line with this, the industry is increasingly focusing on sponsorship contracts, 360-degree contracts and merchandising.

Ticket prices for live concerts have shot up in recent years. This development – and its acceptance by consumers – should be seen in conjunction with the growing commoditization of music, just as the acceptance of port dues is enhanced by the neighboring lighthouse. Conversely, the interviews with active file sharers showed that the sharp increase in the price of live concerts is being used by consumers to justify their file-sharing activities. This development seems to be irreversible, or at least difficult to reverse. At the same time we see that artists, in particular artists at an early stage in their career, are gaining access to new, accessible channels to market their wares, such as MySpace and YouTube. New market concepts such as Sellaband are also successfully responding to the democratization of talent development. More commercially, concepts such as *Idols* manage to combine a successful TV program with talent development and promotion, reducing the commercial risks of the resulting recording in the process. For established artists, marketing and income-generating models are being developed where income is generated not so much directly by music recordings, but increasingly by live concerts, merchandising and sponsorship. Determining the extent to which these sources of income make good the losses in the market for physical audio formats is difficult on the basis of the information publicly available. That said, the new models still cater for music recordings, but show that in the future the industry is not likely to be able to survive profitably on music recordings alone.

In addition to the growing importance of live concerts, sponsorship and merchandising, recent developments in the area of value creation include such initiatives as alliances between the mobile phone and music industries. At the same time we see that file sharing impacts the rest of the economy through spin-off revenues. The current demand and willingness to pay for fast broadband connections, for example, is most probably generated by file sharing. In economic terms, consumers pass on part of the surplus they derive from file sharing in the form of increased demand and a greater willingness to pay for fast internet connections. In view of this, it is clear why internet service providers (ISPs) are inclined to play a backbench role when it comes to combating file sharing. Rather than being each other's natural enemies, ISPs and copyright holders could equally well become each other's allies if they succeed in clinching innovative deals, such as jointly offering internet connections in combination with flat-fee access to content.

Recommendation 1: an urgent need for innovative business models in music

The music industry is suffering from a decline in sales. It is therefore tempting to point the blame at file sharing as the main or sole cause. Yet the challenge is to capitalize on the dynamics of the digital age by responding to the new reality created by users and by reinventing business models. The survey held among Dutch internet users has shown that file sharing is here to stay and that people who download are at the same time important customers of the music industry. The point of no return has been reached and it is highly unlikely that the industry will be able to turn the tide. What is more, there is no guarantee that a situation will ever arise in which a majority of digital downloads will come from an authorized source. Whatever the future brings, the time that will pass between now and a 'clean' future is too long for the industry to sit back and wait, without making an effort to innovate. And so the music business will have to work actively towards innovation on all fronts. New models worth developing, for example, are those that seek to achieve commercial diversification or that match supply and end-user needs more closely. The advance of 360-degree contracts is a step towards greater diversification of sources of income and underlines the clear connection that exists between various revenue sources in different music markets. Innovation in the music business should step outside the box of the traditional value chain and venture into a host of other markets related to the entertainment industry and beyond – for example, through the creation of value networks. It should not be restricted to new distribution or marketing channels – forging new alliances and combinations for newly developed products and services seems to be the only way to successfully tackle the implications of file sharing for the industry, at least for the time being. A strategy that focuses solely on lawsuits and DRM is not the best response, in particular as it remains to be seen whether a fully authorized, paid-for downloading market would generate sufficient revenues to revive the music industry. Even in a hypothetical future without file sharing, a hybrid business model would appear to be the only solution. It is up to government, as part of its cultural policy and its policy to strengthen the country's innovative power and competitive edge, to consider identifying the promotion of innovation in the music industry – in combination perhaps with the film industry – as a key priority. The industries studied here are now necessarily in a phase of transition, given the nature of the business and its products, which could pave the way for similar processes in other domains of the economy. Subsequently, the government should monitor developments with respect to new business models. Will the delivery of official downloads be the most appropriate response to declining sales, or are more radical changes needed? Will the industry sufficiently be able to reinvent itself? This study has also shown that information about certain major sectors of the industries researched here, such as the live music sector, is in short supply. It is often claimed that live concerts are growing at the expense of CD sales, but much remains uncertain about the magnitude of the assumed growth and the degree to which it could make good the loss in CD sales. The industries concerned and the Dutch government would do well to gain a better insight into this issue through systematic data collection, in particular if government intends to keep close tabs on the development of file sharing.

Recommendation 2: don't 'criminalize' individual end users – educate them

File sharing and P2P networks have become generally accepted practices and important drivers for innovation. Moreover, file sharers turn out to be very important, if not the most important, costumers of the music industry. It would therefore be ill advised to criminalize file sharing by end users on the grounds that the content is from an illegal source or because of the uploading aspects of P2P traffic. Experience outside the Netherlands has shown that the effect of enforcement tends to be temporary and may, in fact, have adverse effects, in that it alienates the industry from its customers. Enforcement can be undertaken either by the industry itself (civil actions, rules of liability), or by public enforcement authorities (criminal enforcement). Recent policies (not only at national but also European level) are in favor of civil enforcement by the industry itself, in which case the various interests of the industry as a whole and of individual end users should be carefully weighed. That said, the provision of information and education is still vital, if only because research has shown that there is still much uncertainty among both users and suppliers about what is – and is not – permitted. We also saw that many consumers are ill-informed about the techniques used and unaware of the fact that they are often downloading and uploading at the same time. A better awareness of what is and is not lawful is also important in relation to the acceptance of new business models. There is a role to play here for government – and for the industry itself.

Recommendation 3: enforcement against commercial copyright infringement

The law provides right holders with a range of enforcement measures, in particular with respect to unauthorized uploading on a commercial and large scale – preferably in line with, or after new business models have been developed, thus creating real alternatives. In the case of civil enforcement against large-scale uploaders, right holders and other parties in the distribution chain could join forces. This should not, however, be undertaken at the expense of the basic principles of justice such as proportionality, legal certainty and the protection of fundamental rights and procedural justice. Criminal enforcement should serve only as an ultimate remedy – which is in keeping with current government policy in the Netherlands. An additional problem for enforcement is that it is very difficult to establish a direct relationship between file sharing and purchasing behavior, as was illustrated in the fourth section. This implies that it is virtually impossible to measure the damage caused by the uploading activities of individuals. Effects of individual uploads on the sales of individual albums, films and games, generally range from negative, via neutral to positive. And taking revenues from live concerts and sponsor deals into account, the 'damage' from file sharing becomes even more elusive, particularly with respect to isolated titles or peers. This conclusion has important consequences regarding the proportionality and viability of both civil and criminal enforcement.

Notes

1. To be more precise: the marginal costs are low, but the fixed recording costs (or costs of developing a game) have already been incurred and are 'sunk'. In order to determine the absolute producer surplus, the fixed costs need to be subtracted from total revenues. The current approach suffices for an estimation of relative differences.
2. In some policy areas, such as the supervision of mergers, the producer surplus is not included, assuming that companies are able to look after themselves and that government's primary responsibility is towards consumers/citizens.
3. In Rob and Waldfogel's calculation (2006), the transfer amounted to $25 per student in the period 1999–2003. The welfare gains for society stood at $70 per student, almost three times the transfer.
4. Figure 9.3 also shows at which price maximum turnover from downloading would be achieved – namely €10. Demand drops steeply at higher prices (such as the current average of €12.31).
5. Note also that this is only one side of the coin – namely substitution. A positive contribution of the sampling effect could explain why actual impact on turnover is lower.
6. Note that according to the NVPI, the Dutch market share of classical CD sales has dropped from a stable 10 percent, up until 2002, to 5 percent in 2005. This underlines once again that the relationship between the drop in CD sales and file sharing is an ambiguous one.

References

Ballon, P. (2007) 'Business Modelling Revisited: The Configuration of Control and Value', *The Journal of Policy, Regulation and Strategy for Telecommunications, Information and Media*, Vol. 9, No. 5, pp. 6–19.

Blackburn, D. (2004) 'Online Piracy and Recorded Music Sales' Mimeo available at http://citeseerx.ist.psu.edu/viewdoc/summary?doi=10.1.1.117.2922

Frost, R.L. (2007) 'Rearchitecting the Music Business: Mitigating Music Piracy by Cutting Out the Record Companies', *First Monday*, Vol. 12, No. 8.

Jacobs, D. (2007) *Adding Values: The Cultural Side of Innovation*, Arnhem: Artez Press.

Jain, S. (2008) 'Digital Piracy: A Competitive Analysis', *Marketing Science*, pp. 1–17.

Liebowitz, S.J. (2006) 'File Sharing: Creative Distruction of Just Plain Destruction', *Journal of Law and Economics*, Vol. XLIX, April, pp. 1–27.

Margetta, J. (2002) *What Management Is*, New York: Free Press, quoted in Jacobs (2007).

OECD (2005) *Digital Broadband Content: Music*, Paris: OECD.

Peitz, M. and P. Waelbroeck (2004) 'The Effect of Internet Piracy on Music Sales: Cross-Section Evidence', *Review of Economic Research on Copyright Issues*, Vol. 1, No. 2, pp. 71–9.

Premkumar, G. (2003) 'Alternate Distribution Strategies for Digital Music', *Communications of the ACM*, Vol. 46, No. 9, pp. 89–95.

Rob, R. and J. Waldfogel (2006) 'Piracy on the High C's: Music Downloading, Sales Displacement, and Social Welfare in a Sample of College Students', *Journal of Law and Economics*, Vol. XLIX, April, pp. 29–62.

Rutten, P. and van Bockxmeer, H. (2003) *Cultuurpolitiek, auteursrecht en digitalisering (Cultural Politics, Copyright and Digitization)*, Delft: TNO Strategy, Technology and Policy.

Shapiro, C. and H.R. Varian (1999) *Information Rules: A Strategic Guide to the Network Economy*, Boston: Harvard Business School Press.

Vaccaro, V.L. and D.Y. Cohn (2004) 'The Evolution of Business Models and Marketing Strategies in the Music Industry', *International Journal on Media Management*, Vol. 6, No. 1 and 2, pp. 46–58.

Zentner, A. (2006) 'Measuring the Effect of File Sharing on Music Purchases', *Journal of Law and Economics*, Vol. XLIX, April, pp. 63–90.

10
The Make-or-Buy Decision in ICT Services: Empirical Evidence from Luxembourg

Ludivine Martin

Introduction

In the context of economic globalization, firms need to increase their adaptability and flexibility to assure competitiveness in their market. To manage their activities effectively, firms are resorting increasingly to outsourcing and/or offshoring of activities both for the manufacture of products and for the inputs included in the production process. Outsourcing has been called 'one of the greatest organizational and industry structure shifts of the century' with the potential to transform the way firms organize their activities (Drucker, 1998).

The number of articles dedicated to these phenomena has increased in recent years (Gonzalez et al., 2006; Grossman and Helpman, 2005; Marin and Verdier, 2003). A lot of papers consider the outsourcing of materials (Antras and Helpman, 2004; Hubbard and Baker, 2003), but also there is a large literature on the outsourcing of different business services (Abramovsky and Griffith, 2006; Arnett and Jones, 1994; Barthélemy and Geyer, 2005). The concepts of outsourcing and offshoring suffer from the lack of a common definition as underlined by Loh and Venkatraman (1992) for outsourcing and by Jahns, Hartmann and Bals (2006) for offshoring. The definitions adhered to in this chapter follow Abramovsky and Griffith (2006).

The outsourcing decision occurs when firms choose to 'buy' rather than 'make' in-house (see Figure 10.1). It involves greater specialization as firms switch from sourcing inputs internally to sourcing them from external suppliers. The offshoring decision occurs when firms move production overseas, either made by their own foreign affiliates or purchased from outsourced suppliers.

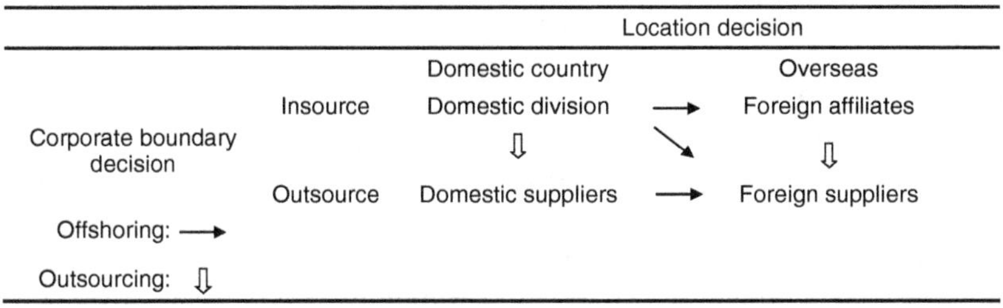

		Location decision	
		Domestic country	Overseas
	Insource	Domestic division ⟶	Foreign affiliates
Corporate boundary decision		⇩ ↘	⇩
	Outsource	Domestic suppliers ⟶	Foreign suppliers
Offshoring: ⟶			
Outsourcing: ⇩			

Figure 10.1   Outsourcing and offshoring concepts
Source: Abramovsky and Griffith (2006, p. 595).

Research conducted on outsourcing and offshoring decisions, in most cases, broadly relates to four topics. The first topic is related to the drivers of a firm's choice (Abramovsky and Griffith, 2006; Arnett and Jones, 1994; Barthélemy and Geyer, 2001, 2005; Diaz-Mora, 2007). The second topic focuses on the characteristics of the products delivered by outsourcers and the management of the relationship between the firm and the outsourcer or the firm located abroad (Bhatnagar and Madon, 1997; Currie and Seltsikas, 2001). The third most important topic concerns the effect on firm success in terms of productivity (Altinkemer et al., 1994; Heshmati, 2003; Holger et al., 2008; Ohnemus, 2007). Finally, the fourth main topic discussed in the literature is the macroeconomic consequences of the phenomena (Amiti and Wei, 2005; Chongvilaivan and Hur, 2008; Chongvilaivan et al., 2008). The literature provides both theoretical background (Chalos and Sung, 1998; Antras and Helpman, 2004) and/or empirical studies (Abramovsky and Griffith, 2006; Diaz-Mora, 2007).

In this chapter we focus on firms that decide to outsource and/or offshore activities related to information and communication technology (ICT) needs. In most firms, ICT is not within the core competencies of the firm, so the phenomena of outsourcing and/or offshoring have grown during the last decade. In 2006, 44 percent of firms located in the European Union (EU with 27 countries) chose to outsource a part or all of their ICT services (Ohnemus, 2007). *The Economist* has published a survey on outsourcing, in which the growing development of IT outsourcing, especially in Asia, is pointed out (*The Economist*, 2004).

As underlined by several papers, the phenomena have undergone a lot of transformations. Ketler and Walstrom (1993), Vassiliadis, Stefani, Tsaknaki and Tsakalidis (2006), Yang and Huang (2000) provide histories of these changes. As underlined by Watjatrakul (2005), the last decade has brought new changes to the phenomena. Indeed, with the e-commerce revolution, the outsourcing of ICT services like Internet service outsourcing, application service outsourcing and business process outsourcing as appeared. The outsourcing (or offshoring) activities studied in this chapter covers three types of ICT services the firm used in the production process. In accordance with Arnett and Jones (1994), these ICT activities can be classified as: hardware, software and 'comprehensive management activities'. Hardware covers ICT systems integration, installation, development and administration of firm's networks and technical support. Software activities include software development, programming and user help and support. 'Comprehensive management activities' concerns e-business, database, website, ICT systems management and administration.

Moreover, technological changes favor the compatibility and tradability of many services across the world (Goodman and Steadman, 2002; Abramovsky et al., 2004). Many services can be performed thousands of miles away from the customer. Consequently, a lot of firms outsource abroad – for example, their call centre or invoice and payroll services. With a quick skimming over of the literature we can observe that outsourcing is extensively documented concerning the motivations behind outsourcing, in particular, the benefits (i.e., cost reduction, the ability to focus on core competencies, technological leadership etc.) and the risks (i.e., vendor opportunism, lock-ins, contractual difficulties etc.). The ICT services studied in our analysis can be easily transferred across firms, especially the programming and network needs of the firm. Consequently, the costs of transaction between the firm and its supplier are reduced and beyond the cost of outsourcing. As firms are cost minimizing, the demand for outsourced services depends on the relative cost of producing the services in-house compared to outsourcing. This cost may vary across firms depending on, notably, the size of the firm and its investment in ICT. Concerning ICT investment we can formulate an ambivalent hypothesis. First, according to Abramovsky and Griffith (2006), we can suppose that a firm's investment in ICT can diminish the cost of outsourcing and favor this phenomenon. Second, conversely, if the firm has internal ICT competencies it can reduce the cost of managing in-house ICT services and thus reduce the resort to outsourcing.

We conduct our empirical analysis using a large and nationally representative dataset at the firm unit level. The dataset comes from the Luxembourg part of the 'ICT Usage and e-Commerce in Enterprises' survey collected in 2007. It gives some information about the characteristics of the firm surveyed and covers: computers and communication technologies use; Internet access and use; purchases via the Internet or other computer networks. Thanks to a specific topic included in 2007 in the survey we have information on ICT competencies in the firm unit and the demand for ICT services produced by external suppliers and/or by foreign firms.

In order to empirically analyze the impact of ICT usage on decisions to outsource ICT services, and as we have a lot of information on firms' ICT usage, a data-mining technique (a multiple correspondence analysis followed by a cluster analysis) is performed to form groups of ICT users relative to how much they use 20 ICTs (such as, intranet, enterprise resource planning, usage of Internet to make purchase online etc.). We analyze the make-or-buy choices of firms through a bivariate probit on non-exclusive choice of outsourcing and offshoring. To take care of the potential endogeneity of ICT investment, as underlined by Abramovsky and Griffith (2006), we construct predicted value of ICT investment choices through a multinomial probit and include these variables in the bivariate probit (Angrist, 2001).

The results show that resources play a positive role on the choice to outsource and offshore ICT activities. Concerning ICT investment, after the control of its potential endogeneity, we observe that firms with the highest specific ICT needs choose to find these services from external suppliers or firms located abroad, especially when their ICT competencies measured by the presence of ICT/IT specialists are low. Conversely, firms which have also high ICT needs but associated with the employment of ICT/IT specialists don't seem to resort to external services providers. Finally, it appears that a high trust in data transfer favors the choice of outsourcing ICT services.

The remainder of this chapter is organized as follows. In the next section we present both theoretical and empirical literatures concerning the outsourcing and offshoring of ICT services in order to formulate our research hypotheses. The third section details the database. In a fourth section, we present the empirical methodology used to analyze the factors that can affect the decision to outsource and/or offshore ICT services. The fifth section presents the empirical results of regressions computed. Finally, the sixth section concludes.

Research hypotheses

The objective of our study is to explore the determinants of outsourcing and/or offshoring decisions concerning ICT services. As underlined by Diaz-Mora (2007), Curzon Price (2001) and Kimura and Ando (2005), the first phenomenon concerns the ownership dimension of the production of ICT services and the second, the geographical dimension of the choice. As firms are cost minimizing, their decisions depend on the relative costs to produce in-house or to purchase services on the market for the first dimension. The second dimension concerns the location of the production of the services: the firm has to choose between the production by a foreign subsidiary or by an independent foreign firm.

Built on Abramovsky and Griffith (2006) and Grossman and Helpman (2005), we can make clear the various costs firms need to evaluate before taking their decisions to insource or outsource their activities and the relative costs of resident production against foreign production. The costs of the firm when it chooses to produce in-house depend on drivers such as its resources, its needs, its competencies, its productivity and its size. The cost of purchasing goods or services on the market includes the market price and other costs of outsourcing that are firm-specific. These costs cover identifying needs, adjusting the services to the real needs of the firm, finding the best provider on the market, the transaction costs on market and the costs of writing contracts and monitoring their execution. These costs can be diminished by the bargaining power of the firms for negotiation and renegotiation of contracts. Transaction cost theory assumes that the market is always the lowest-cost producer of a good or a service (Coase, 1937). However, factors like internal competencies can lead firms to choose an internal governance mode.

Focusing on ICT outsourcing, we analyze services inducing both short-term or long-term contracts. If the ICT activity the firm wants to outsource concerns software without maintenance, spot transaction on the market can be used. However, for other activities such as network maintenance the relationship has to be a long-term one. Consequently, market transaction costs can be higher than internal ones if the relationship between firms has a long-term nature and if it concerns a very specific need. Moreover, if the need is very specific, it involves giving a great quantity of information to the outsourcer, such as detailed instructions and specifications, but ICT facilitates the communication of such information. The trade-off between in-house production of ICT needs and outsourcing depends on the characteristics of the firm. In accordance with their business activities, firms have greater or lesser needs in terms of software sophistication and of security of data management. Large firms have more available resources to produce internally but at the same time their needs are bigger than those of small ones. Furthermore, the larger the resources and competencies of the firm, the higher its bargaining power. Consequently, transaction costs are reduced for negotiation and renegotiation of contracts. Thus, we can formulate the following hypothesis concerning resources.

Hypothesis 1

Firms with large resources and needs in particular should favor the outsourcing of business activities. The choice between in-house and external production can vary according to the firm's investment in ICT. Following Abramovsky and Griffith (2006) and Magnani (2006), we can suppose that technologies affect the cost of outsourcing. Technological diffusion in firms seems to facilitate outsourcing because it 'induces convergence of firm-specific skill to general skill over time' (Magnani, 2006, p. 618). So it increases the transferability of services across firms and reduces the specificity of the transaction. Moreover, investments and usages of ICT, especially those devoted to Internet, are likely to influence others costs of outsourcing such as the costs of finding the best outsourcer in the market and the costs of monitoring the execution of the contract. ICT competencies and skills should also reduce the adjustment costs of the services purchased to the firm's needs. Furthermore, as underlined by Willcocks, Lacity and Fitzgerald (1995), firms need to retain sufficient in-house capability in order to be able to manage the outsourcer and the measurement systems to make sure that the contract goes smoothly. ICT activities induce, indeed, hidden cost and uncertainty about the quality of the services provided by the outsourcer. So, it is not surprising that some firms choose to retain in-house a part of their ICT activities.

But if the firms have enough internal ICT competencies the costs of producing in-house can be lower than those induced by outsourcing. However, ICT competencies can affect the needs of the firm. When the firm accumulates ICT competencies, it can develop new needs that are more specific and that induce the firm to resort to an external service provider. We can therefore formulate an ambivalent hypothesis.

Hypothesis 2

As a firm's investment in ICT tends to diminish the cost of outsourcing it can favor the phenomenon. Conversely, if the firm has sufficient ICT competencies it can reduce the cost of managing in-house ICT services.

Data

The data used to analyze the characteristics of enterprises which have decided to outsource and/or offshore ICT activities during 2006 have been collected by CEPS/INSTEAD, with the support of STATEC and EUROSTAT. The survey was conducted by post during the second quarter of 2007 among firms employing ten persons and more and operating in almost all sectors of the economy. Among the 3,144 firms surveyed, 1,955 responded – that is to say, a response rate of 62 percent. The data collected give information about the characteristics of the firm and its business and about the investment and use of different ICTs (computer, Internet etc.).

The data used do not apply to firms that are not computerized (50 firms) because without this tool they cannot adopt any ICT. Our sample consists of 1,905 enterprises computerized and employing ten persons or more.

Firms' characteristics

The descriptive statistics concerning the characteristics of the firms surveyed are available in the Appendix. We have information on the business in which the firm operates. The sectors surveyed are: industry, construction, trade, tourism,[1] transport (of merchandise), finance[2] and services. The most represented sectors in our sample are trade and construction, with each one nearly 25 percent of the sample. We also know the size of the firms. We use the classification of the European Union concerning small (10–49 employees), medium-sized (50–249) and large firms (250 and more). The large majority (78 percent) of the firms surveyed are small ones. In order to capture the organizational structure, we introduce two dummy variables: the first equals one when the firm is a subsidiary of a group and the second equals one when the firm has more than one legal unit in its organization. Of the firms in the sample, 12 percent are multi-unit firms.

ICT investment

In order to analyze the impact of ICT usage on decisions to outsource and offshore IT services, and as we have a lot of information on firms' ICT usage, a data-mining technique is used to form groups of ICT users based on their usage of 20 ICTs. We can distinguish four groups of ICT variables:[3] common ICT essentially used to communicate in the firm and with external partners;[4] management ICT used to manage the production and distribution processes;[5] firms' trust in the security of data transfer on virtual networks thanks to their use of e-government and e-commerce;[6] and the fact of having ICT/IT specialists among employees. As these ICT uses are binary qualitative variables, a multiple correspondence analysis followed by a cluster analysis is performed. The cluster analysis allows the grouping of individuals into classes that are as homogeneous as possible according to their similarities with respect to all variables. The classification was based on the coordinates of individuals on the axes we obtain with a multiple correspondence analysis (MCA).[7] The hierarchical clustering method we perform uses the Ward index to measure the distance between two classes.[8] Table 10.1 summarizes the main characteristics of ICT classes created by the hierarchical clustering methodology. We perform a Student T-test to find significant differences between classes in terms of ICT investment.[9]

The class A groups together small ICT users, for which all averages are below those calculated on the whole sample. For all types of ICT studied, this class always exhibits a significantly less use of ICT than other classes. Class B uses less common ICT and management ICT than the whole

Table 10.1 ICT usage in the 'ICT classes'

	Class A	Class B	Class C	Class D	Whole sample
Sum of common ICT	0.67	1.97	2.41	4.83	2.14
	(0.815)	(1.144)	(1.278)	(1.465)	(0.566)
T-test	A<B<C<D				
Sum of management ICT	0.90	1.50	4.61	3.19	2.22
	(1.122)	(1.510)	(1.667)	(2.408)	(2.123)
T-test	A<B<D<C				
Indicator of trust (sum of Internet use)	0.59	1.78	2.19	2.13	1.71
	(0.762)	(0.848)	(0.942)	(0.977)	(1.030)
T-test	A<B<C=D				
Employment of ICT/ IT specialists	0.01	0.17	0.20	0.58	0.20
	(0.077)	(0.375)	(0.400)	(0.495)	(0.402)
T-test	A<B=C<D				
Observations	332	936	352	280	1900

Note: Standard development are in parentheses. T-test: '=' when there is no significant difference between classes.

sample average, but has a level of trust in data transfer and of employment of ICT/IT specialists close to the sample average. Compared with other classes, this class use less ICT than classes C and D, but it is not different from C in the employment of ICT/IT specialists. Class C includes firms that use ICT intensively and for which the average adoption rates are greater than the sample average, except for the employment of ICT/IT specialists. Compared with other classes, class C uses management ICT more extensively, but it is not different from B in the employment of ICT/IT specialists, or from D in the trust in data transfer on the Internet. Firms in class D use common ICT intensively, as well as a lot of management ICT (but less than class C). Firms in this class have a high trust in data transfer on the Internet, but this does not differ from class C. D is the class in which a majority of firms employs ICT/IT specialists.

If we turn again to Hypothesis 2, formulated above, we can expect that classes that use ICT intensively should choose to resort to external service providers more than others as ICT diminishes the costs of outsourcing (Abramovsky and Griffith, 2006). Moreover, the classes for which the use of ICT seems specifically targeted – such as class C, which uses a lot of management ICT – can benefit from external firms specializing in advanced ICT/IT services. In contrast, firms that decide to employ ICT/IT specialists are expected to have low internal costs when they choose to produce in-house and consequently they are expected to resort less to outsourcing. Moreover, the higher the confidence in online transfer of data, the less the risk aversion to using networks to manage relationships with external providers or with firms located abroad. This trust should favor outsourcing and offshoring decisions.

Econometric methodology

The control of the potential endogeneity of ICT investment

We correct for potential endogeneity of ICT usage in the decision to buy ICT services by using results of a multinomial probit of the ICT class the firm belongs to. We construct predictions of ICT class membership and include these variables in the outsourcing and offshoring choice regression (Angrist, 2001). For identification, we need independent variables that affect ICT class membership without affecting make-or-buy decisions directly. Short of instruments like ICT usage of the firm one year before or 'input prices', we are only able to propose imperfect instruments. Nevertheless, we construct variables of ICT diffusion in the town where the firms are located one year before the conduct of the survey we use.

The choice of these instrumental variables gives the best indication of the adoption of ICT by the firm in *t-1* and is justified by various empirical studies on ICT diffusion. The importance of spatial effects on ICT adoption as been, indeed, notably underlined by Galliano and Roux (2008) and Forman, Goldfarb and Greenstein (2005). Thus we construct five new variables relating to the average number of common ICTs in the town in 2006, the percentage of firms: having at least one ICT management system; undertaking e-commerce (purchasing and selling); and using at least one e-government practice. As some of these variables are drivers of the determination of ICT class membership, they could serve as potential instruments.

The latent variables for the kth alternatives, $k=1,...,K$ is:

$$\eta_{ik} = \alpha' Z_i + \beta' X_i + \xi_k \tag{1}$$

with X_i a vector of firms' (*i*) characteristics and Z_i the 'instruments'. The $\xi_1,...,\xi_K$ are distributed independently and identically standard normal. The firm chooses the alternatives q such that $\eta_{iq} > \eta_{ik}$ for $q \neq k$. The probability that the alternative q is chosen is:

$$\Pr(\text{choice of q}) = \Pr(\eta_{iq} > \eta_{ik}, k=1,...,K, k \neq q) \tag{2}$$

The choice of outsourcing and offshoring

To analyze outsourcing and offshoring decisions we chose to perform a bivariate probit model.

This model estimates jointly the choices of firms. Thus, there exists for every choice j ($j = 1$ if the firm outsources, $j = 2$ if the firm offshores) a latent variable (y^*_{ji}), a vector of firms (*i*) characteristics X_i and ICT_i the ICT class of the firm, such as:

$$y^*_{ji} = \beta'_j X_{ji} + \varphi'_{ji} ICT_{ji} + \varepsilon_{ji} \tag{3}$$

As y^*_{1i} and y^*_{2i} are unobserved, instead we observe y_{ji} if $y^*_{ji} > 0$ and $y_{ji=0}$. And we assume that $E(\varepsilon_j)=0$, $var(\varepsilon_j)=1$ and $cov(\varepsilon_1, \varepsilon_2)= \rho$.

The errors of the two equations are jointly distributed and not independent, as in the binary probit model. The coefficient ρ reflects the correlation that can exist between the error terms of the two equations. This methodology is performed with and without the control of the potential endogeneity of ICT investment. First, we introduce the ICT classes created by the data-mining procedure we mobilized. Second, we introduce the predictions of ICT class membership calculated from the multinomial probit. When we introduce predicted variables, the stand-ard errors are bootstrapped in order to correct for biases arising from the inclusion of predicted variables in the explanatory variables.

Econometric analysis

Multinomial probit regression to control of the potential endogeneity of ICT investment

To take care of the potential endogeneity of ICT investment on out-sourcing and offshoring as underlined by Abramovsky and Griffith (2006), we construct predictions of ICT class membership and use these as instruments in the bivariate probit analysis (Angrist, 2001; Mairesse and Robin, 2009). Table 10.2 presents the results of a multinomial probit (10) where we use the exclusive ICT classes as the dependent variables. E-government usage in the town of the firm in *t-1* drives belonging to class B and C, two classes for which the indicator of trust in data trans-fer is above the sample average. For the class D, it is the use of common ICT in the town in *t-1* that is the main driver among instruments. As this class has a high average number of ICT, it is not surprising that this instrument is determinant. Concerning firms' characteristics, Table 10.2 shows that, relative to belonging to class A (small users), evolving in the sector of industry, finance or services favors belonging to class D. The size of the firm influences the class of ICT user the firm is likely to be. Thus, medium size indicates belonging to the top classes (C and D) and large size increases the firm's predisposition to be in class D. Moreover, multinomial probit reveals that belonging to a group posi-tively affects belonging to classes B, C or D relative to belonging to class A (small users).

As underlined by various empirical studies about ICT diffusion, resources play an important positive role on ICT investment (Dholakia and Kshetri, 2004; Lal, 1999; Lucchetti and Sterlacchini, 2004). Thus, the probability of belonging to class D (large users of ICT) and employ-ing at least one ICT/IT specialist is higher when the firm belongs to a group or employs 50 persons or more. Finally, the multi-unit dummy introduced to capture the effect of the coordination needs of firms located in various places doesn't reveal any effect, whatever the class considered. The model is significant but the predictive power is rela-tively poor. Overall, the percentage of correctly predicted cases is 51 percent. This problem is often met in papers using such a method to calculate some variables (e.g., Cassiman and Veugelers, 2006) and, thus, seems to be inherent to the method employed.

Table 10.2   Multinomial probit of 'ICT classes'

	Class B	Class C	Class D
Instruments			
Average sum of common ICT in the town in t–1	0.063 (0.112)	0.014 (0.125)	0.317** (0.149)
Percentage of firms with at least one management ICT in the town in t–1	0.284 (0.387)	1.216*** (0.438)	–0.004 (0.594)
Percentage of firms using e-government in the town in t–1	1.128** (0.499)	1.281** (0.566)	0.524 (0.749)
Percentage of firms doing online purchases in the town in t–1	–0.111 (0.388)	0.102 (0.458)	–0.272 (0.515)
Percentage of firms selling online purchases in the town in t–1	0.085 (0.591)	0.966 (0.662)	0.072 (0.807)
Firms' characteristics			
Business sector (Ref.: Trade)			
Industry	0.441** (0.185)	0.09 (0.196)	0.51** (0.227)
Construct	0.222* (0.133)	–0.375** (0.146)	–0.178 (0.195)
Tourism	0.552** (0.246)	–0.604* (0.309)	0.061 (0.349)
Finance	1.192*** (0.390)	0.37 (0.419)	2.053*** (0.403)
Transports	0.24 (0.177)	–0.759*** (0.211)	0.202 (0.235)
Services	0.714*** (0.161)	0.058 (0.177)	1.294*** (0.192)
Size (Ref.: Small)			
Medium	0.208 (0.139)	0.313** (0.152)	0.587*** (0.163)
Large	0.338 (0.447)	0.779 (0.482)	1.561*** (0.466)
Belonging to a group	0.262** (0.130)	0.405*** (0.143)	0.984*** (0.149)
Multi-unit organization	0.196 (0.157)	0.156 (0.173)	0.261 (0.191)
Constant	–0.809** (0.404)	–1.762*** (0.466)	–2.222*** (0.592)
Observations	1900		
LL full	–2141,17		
% correctly classified	51%		

Class A is the base outcome. Robust standard errors in parentheses.
Coefficient significant at 10%*; 5% **; and 1%***.
Class A is the base outcome. Robust standard errors in parentheses.

Bivariate probit to analyze the choice of outsourcing and/or offshoring

The results obtained with a bivariate probit about the non-exclusive outsourcing and offshoring choices concerning ICT services are presented in Table 10.3.

The fact that the coefficient of correlation (ρ) is significant, no matter what the specification, underlines that our choice of econometric modeling that estimates simultaneously the two equations instead of two unrelated probit models is justified.

The main coefficients of interest in the study are those concerning ICT investment, but control variables capturing firms' characteristics are also included. Main effects of characteristics are stable despite the introduction of ICT classes. As we can observe, industry, construction, tourism and transport seem to resort less, as compared to the trade sector, to outsourcing and offshoring. Conversely, firms which evolve in financial and insurance activities seem to resort more than others to outsourcing but are not different from trade for the offshoring decision.

This result is not surprising given that, since 2003 (Law of 2 August 2003), a specific Luxembourgish regulation governs the conditions under which financial firms can outsource ICT services. Thus, service providers must be accredited by the 'Commission de Surveillance du Secteur Financier' (CSSF). This regulation aims to ensure the security and confidentiality of data managed by these firms. Furthermore, public authorities wish to develop efficient ICT services providers that can provide their services to firms in the financial sector located abroad. Firms employing 50 persons and more seem to resort more to subcontracting and offshoring than small ones. The fact of belonging to a group seems to play in the same direction, and it increases the probability of outsourcing by around 10 percent. As formulated in Hypothesis 1, large resources are synonymous with the choice to outsource and offshore at least some of the ICT services that the firm needs. All ICT classes seem to choose to outsource and offshore their ICT services to some degree, more frequently compared to class A (small users). As we suspect ICT investment choices are endogenous, we introduce predicted values of ICT investment in our analysis to formulate a conclusion about Hypothesis 2. Table 10.5 presents the results of our analysis of outsourcing and offshoring decisions where the exclusive classes of ICT usage are calculated based on the predicted probabilities of the multinomial probit results (11). This correction procedure minimizes the effect of firms' characteristics impacting on outsourcing decisions.

As underlined by Abramovsky and Griffith (2006), the results without the introduction of instruments are downward biased. Thus, apart from for transport, sectors are always significant. Thus, industry, tourism and construction still have a smaller probability of resorting to external firms than trade, and finance seems to resort more than other sectors to outsourcing.

Firms' size and the fact of belonging to a group, variables that capture resources, still have a positive influence, as we expect when we formulate Hypothesis 1. Conversely, for the offshoring regressions, some of the results obtained without the introduction of instruments have disappeared. With the introduction of instruments instead of ICT class, except construction, all sectors are non-significant. However, for variables concerning resources, the effects are confirmed by the two-step analysis and thus substantiate Hypothesis 1. Concerning the coefficients of predicted value of ICT classes, the correction of endogeneity induces some results that differ from the analysis without instrumentation. Table 10.4 shows that the results on ICT investment are more in line with those expected than those obtained without endogeneity correction. Thus, ICT classes are no longer all significant. Thus, being an ICT user of class D has no impact on outsourcing or even on offshoring. This result confirms the ambivalence that we assess, in Hypothesis 2. Thus, employing ICT/IT specialists seems to reduce in-house costs of production and consequently leads firms not to use external service providers or firms located abroad, as in class A (small ICT users).

Conversely, firms which belong to class B or class C have the biggest probability, relative to class A, of resorting to outsourcing. For class B, the positive effect can be linked to their high trust in data transfer on virtual networks; even if their ICT needs seem to be low, the absence of ICT/IT specialists drives those firms to appeal to external firms to manage their internal network of communication, for example. Moreover, as their needs are not very specialized, the transactions are often one-off deals or can be executed via short-term contracts. Thus, the market can produce such services cheaper than internal production. For class C, the positive effect can be linked to their high trust in data transfer and to their heavy use of management ICT, which is more specialized and needs to be tailored to the firm's high need for security for payments of invoices, for example.

Class C is the only class with a significant coefficient for the offshoring decision. This effect can be linked with their high use of ICT, which reduces the cost of using providers located abroad, and to the fact that they don't have enough internal competencies to cover their specific

Table 10.3 Biprobit of outsourcing and offshoring decisions without instrumental variables

	Outsource	Marg. eff.	Offshore	Marg. eff.	Outsource	Marg. eff.	Offshore	Marg. eff.
Firms' characteristics								
Business sector (Ref.: Trade)								
Industry	-0.262** (0.112)	-0.1010	-0.292** (0.126)	-0.0687	-0.308*** (0.114)	-0.1177	-0.349*** (0.130)	-0.0759
Construct	-0.494*** (0.085)	-0.1887	-0.638*** (0.105)	-0.1450	-0.493*** (0.088)	-0.1876	-0.602*** (0.109)	-0.1309
Tourism	-0.392** (0.157)	-0.1474	-0.444** (0.183)	-0.0952	-0.39** (0.162)	-0.1461	-0.404** (0.184)	-0.0836
Finance	0.7*** (0.150)	0.2699	0.203 (0.135)	ns	0.618*** (0.157)	0.2412	0.025 (0.144)	ns
Transports	-0.364*** (0.116)	-0.1383	-0.315** (0.130)	-0.0731	-0.35*** (0.118)	-0.1328	-0.311** (0.134)	-0.0685
Services	0.08 (0.089)	ns	-0.142 (0.098)	ns	0.011 (0.092)	ns	-0.261** (0.104)	-0.0608
Firms size (Ref.: Small)								
Medium	0.291*** (0.079)	0.1157	0.21** (0.085)	0.0586	0.253*** (0.079)	0.1004	0.141* (0.086)	0.0370
Large	0.642*** (0.180)	0.2488	0.433** (0.185)	0.1335	0.567*** (0.181)	0.2219	0.247 (0.185)	ns
Belonging to a group	0.28*** (0.073)	0.1111	0.662*** (0.078)	0.1942	0.224*** (0.075)	0.0887	0.581*** (0.078)	0.0318
Multi-unit organization	0.143 (0.093)	ns	0.133 (0.100)	ns	0.122 (0.094)	ns	0.121 (0.101)	ns

ICT class (Ref.: Class A)

Class B	-0.176*** (0.063)		0.662*** (0.091)	0.2564	0.689*** (0.139)	0.1741
Class C			0.82*** (0.106)	0.3169	0.965*** (0.148)	0.3027
Class D			0.745*** (0.123)	0.2890	1.155*** (0.158)	0.3809
Constant	-0.918*** (0.071)		-0.723*** (0.095)		-1.579*** (0.132)	
Pr(Yi=1) predicted	0.4425	0.181	0.4473		0.1681	
Observations	1905		1905			
Mac Fadden R2	0.076		0.105			
LL null	-2081.18		-2081.18			
LL full	-1923.66		-1864.43			
Correlation (rho)	0.696*** (0.029)		0.682*** (0.03)			
Wald test of rho=0	chi2(1) = 240.579***		chi2(1)= 221.824***			
% Correctly classified	89.40%		91.23%			

Coefficient significant at 10%*; 5% **; and 1%***; ns: coefficient not significant.

Table 10.4 Costs of outsourcing and offshoring decisions with prediction of 'ICT classes'

	Outsource	Marg. eff.	Offshore	Marg. eff.
Firms' characteristics				
Business sector (Ref.: Trade)				
Industry	−0.345**	−0.1314	−0.269	ns
	(0.170)		(0.196)	
Construct	−0.575***	−0.2176	−0.549***	−0.1263
	(0.175)		(0.198)	
Tourism	−0.638**	−0.2276	−0.391	ns
	(0.322)		(0.358)	
Finance	1.273***	0.4408	0.682	ns
	(0.440)		(0.491)	
Transports	−0.345	ns	−0.099	ns
	(0.255)		(0.277)	
Services	0.249	ns	0.089	ns
	(0.296)		(0.343)	
Size (Ref.: Small)				
Medium	0.361***	0.1432	0.228*	0.0633
	(0.114)		(0.131)	
Large	1.296***	0.4424	0.732*	0.2426
	(0.373)		(0.411)	
Belonging to a group	0.503***	0.1983	0.755***	0.2224
	(0.173)		(0.194)	
Multi-unit organization	0.094	ns	0.112	ns
	(0.101)		(0.112)	
Predicted ICT class (Ref.: Predicted class A)				
Predicted class B	2.163*	0.8535	1.099	ns
	(1.152)		(1.362)	
Predicted class C	1.704*	0.6723	1.907*	0.4976
	(0.917)		(1.085)	
Predicted class D	−0.763	ns	−0.252	ns
	(1.377)		(1.635)	
Constant	−1.573**		−1.946**	
	−0.643		(0.789)	
Pr(Yi ™ = 1) predicted	0.4408		0.1785	
Observations		1900		
Mac Fadden R2		0.084		
LL null		−2081.18		
LL model complete		−1906.6591		
Correlation		0.696***		
		(0.029)		
Wald test of rho = 0		chi2(1) = 238.152***		
% correctly classified		90.05%		

Bootstrapped standard errors in parentheses.
Coefficient significant at 10%*; 5% **; and 1%***; ns: coefficient not significant.

needs, especially in management ICT. As they have the same average as the whole sample for the employment of ICT/IT specialists, it is a sign of the presence of the effect underlined by Willcocks et al. (1995).

According to these authors, some firms choose to retain in-house a part of their ICT competencies to facilitate the adjustment of purchase services on the market and to ensure the execution of contracts with external services providers functions well, especially when the distance is high. The absence of impact of class B can be linked with of the fact that these firms' ICT needs are smaller than the sample average (see Table 10.1) and can be covered by external suppliers mostly located in the country.

Conclusion

In this chapter, we sought to analyze the determinants of firms' choice in terms of outsourcing and/or offshoring of ICT activities. As underlined by Watjatrakul (2005), the decade starting in 2000 saw the phenomena evolve significantly, with, notably, the e-commerce revolution. At present, the outsourcing of ICT services is quite large. The outsourcing (and/or offshoring) of ICT activities studied in this chapter covers three types of ICT services. In accordance with Arnett and Jones (1994), these ICT activities can be classified as: hardware, software and 'comprehensive management activities'. Hardware covers ICT systems integration, installation, development and administration of a firm's networks and technical support. Software activities include software development, programming and user help and support. 'Comprehensive management activities' concerns e-business, database, website, ICT systems management and administration. As underlined by Diaz-Mora (2007), Curzon Price (2001) and Kimura and Ando (2005), the outsourcing phenomenon concerns the ownership dimension of the production of ICT services and the offshoring phenomenon concerns the geographical dimension of the production of these services. As firms are cost minimizing, their decisions depend on the relative costs of producing in-house or purchasing services on the market, in the first place. Second, we looked at the location of the production of the services: the firm has to choose between using a foreign subsidiary or an independent outside firm.

First, we try to find in the theoretical and the empirical existing literature the drivers that can modify the cost of producing in-house and those of purchasing the services on the market, as well as the drivers that sustain the choice of outsourcing and/or offshoring. To facilitate the formulation of research hypotheses, we studied a database collected in 2007 in Luxembourg.

Second, in order to empirically analyze the impact of ICT usage on decisions to outsource ICT services, and as we had a lot of information on firms' ICT usage, a data-mining technique (a multiple correspondence analysis followed by a cluster analysis) is performed to form groups of ICT users based on how much they used nearly 20 ICTs (like intranet, enterprise resource planning, usage of Internet to make purchase online etc.). We analyze the make-or-buy choices of firms through a bivariate probit on non-exclusive choice of outsourcing and offshoring.

To take care of the potential endogeneity of ICT investment, as underlined by Abramovsky and Griffith (2006), we construct predicted value of ICT investment choices trough a multinomial probit and use these as instruments in the bivariate probit (Angrist, 2001). The results show that firms' resources positively influence the probability of choosing the outsourcing and offshoring of ICT activities. Concerning ICT investment, after the control of its potential endogeneity, we observe that firms with the most specialized ICT needs choose to find these services from external suppliers or firms located abroad, especially when their ICT competencies measured by the presence of ICT/IT specialists is low. Conversely, firms which have also high ICT needs but who employ higher numbers of ICT/IT specialists don't seem to resort to external services providers. Finally, it appears that a high trust in data transfer favors the choice of outsourcing ICT services. As we mentioned earlier, the predictive power of the first stage of our analysis, conducted to take into account the endogeneity of ICT investment, is poor. Consequently, we need to pursue research on methods to improve the determination of the various probabilities of belonging a class of small or high users. However, this limit doesn't seem to affect the results of the bivariate probit with the introduction of instruments, given that most of the results on resources remain the same. Another limitation of our study lies in the measure of the outsourcing and offshoring phenomena. Indeed, we only have global information on the fact of using these possibilities to obtain ICT services. Further research should address this limitation by finding precise information on the degree or the number of ICT functions outsourced or offshored by firms.

Appendix

Table A 10.1   Descriptive statistics of the variables introduced in the MCA

Variable	Mean	Std. Dev.
Common ICT		
Broadband connection	84.35%	0.3634
Intranet	47.55%	0.4995
Extranet	27.59%	0.4471
Video conference	9.16%	0.2886
Electronic forum	8.92%	0.2851
Electronic working group calendar	30.17%	0.4591
Group project scheduler	14.87%	0.3559
Management ICT		
Internal systems for re-ordering replacement supplies	22.75%	0.4193
Systems of invoices and payment, systems for managing	56.73%	0.4956
Logistics or services operations	29.14%	0.4545
ICT linked with suppliers' business systems	20.51%	0.4039
ICT linked with customers' business systems	23.99%	0.4271
Use of software for CRM	25.33%	0.4350
Use of ERP	19.17%	0.3937
Automatic processing of the reception or the sending of invoices in digital format	24.69%	0.4313
Firms' trust in the security of data transfer on virtual networks		
Use of Internet for interaction with public authorities for obtaining forms (tax forms)	83.47%	0.3716
Use of Internet for interaction with public authorities returning filled in forms	37.84%	0.4851
Selling product or services on Internet or on external computer networks	13.48%	0.3416
Doing purchases on Internet or on external computer networks.	35.89%	0.4798
Employment of ICT/IT specialists	20.26%	0.4020
Number of observations (weighted)	1905	(3075)

Table A 10.2   Descriptive statistics of the variables introduced in the econometric analysis

Variable	Mean	Std. Dev.
Outsource	44.44%	0.4970
Offshore	20.70%	0.4053
Firms' characteristics		
Trade	24.84%	0.4322
Industry	10.04%	0.3006
Construct	26.31%	0.4404
Tourism	3.46%	0.1828
Finance	5.51%	0.2282
Transports	8.82%	0.2837
Services	21.01%	0.4075
Small	77.71%	0.4163
Medium	18.50%	0.3884
Large	3.79%	0.1910
Belonging to a group	29.40%	0.4557
Multi-unit organization	12.39%	0.3295
ICT class		
Class A	17.88%	0.3833
Class B	48.79%	0.5000
Class C	18.77%	0.3906
Class D	14.55%	0.3527
Predicted ICT class		
Predicted class A	17.90%	0.0945
Predicted class B	48.81%	0.0893
Predicted class C	18.78%	0.0803
Predicted class D	14.52%	0.1583
Instruments		
Average sum of common ICT in the town in t-1	2.1399	0.5660
Percentage of firms with at least one management ICT in the town in t-1	43.00%	0.1260
Percentage of firms using e-government in the town in t-1	84.87%	0.1024
Percentage of firms doing online purchases in the town in t-1	36.36%	0.1355
Percentage of firms selling online in the town in t-1	11.71%	0.0787
Number of observations (weighted)	1900	(3067)

Notes

1. The tourism sector includes hotels, restaurants, travel agencies and companies operating in the market for passenger transport (by train, by car, by boat and by plane).
2. This sector includes both financial and insurance activities.
3. Descriptive statistics concerning these variables are available in the Appendix.
4. These common ICTs relate to having a broadband connection, the use of an intranet, an extranet, video-conference tools, electronic forums, electronic working group calendar and/or a group project scheduler.
5. These management ICTs are related to the use of tools for reordering replacement supplies, for managing invoices and payment, for monitoring logistics or service operations, to the use of ICT to be linked with suppliers' business systems and/or with customers' business systems, the use of enterprise resource planning (erp), the use of software application or customer relationship management (CRM) and/or, finally, the use of automatic processing of the reception or the sending of invoices in digital format.
6. In order to capture the trust of firm in data transfer on the Internet, we insert in our analysis their use of Internet for obtaining official forms (tax forms), for returning filled-in forms to public authorities and their use of Internet and other networks in order to sell products and to make purchases.
7. We retain the maximum number of axes of the calculations by the MCA.
8. The choice of the number of classes has been determined according to three rules: Je(2)/Je(1) and pseudo T-squared of Duda and Hart (1973) and pseudo-F of Calinski and Harabasz (1974). The number of classes retained is four.
9. We choose to build a score for the three groups of ICT (common ICT, management ICT, trust in data transfer) in order to summarize all the information given by the various ICT firms involved.
10. The benchmark case is the class A of small ICT users. Unlike the multinomial logit, this model with correlation between structural residuals does not suffer from the irrelevance of independent alternatives (IIA) problem.
11. As a robustness check, we estimate the model as a system of simultaneous equations, using full information maximum likelihood. With such a method we don't take into account the potential endogeneity and the results are close to those of model 2 with ICT classes.

References

Abramovsky, L. and R. Griffith (2006) 'Outsourcing and Offshoring of Business Services: The Role of ICT', *Journal of the European Economic Association*, Vol. 4, No. 2–3, pp. 594–601.

Abramovsky, L., R. Griffith and M. Sako (2004) 'Offshoring of Business Services and its Impact on the UK Economy', *Tech. Rep. IFS Briefing Note BN51*, AIM Briefing Note.

Altinkemer, K., A. Chaturvedi and R. Gulati (1994) 'Information Systems Outsourcing: Issues and Evidence', *International Journal of Information Management*, Vol. 14, pp. 252–68.

Amiti, M. and S.J. Wei (2005) 'Fear of service outsourcing: is it justified?' *Economic Policy*, CEPR, CES, MSH, Vol. 20, No. 42, pp. 308–47, 04.

Angrist, J. (2001) 'Estimation of Limited Dependent Variable Models with Dummy Endogenous Regressors: Simple Strategies for Empirical Practice', *Journal of Business & Economic Statistics*, Vol. 19, No. 1, pp. 2–16.

Antras, P. and E. Helpman (2004) 'Global Sourcing', *Journal of Political Economy*, Vol. 112, No. 3, pp. 552–80.

Arnett, K.P. and M.C. Jones (1994) 'Firms that choose outsourcing: A profile', *Information and Management*, 26, 179–88.

Barthélemy, J. and D. Geyer (2001) 'IT Outsourcing: Evidence from France and Germany', *European Management Journal*, Vol. 19, No. 2, pp. 195–202.

Barthélemy, J. and D. Geyer (2005) 'An Empirical Investigation of IT Outsourcing Versus Quasi-outsourcing in France and Germany', *Information & Management*, Vol. 42, pp. 533–42.

Bhatnagar, S. and S. Madon (1997) 'The Indian Software Industry: Moving Towards Maturity', *Journal of Information Technology*, Vol. 12, No. 4, pp. 277–88.

Calinski, T. and J. Harabasz (1974) 'A Dentrite Method for Cluster Analysis', *Communications in Statistics*, Vol. 3, pp. 1–27.

Cassiman, B. and R. Veugelers (2006) 'In Search of Complementarity in Innovation Strategy: Internal R&D and External Knowledge Acquisition', *Management Science*, Vol. 52, No. 1, pp. 68–82.

Chalos, P. and J. Sung (1998) 'Outsourcing Decisions and Managerial Incentives', *Decision Sciences*, Vol. 29, No. 4, pp. 901–19.

Chongvilaivan, A. and J. Hur (2008) 'Outsourcing, Labor Productivity, and Wage Inequality in US: A Primal Approach', *Applied Economics*, forthcoming.

Chongvilaivan, A., J. Hur and Y. Riyanto (2008) 'Outsourcing Types, Relative Wages, and the Demand for Skilled Workers: New Evidence from US Manufacturing', *Economic Inquiry*, Vol. 47, No. 1, pp. 18–33.

Coase, R. (1937) 'The Nature of the Firm', *Economica*, Vol. 4, No. 16, pp. 386–405.

Currie, W.L. and P. Seltsikas (2001) 'Exploring the Supply-side of IT Outsourcing: Evaluating the Emerging Role of Application Service Providers', *European Journal of Information Systems*, Vol. 10, No. 3, pp. 123–34.

Curzon Price, V. (2001) 'Some Causes and Consequences on Fragmentation: New Production Patterns in the World Economy', in S.W. Arndt and H. Kierzkowski (eds), *Fragmentation: New Production Patterns in World Economy*, Oxford: Oxford University Press.

Dholakia, R.R. and N. Kshetri (2004) 'Factors Impacting the Adoption of the Internet among SMEs', *Small Business Economics*, Vol. 23, No. 4, pp. 311–22.

Diaz-Mora, C. (2007) 'What Factors Determine the Outsourcing Intensity? A Dynamic Panel Data Approach for Manufacturing Industries', *Applied Economics*, Vol. 1, pp. 1–13.

Drucker, P. (1998) *Peter Drucker on the Profession of Management*, Cambridge, MA: Harvard Business School Press.

Duda, R. and P. Hart (1973) *Pattern Classification and Scene Analysis*, New York: Wiley.

Forman, C., A. Goldfarb and S. Greenstein (2005) 'How did Location Affect Adoption of the Commercial Internet? Global Village vs Urban Leadership', *Journal of Urban Economics*, Vol. 58, No. 3, pp. 389–420.

Galliano, D. and P. Roux (2008) 'Organisational Motives and Spatial Effects in Internet Adoption and Intensity of Use: Evidence from French Industrial Firms', *The Annals of Regional Science*, Vol. 42, pp. 425–48.

Gonzalez, R., J. Gasco and J. Llopis (2006) 'Information Systems Outsourcing: A Literature Analysis', *Information & Management*, Vol. 43, pp. 821–34.

Goodman, B. and R. Steadman (2002) 'Services: Business Demand Rivals Consumer Demand in Driving Job Growth', *Monthly Labor Review*, Vol. 125, No. 4, pp. 3–16.

Grossman, G.M. and E. Helpman (2005) 'Outsourcing in a Global Economy', *Review of Economic Studies*, Vol. 72, No. 1, pp. 135–59.

Heshmati, A. (2003) 'Productivity Growth, Efficiency and Outsourcing in Manufacturing and Services Industries', *Journal of Economic Surveys*, Vol. 17, No. 1, pp. 79–112.

Holger, G., A. Hanley and E. Strobl (2008) 'Productivity Effects of International Outsourcing: Evidence from Plant-level Data', *Canadian Journal of Economics/ Revue canadienne d'Economique*, Vol. 41, No. 2, pp. 670–88.

Hubbard, T. and G. Baker (2003) 'Make or Buy in Trucking: Asset Ownership, Job Design, and Information', *American Economic Review*, Vol. 93, No. 3, pp. 551–72.

Jahns, C., E. Hartmann and L. Bals (2006) 'Offshoring: Dimensions and Diffusion of a New Business Concept', *Journal of Purchasing & Supply Management*, Vol. 12, pp. 218–31.

Ketler, K. and J. Walstrom (1993) 'The Outsourcing Decision', *International Journal of Information Management*, Vol. 13, pp. 449–59.

Kimura, F. and M. Ando (2005) 'Two-dimensional Fragmentation in East Asia: Conceptual Framework and Empirics', *International Review of Economics and Finance*, Vol. 14, pp. 317–48.

Lal, K. (1999) 'Determinants of the Adoption of Information Technology: A Case Study of Electrical and Electronic Goods Manufacturing Firms in India', *Research Policy*, Vol. 28, No. 7, pp. 667–80.

Loh, L. and N. Venkatraman (1992) 'Determinants of Information Technology Outsourcing: A Cross-sectional Analysis', *Journal of Management Information System*, Vol. 9, No. 1, pp. 7–24.

Lucchetti, R. and A. Sterlacchini (2004) 'The Adoption of ICT Among SMEs: Evidence from an Italian Survey', *Small Business Economics*, Vol. 23, No. 2, pp. 151–68.

Magnani, E. (2006) 'Technological Diffusion, the Diffusion of Skill and the Growth of Outsourcing in US Manufacturing', *Economics of Innovation and New Technology*, Vol. 15, No. 7, pp. 617–47.

Mairesse, J. and S. Robin (2009) 'Innovation and Productivity: A Firm-level Analysis for French Manufacturing and Services using CIS3 and CIS4 Data (1998–2000 and 2002–2004)', under reviewed for *Economie et Prévision*.

Marin, D. and T. Verdier (2003) 'Globalization and the New Enterprise', *Journal of the European Economic Association, Paper and Proceedings*, Vol. 1, No. 2, pp. 337–44.

Ohnemus, J. (2007) 'Does IT Outsourcing Increase Firm Success? An Empirical Assessment using Firm-level Data', *Discussion Paper 07-087*, ZEW.

The Economist (2004) 'Faster, Cheaper, Better', 13 November 2004, p. 373 (Issue No. 8401).

Vassiliadis, B., A. Stefani, J. Tsaknaki and A. Tsakalidis (2006) 'From Application Service Provision to Service-oriented Computing: A Study of the IT Outsourcing Evolution', *Telematics and Informatics*, Vol. 23, pp. 271–93.

Watjatrakul, B. (2005) 'Determinants of IS Sourcing Decisions: A Comparative Study of Transaction Cost Theory versus the Resource-based View', *Journal of Strategic Information Systems*, Vol. 14, pp. 389–415.

Willcocks, L., M. Lacity and G. Fitzgerald (1995) 'Information Technology Outsourcing in Europe and the USA: Assessment Issues', *International Journal of Information Management*, Vol. 15, No. 5, pp. 333–51.

Yang, C. and J.-B. Huang (2000) 'A Decision Model for IS Outsourcing', *International Journal of Information Management*, Vol. 20, pp. 225–39.

11
An Empirical Analysis of Organizational Innovation Generated by ICT in Japanese SMEs

Hiroki Idota, Masaru Ogawa, Teruyuki Bunno, and Masatsugu Tsuji

Introduction

Small and medium-sized enterprises (SMEs) play an important role in Japanese economic development by supplying high-quality parts to the manufacturing sector. In fact, the superior quality of Japanese products can largely be attributed to SMEs. In the information age, Japanese SMEs must meet the challenges of global competition in order to survive. In this context, Japanese SMEs need to increasingly rely on information and communication technology (ICT) as a basis for organizational restructuring to improve performance and efficiency in all aspects of business activities.

In the present investigation, we conducted field surveys, a mail survey and in-depth interviews in two of Japan's most prominent SME clusters, located in Higashi-Osaka city in Osaka prefecture, and Ohta ward in the Tokyo metropolitan area. In 2004, questionnaires were sent to more than 6,000 SMEs in the two clusters, yielding nearly 1,200 responses. ICT use and innovative organizational restructuring were not extensive in those SMEs. Therefore, in 2005, we also sent a mail survey containing the same questions as the above field survey to SMEs identified as being among the 'top 100 SME business practices in the Kansai area' and the '100 best SMEs as selected by the Ministry of Economy, Trade and Industry (METI)' (subsequently referred to as the IT Hyakusen). We suspected that these SMEs would be using ICT extensively. Of the 336 SMEs contacted, we received 137 responses. The questions in the field and mail surveys dealt with (i) company characteristics (amount of capital, number of employees, etc.); (ii) managerial orientation (used to classify SMEs as expanding, incentive-providing, adapting, or data-using); (iii) business environment (e.g., degree of competition); (iv) purposes of ICT use (e.g., increasing profitability or productivity); (v) expectations for future ICT use; and (vi) other issues such as ICT investment in the previous fiscal year and perceived importance of ICT in business management.

Previous papers by Tsuji et al. (2005, 2010), Bunno et al. (2006a, 2006b, 2007) and Ogawa et al. (2009) attempted to construct a suitable index for ICT use by SMEs in order to identify factors, particularly management type and policies, that promote ICT use. Tsuji et al. (2005) identified the following items as good measures of ICT use by SMEs: (i) the amount of software to optimize use of managerial resources and (ii) Internet usage. Tsuji et al. (2005) constructed an index whereby each instance of simple software or the Internet was assigned a score of one point, while more complicated and integrated utilization was assigned a score of ten. While this scoring may seem somewhat arbitrary, it is consistent with Bunno et al.'s (2006a) contention that commonly used software or Internet usage, which occurs in many small SMEs, is less important and should contribute less to the ICT score. The point value for each type of software was assigned according to the percentage of SMEs that use it – that is, the number of points is reciprocal to percentage use. In other words, the more advanced and integrated the use, the more points were assigned to them.

Bunno et al. (2006b, 2007), Ogawa et al. (2009) and Tsuji et al. (2010) developed an index of ICT use by SMEs by applying the analytical hierarchical process (AHP). This ICT usage index is based primarily on the use of hardware and information systems, with 'hardware' including items such as (i) the number of PCs owned by the SME and (ii) the number of network-connected PCs, while 'information systems' include local area networks (LAN), software use, Internet use and security measures. The index also takes into account use of software for routine and non-routine work, use of the Internet to collect and distribute information or for e-commerce, and use of information systems for technical and organizational security measures. In order to calculate AHP level, 11 ICT experts were asked to reply to questions about the importance of each of these items.

One of the most important predictors of ICT usage was identified as the level of 'ICT expectation', which included such items as the perceived potential of ICT for 'restructuring the whole business process'. SMEs that use ICT extensively believe in its effectiveness and invest a significant amount in it. It follows then, that the most important way to promote ICT use among SMEs is to encourage them to be forward-thinking. Once they adopt such an outlook, SMEs can determine the specific ways in which they will implement ICT to meet their goals. Consistent with previous research (Delone, 1988; Martin, 1989; Yap et al., 1992; Thong and Yap, 1995; Igbaria et al., 1998; Caldeira and Ward, 2002), probit analysis revealed that the attitude and behavior of CEOs or top managers was also an important predictor of ICT adoption. Since ICT use is a function of business management and strategy, the decisions made by senior managers are crucial. Even if SMEs operate under optimal conditions, they will not be able to use new technologies to their advantage unless their managers make correct decisions. It was also found that certain policies, including tax and subsidy schemes as well as various deregulation measures, promoted ICT investment by SMEs.

We identified the level of ICT usage by each SME by applying the ICT index based on AHP, with the goal of identifying factors promoting ICT use. In addition, difference in ICT use and characteristics of two groups of SMEs, developed and underdeveloped SMEs, are analyzed using a variety of regression models, with the former group comprising SMEs in Higashi-Osaka/Ohta and the latter comprising the IT Hyakusen. In so doing, this chapter fully utilizes dummy variables to clarify the differences between two SME clusters; especially, in addition, to add dummy variables to the constant term, we attach them to coefficients of independent variables.

The chapter consists of seven sections. In the second section, we present a case study of a Japanese SME successfully implementing ICT. In the third section, we construct an ICT index of use by SMEs based primarily on AHP. We explain, in addition, the independent variables that are used to predict differences in ICT usage by SMEs. In the fourth section, we describe the ordinary least squares (OLS), logit and probit regression analyses employed to predict ICT use and identify factors that promote ICT use based on survey responses. In the fifth section, we discuss the influence of policies in promoting ICT adoption along with problems encountered by SMEs when implementing ICT. In the final section, we make concluding remarks and suggestions for future research.

Case study: a supply chain system that facilitates Japanese SME exports

Although SMEs were once the primary force behind Japanese exports, they were eventually supplanted by large companies. However, with the wider adoption of ICT, the pendulum appears to be swinging back. This section examines the case study of an SME that successfully implemented ICT as part of its organizational restructuring to create its own international supply chain.

Profile of the firm

Tabio is a sock manufacturer, wholesaler and retailer, established in 1968. The company sells its products through its own retail shops in London, as well as Japan. The company's head office is located in Osaka. Its total capital is approximately ¥333 million and it employs 82 workers (it is classified as an SME since it has is fewer than 100 employees).

Sock manufacturers can be divided into three categories:

- highly competitive national brands;
- specialized sock makers; and
- SME sock makers.

Tabio's socks are priced from ¥850–900 (approximately US$9–9.50) at its retail shops.

Since most of its customers – mainly schoolgirls – usually make monthly visits to the store, Tabio changes its stock every month. Customer information is collected through the firm's POS system, which is directly connected to its distribution centre as well as its suppliers (sock knitters). Tabio offers a wide range of designs and colors, 500 items in 12 colors for a total of 6,000 products, although it produces relatively few of each item. Store managers monitor sales in their stores and order products on a weekly basis, so as to ensure that they can offer a full range of socks to its young customers. Unlike many Japanese SMEs that have outsourced production to countries such as China, Tabio manufactures mainly in Japan.

Supply chain

Tabio's president initially wanted to locate its factories near the company's retail outlets, but this proved to be unfeasible. However, the company achieved a similar result by using ICT. It created its own supply chain system capable of transmitting customer information through the POS system in real time, which enables the factories, distribution centers and marketing departments to receive and utilize this information for decision-making. Tabio has 40 knitters under contract, seven of which manufacture exclusively for Tabio. These knitters employ between eight to 25 workers and are located close to distribution centers – typically within a ten-minute drive. Sales information transmitted through the POS is received by the knitters, allowing them to update their own production plans. Tabio has installed counters on its suppliers' knitting machines, and production data are automatically transmitted to Tabio's managers, enabling them to monitor the production process. The total cost of creating the distribution and supply chain networks was ¥1.35 billion, most of which was covered by government subsidies.

Tabio's supply chain is vertically structured, with Tabio at the top and the knitters below. Tabio cannot organize upstream networks, such as its thread suppliers, since codes and purchase units vary from one company to another, and Tabio's supply system is unable to manage these transactions. Tabio has implemented unique purchasing and ordering schemes. Rather than ordering socks from its knitters, Tabio requires the knitters to determine the amount of product they need to bring to the distribution centre themselves using information provided through the POS system. If products go unsold, the knitters must absorb the losses. This high degree of risk avoidance with respect to inventory also precludes Tabio from taking advantage of potential opportunities for large sales. After conducting a risk analysis, Tabio's management chose to emphasize inventory management at the expense of potentially losing large orders. Although this marketing strategy could be criticized for being overly conservative, the company believes that it is a safe one for an SME.

Overseas shops and the international supply chain

Tabio is one of only three Japanese sock manufactures with overseas retail outlets. The company established Tabio Socks, United Kingdom, in London in 2001, and opened its first shop in March 2002. It also sells its socks through department stores such as Harrods. Tabio's overseas marketing strategy differs from that of other Japanese companies. Instead of relying on large trading firms for overseas sales, Tabio manages its overseas business directly. Prior to opening its London shop, Tabio gleaned important lessons from trading firms, including the importance of performing tasks internally as much as possible in order to reduce costs. The London shops are connected with the company's home offices in Japan through the Internet-based POS system. The King Street shop has IBM computers, and the one on Neal Street has Dell computers. Both King Street and Neal Street shops report data such as number of items sold, time of each sale and customers' gender and age, and can automatically calculate the value added tax. All data are also transmitted to the knitters via Tabio's home offices. If additional socks are needed in London, the knitters can deliver them to the distribution centre at 24 hours' notice. Once customs declarations for export to the United Kingdom have been completed, the products are delivered to Kansai International Airport. Although Tabio tried to find suitable knitters in the United Kingdom, their quality did not meet the company's standards. Due to British regulations prohibiting the import of assembled machinery from Japan, as well as differences in voltage and safety standards, Tabio gave up its efforts to establish its own factory in the UK. As a result, Tabio ships all its products from Japan. The software for the POS system in the London shops was designed by six employees. Tabio prefers to utilize local manufacturers rather than outsource, despite the large cost differential. Although the ability to outsource to foreign manufacturers – one of the commonly cited advantages afforded by IT – purportedly allows firms to increase efficiency, such outsourcing also requires a substantial investment. Hence, Tabio has found it more economical to subcontract with local companies in Japan.

ICT use in two groups of SMEs

Characteristics of the Higashi-Osaka/Ohta SMEs

Japanese manufacturing SMEs have supported the entire Japanese *Monozukuri* (manufacturing) sector by supplying high-quality parts, and the well-known superiority of Japanese products is based largely on the SMEs' technological know-how and accumulated skills. In this chapter, we compare ICT use in two groups of SMEs, Higashi-Osaka/Ohta and IT Hyakusen, and identify factors that affect the adoption of ICT. The latter group represents advanced SMEs, while the former represents less-advanced ones in terms of their ICT use. We conducted field surveys, a mail survey and in-depth interviews in two of Japan's most prominent SME clusters located in Higashi-Osaka city and Tokyo's Ohta ward. In 2004, questionnaires were sent to more than 6,000 SMEs in these two clusters, which yielded nearly 1,200 replies. The two regions, representing the two largest SME clusters having highly specialized technologies and regional collaboration networks, however, differ in a number of ways. SMEs in Higashi-Osaka manufacture completed products for the machinery and metalwork industries. More than 100 SMEs in Higashi-Osaka manufacture unique products and maintain the largest shares of the markets for these products in Japan, as well as abroad. Core sectors of SMEs located in Higashi-Osaka include metalwork, plastics, electronics, general machinery and printing/publishing. Although these SMEs subcontract with some large 'demand transporter' companies such as Panasonic, Sanyo and Sharp, they tend to be more independent-minded and less-focused on subcontracting than their counterparts in Ohta ward. In Higashi-Osaka, SMEs have created local networks through horizontal cooperation among SMEs producing unique niche products and the accompanying peripheral products. The SMEs proactively participate in cross-industrial exchange in order to assimilate ideas for new technologies, increase product marketability, etc. These exchanges are strongly oriented towards creating and introducing novel products to the market.

Most SMEs in Ohta ward specialize in metalworking and processing, and are known to possess a high level of technical capability. Both large and leading medium-sized companies in the electronic and automobile industries, such as Toshiba, Sony, NEC and Nissan, have benefited from the superior parts manufactured by these SMEs. Historically, large companies have chosen to locate in the Tokyo metropolitan area, which has enabled the SMEs in Ohta ward to develop strong ties and collaborations with them. These collaborations increase the SMEs' effectiveness, but, in turn, restrict their behavior. As a result, SMEs in Ohta ward tend to be more passive and accepting of the subcontractor role than their counterparts in Higashi-Osaka. Summarizing these characteristics of the two clusters, the SMEs in Higashi-Osaka can be referred to as a 'horizontal cluster', while those in Ohta ward are a 'vertical cluster'.

Characteristics of IT Hyakusen SMEs

Higashi-Osaka and Ohta were both found to be less advanced with regard to ICT use in our previous studies (Bunno et al., 2006b), while the group of high ICT adopting SMEs were chosen from among those selected as the 'Top 100 SME business practices in the Kansai area' and the '100 best SMEs, as selected by the Ministry of Economy, Trade and Industry (METI)'. The former 100 SMEs were selected by the Kansai IT Strategic Committee based on their use of ICT for management and business. The latter 100 SMEs were selected from all over Japan using the same criteria. As a result, some SMEs were included in both lists. In December 2005, we sent a mail survey to 336 SMEs identified as high-adopters of ICT, including those in the two groups above. In the remainder of the chapter, we will refer to this group of 336 SMEs as the 'IT Hyakusen'. Of the 336 contacted, we received 137 responses.

Index of ICT adoption

ICT index based on AHP

ICT utilization cannot be assessed with a single index because usage varies substantially with a number of controlling factors such business size, industrial sector, business practices, etc. A number of previous studies used 'user satisfaction' as a measure of ICT use (Yap et al., 1992; Palvia, 1996). However, this measure is highly subjective. Therefore, in these surveys, we chose the following as indicators of ICT usage:

- number of PCs owned;
- number of PCs connected to networks, including LAN;
- amount of software intended to optimize use of managerial resources;
- Internet use.

The first point is a simple quantitative proxy for ICT use, based on the assumption that the number of PCs is positively correlated with the degree of business activity. The fourth point is more of a qualitative measure, while the second and third points are intended to more directly measure ICT use, since having a large number of computers does not necessarily mean that they are being used efficiently.

Early on, software was adopted to streamline internal tasks such as accounting and marketing. These applications were generally used on individual PCs and not on computer networks. More advanced ICT systems require users to be connected and to be able access shared databases. Subsequently, the PCs in one or several locations may become connected to each other, generally through use of a groupware program.

In previous studies by Tsuji et al. (2005) and Bunno et al. (2006a), the index was constructed in such a way that questions one to eight were worth one point, and questions nine to 13 were worth ten points. The description of ICT use in questions one to eight was quite different from nine to 13 since the latter dealt with more complicated and integrated utilization. This scoring may seem somewhat arbitrary. In this chapter, we utilize AHP, which is a more rigorous methodology for constructing an index (Saaty, 1980, 1986).

Software and Internet use

Questions about software and Internet use included in the survey, presented in Tables 11.1 and 11.2, respectively, are explained here. The number of questions on the survey made it impossible to ask pair-wise

Table 11.1 Questions on software use

Routine Works	Non-routine Works
1. Sales management (including POS and bar code)	9. Enterprise resource planning (ERP) package
2. Accounting	10. Customer Relations Management (CRM)
3. Payroll management	11. Groupware (office information sharing system)
4. Purchase management	12. Sales Force Automation (SFA)
5. Inventory management	13. Supply Chain Management (SCM)
6. Design management (include CAD/CAM)	
7. Production management	
8. Logistics	

Source: Authors.

Table 11.2 Questions on Internet use

Collection/exchange of information	e-Commerce
1. Collection /exchange of information	4. Net-banking
2. PR of company and products	5. e-commerce with companies (BtoB)
3. Efficient business management	6. e-commerce with consumers (BtoC)

Source: Authors.

questions for the determination of relative weights, which is basic to AHP. Therefore, in order to keep the questions to a reasonable number, we divided the questions into layers, as indicated in Figure 11.1.

Weight of items derived by AHP

In the AHP, the questions were divided into layers and assigned weights by 11 ICT experts (Figure 11.2). For example, 'establishment and operation of an information system' (0.801) was weighted higher – that is, more important – than 'hardware' (0.199) by the experts. The former factor included sub-factors such as software use and Internet use which were weighted 0.444 and 0.357, respectively. Next, based on the AHP weighting, we calculated an ICT use score for each SME and compared the scores of the Higashi-Osaka/Ohta and IT Hyakusen SME groups. The results are summarized in Table 11.3 and Figure 11.3. The average ICT use score for the IT Hyakusen and Higashi-Osaka/Ohta groups were

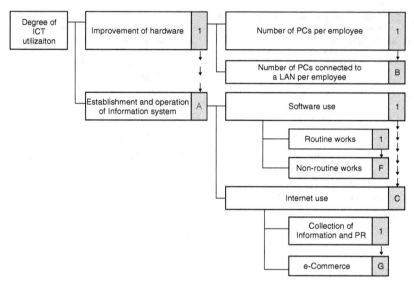

Figure 11.1   Layer of questions in AHP
Source: Authors.

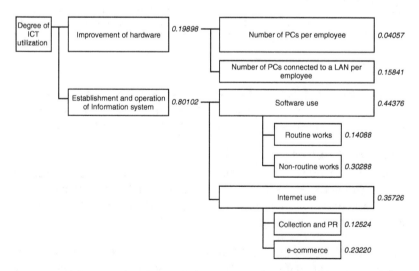

Figure 11.2   Weight obtained by AHP
Source: Authors.

Table 11.3 Index of ICT use of two groups

Degree of ICT utilization	Frequency			Ratio(%)		
	IT Hyakusen	Higashiosaka/Ohta	Total	IT Hyakusen	Higashiosaka/Ohta	Total
0–0.05	1	553	554	0.73	46.16	41.5
0.05–0.1	10	368	378	7.3	30.72	28.31
0.1–0.15	31	173	204	22.63	14.44	15.28
0.15–0.2	36	63	99	26.28	5.26	7.42
0.2–0.25	26	28	54	18.98	2.37	4.27
0.25–0.3	16	11	27	11.68	0.92	2.02
0.3–0.35	17	2	19	12.24	0.17	0.22
Total	137	1198	1335	100.00	100.00	100.00

Degree of ICT utilization	Avg.	Std. Dev.
IT Hyakusen	0.39	0.15
Higashiosaka/Ohta	0.13	0.11
Total	0.16	0.14

Source: Authors.

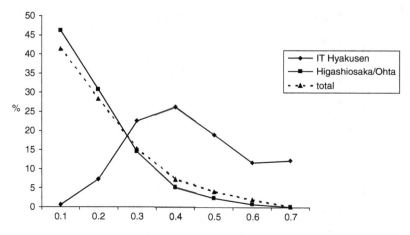

Figure 11.3   Degree of ICT use

0.17 and 0.07, respectively, indicating that SMEs in the IT Hyakusen had adopted ICT to a greater extent.

Using this ICT use index, we were then able to identify factors that promoted ICT usage.

Factors that promote ICT use

Here, we explain variables which encourage ICT use. In the questionnaires and surveys, SMEs were asked about (i) company characteristics, (ii) managerial orientation, (iii) business environment, (iv) importance of ICT, (v) expected results from ICT use and (vi) ICT investment in the last fiscal year. A list of these variables and questions are presented in Table 11.4. The first four of these six variables are explained as follows: (i) company characteristics included variables such as amount of capital, numbers of full- and part-time employees, year of business establishment and the generation of the present owners. A detailed explanation is required to understand why (ii) management orientation is considered to be one variable. The questionnaires contained ten questions regarding managers' daily activities (Table 11.4). Since there was overlap between the ten questions, an attempt was made to identify the subcomponents of management orientation through component analysis of the pooled responses of both Higashi-Osaka/Ohta and IT Hyakusen groups regarding management type. Four subcomponents, accounting for 70.7 percent of the total responses, were determined in this manner. The first of these, which we refer to as 'orientation towards

Table 11.4   Result of component analysis

Management Behavior	Common Factors			
	Training/expansion type	Information-sharing type	Adaptive type	Data-using type
There is training and rotation to utilize each employee's ability and knowledge	0.790	0.127	0.256	0.116
The company offers ICT training to executives, managers and employees	0.662	0.187	0.202	0.142
Employees are apprised of the company's plan for next 2-3 years	0.566	0.306	0.179	0.382
New lines of business are constantly being sought and products developed	0.453	0.322	0.206	0.198
Company's business performance is disclosed to employees	0.243	0.684	0.221	0.256
Senior managers are provided broad responsibility and authorities	0.210	0.355	0.444	0.290
Company studies competitors' mistakes and learn from them	0.180	0.404	0.486	0.280
Company listens to any employee's opinion on how to improve management	0.261	0.182	0.708	0.276
Past business data is extensively utilized in company's management	0.175	0.239	0.245	0.567
Monthly business data are utilized to improve management	0.349	0.217	0.237	0.428
Eigen Value	4.568	1.049	0.774	0.765
Rotated Factor Pattern (%)	41.045	6.065	3.050	2.214
Cumulative Proportion (%)	70.670			

Source: Authors.

training/expansion', comprised questions to determine the extent to which an SME is geared towards expansion as well as ICT training and education.

The second subcomponent, 'orientation towards information-sharing', comprised a single question related to disclosure of business performance to employees. The third subcomponent, 'orientation towards adapting', included questions probing the extent to which firms learn from their mistakes and the degree to which top management consider their employees' suggestions. As such, they were indicative of management's responsiveness – that is, its willingness to 'adapt'. The last subcomponent, 'orientation towards data use', included questions related to how firms make use of data for decision-making. A summary of the statistics for all variables is shown in Table 11.5.

Statistical analysis

Effect of SME group membership on ICT usage

Using pooled ICT usage index data for both SME groups as the response variable, we examined the main factors predicting overall ICT use in both groups with the following OLS model.

$$Y_i = \beta_0 + \beta_1 X_{1i} + \beta_2 X_{2i} + \beta_3 X_{3i} + \dots \dots + \beta_n X_{ni} + \beta_d IT \ dummy + e_i, \qquad (1)$$

where the dependent variable Y_i is the ICT index; X_{ji} denotes variables such as the characteristics of the SMEs, managerial behavior, expectations for ICT use, etc.; β_i indicates the coefficients to be estimated; *IT dummy* is a dummy variable indicating group membership; and e_i is the residual. The variables included in this model were selected from among those found to co-vary with the ICT use index. With respect to group membership, the Higashi-Osaka/Ohta group was considered to be the reference group. The IT Hyakusen group was considered to be the test group and dummy coded as one. After accounting for the effect of all other factors, OLS regression indicated that membership in the IT Hyakusen group predicted a 0.26 increase in ICT index score over membership in the Higashi-Osaka/Ohta group ($P < 0.01$) (Table 11.6).

Factors predicting ICT use in in each group of firms

In this analysis, we identified factors that predicted ICT use both SME groups, as well as those that predicted ICT use only in the IT Hyakusen group. The regression model included both main effects, including group membership, and two-way interactions between variables and group membership. As in the earlier regression model, the Higashi-Osaka/Ohta group was considered the reference group and coded zero, and the IT Hyakusen group was coded one.

All other variables included in the model were selected after checking their covariance with the ICT index. The main effect variables indicated those predicting ICT use for all SMEs (i.e., 'common effects'), while the interactive terms represented variables that predicted ICT use in the IT Hyakusen group (i.e., 'cross-effects').

$$Y_i = b_0 + \sum_{j=1} b_j X_{ji} + \sum_{j=1} b_j{}'(X_{ji}ITdummy_i) + b_0{}'ITdummy_i + \varepsilon_i \qquad (2)$$

The results of this second OLS regression are presented in Table 11.7. The main variables – 'capital', 'recognition of ICT importance', 'amount of ICT investment' and managerial behavior-related variables such as 'training/expansion type' and 'data-using type' – were found to predict ICT usage of all SMEs at the significant at the 1 percent level, while 'ability to determine prices' and 'precise understanding of customer needs' were significant at the 10 percent level. The interaction between 'capital' and group membership was significant at the 5 percent level, while the interaction of 'ability to determine prices', 'frequency of shipment of new products', 'efficiency of routine work' and 'training/expansion type' and group membership were significant at the 10 percent level. In order to better classify the influence of the factors included in the regression models on ICT usage, we categorized them into four groups according to their significant impact.

Group I variables had a common effect (on both groups) as well as an additional cross-effect on the IT Hyakusen group. Group II variables had only a significant cross-effect – that is, they affected only the IT Hyakusen group. Group III variables had only a common effect on both groups; and Group IV variables had no significant effect on ICT use.

Group I variables (see Table 11.8) – 'capital', 'ability to determine prices' and 'training/expansion type' – were predictive of ICT use in both SME groups. In addition, the first two variables had an additional positive influence and the third variable had an additional negative influence on ICT use within the IT Hyakusen group. These results suggest that, while larger SMEs tend to make more extensive use of ICT, for SMEs with already developed ICT, such as those in the IT Hyakusen group, the amount of capital is less relevant to ICT use.

Group II variables – 'efficiency of routine work' and 'frequency of shipment of new products' – were found to be predictive of ICT use

Table 11.5 Summary statistics

Variables		Higashiosaka/Ohta		IT Hyakusen		Pooled data	
		Avg.	Std. Dev.	Avg.	Std. Dev.	Avg.	Std. Dev.
Degree of ICT utilization*		0.13	0.11	0.39	0.15	0.16	0.142
Characteristics of firm	Capital (10 thousand Yen)	1,963.66	2,612.46	13,356.10	40,297.08	14,070	40,297
	The number of Employees	20.491	31.078	78.938	108.45	48.866	108.45
	The number of Part-time job Employees	5.719	10.778	32.734	74.729	27.639	74.729
	Operation years	44.09	79.863	49.11765	40.24814	7.575	40.248
	CEO's generation	1.79	0.848	2.199	0.091	0.876	0.091
Managerial behavior**	Training/expansion type	0	1	0	1	0	1
	Information-sharing type	0	1	0	1	0	1
	Adaptive type	0	1	0	1	0	1
	Data-using type	0	1	0	1	0	1
Business Environment	We obtain new business partners every year	3.106	1.33	3.689	1.034	1.31	1.034
	The share of new products and services in our business is larger than before	3.055	1.214	3.008	1.044	1.014	0.95
	Many purchase orders are repeatedly from the same business partners	3.932	1.01	3.91	0.95	1.263	1.193
	We can price our own products	3.323	1.26	3.403	1.193	1.212	1.044
	In recent years, we have not been able to employ younger (30-year-old or younger) workers	2.938	1.59	2.121	1.214	1.587	1.214
Importance of the introduction of ICT in business management		3.974	1.122	4.728	0.051	3.968	1.162

Expectation of ICT usage						
Increased profit	2.712	0.964	3.44	0.072	1.133	0.072
Higher productivity of routine works, such as administrative works	3.292	0.828	3.744	0.046	0.895	0.046
Higher productivity of non-routine business, such as project planning	2.536	0.956	3.069	0.08	1.233	0.08
Higher speed of decision-making in management and business development	2.867	0.902	3.45	0.064	1.081	0.064
Restructuring of the whole business process	2.598	0.9	3.252	0.067	1.183	0.067
Active communication and accumulation sharing of information knowledge	3.012	0.895	3.511	0.06	1.046	0.06
Precise understanding of customer needs	2.733	0.91	3.183	0.076	1.124	0.076
Better customer satisfaction by improvement in services and products	2.697	0.918	3.323	0.068	1.143	0.068
Company's IT investment last Fiscal Year (10 thousand Yen)	292.735	1,646.98	2,781.20	5,591.50	1,574	22,361
Amount of samples		1,198		137	1,335	

Notes: *shows the result of Analytic Hierarchy Process.
    **shows the four types of corporate management which was clarified by the method of the factor analysis.

Source: Author.

Table 11.6   Result of OLS estimation

Variables	Coefficient	t-value
Manufacturing	0.009	1.338
Retail	0.019	1.401
Capital	0.016	4.382***
We can determine prices	0.006	2.261**
Frequency of shipment of new products	0.005	1.756*
Recognition of ICT importance	0.020	6.352***
Improve profitability	−0.001	−0.380
Efficiency of routine works	−0.005	−1.291
Precise understanding of customer needs	−0.004	−1.266
Amount of ICT investment	0.034	10.825***
Training/expansion type	0.025	5.975***
Adaptive type	0.002	0.544
Data-using type	0.021	4.020***
Dummy variable attached to IT Hyakusen Group	0.146	12.389***
Constants	−0.022	−1.085
R^2		0.571

Note: ***, **, and * indicate the significance at the 1, 5, and 10 % level.
Source: Authors.

only within the IT Hyakusen group. Well-developed SMEs ship new products to the market more frequently and are eager to increase efficiency through ICT use. Group III variables – 'recognition of ICT importance', 'data-using type', 'precise understanding of customer need' and 'amount of ICT investment' – were predictive of ICT use in both IT Hyakusen and Higashi-Osaka/Ohta groups.

Probit/logit estimation of factors that affect the ICT use index

To further examine factors influencing ICT usage, we divided the SMEs into those with higher-than-average and lower-than-average ICT indexes. We, then, constructed logit and probit regression models with odds of membership in the higher-than-average group as the response and the same variables used in the OLS regression above, including a dummy variable for membership in the IT Hyakuen group, as independent variables.

Logit model: $$F(x_i'\beta) = \frac{\exp(x_i'\beta)}{1 + \exp(x_i'\beta)} \tag{3}$$

Probit model: $F(x_i'\beta) = \Phi(x_i'\beta)$ (4)

Table 11.7 Factors affecting ICT use: OLS estimation with cross effects

Variables: Common effect	Coefficient	t-value	Variables: Cross-effect (dummy X variable)	Coefficient	t-value
Manufacturing	0.012	1.641	Manufacturing	-0.026	-1.232
Retail	0.002	0.138	Retail	0.025	0.801
Capital	0.023	5.520***	Capital	-0.022	-2.374**
We can determine prices	0.004	1.703*	We can determine prices	0.017	1.877*
Frequency of shipment of new products	0.005	1.544	Frequency of shipment of new products	0.018	1.768*
Recognition of ICT importance	0.020	6.243***	Recognition of ICT importance	0.022	1.224
Improve profitability	-0.001	-0.394	Improve profitability	-0.006	-0.444
Efficiency of routine works	-0.006	-1.512	Efficiency of routine works	0.035	1.851*
Precise understanding of customer needs	-0.006	-1.784*	Precise understanding of customer needs	0.013	1.026
Amount of ICT investment	0.033	9.814***	Amount of ICT investment	0.005	0.564
Training/expansion type	0.021	4.987***	Training/expansion type	0.026	1.653*
Adaptive type	0.002	0.547	Adaptive type	0.028	1.407
Data-using type	0.021	4.038***	Data-using type	-0.010	-0.443
Dummy variable attached to IT Hyakusen Group	-0.196	-1.636			
Constant	-0.019	-0.936			
R^2	0.591				

Table 11.8   Factors affecting ICT use in Group I*

Variables	Higashioska/Ohta (Coefficient)	IT Hyakusen (Coefficient)
Capital	0.023	0.001
We can determine prices	0.004	0.021
Training/expansion type	0.021	0.047

*Variables to which cross and own effects are significant.
Source: Authors.

where F denotes the standard normal distribution function, and the X_i variables are similar to those in the OLS estimation. The results of logit and probit regressions (Table 11.9) were similar to that of OLS regression (Table 11.8). 'Amount of capital' (marginal effect: 0.0648 and 0.0656), 'amount of ICT investment' (marginal effect: 0.1324 and 0.1306), 'data-using type' (marginal effect: 0.0760 and 0.0798) and IT Hyakusen dummy (marginal effect: 0.2934 and 0.2984) were all significant at the 1 percent level. 'Recognition of ICT importance' (marginal effect: 0.0399 and 0.0418) was significant at the 5 percent level. In addition, 'ability to determine prices' (marginal effect: 0.0247 and 0.0259) and 'training/expansion type' (marginal effect: 0.0431 and 0.0452) were significant at the 1 percent level. These results are consistent with those of the OLS analysis.

Obstacles to ICT adoption: implications for policy

Factors hindering ICT adoption

The analysis thus far has focused on factors that encourage ICT use. In this section we identify factors that hinder SMEs from adopting ICT in order to be able to develop policies aimed at overcoming specific obstacles.

Potential obstacles to ICT adoption are summarized in Q9 of the questionnaire. Based on previous studies, it is expected that low adoption of ICT is due to lack of leadership by top management, absence of ICT experts or advisors, lack of knowledge regarding ICT or ICT know-how, low investment in ICT, etc. (Yap et al., 1992; Cragg and Zinatelli, 1995; Mata et al., 1995; Thong and Yap, 1995; Doukidis et al., 1996; Ruiz-Mercader et al., 1996; Delone, 1988; Igbaria et al., 1998; Levy and Powell, 2000; Caldeira and Ward, 2002; Kauremaa et al., 2009). To identify factors that predict low ICT adoption, we utilized an OLS regression model similar that used in the previous section, including

Table 11.9 Logit/probit estimation

Variables	Logit-model			Probit-model		
	Coeff.	z-value	Marginal effect	Coef.	z-value	Marginal effect
Manufacturing	0.271	1.36	0.057	0.153	1.28	0.055
Retail	0.731	1.56	0.129	0.430	1.59	0.134
Capital	0.314	2.90***	0.065	0.187	3.00***	0.066
We can determine prices.	0.120	1.71*	0.025	0.074	1.76*	0.026
Frequent shipment of new products	0.097	1.26	0.020	0.060	1.30	0.021
Recognition of ICT importance	0.193	2.04**	0.040	0.119	2.07**	0.042
Improve profitability	0.131	1.29	0.027	0.080	1.31	0.028
Efficiency of routine works	-0.021	-0.19	-0.004	-0.016	-0.23	-0.006
Precise understanding of customer needs	-0.069	-0.71	-0.014	-0.032	-0.55	-0.011
Amount of ICT investment	0.642	6.30***	0.132	0.373	6.64***	0.131
Training/expansion type	0.209	1.87*	0.043	0.129	1.93*	0.045
Adaptive type	0.006	0.05	0.001	0.000	0.00	0.000
Data-using type	0.368	2.63***	0.076	0.228	2.72***	0.080
Dummy variable attached to IT Hyakusen Group	2.178	3.55***	0.293	1.185	3.93***	0.298
Constants	-2.938	-4.99***		-1.786	-5.03***	
Log likelihood	-412.66702			-412.13722		

Note: ***, ** and * indicate the 1 %, 5 % and 10 % significance level.

Source: Authors.

interactions of independent variables with SME group membership to identify 'cross-effect' variables. ICT use index was again used as the response variable. However, in this analysis, independent variables consisted of potential obstacles to ICT adoption (Table 11.10). Since the response variable is the degree of ICT use and the independent variables are potential obstacles, coefficients are expected to be negative. In other words, it is expected that higher obstacle scores will result in lower ICT adoption. Factors with positive coefficients, then, can be interpreted as negative factors that act as incentives for, rather than deterrents of, ICT adoption.

As in the previous analysis, we grouped variables based on significance of 'common' and 'cross-effects'. The Group I variables 'unclear objectives of management' and 'ICT security is a major concern' influenced ICT use in the Higashi-Osaka/Ohta group and had an additional effect on IT Hyakusen group. Care needs to be taken in interpreting coefficients in this model. Coefficients of main effect variables represent the effects in the Higashi-Osaka/Ohta group, while the coefficients of the interactive terms represent effects in the IT Hyakusen group relative to that of the Higashi-Osaka/Ohta group. The direct effect of a given variable in the IT Hyakusen group on the ICT use, then, is calculated as the sum of the coefficients for both main and interaction terms. Thus, the direct effects of 'unclear objectives of management' and 'ICT security are a major concern' on ICT use index are −0.029 and −0.034, respectively.

We note that the direction of impact (sign) of the 'unclear objectives of management' and 'ICT security is a major concern' differs between SME groups, which we interpret as follows. For the Higashi-Osaka/Ohta group, these two factors appear to act as incentives for increased ICT adoption. However, in the IT Hyakusen group, SMEs have already achieved higher levels of ICT use, and these two might not be major reasons to introduce ICT (the coefficient expresses the marginal contribution of an independent variable to the index, and its amount depends on the current level of the index). This is one interpretation, but a more rigorous analysis is required to understand the differential impact of these factors on ICT usage. Group II variables 'employees' lack of ICT knowledge', 'introduction to ICT is left up to the hardware/software makers' and 'lack of workers' cooperation with ICT usage at the office' had a significant impact on ICT usage in the IT Hyakusen group, but not in the Higashi-Osaka/Ohta group. The first two had negative coefficients, implying that they were less serious issues for the IT Hyakusen group.

Table 11.10 Problems of ICT use by SMEs (1)

Variables: Common effect	Coefficient	t-value	Variables:Cross-effect (dummy X variable)	Coefficient	t-value
Lack of leadership regarding ICT use	-0.025	-3.139***	Lack of leadership regarding ICT use	-0.013	-0.391
Unclear objectives of management	0.014	1.696*	Unclear objectives of management	-0.043	-1.676*
ICT has been introduced without any restructuring of works	0.015	1.694*	ICT has been introduced without any restructuring of works	-0.029	-1.028
Lack of employees who can use ICT	0.007	0.887	Lack of employees who can use ICT	-0.013	-0.527
Lack of employees' ICT Knowledge	0.010	1.302	Lack of employees' ICT Knowledge	-0.060	-2.315**
Lack of employees' cooperation with ICT usage at the office	0.007	0.551	Lack of employees' cooperation with ICT usage at the office	0.095	1.763*
Lack of ICT advisers	-0.008	-0.998	Lack of ICT advisers	0.033	0.928
We leave everything of ICT introduction to ICT adviser(s)	0.031	2.177**	We leave everything of ICT introduction to ICT adviser(s)	-0.085	-1.450
We leave everything of ICT introduction to ICT makers	0.009	0.834	We leave everything of ICT introduction to ICT makers	-0.100	-2.101**
Lack of software that we need	0.017	2.025**	Lack of software that we need	0.026	0.914
We can't keep up with technological innovation	-0.026	-2.917***	We can't keep up with technological innovation	0.042	1.303
Each business partner wants to adopt its own ICT systems	0.046	4.895***	Each business partner wants to adopt its own ICT systems	-0.043	-1.462
ICT investment does not yield explicit profit	-0.013	-1.626	ICT investment does not yield explicit profit	-0.001	-0.019
ICT investment is very costly	0.022	2.872***	ICT investment is very costly	-0.010	-0.424
We have deep concern for information security, if ICT is introduced	0.051	6.831***	We have deep concern for information security, if ICT is introduced	-0.060	-2.764***
It takes time to introduce ICT	-0.024	-2.290**	It takes time to introduce ICT	0.015	0.313
Others	-0.032	-1.655*	Others	0.110	2.488**
IT Hyakusen dummy variable	0.302	15.589***			
Constants	0.107	18.94***			
R^2	0.390				

Note: ***, **, and * indicate the significance at the 1, 5, and 10 % level.

Source: Authors.

The third factor had a positive coefficient, indicating that it may serve as an incentive for increased ICT adoption. Group III variables were significant predictors of level of ICT use in both the Higashi-Osaka/Ohta and IT Hyakusen groups. 'ICT has been introduced without any restructuring of work', 'introduction of ICT is left to the ICT adviser(s)', 'lack of necessary software', 'each business partner wants to adopt its own ICT systems' and 'ICT investment is very costly' had positive coefficients, indicating that they served as incentives for SMEs to adopt ICT. On the other hand, 'lack of leadership regarding ICT use', 'we can't keep up with technological innovation' and 'it takes time to introduce ICT' had negative coefficients, suggesting that these were factors that hindered ICT adoption. The last three variables in particular seem to be common hurdles for the introduction of ICT into small SMEs.

From the above analysis it appears that 'lack of leadership regarding ICT use' remains a significant obstacle to ICT adoption among Japanese SMEs. Our surveys revealed that both ICT knowledge of the employees and ICT leadership by top management need to be improved. Thus, these two areas, which are related to human resources, should be the targets of policy aimed at promoting ICT in SMEs.

Policies to promote ICT use suggested by empirical research

In this section we analyze the kinds of policies that would encourage ICT adoption by SMEs. We performed OLS regression using a model similar to that used in the previous analyses (equation 2) to identify policies that predict level of ICT usage (Tables 11.12 and 11.13). 'Tax exemptions for ICT investments', 'grants and other financial support for ICT investments', 'commendation of small company business models that make use of ICT', 'introduction of an e-bidding system', 'low-interest loans for ICT', 'low-interest leases for ICT' and 'deregulation' were policies desired by both SMEs groups, and were positively related to the ICT use index. In the IT Hyakusen group, desire for introduction

Table 11.11   Problems of ICT use by SMEs (2)

Variables	Higashioska/Ohta Coefficient	IT Hyakusen Coefficient
Unclear objectives of management	0.014	−0.029
We have deep concern for information security, if ICT is introduced*	0.051	−0.034
Others	−0.032	0.078

Variables which cross and own effects are significant.

Table 11.12 Policy desired for ICT introduction

Variables: Common effect	Coefficient	t-value	Variables: Cross-effect (dummy X variable)	Coefficient	t-value
Opening of ICT seminars	0.007	0.969	Opening of ICT seminars	-0.013	-0.476
Implementation of education for PC operation	-0.002	-0.205	Implementation of education for PC operation	-0.072	-2.082**
Adviser system	0.005	0.656	Adviser system	-0.046	-1.764*
Low-interest loans for ICT	0.016	2.090**	Low-interest loans for ICT	-0.019	-0.736
Low-interest lease for ICT	0.016	2.199**	Low-interest lease for ICT	-0.004	-0.152
Tax exemptions on ICT investment	0.064	8.887***	Tax exemptions on ICT investment	-0.042	-1.943*
Support for opening new portals	-0.002	-0.132	Support for opening new portals	0.061	1.405
Deregulation	0.039	4.469***	Deregulation	0.009	0.378
Commendation of small company business models that make use of ICT	0.059	3.546***	Commendation of small company business models that make use of ICT	-0.073	-2.453**
Introduction of e-bidding system	0.031	2.482**	Introduction of e-bidding system	0.119	2.740***
Others	0.012	0.834	Others	0.077	2.053**
Dummy variable attacked to IT Hyakusen	0.277	15.199***			
Constants	0.088	15.795***			
R^2	0.404				

Note: ***, **, and * indicate the significance at the 1, 5, and 10 % level.

Source: Authors.

Table 11.13 Policy desired by SMEs

Variables	Higashiosaka/Ohta Coefficient	IT Hyakusen Coefficient
Tax exemptions on ICT investment	0.064	0.022
Commendation of small company business models that make use of ICT*	0.059	−0.014
Introduction of e-bidding system	0.031	0.15

Variables which cross and own effects are significant
Source: Authors.

of an e-bidding system was strongly related to a higher rate of ICT use. In contrast, SMEs in the IT Hyakusen group are less interested in subsidies, such as tax exemption and training and education, since they have already achieved a certain level of ICT use.

Conclusion

We conducted field surveys in two major SME clusters in Higashi-Osaka and Ohta ward and by mail surveys of selected high ICT adopting SMEs around the country, which we referred to as the IT Hyakusen. The data collected were used to create an index of ICT usage using AHP in order to identify factors that promote ICT use among Japanese SMEs. High ICT adopting SMEs were found to believe strongly in the importance of ICT for improving their business efficiency and to invest significant money in ICT. Among the factors identified as promoting or hindering ICT adoption, our analysis revealed the leadership, or lack thereof, by top management played the most significant role in predicting ICT use. It follows, then, that the best way to promote ICT use among SMEs would be to encourage top management to better understand, value and proactively pursue ICT. Once management adopts a positive perception of ICT, they can determine the exact ways in which they will implement ICT to meet their specific goals.

In our analysis of obstacles to ICT adoption, which was particularly relevant to the low ICT adopting SMEs in the Higashi-Osaka/Ohta group, 'each business partner wants to adopt its own ICT systems' or 'information security is a major concern' were found to be related to lack of ICT adoption. These results indicate the following underlying issues:

• large firms want subcontractors to use the firms' ICT systems;

- a large amount of money is required to comply with the ICT demands of these large firms;
- there is a lack of human resources to handle ICT;
- firms are concerned with the security and privacy of data related to customers and business transactions.

SMEs in this group that use ICT extensively tend to shift all of their business activities or solve managerial problems by drastic restructuring of their businesses. In doing so, they encounter problems involving customer relationships and ICT utilization by employees.

IT Hyakusen SMEs, on the other hand, which already have a strong ICT base, tend to introduce and operate new ICT without help from outside experts, but rely more on their own employees. In addition, introduction of new ICT tends not to require drastic restructuring of business activities, but, rather, can be done gradually leading to incremental improvements in business operation. In this way, both ICT and the ICT know-how of these SMEs can be continuously improved. This chapter focused on identifying factors that promote ICT use by SMEs in order to develop suitable policy recommendations. SMEs in Higashi-Osaka/Ohta desired tax exemptions and subsidies for ICT investment, indicating that shortage of funds for ICT investment is the most serious obstacle in this group of SMEs for ICT adoption. This problem is doubled because of the need for ICT updates as technology improves. IT Hyakusen SMEs, on the other hand, are interested in policies including the introduction of an e-bidding system, which will expand their business opportunities.

These findings serve as an empirical basis on which to formulate more effective policies. The policies implemented so far by various ministries of the government (Tsuji et al., 2005; Small and Medium Enterprise Agency, 2001, 2002, 2003, 2004b) can hardly be considered successful. New policies, based on rigorous empirical research, are required to more effectively promote ICT adoption and maintain the competitiveness of Japanese SMEs in the increasingly competitive global market.

References

Bunno, T., H. Idota, M. Tsuji, H. Miyoshi, M. Ogawa and M. Nakanishi (2006a) 'An Empirical Analysis of Indices and Factors of ICT Use by Small- and Medium-sized Enterprises in Japan', Proceedings of 16th ITS Biennial Conference, Beijing, China, June.

Bunno, T., H. Idota, M. Tsuji, H. Miyoshi, M. Ogawa and M. Nakanishi (2006b) 'Index of the Diffusion of Information Technology among SMES: An AHP

Approach', Proceedings of the 17th European Regional ITS Conference, Amsterdam, the Netherlands, August.

Bunno, T., H. Idota, M. Tsuji and M. Nakanishi (2007) 'Factors and Policies for the Diffusion of Information and Communications Technology among Japanese SMEs', Proceedings of the 18th European Regional ITS Conference, Istanbul, Turkey, September.

Caldeira, M.M. and J.M. Ward (2002) 'Understanding the Successful Adoption and Use of IS/IT in SMEs: An Explanation from Portuguese Manufacturing Industries', *Information Systems Journal*, Vol. 12, No. 2, pp. 121–52.

Cragg, P.B. and N. Zinatelli (1995) 'The Evolution of Information Systems in Small Firms', *Information & Management*, Vol. 29, No. 1, pp. 1–8.

Delone, W. (1988) 'Determinants of Success for Computer Usage in Small Business', *MIS Quarterly*, Vol. 12, No. 1, pp. 51–61.

Doukidis, G.I., P. Lybereasand R.D. Galliers (1996) 'Information Systems Planning in Small Business: A Stages of Growth Analysis', *Journal of Systems and Software*, Vol. 33, No. 2, pp. 189–201.

Giovannetti, E., M. Kagami and M. Tsuji (eds) (2003) *The Internet Revolution: A Global Perspective*, Cambridge, MA: Cambridge University Press.

Igbaria, M., N. Zinatelli and A.L.M. Cavaye (1998) 'Analysis of Information Technology Success in Small Firms in New Zealand', *International Journal of Information Management*, Vol. 18, No. 2, pp. 103–19.

Japan Small and Medium Enterprise Management Consultants Association (2003) Report of Research on SCM Business Models for SMEs (in Japanese), Tokyo.

Kauremaa, J., M. Kärkkäinen and T. Ala-Risku (2009) 'Customer Initiated Interorganizational Information Systems: The Operational Impacts and Obstacles for Small and Medium Sized Suppliers', *International Journal of Production Economics*, Vol. 119, No. 2, pp. 228–39.

Kuchiki, A. and M. Tsuji (eds) (2004) *Industrial Clusters in Asia: Competition and Coordination*, Basingstoke and New York: Palgrave Macmillan.

Kuchiki, A. and M. Tsuji (2008) *The Flowchart Approach to Industrial Cluster Policy*, Basingstoke and New York: Palgrave Macmillan.

Levy, M. and P. Powell (2000) 'Information Systems Strategy for Small and Medium Sized Enterprises: An Organizational Perspective', *The Journal of Strategic Information Systems*, Vol. 9, No. 1, pp. 63–84.

Martin, C.J. (1989) 'Information Management in the Smaller Business: The Role of the Top Manager', *International Journal of Information Management*, Vol. 9, No. 3, pp. 187–97.

Mata, F.J., W.L. Fuest and J.B. Barney (1995) 'Information Technology and Sustained Competitive Advantage: A Resource-Based Analysis', *MIS Quarterly*, Vol. 19, No. 4, pp. 487–505.

Ogawa, M., H. Idota, T. Bunno and M. Tsuji (2009) 'Indices of the Diffusion of Information Technology among Japanese Small- and Medium-sized Enterprises: An AHP Approach', Proceedings of the ISAHP2009, Pittsburgh, Pennsylvania, USA, July–August.

Palvia, P.C. (1996) 'A Model and Instrument for Measuring Small Business User Satisfaction with Information Technology', *Information & Management*, Vol. 31, No. 3, pp. 151–63.

Ruiz-Mercader, J., A.L. Meroño-Cerdan and R. Sabater-Sánchez (2006) 'Information Technology and Learning: Their Relationship and Impact on Organizational Performance in Small Businesses', *International Journal of Information Management*, Vol. 26, No. 1, pp. 16–29.

Saaty, T.L. (1980) *The Analytic Hierarchy Process: Planning, Priority Setting, Resource Allocation*, New York: McGraw-Hill.

Saaty, T.L. (1986) 'Absolute and Relative Measurement with the AHP: The Most Livable Cities in the United States', *Socio-Economic Planning Sciences*, Vol. 20, No. 6, pp. 327–31.

Small and Medium Enterprise Agency (2004a) Project II for Promotion of ICT Use by SMEs (in Japanese), Tokyo, Ministry of Economy, Trade and Industry.

Small and Medium Enterprise Agency (2001, 2002, 2003, 2004b) White papers on small and medium enterprises in Japan (in Japanese), Tokyo, Ministry of Economy, Trade and Industry.

Thong, J.Y.L. and C.S. Yap (1995) 'CEO Characteristics, Organizational Characteristics and Information Technology Adoption in Small Businesses', *Omega*, Vol. 23, No. 4, pp. 429–42.

Tsuji, M., H. Miyoshi, T. Bunno, H. Idota, M. Ogawa, M. Nakanishi, E. Tsutsumi and N. Smith (2005) 'ICT Use by SMEs in Japan: A Comparative Study of Higashi-osaka and Ohta Ward, Tokyo', in M. Kuwayama, Y. Ueki and M. Tsuji (eds), Information Technology for Development of Small and Medium-sized Exporters in Latin America and East Asia, Santiago, Chile: ECLAC/IDE-JETRO/ United Nations, pp. 345–74.

Tsuji, M., E. Giovannetti and M. Kagami (eds) (2007) *Industrial Agglomeration and New Technologies: A Global Perspective*, Basingstoke: Edward Elgar.

Tsuji, M., T. Bunno, H. Idota, M. Ogawa, H. Miyoshi and Y. Ueki (2010) 'An Empirical Analysis of Indices and Factors of ICT Use by Small- and Medium-sized Enterprises in Japan', in M. Karatas and M.Z. Tunca (eds), *Sustainable Economic Development and Influence of Information Technologies: Dynamics of Knowledge Society Transformation*, Hershey, PA: IGI Global, pp. 161–74.

Yap, C.S., C. Soh and K. Raman (1992) 'Information Systems Success Factors in Small Business', *Omega*, Vol. 20, No. 5–6, pp. 597–609.

12
Determinants of Intra-firm Diffusion Process of ICT: Theoretical Sources and Empirical Evidence from Catalan Firms

Adel Ben Youssef, David Castillo Merino, and Walid Hadhri

Introduction

The potential for information and communication technology (ICT) usage in business has been a well-covered topic during the last decade. Since ICTs are considered to be 'general purpose' technologies (Bresnahan and Trajtenberg, 1995; Antonelli 2003), they are shaping the internal organization of firms, their boundaries and also their productivity and performance. International literature gives empirical evidence that adopting a new technology influences firms' productivity rates in the short and long term. Short-term productivity losses may affect the decision process of adopting a new technology. In fact, it involves three main decisions:

- whether to adopt or not;
- the replacement speed of old technology with a new one; and
- the extent to which the capabilities of the new technology will be exploited by a firm, which is usually known as 'depth of adoption' (Astebro, 2004).

At least three views of these dynamics are expressed in economic theory. The first one is known as the non-equilibrium theory and is related to the seminal work of Mansfield (1963). Firms' usage dynamics follows an S-shaped curve, depending on time. Epidemic models (non-equilibrium) are in general presented as the main explanation of these dynamics. The second one is known as the equilibrium theory (Battisti and Stoneman, 2003, 2005). The adoption and usage of technology depend on the trade-off between the cost of additional usage and the benefits of this additional usage. Since then there's no need for an S-curve describing the usage over time. The patterns of usage are random, depending on the opportunity costs of the usage. Finally, and recently Battisti et al. (2007), have tried to link these two views by supposing that in an earlier stage of technology diffusion patterns follow evolutionary dynamics (epidemic effect) and then, when the technology is generalized and adopted, the equilibrium theory becomes applicable. Recently empirical literature has tried to confirm this view by examining these dynamics in different settings (Bocquet and Brossard, 2007, in France, Battisti and Stoneman, 2005, in Italy, for example). In this sense, the objective of our study is to contribute to a better understanding of the determinants and patterns of ICT intra-firm diffusion by adapting Bocquet and Brossard's (2007) approach and testing it using a single year (2003) cross-section dataset on the intra-firm diffusion of digital technologies in Catalan companies. In fact, in 2003 the adoption of ICT by Catalan firms was important; however, the usage was sub-optimal. By separating the dynamics of usage and adoption we will show how the two views are valid. Our chapter aims also to verify the standard effects of technology adoption on the extent of ICT depth of adoption. Hence, we focus on firm's size, organization, its absorptive capacity, cooperation and innovation. The main contribution is to verify how standard arguments for ICT adoption behavior work in the context of Catalan firms in 2003 and to highlight the difference between digital technology adoption and usage patterns.

In order to reach this objective, this chapter is divided into five sections. the first section summarizes the main findings in the economic theory related to intra-firm diffusion. The second section explains how data was collected and the theoretical model used. The third section identifies the main explanatory variables and specifies the empirical models. The fourth section discusses the results and the findings. The fifth section concludes.

The intra-firm diffusion of ICT literature review

The intra-firm diffusion of ICT is nowadays at the centre of a fruitful international discussion, focused on a theoretical analysis of the determinants of the digital technology diffusion process – that is, trying to identify a diffusion pattern and the main factors that may explain it – and on gathering empirical results from diverse theoretical approaches. This diffusion process of new technology within a firm involves the depth of adoption, a construct that can be defined as the extent to which a firm is able (or decides) to exploit an innovation's potential technological capabilities (Astebro, 2004). The majority of the extant diffusion literature (Stoneman, 2001) is mainly concerned with inter-firm diffusion. However, there is an increasing number of recent papers proposing approaches to modeling the intra-firm diffusion of a new technology (Battisti and Stoneman, 2003, 2005), as well as focusing on giving empirical evidence on this phenomenon, particularly on the diffusion of digital technologies within a firm (Bocquet and Brossard, 2007; Hollenstein, 2004). As Battisti and Stoneman (2003) demonstrated empirically, the inter-firm effect (i.e., the time profile of the number of firms using the technology) is more important in the early stages, while the intra-firm effect (i.e., the time profile of the extent of use by individual firms) is more important in the later stages of the whole diffusion process.

Our data about Catalan companies gives support to this assumption. There is broad consensus in fixing the middle of the 1990s (as in other developed economies) as the starting point of a general diffusion of information and communication technology among industries and businesses in Catalonia.[1] After a decade of digitalization, it can be confirmed that the adoption of digital technologies among Catalan firms was a reality.[2] But if we look at digital use by firms, the picture appears to be quite opposite. ICT was a basic work tool for just 15.6 percent of Catalan companies, a statistic that gives us a more detailed idea of this early stage of implementation of the digital business in the Catalan economy; the main uses were in management, administration and accounting tasks and obtaining information.[3] This empirical evidence may question the epidemic effects (Mansfield, 1963) approach as the sole theory able to explain determinants of ICT use diffusion in companies. As can be deduced from this data description, inter-firm diffusion of digital technologies (measured here as ICT adoption) may be identified as a prior step to deeper adoption. In fact, it can be said that 2003 conforms to an early stage pattern in terms of the diffusion of ICT uses within Catalan firms.

Together with epidemic effects, rank, stock and order effects are the main and widely accepted factors affecting intra-firm diffusion of a new technology (Karshenas and Stoneman, 1993). As has been outlined by Battisti and Stoneman (2005), it is difficult to see the relevance of an order effect on the intra-firm diffusion process, as any order effects may be internalized by a firm. Thus, our general framework for the 'diffusion' approaches relies on epidemic, rank and stock effects.

Epidemic effects

Epidemic effects explain the intra-firm diffusion process as the result of risk reduction of the depth of adoption over time (Mansfield, 1961, 1963). The main predictions of this type of models are:

- the level of intra-firm diffusion is a growth function of time since first adoption by the firm;
- the depth of adoption follows a logistic S-shaped path, increasing with time as use reduces the risk of adoption; and
- different diffusion paths for different firms and technologies reflect diverse levels of adoption profitability and initial risk levels (Battisti and Stoneman, 2003).

Thus, epidemic models consider that the diffusion of a new technology requires the spreading of information about efficient uses of a new technology (Bocquet and Brossard, 2007). Battisti and Stoneman (2003, 2005) have shown that epidemic effects are not empirically significant to explain intra-firm diffusion processes. Thus, if these effects have any influence on this process, it is due to the development of a technological absorption capacity within the firm. Following evolutionary approaches (Hannan and Freeman, 1989), this particular interpretation of epidemic models will lead to a connection between human capital and the diffusion of ICT use by firms. We use here only those variables that can be understood as a proxy of human capital. The first set of variables is higher education degree of managers and workers. Educational-level attainment is a factor that may influence digital technology investment and use, as it conditions managers and workers' vision towards new technologies, which also depends on their own convictions. However, the importance of education is obvious, since new technologies require high-skilled workers. Furthermore, we try to analyze whether the fact that workers are enrolled in training programs has an effect on ICT uses. The second variable is the average age of managers and workers. These variables can also give an idea of the effect of workforce experience on ICT usage. Experience is also summarized in a last variable defined as the average wages in a firm. We suppose here that human capital is not depreciating and age summarizes experience and learning. Then, the stock of 'human capital' is approximated by these variables. The absorptive capacity effect refers also to the capability of a firm to develop its own mix of inputs and to adapt technologies to productive uses. Therefore, we use training inside the firm and employees' and managers' training as indicators of the ability to develop and use these technologies.

Rank effects

Rank effects link with a benefit function approach and result from the fact of firms' differences in terms of returns on technology investment. The trade-off between expected benefits and costs from technology adoption leads to consideration of sunk costs, as well as costs spreading among products' incomes, as critical factors to explain the diffusion of technology use. From this point of view, the most important effect summarizing the depth of adoption is a firm's size. Different explanations are given in order to justify why large firms are more able to adopt and use new technologies (Fabiani et al., 2005; Morgan et al., 2006; Thong, 1999). Generally, small firms readily embrace daily use of digital technology, but they need to be assisted to make the most efficient and comprehensive use of them. Therefore, the larger a company is, the greater is the depth of ICT adoption and use. In our estimation, we took into account firms' size by the logarithm of the number of workers employed.

Stock effects

Stock effects results from the evidence indicate that low ICT uses may be the optimal choice for some firms, as marginal benefits, as well as productivity, tend to decrease after new technology adoption. This situation leads to uncertainty about the impact of increasing digital use in terms of future benefits. This effect may be identified by comparing different intensity use related to diverse cost and benefit functions. As we have available a cross-section database, the time dimension cannot be considered in our model and, therefore, stock effects will not be distinguished from rank effects (Bocquet and Brossard, 2007). This is the main reason why this type of effect will not be measured and estimated here.

In addition to epidemic and 'diffusion' effects, the ICT complementarities approach has been demonstrated as being useful in analyzing the digital spread within a firm (Bresnahan et al., 2002a, 2002b; Cristini et al., 2003). There is a mutually beneficial relationship between organizational change and ICT investment. Digital technology is a key element in facilitating new organizational practices, such as lean production, team-working, more decentralization in strategic decision-making activities, or a closer interaction with customers and providers of intermediate inputs. Therefore, ICT availability and usage increase firms' capacity to adapt their organizational structure to these new network requirements. At the same time, efficient ICT use by firms require some specific organizational changes in order to maximize the exploitation of their technological capabilities. How ICT and organizational change are combined within a firm will determine the efficiency level achieved and, therefore, the degree of productivity gained. Firm-level organizational change can take many forms, but generally can be classified into two broad systems (Murphy, 2002).

Organizational effects

Organizational effects illustrate that the extent to which ICT is used within a firm depends on its organizational design and its management practices. Since digital technologies are 'network' technologies they are more efficient in a decentralized setting. They fit well with the connectivity effects arising from belonging to a group of companies and with the external links of importer firms. The variable 'belonging to a group', which indicates whether a firm belongs to a group or not, anticipates advantages from improving external relationships and coordination with others firms of its group; this should not be neglected.

In addition, labor management practices connect firms' organization with ICT through new management practices and employees' schemes. In this sense, previous studies (Milgrom and Roberts, 1992; Osterman, 2000; Foss et al., 2007) have demonstrated that interaction among decision-makers and executives leads to less hierarchical structures. Moreover, the transition from hierarchical structures towards more decentralized ones, in which knowledge and the power of decision-making are clearly imbricated, is very useful in terms of understanding how the organization solves its problems of coordination, motivation and incentives. Therefore, the type of workforce control applied by the company is a critical variable for a better understanding of a firm's technological diffusion process. Digital technologies induce new forms of indirect employee control or supervision (being reachable constantly), which are replacing the traditional forms of direct control based on hierarchical supervision (Acemoglu and Newman, 2002). ICT, thus, tends to replace modes of control of the employees based on the input (attendance time in the company, direct or visual monitoring by a superior) by modes of control based on different measures of output or performance (objectives to be filled, times to be respected, answering a request etc.). The variable 'control by objectives or result', as an indication of the adoption of new organizational design, is represented here by a variable denoting whether the firm has adopted a control based on objectives or results within its organization or not.

Network effects

Network effects results are fundamental to digital technologies. ICTs are network technologies. Thus, we expect a positive correlation for importer firms. We also consider the number of customers and the number of providers as factors, which can influence ICT adoption and use. This fact should tend to increase the probability of integration in a broader network and thus the probability of ICT usage by firms. We try to approximate here the connectivity of a firm by the number of the relationships (customers, suppliers, importers and plants). We expect a positive effect between the connectivity of a firm and the ICT adoption process. In other words, if size gives us the internal dimension of a firm's connectivity, the above-mentioned factors give us the external dimension of this connectivity. Within network approach, the effect of the sector affiliation on ICT adoption can also be considered. The economic sector should also constitute an important factor of adoption as it reflects production and organizational logics. Thus, we distinguished in our study between firms belonging to the information sector and others.

Furthermore, network effects can be also understood as a firm's cooperation effort to innovate. Cooperation needs coordination and communication technology. In this sense, the more the firm is engaged in cooperation, the more it uses ICT. So, in our explanatory variables, we consider if a firm is cooperating with others institutions, such as other firms, universities, research and innovation centers, with competitors, with suppliers, with customers, or not. We also try to explain the difference in ICT use and adoption between innovative and not non-innovative firms and, in particular, between those firms using digital technologies to innovate and others. Complementary investments in innovation are essential for the advantages of the ICT adoption to be apparent; therefore, firms' investment in digital technology will impact performance only if it is accompanied by a set of organizational changes and complementary investments, otherwise the economic impact of ICT will be limited (OECD, 2004). An innovative company reaches, through innovation, new market opportunities, either because innovation will have enabled it to reduce costs, or because new products or services will answer better the demand requirements, while making it possible for customers to profit from more complete services, adapted better to their requirements or more respectful of the environment. The use and diffusion of ICT facilitates and supports innovation for all companies. Indeed, the innovating firm had more probability of being well equipped with ICT. ICT allows trial and error without costs ('learning before doing'). At the same time, ICT allows the generalization of the exploration–exploitation process and the involvement of non-manager workers (Bellon et al., 2006, 2007). These facts increase the speed of the innovation. Three variables are used in our chapter: innovation led by ICT, cooperation with other firms through ICT and whether the firm is innovative or not.

ICT diffusion is a complex issue as digital technologies include a huge number of different tools and devices (computers, Internet, LAN/WAN, EDI systems, websites, CRM systems, etc.) which allow general and specific uses. It is a fact that firms won't necessarily use of all them and that use of various aspects of ICT won't occur at the same time. Therefore, it is difficult to define a measure of digital use within a firm. Given that we aim to identify determinants of different ICT diffusion patterns, we propose to use a twofold measurement system here:[4] the first considers specific ICT tools (such as CRM, EIS or ERP) adopted by a firm (as they are specific and complex, we assume that a firm will only adopt them if an 'appropriate' use has been planned before adoption); a second measure relies on different business uses of digital technologies that have been declared by firms.

Hypothesis

The explanation of intra-firm diffusion of digital technologies has been usually based on epidemic effects, together with rank, stock and order effects; there is broad consensus on this. And it conforms to the general framework of the 'diffusion' approaches. But if we consider the particular traits of digital technologies, the depth of uses by firms can be better explained if we add to the 'diffusion' perspective an ICT complementarities approach and the theory of technological choices based on epidemic evolutionary models.

> *H: technological diffusion theories, together with organization and network complementarities approach and epidemic evolutionary models, lead to a better understanding of the main determinants of ICT intra-firm diffusion.*

Sample, data description, and econometric models

Data

The analysis is based on the data of a survey conducted between January and May 2003 on firms developing their activity in Catalonia. Its general objective is to analyze the transformation of the strategy and the organization of the companies linked to the use of information and communication technology (ICT). The survey has been carried out by means of a questionnaire, consisting of a face-to-face interview of one-hour duration, on a representative sample of 2,038 Catalan firms. The interviews, held with entrepreneurs or company directors who have a global vision of the whole activity, were generally well received and the collaboration of the interviewed was high. In addition, the questionnaire information was completed with economic and financial information available to the general public in the *Registre Mercantil* (Mercantile Register), obtained through the SABI programme. The questionnaire yielded data, for all firms, on: ICT equipment, such as the Internet, email, intranet, LAN/WAN/; the objective pursued by using ICT, such as, information, communication, administration. – and many other variables which may also serve as determinants of ICT adoption. The dataset contains information on firms' characteristics, such as size, industry affiliation, number of customers, number of providers, human capital composition or financials characteristics.

The models

In order to study the factors influencing intra-firm diffusion of ICT in Catalan firms, we use an ordered probit econometric model. The aim of the model is to determine the effect of different factors on the probability of the ICT adoption and use by the firm (i.e., age, size and networks effects, firm's organizational structure, absorptive capacity and human capital effect and the innovation and cooperation effect). Indeed, this method makes it possible to study the exerted influence by series of factors on a multinomial ordered variable.

The basic variables of our study are binary and qualitative (they take the value one if the firm uses an ICT tool and value zero if not). Firms' answers give us information on whether they adopt or use a particular technology or a tool of communication or not. For example, a firm indicates if it chooses the use of intranet or not. Since we have various types of binary variables, they are gathered, then, in different types of scores, in order to formulate a total score of adoption and a total score of ICT use. This gives us the multinomial character of this distribution (because it is composed of various methods) and the ordered character (because it is deduced starting from other binary variables).

From these particular hypotheses, we use ordered probit models. Indeed, the explained variable is subscripted from 1 to 18 for the adoption score and from 1 to 11 for the usage score. These variables are thus discrete and ordinate. A probit multinomial model would thus neglect the ordinality of the dependent variable while a linear regression, in contrast, would treat the difference between indices 3 and 4 in the same way as the difference between indices 1 and 2, whereas this corresponds only to one classification. In these two cases, the estimators would be thus biased (Greene, 2000; Thomas, 2000). The models commonly used for this type of variable are, therefore, the ordered logit and probit models. These models are founded on the estimation of a continuous latent variable, subjacent with the subscripted variable of interest. In an ordered probit model, the residual associated with this latent variable is supposed to follow a normal distribution.

Indeed, this method makes it possible to study the influence exerted by series of factors on a multinomial ordered variable (Greene, 2000; Thomas, 2000). The ordered probit models are generally based on probability. The latent model is similar to that of a binomial probit.

$$y_i^* = \beta x_i + \varepsilon_i \qquad (1)$$

where y_i^* is unobserved, continuous and latent measurement of ICT use, x_i a vector of endogenous variables, β the vector of the parameters and, ε_i the residual error, which follows a normal distribution. In the case of the probit multinomial ordered, one observes:

$$y_i = j \quad if \quad c_j < y_i^* < c_{j+i} \qquad (2)$$

where $j = 0, 1, J$ represent the various methods of the endogenous variable. The observed coded variable y_i is determined by the following model:

$$
\begin{aligned}
y_i &= 0 & if \ -\infty < y_i^* < \mu_1, \\
&= 1 & if \ \mu_1 < y_i^* < \mu_2, \\
&= 2 & if \ \mu_2 < y_i^* < \mu_3, \\
&\vdots \\
&= J & if \ \mu_{J-1} < y_i^* < \mu_J,
\end{aligned}
\qquad (3)
$$

where μ_k is an unknown parameter that must be estimated with the vector β.

The estimation of the model enables us to obtain the probabilities of realization of each index of the dependent variable. These probabilities are given by:

$$\text{Prob}(y_i = 0) = \phi(-\beta' x_i)$$
$$\text{Prob}(y_i = 1) = \phi(\mu_1 - \beta' x_i)$$
$$\text{Prob}(y_i = 2) = \phi(\mu_2 - \beta' x_i) - \phi(\mu_1 - \beta' x_i)$$
$$\text{Prob}(y_i = 3) = \phi(\mu_3 - \beta' x_i) - \phi(\mu_2 - \beta' x_i) \qquad (4)$$
$$\vdots$$
$$\text{Prob}(y_i = J) = 1 - \phi(\mu_{J-1} - \beta' x_i)$$

with ϕ representing the normal law function distribution. The adjustment of the model is done by the maximum likelihood estimation (Maddala and Flores-Lagaunes, 2001):

$$L = \prod_{i=1}^{N} \prod_{j=0}^{J} F_{ij}(x, \beta)^{y_{ij}} \qquad (5)$$

Let us note that the marginal effects of the explanatory variables x_i on the probabilities are not equal to the coefficients.

Thus, only the sign of the coefficient will be interpreted here and not its value. We try to model, first, the intensity of equipment or adoption of ICT and, second, the intensity of usage of various ICT tools.

The variables

Dependent variables

In our study we considered three models for three different dependent variables. Our dependent variables are obtained starting from the calculation of a total score of equipment and uses, which is obtained by summing two sub-scores (general equipment and specific equipment) and a score of ICT uses (Table 12.1).

Table 12.1   Definition of the dependent variables

Variable	Definition
❶ General equipment	Number of ICT general equipment adopted by the firm in 2003
❷ Specific equipment	Number of ICT specific equipment adopted by the firm in 2003
❸ ICT usage	Number of ICT equipment already in use by the firm in 2003

Variables measuring ICT tools adopted by firms

The first variable (score of general equipment: *Model 1*) gathers the basic or general purpose ICT tools that the firm has, such as: 1 – mobile phone, 2 – computers, 3 – Internet, 4 – LAN/WAN, 5 – EDI, 6 – website, 7 – email, 8 – intranet, 9 – firewall or antivirus (any of the nine types of use). The second variable (score of specific equipment: *Model 2*) gathers the specific ICT tools for each firm, such as: 1 – information processing system of production planning, 2 – information processing system of production planning to providers, 3 – information processing system of production planning to distributors, 4 – CRM, 5 – operational system of accounting and invoicing, 6 – system of payment by ICT tools, 7 – system or control program of data or exploitation of information, 8 – EIS, 9 – ERP (any of the nine types of use).

Each variable is presented, therefore, as follows:

$$\begin{cases} y_i = 0 & \text{if} \quad \text{zero equipment} \\ y_i = 1 & \text{if} \quad \text{one equipment} \\ y_i = 2 & \text{if} \quad \text{two equipments} \\ \quad \vdots \\ y_i = n & \text{if} \quad n \quad \text{equipments} \end{cases} \tag{6}$$

with n = 9 for variables score general equipment, n = 9 for the variable score specific equipment and N = 18 for the total score variable (score of adoption). y_i represents the dependant variable of the adoption of ICT by the firm i. This variable will be estimated by different explanatory variables (X_i).

Variables measuring intensity of ICT business uses

In this section, we chose to distinguish between the uses of the ICT, not according to the tool used (Internet, computers, EDI etc.), but according to the real usage expressed by the firm via their answers on this topic. In order to obtain this variable we gathered 11 purposes of ICT use by the firms, such as: communication, information, management, e-commerce, email and so on. Every firm has a score between zero and 11.

The variable used here (score of ICT uses: *Model 3*) is also an ordered polytomic variable characterizing the finality of the ICT usage by the firm. It gathers the uses which meet specific needs for the company, such as: 1 – communication, 2 – communication with costumers and providers, 3 – information via Internet, 4 – email, 5 – e-banking, 6 – web page and online marketing, 7 – internal communication, 8 – management, administration, accounting, 9 – basic tool in work/tasks, 10 – e-commerce, 11 – e-procurement (any of the 11 types of use). Therefore, this variable is presented as follows:

$$\begin{cases} y_i = 0 & if \quad zero\ usage \\ y_i = 1 & if \quad one\ usage \\ y_i = 2 & if \quad two\ usages \\ \quad \vdots \\ y_i = 11 & if \quad 11\ usages \end{cases} \tag{7}$$

y_i represents the dependant variable which summarizes the intensity of ICT usage by the firm i. We test the estimation in function of the same explanatory variables (X_i) of the first model. Explanatory variables are summarized in Table 12.2.

Determinants of intra-firm ICT diffusion in Catalan firms

This section presents the empirical results of a probit ordered model of the determinants of ICT adoption and use by Catalans firms. These determinants are gathered according to the different approaches quoted above. In order to characterize the adoption process we divide our investigation in three different models. Model 1 estimates the adoption of general purpose technologies. Model 2 estimates the adoption of specific technologies. Model 3 estimates the intensity of different business uses of ICT (Table 12.3).

By observing all the explanatory variables, we can outline the importance of ICT complementarities approach and evolutionary models in improving the explanation of the main determinants of businesses' digitalization process. In fact, we have demonstrated that some particular organizational practices are critical in the early adoption stage, while network effects offer further explanation of the diffusion of ICT use within a firm. Our results confirm the expected effects stated above. Let's see it step by step.

Epidemic effects

From an epidemic model point of view, we have demonstrated in this chapter a positive contribution made by managers' education attainment and worker profile. In fact, those firms with more qualified managers and younger workers are those showing a higher probability of using more digital technologies. In addition, managers' profiles (educational level, age, style of leadership, position regarding ICT etc.) impact

Table 12.2 Description of the explanatory variables

Explanatory variables	Definition
Epidemic effects	
HE degree of managers	Dummy variable: equal to 1 if the director has a university level and 0 so not.
Average age of managers	The age average of the directors
HE degree of workers	Dummy variable: equal to 1 if the employees have a university degree and 0 if not.
Average age of workers	The average age of the employees
Average wage	The logarithm of the average wage in the firm
Rank effects	
Age	The age of the firm
Size	The logarithm of the number of establishment's workers.
Learning effect	
Workers training	Dummy variable: equal to 1 if the employees are implied in training programs
Organizational effects	
Control by objective or result	Dummy variable: equal to 1 if the firm admits a control of payment by objective or result and 0 if not
Belonging to a group	Dummy variable: equal to 1 if the firm belong a group and 0 if not
Network effect	
Importer Firm	Dummy variable: equal to 1 if the firm is an importer and 0 if not
Number of customers	The logarithm of the number of the customers of the firm
Number of providers	The logarithm of the number of providers of the firm
Information industry sector	Dummy variable: equal to 1 if the firm belongs to the sector of information and 0 if not
Innovation process led by ICT use	Dummy variable: equal to 1 if the firm starts its innovation process by the use of ICT and 0 if not.
Innovative Firm	Dummy variable: equal to 1 if the firm is innovating and 0 if not.
Firm which cooperates with other firms/ institutions	Dummy variable: equal to 1 if the firm has a co-operation with other companies or institutions

Table 12.3 Determinants of ICT intra-firm diffusion

Explanatory Variables		ICT diffusion score		
		General Model 1	Specific Model 2	ICT uses Model 3
I. Epidemic effects				
HE degree of managers	No	Ref.	Ref.	Ref.
	Yes	0.3142***	0.0422	0.1491**
Average age of managers		−0.0091**	−0.0049	−0.0054*
Average age of workers		−0.0134***	−0.0083*	Ref.
Average wage		0.4093***	0.0536	0.1868**
II. Rank effects				
Age		−0.0044	0.0432	−0.0620*
Size		0.2553***	0.1482***	0.0613**
III. Learning effect				
Workers training	No	Ref.	Ref.	Ref.
	Yes	0.1982**	0.0629	0.0847
IV. Organizational effects				
Belonging to a group	No	Ref.	Ref.	Ref.
	Yes	0.1739**	0.0201	0.0539
Control by objective or result	No	Ref.	Ref.	Ref.
	Yes	0.1361**	0.0949	−0.0280
V. Network effects				
Importer Firm	No	Ref.	Ref.	Ref.
	Yes	0.2932***	0.2927***	0.2026***
Number of customers		0.0575***	0.0009	0.0335***
Number of providers		0.05210**	0.0318	0.0087
Information industry sector	No	Ref.	Ref.	Ref.
	Yes	0.1638**	0.0457	0.3330***
Innovation process led by ICT use	No	Ref.	Ref.	Ref.
	Yes	0.2215***	0.1508**	0.1763***
Innovative Firm	No	Ref.	Ref.	Ref.
	Yes	0.3732***	0.0958	0.2218***
Firm which cooperate with	No	Ref.	Ref.	Ref.
Other firms/ institutions	Yes	0.1299*	0.1620**	0.1083*

Ref.: Reference group.
*Significant at 10% level, **significant at 5% level, ***significant at 1% level.

strongly the technology adoption process. Managers are the main element responsible for the success of ICT introduction in small and medium firms.

In fact, higher education attainment by managers has a positive link with the probability of ICT adoption. Firms whose managers have attained higher education studies implement more rapidly these technologies since they are more likely to understand their aims and more able to foresee the impact on their collaborators; thus, degree of adoption of ICT in their companies is higher on average.

Our results also show a negative relationship between the age of both, managers (with $p<0.05$) and workers ($p<0.00$) and the willingness of firms to adopt digital technologies, indicating that firms with younger workers, younger and highly qualified managers and workers following training programs have a higher willingness to invest in digital technologies.

In terms of digital use, we have found that the intensity of usage is positively correlated with the absorptive capacity of the firm. In our sample of Catalan firms, one notices that firms with managers that have attained a university degree have higher intensity of use of more specialized ICT. The use of digital technologies by managers is far from being uniform and shows disparities.

However, the use of ICT increased for all the categories of age, even if the phenomenon is more significant in young people of less than 30 years. The intensity of ICT use by directors decreases with age, which is the case in our chapter.

In addition to those factors, a firm's efficiency plays an important role in the explanation of ICT adoption by firms. Moreover, the use of ICT is more important in those firms showing a higher level of average wages. Therefore, both in terms of acquirement of digital equipment and use, ICT is mainly adopted and used by those companies with high-skilled workers.

The implementation of ICT requires mid-term, and sometimes short-term, specific competences within the firm, especially those related to data processing and computer problem-solving. We observe that the average wage in a firm has a positive effect on ICT equipment or adoption. Since wages are considered as an imperfect measure of workers' productivity based on their competencies and qualifications, this may allow us to interpret this correlation as a relationship between ICT adoption and qualifications. Therefore, it is important to note that ICT is more likely to be adopted by firms with higher levels of employees' skills.

Rank effects

First, we verify a strong, positive and significant relationship between size and the probability of ICT adoption by a firm. As it was expected, there is a positive correlation between a firm's size and ICT capital stock, showing the existence of scale economies for digital investment. Similar to industrial technologies, large firms have more incentive to adopt ICT, as they have the chance to spread adjustment costs over a more substantial output volume.

Firm size has a positive and significant effect on the adoption of the two kinds of ICT equipment in econometric models (general and specific). This result is mainly due to two relevant factors: depth of technology and importance of internal coordination and communication within the firm. This finding is also consistent with the evidence that larger firms are more likely to adopt digital technology because they show lower levels of financial constraints. Moreover, the size of the firm exerted a positive and significant effect on the intensity of use of ICT, as in the case of the equipment. The intensity of use by a firm is positively correlated with its size. Our result confirms most of the well-established literature on this subject (OECD, 2004). In this sense, it is important to outline that firms' size and productivity levels have also, in our ICT usage model, a positive and significant effect on the explanation in terms of depth of adoption of digital technology, but the relationship is weaker than in our ICT equipment models. This means that the chance to obtain scale economies and firms' economic results seem not to be critical factors in explaining the willingness regarding and intensity of ICT use by a firm.

Learning effect

We have theoretically complemented epidemic effects with firms' technological absorption capacity based on learning, as a means of explaining the intra-firm diffusion process. Our results also show a positive relation with a firm's investment in workers' training; employees can acquire various qualification levels in ICT. These competences can be acquired in different ways, including various stages of conventional teaching in schools or universities or by workplace-specific training. This result is also confirmed in our estimation. Thus, it is found that firms with employees enrolled in training programs have more intensity of ICT use. And it confirms Bresnahan et al.'s (2002a, b) virtuous circle between ICT use and workers' skills; the positive effect of firms' networking structure on the depth of ICT adoption is complemented by the positive and significant contribution of human capital formation as determinants of economic digital use by firms.

Organization effects

We have divided complementarities approach into two different classes: organizational practices and network effects. As it was expected, we have found a positive and significant effect of new organizational practices, workers' skills and the existence of innovation policies on firms' willingness to invest in digital technologies.

Concerning organization, we have found that an organizational structure based on flexibility and decentralization of task execution and on the assessment of objectives reached leads to a higher probability of ICT adoption. It is interesting to note that network structure seems to be particularly appropriate for knowledge diffusion in all firm levels. This kind of organization gives firms the necessary flexibility to adjust their structures and to ensure a faster circulation of information, in which ICT plays a crucial role. It is also important to stress that the fact that a firm carries out its control by objectives or result, which requires important coordination, has a positive impact on the probability of ICT adoption. Organizational synergies are here confirmed by the positive sign of the coefficient of the variable 'belonging to a group'. When a firm is a large, multi-plant firm, the adoption of ICT facilitates internal coordination and communication. Indeed, the need for good coordination between firms within a group increases the probability of ICT adoption by firms. Concerning organization in the context of use of ICT by Catalan firms, we have found that the organizational structure of labor relations (the application of assessing by objectives or results) does not have an influence on the intensity of use of these tools, but does have a positive effect on ICT equipment present. This may mean that, at an earlier stage of adoption, firms have not reorganized to maximize efficiency by ICT use. This requires more time and may explain why productivity is negatively affected in the short run.

Network effects

We also observe that the degree of ICT adoption is higher for importing firms. This is explained by the fact that importation requires the automation of the relationship with providers and perhaps more information processing. This international effect is observed in all studies. We have found a significant and positive coefficient of the variable 'importer firm'.

The connectivity effect is also validated in our study. Indeed, an important result appears when analyzing external links of a firm. External communication is measured by the number of customers and providers. The pressures by customers and providers to improve communication and to use specific software to manage this kind of relationship increases the probability of ICT adoption; firms encourage their suppliers to adopt compatible technologies in order to coordinate transactions more effectively and to improve their information-processing capacity and reliability. This theoretical effect has been validated for Catalan firms in our estimate. Thus, we have found that the greater the number of customers and suppliers, the higher the degree of ICT adoption by firms. Firms' networking structure results contrast with firm size and productivity. Those firms that are more connected with foreign markets ('importer firms') demonstrate a noticeably higher probability of deeper ICT adoption. Therefore, it can be said that the promotion of net organizational structures leads to a positive and significant effect on a firm's willingness to show more advanced use of digital technology.

Another interesting result is the weak link between industry belonging and the probability to adopt ICT. Our results show that only one out of three ICT equipment models specified (the general model) have a coefficient that is significant, with $p<0,05$, confirming the idea of general diffusion of ICT among industries. However, in our general model, we have found some significant differences between industries, demonstrating that ICT industry willingness to increase its digital capital stock is higher than the average probability for the rest of industry. But, contrary to the determinants of ICT investment, the industrial approach plays an important role here. Our results show that ICT and digital content producers are also those firms showing a higher intensity of use of this kind of technology than the rest of industry in their production processes.

Nowadays, innovation is the main driver of change in business and in the whole economy. In an environment of globalization, knowledge and the development of capital value added become extremely important factors of competition. Consequently, in a knowledge-based economy, where coordination and communication intra- and inter-firm is required, investment in digital technologies is consistent with business innovation.

The capability and willingness of a firm to innovate is another significant variable in the explanation of firms' investment in ICT equipment. In this sense, we have found a positive and significant effect from innovative firms (those that have innovated in the last two years), from those firms that are used to innovation by using digital technologies, and from cooperation to innovate. The latter issue is particularly important in the case of SMEs, which usually do not have a formal department devoted to R&D activities.

We can also confirm that those firms that have innovated during the last two years, especially those whose innovation has been led by ICT use, show more willingness to have higher levels of depth of digital technology adoption. So, the results in Table 12.3 indicate that cooperation and innovation have a statistically significant effect on the use of the ICT, innovation in particular, which has a significant coefficient at 1 percent level.

In this same context, one of the main advantages of innovation is the incentive that it gives to companies to become a part of networks of cooperation. Thus, as confirmed by the results in Table 12.3, it is noticed that the degree of cooperation of the firm with other companies or institutions (universities, research centers, public authorities etc.) has a positive impact on the diffusion of ICT. Therefore, we can conclude that innovation and firms' cooperation have a positive effect on ICT adoption by Catalan companies.

As an example of innovation in the process, a firm might adopt new online shop software. This may allow the firm to deliver its products to customers in a new way or to offer additional services, such as tracking orders online or getting immediate information about availability. This new process thus requires significant use of digital technology; ICT not only makes the innovation process more dynamic, but also more interactive and interdependent. This justifies the higher coefficient of the variable 'innovation process led by ICT use' in our results. These unidirectional relationships are consistent with results available in the international literature, which evidence positive complementary effects from ICT investment, organizational change and the demand for skilled labor on the improvement of firms' efficiency (Bresnahan et al., 2000a, 2000b; Cristini et al., 2003).

The dynamic of use may not follow the same pattern as the adoption of technology. This lag between adoption and use is due to a required adjustment to incorporate new technology into the routines of firms. Our estimate verifies most of the effect for use dynamics. Three main reasons describe the positive correlation between ICT use and innovation for Catalan companies. First, because ICT stimulates innovative dynamism in partially reducing existing constraints on innovation and making interaction between the agents involved in the innovative process – both inside and outside the company – more efficient. Second, ICT modifies the nature of innovations and allows the development of more sophisticated and interdependent innovative processes. Third, because the complexity of innovative processes induced by ICT means that their use can be considered a sustainable competitive advantage only if these technologies are used in an integrated structure with the available resources and capacities.

With regard to the influence of the cooperation effect, we observe that firms which cooperate with others institutions or firms have a higher probability of using ICT than those that do not. One of the main positive effects of ICT usage as an innovation tool is the incentive it represents for Catalan firms to build new cooperation networks or to make the existing ones more efficient.

In this sense, from our results, it can be stated that there is a positive and significant relationship between ICT use by firms, networking structure, workers' skills and profile, and innovation capabilities and background, as these are the main determinants of the intensity of use of digital technology.

Conclusion

In this chapter, we try to understand the main forces behind the ICT intra-firm diffusion process. To achieve this, we analyze a representative sample of Catalan firms through a single year (2003) cross-section database and propose an approach to modeling the determinants of ICT intra-firm diffusion by combining diffusion theories with complementarities approaches and technical choices perspectives. Our main contribution lies in the measurement and estimation of organizational network effects to explain the depth of digital technology adoption by firms. In order to achieve consistent results, given the important difficulties of defining a measure of digital uses within a firm, we propose a twofold measurement system: i) first, one that considers specific ICT tools (such as CRM, EIS or ERP) adopted by a firm (as they are specific and complex, we assume that a firm will only adopt them if an 'appropriate' use has been planned before adoption); ii) and, second, a measure that relies on different business use of digital technology that has been declared by firms. Our results confirm that inter-firm diffusion of ICT, estimated in our work with a general model of digital tools' adoption, can be identified as a previous step to depth of adoption in firms. Thus, inter-firm and intra-firm diffusion processes have different determinants, although they share some common traits based on the existence of complementary effects between digital technologies, innovation, organizational structure and workers' skills within a firm.

On the one hand, inter-firm diffusion of ICT mainly depends on the chance of obtaining scale economies and the firm's ability to achieve positive returns on its investment through efficiency levels. Thus, the effect of firm size and productivity level is confirmed here. However, ICT capital is characterized by representing general purpose technology and by being complementary to some advanced organizational practices and to analytic, interactive and computing skills. These particular traits can explain why, in contrast to other industrial technologies, there is an important relationship between ICT adoption in firms and: i) decentralization of the decision-making processes, ii) human capital formation through the demand for managers with higher education attainment and investment in workers' training programs and iii) firms' willingness to innovate, to use ICT as an innovation tool or mechanism, and to cooperate with other organizations in innovating.

On the other hand, intra-firm diffusion of ICT is more related to firms' ability to improve their efficiency through digital business uses. This is the reason why complementing technological diffusion theories with organizational network complementarities and epidemic evolutionary models allows us to explain much better the main determinants of the depth of ICT adoption within firms. Empirically, these approaches can be identified in five critical variables: i) firms' networking organizational structure, ii) the demand for highly qualified managers, iii) the existence of young workers, iv) the innovation background and v) belonging to the ICT industry.

We have also found a difference concerning some organization effects between inter-firm and intra-firm diffusion patterns. The recombination and the modification of technologies were not optimal at the earlier stage of adoption. The study is based upon a questionnaire concluded in an earlier period of ICT diffusion in Catalonia; a new survey may reveal changes in these dynamics. Our study confirms the lag between adoption and usage of these technologies in the earlier stage of adoption.

Notes

1. As it will be explained in the fourth section, the survey's sample contains 2,038 Catalan companies that are significant in terms of size (number of employees – including micro-companies (i.e. less than 10 employees)).
2. Most Catalan companies, 93.2 percent, used mobile phones in 2003, regardless of the size of the firm; 97.3 percent had a computer; 90.9 percent had an Internet connection (67.0 percent of firms connected to the Internet and 60.9 percent of Catalan companies were connected to the Internet via an ADSL connection) and 87.4 percent of companies have email. Among the reasons that companies gave for not having a website or email – that is, the fact of not using the Internet as a possible channel by which to interact directly with suppliers and customers – it should be highlighted that the main reason was that they did not need it. In fact, this reason was given by 77.4 percent of companies that had neither website nor . Other reasons – such as still being in the construction phase or the lack of finance – were cited by 11.0 percent and 9.4 percent of Catalan companies, respectively.
3. 44.4 percent of companies mention these tasks, compared to other options, such as principal digital uses. Next, 29.3 percent of Catalan companies declared using digital technologies, especially the Internet, to obtain

information, while an additional 27.4 percent employed it in their relationship with customers and suppliers. Communication is a fourth significant element. This use was cited by 23.4 percent of Catalan firms. Therefore, at first sight, Catalan companies used digital technologies in production to become more efficient in internal administrative tasks and to improve their external relations through the communication, particularly with the customers in general, with the two external agents most directly linked to the business activity: customers and suppliers.

4. This measurement system will be developed in the fifth section.

References

Acemoglu, D. and F. Newman (2002) 'The Labor Market and Corporate Structure', *European Economic Review*, Elsevier, Vol. 46, No. 10, pp. 1733–56.

Antonelli, C. (2003) 'The Economics of Innovation, New Technologies and Structural Change', London: Routledge.

Astebro, T.B. (2004) 'Sunk Costs and the Depth and Probability of Technology Adoption', *Journal of Industrial Economics*, Vol. 52, pp. 381–99.

Battisti, G. and P. Stoneman (2005) 'The Intra-firm Diffusion of New Process Technology', *International Journal of Industrial Organization*, Vol. 23, pp. 1–22.

Battisti, G. and P. Stoneman (2003) 'Inter- and Intra-firm Effects in the Diffusion of New Process Technology', *IResearch Policy*, Vol. 32, pp. 1641–55.

Battisti, G., H. Hollenstein, P. Stoneman and M. Woerter (2007) 'Inter and Intra Firm Diffusion of ICT in the United Kingdom (UK) and Switzerland (Ch): An Internationally Comparative Study based on Firm-level Data', *Economics of Innovation and New Technology*, Vol. 16, No. 8, pp. 669–87.

Bellon, B., A. Ben Youssef and H. Mhenni (2006) 'Le maillon manquant entre adoption et usage des TIC dans les fonctions managériales des économies du sud méditerranéen', *Revue Française de Gestion*, Vol. 166, pp. 173–89.

Bellon, B., A. Ben Youssef and H. Mhenni (2007) 'Les capacités d'usage des Technologies de l'information et de la communication dans les économies émergentes', *Revue Tiers Monde*, Vol. 192, pp. 919–36.

Bertschek, I. And H. Fryges (2002) 'The Adoption of Business-to-business e-commerce: Empirical Evidence for German Companies', Discussion Paper No. 02-05, Centre for European Economic Research, Mannheim.

Bocquet, R. and O. Brossard (2007) 'The Variety of ICT Adopters in the Intra-firm Diffusion Process: Theoretical Arguments and Empirical Evidence', *Structural Change and Economic Dynamics*, Vol. 18, pp. 409–37.

Bresnahan, T.F., E. Brynjolfsson and L.M. Hitt (2002a), 'Technology, Organization, and the Demand for Skilled Labor', in M.M. Blair and T.A. Kochan (eds), *The New Relationship: Human Capital in the American Corporation*, Washington DC: Brookings Institution Press.

Bresnahan, T.F., E. Brynjolfsson and L.M. Hitt (2002b), 'Information Technology, Workplace Organization and the Demand for Skilled Labor: Firm-level Evidence', *The Quarterly Journal of Economics*, Vol. 117, No. 1, pp. 339–76.

Bresnahan, T.F. and M. Trajtenberg (1995) 'General Purpose Technologies: Engines of Growth', *Journal of Econometrics*, Vol. 65, No.1, pp. 83–108.

Brousseau, E. (1994) 'EDI and Inter-firm Relationships: Toward a Standardization of Coordination Process?', *Information Economics and Policy*, Vol. 6, pp. 319–47

Brynjolfsson, E. and L.M. Hitt (2000) 'Beyond Computation: Information Technology, Organizational Transformation and Business Performance', *Journal of Economic Perspectives*, Vol. 14, No. 4, pp. 24–48.

Caroli, E. and J. van Reenen (2001) 'Skill-Biased Organizational Change? Evidence from a Panel of British and French Establishments', *The Quarterly Journal of Economics*, Vol. 116, No.4, pp. 1449–92.

Cohen, W. and D. Levinthal (1989) 'Innovation and Learning: The Two Faces of R&D', *Economic Journal*, Vol. 99, pp. 569–96.

Cristini, A., A. Gaj, S. Labory and R. Leoni (2003) 'Flat Hierarchical Structure, Bundles of New Work Practices and Firm Performance', *Rivista Italiana degli Economisti*, Vol. 8, No. 2, pp. 313–41.

Davies, S. (1979) *The Diffusion of Process Technologies*, Cambridge, MA: Cambridge University Press.

Doms, M.E. and T. Dunne (1998) 'Capital Adjustment Patterns in Manufacturing Plants', *Review of Economic Dynamics*, Vol. 1, No. 2, pp. 409–29.

Dunne, T. (1994) 'Plant Age and Technology Use in US Manufacturing Industries', *Rand Journal of Economics*, Vol. 25, pp. 488–99.

Fabiani, S., F. Schivardi and S. Trento (2005) 'ICT Adoption in Italian Manufacturing: Firm Level Evidence', *Industrial and Corporate Change*, Vol. 14, No. 2, pp. 225–49.

Fichman, R.G. and C.F. Kemerer (1997) 'Object Technology and Reuse: Lessons from Early Adopters', *IEEE Computer*, Vol. 30, No. 10, pp. 47–59.

Foray, D. (2004) *The Economics of Knowledge*, Cambridge, MA: MIT Press.

Foss, K., N.J. Foss and P.G. Klein (2007) 'Original and Derived Judgment: An Entrepreneurial Theory of Economic Organization', *Organization Studies*, Vol. 28, No. 12, pp. 1893–912.

Freeman, C. and L. Soete (1997) *The Economics of Industrial Innovation*, 3rd edn, Cambridge, MA: MIT Press.Galliano, D. and P. Roux (2006) 'Les inégalités spatiales dans l'usage des TIC: Le cas des firmes industrielles françaises', *Revue Economique*, Vol. 57, No. 6, pp. 1449–75.

Galliano, D., P. Roux and M. Filippi (2001) 'Organisational and Spatial Determinants of ICT Adoption: The Case of French Industrial Firms', *Environment and Planning*, Vol. 33, No. 9, pp. 1643–63.

Greene, W.H. (2000) *Econometric Analysis*, 4th edn, New Jersey: Prentice International Hall.

Greenan, N. (2003) 'Organizationnal Change, Technology, Employment and Skills: An Empirical Study of French Manufacturing', *Cambridge Journal of Economics*, Vol. 27, pp. 287–316.

Hannan, M.T. and J. Freeman (1989) *Organizational Ecology*, Cambridge, MA: Harvard University Press.

Hollenstein, H. (2004) 'The Determinants of the Adoption of ICT', *Structural Change and Economics Dynamics*, Vol. 15, pp. 315–42.

Huggett, M. and S. Ospina (2001) 'Does Productivity Growth Fall After the Adoption of New Technology?', *Journal of Monetary Economics*, Elsevier, Vol. 48, No. 1, pp. 173–95.

Jorgenson, D.W., M.S. Ho, K.J. Stiroh (2005), *Productivity: Information Technology and the American Growth Ressurgence*, Vol. 3, Cambridge, MA: MIT Press.

Karlsson, C. (1995) 'Innovation Adoption, Innovation Networks and Agglomeration Economies', in C.S. Bertuglia, M.M. Fischer and G. Preto (eds), *Technological Change, Economic Development and Space*, New York: Springer, pp. 184–206.

Karshenas, M. and P.L. Stoneman (1993) 'Rank, Stock, Order, and Epidemic Effects in the Diffusion of New Process Technologies: An Empirical Model', *RAND Journal of Economics*, The RAND Corporation, Vol. 24, No. 4, pp. 503–28, Winter.

Lange T., M. Ottens and A. Taylor (2000) 'SMEs and Barriers to Skills Development: A Scottish Perspective', *Journal of Industrial Training*, Vol. 24, pp. 5–11.

Leduc, K. (2006a) 'L'intégration des TIC dans les entreprises: quel impact sur leurs partenariats? Une analyse sur des entreprises implantées au Luxembourg', Working Paper Département 'Entreprises', No. 2006-02.

Leduc, K. (2006b) 'Les travailleurs âgés face aux TIC', EPS/INSTEAD Working Paper Département 'Entreprises', No. 2006-03.

Levine, D.I. (1998), *Working in the Twenty-first Century: Policies for Economic Growth through Training, Opportunity, and Education*, Armonk, NY: M.E. Sharpe.

Love, P., Z. Irani, C. Standing, C. Lin and J.M. Burn (2005) 'The Enigma of Evaluation: Benefits, Costs and Risks of IT in Australian Small-Medium-Sized Enterprises', *Information and Management*, Vol. 42, No. 7, pp. 947–64.

Maddala G. and A. Flores-Lagaunes (2001) 'Qualitative Response Models', in B. Baltagi (ed.), *A Companion to Theoretical Econometrics*, Oxford: Blackwell.

Mansfield, E. (1963) 'The speed of response of firms to new techniques', *The Quarterly Journal of Economics*, Vol. 77, No. 2, pp. 290–311.

Milgrom, P. and J. Roberts (1992) *Economics, Organization and Management*, Englewood Cliffs: Printice-Hall International.

Morgan, A., D. Colebourne and B. Thomas (2006) 'The Development of ICT Advisors for SME Business: An Innovative Approach', *Technovation*, Vol. 26, No. 8, pp. 980–87.

Murphy, M. (2002) 'Organisational Change and Firm Performance', STI Working Paper 2002/14.

OECD (2004) *The Economic Impact of ICT, Measurement, Evidence and Implications*, Paris: OECD.

Osterman, P. (2000) 'Work Reorganization in an Era of Restructuring: Trends in Diffusion and Effects on Employee Welfare', *Industrial and Labor Relations Review*, Vol. 53, No. 2, pp. 176–96.

Raymond, L. and G. Paré (1992) 'Measurement of Information Technology Sophistication in Small Manufacturing Businesses', *Information Resources Management Journal*, Vol. 5, No. 2, pp. 4–16

Rogers, E.M. (1995) *Diffusion of Innovations*, 4th edn, New York: Free Press.

Stoneman, P. (2001) 'Technological Diffusion and the Financial Environment' *EIFC – Technology and Finance* Working Papers 3, Institute for New Technologies, United Nations University.

Swanson, E.B. (1994) 'Information Systems Innovation among Organizations', *Management Science*, Vol. 40, No. 9, pp. 1069–92.

Thomas, A. (2000) *Econometric of the Qualitative Variables*, Paris: Dunod.

Thong, J.Y.L. (1999) 'An Integrated Model of Information Systems Adoption in Small Business', *Journal of Management Information Systems*, Vol. 4, No. 15, pp. 187–214.

Windrum, P. and P. de Berranger (2003) 'Factors Affecting the Adoption of Intranets and Extranets by SMEs: A UK Study', Research Memorandum 2003-023, MERIT, Maastricht.

13
Does ICT Enable Innovation in Luxembourg? An Empirical Study

Leila Ben Aoun and Anne Dubrocard

Introduction

This study aims to analyze the impact of information and communication technology (ICT) on the ability to innovate of Luxembourgish firms. On the one hand, ICT can be viewed as an accelerator of technological and organizational innovations; on the other hand, ICT is itself changing fast and in a complex relationship with innovation activities and results. Indeed, ICT can speed up the diffusion of information, favor networking among firms, reduce geographic limitations and increase efficiency in communication. In addition, ICT provides a platform for scientific and technological innovation and organizational changes. Knowledge transfer and sharing made possible through networks in real time increase scientific and technological innovation capacities and reinforce new organizational practices and arrangements such as e-management, e-business and e-commerce. These practices are both organizational innovations in themselves and drivers for improving firms' performance.

A significant number of studies attempting to illustrate the impact of ICT on growth have been conducted on both macroeconomic and microeconomic levels. An overall assessment of the results and international comparisons is offered in the OECD report (2003). Pilat's literature review (2004) tends to confirm that the extent to which ICT tools are used, combined with organizational modifications or increases in employees' qualifications, contributes to growth through improvement of firms' performance. In order to measure and modelize this kind of phenomenon, it is necessary to engage micro data analysis.[1] The main objective is to highlight and understand any link that may exist between the intensity of ICT use and the propensity to innovate.

313

The most recent version of the Oslo manual sets out four innovation categories:

- a product or service innovation – when a company in the business or services sector is concerned – that results in putting out a new product or offering a new business service;
- a process innovation – that is, the implementation of new techniques for producing goods or for providing services;
- organizational innovation;
- innovation in marketing, such as creating a franchise or promoting a product on the Internet.

The sample of Luxemburgish firms set up from two statistical sources merging the ICT survey 2007 (ICT2007) with the latest Community Innovation Survey (CIS) 2006 (CIS2006). Both surveys are coordinated by Eurostat and provide harmonized statistics in European Union countries. The merger resulted in a sample of 349 observations representing about 60 percent of companies with at least ten employees in the 2006 CIS survey. A probit model of dichotomic variables is estimated. For each technological and non-technological innovation type, the decision to innovate is explained by firms' ICT equipment, ICT use and by other individual characteristics.

Literature review

ICT improves firm performance

For years, studies failed to identify and measure the impact of ICT investment on national growth and productivity. Substantial ICT investment undertaken in order to decrease the cost of communication and coordination within and outside firms, changing work and life every day, seems to have had no impact on productivity growth. To assess issues related to measurement and identification of the impact of ICT investment on growth at macro level, studies have been undertaken at micro level, providing new evidence from different countries. On the one hand, recent literature analyses the adoption and diffusion of ICT at firm level (Mansfield, 1963; Hollenstein, 2004; Bocquet and Brossard 2007). Nevertheless, how ICTs drive innovation is a relevant question that has not been developed so much through quantitative approaches. On the other hand, based on different indicators and measures, the relationship between ICT and productivity at the firm level is most often positive (Black and Lynch, 2001; Bresnahan, 2002, for the US; Greenan et al., 2001, for France; Bugamelli and Pagano, 2004; and, more recently, Castiglione, 2009, for Italy). Nevertheless, most studies reveal also that ICT alone is not sufficient to affect productivity. Moreover, micro-level data made it possible to highlight 'intangible organizational investment and products and service innovation associated with computer' (Brynjolfsson and Hitt, 2000, p. 25).

It seems to be clear now that, beyond delay effect and difficulties to catch intangibles throughout national statistics, impact and efficiency of ICT investment are closely related to other factors. Thus, the OECD (2003) points out the complementarities between skills, organizational change and innovation at firm level, while Brynjolfsson and Hitt (2000) investigate the complementarities of investment needed in business processes and work practices to match organizational structure and technology capabilities. Some authors emphasize that skill composition impacts on firm performance. Moreover, the contribution of innovation in achieving effective results from ICT investment is not the easiest to analyze.

Innovation improves firm performance

Drivers of innovation have been of interest for the Luxembourg National Statistics office for several years. Asikainen (2008) aims to determine whether and how factors like firm and market characteristics influence innovative performance (direct effect) and firm performance (indirect effect).

Using data from the CIS2004, it had been found that different variables linked to innovation activities significantly influence firm performance in terms of innovation. Namely:

- firm size;
- sectors;
- market structure;
- research and development intensity;
- trade share;
- foreign ownership.

More precisely, propensity to innovate increases with size of firm, but investment per employee and results obtained decrease. Belonging to a group (holding) increases significantly the probability, as well as propensity, to innovate. Competition and demand pressures are important factors in the decision to innovate.

These results are in accordance with numerous studies conducted in other countries, such as Sweden (Lööf and Heshmati, 2002), France,

Germany, Spain, the UK (Griffith et al., 2006), Chile (Benavente, 2006) and China (Jefferson et al., 2006). These numerous and recent studies show that determinants (direct through innovation and indirect through R&D) of firm performance are of major interest in many countries. The number of studies that focus their attention on the indirect effect of ICT investment or usage is much lower.

ICT use enables innovation and, to an extent, productivity...

Issues in identification and measurement of the relationship between ICT and innovation come from the double nature of information technology. First, ICT is a major technological innovation (or cluster of innovations), which in turn, throughout new application and processes, allows faster development in the innovation process itself. ICT enables innovation and productivity by its input. But, in turn, innovation processes and producers accelerate and modify ICT deployment in a 'co-inventory' process to make ICT useful. Various relationships and variables are studied, as summarized in Figure 13.1.

At the European level some studies have been performed regarding the impact of being ICT-based innovators on firm performance. Koellinger (2008), using a sample with more than 7,000 European enterprises, shows that all studied types of innovation, including Internet-enabled and non-Internet-enabled product or process innovations, are positively associated with turnover and employment growth. Firms that rely on Internet-enabled innovations are at least as likely to grow as those that rely on non-Internet-enabled innovations. The impact of being innovative on ICT adoption has been explored by Hempell (2002). Using

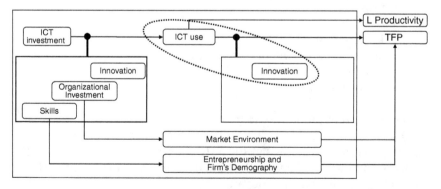

Figure 13.1   Productivity drivers
Source: Authors elaboration.

German data, he shows that the impact of ICT on productivity is much higher for firms that have deployed process innovation in the past. In the end, efficiency of ICT investment depends on complementarities of ICT use. Moreover, Hempell et al. (2004) find that ICT investment has to be coupled with product or process innovation or with change in organization or with permanent non-technological innovations, to increase impact measured on productivity. From German data, they obtain the maximum impact on total factor productivity (TFP) for services enterprises with permanent innovation activities.

Using a balanced panel data of market services firms in the Netherlands, van der Wiel and van Leeuwen (2003) explore also the impact of ICT on innovation capabilities. They show that the average productivity of innovators increases for those identified as high intensity in ICT use. It means that, in order to obtain full benefit from their innovation efforts, firms have to achieve beforehand a high level of ICT adoption. Abello and Prichard (2008), from the Australian Bureau of Statistics, explore business use of IT and innovation using linked firm-level data, and they find important correlation between being an innovator and different measurements of ICT use such as IT skills, broadband connection, web presence, ordering via Internet and linking this process to other business systems. From different logistic regressions, it appears that different IT and non-IT factors significantly explain each type of innovation. Thus, while hiring IT specialists remains a parameter enforcing propensity to innovate in a broad sense, it fails in explaining each type of innovation separately except organizational/managerial innovation.

...depending on its combination with other factors

Since IT and Internet are network features, they have also specific economic property – constant fixed costs and zero marginal costs – whose generalization has a huge impact on market structure. Varian (2005, p. 11) analyses the relationship between technology and market structure and points out: 'the challenge facing us now is to re-engineer the flow of information through the enterprise, and not only within the enterprise – the entire value chain is up for grabs'. It seems that the diffusion of ICT, and especially network technologies, is changing shares of the gains along the value chain and, moreover, has an impact redesigning the firm's frontiers and market competition. Brynjolfsson and Hitt (2000) highlight those transformations with examples of vertical integration or renewed definition of business for existing firms directly induced by ICT technical and organizational capabilities. ICT modifies organizational practice changes, as well the pace of change in producing new technologies and, as a result, market conditions. Askenazy et al. (2006) explore the role of time-based competition allowed by new technologies of information. Widespread ICT diffusion boosts the value of innovation and R&D investment among firms, increasing, at the same time, the competitive pressure on the product market, which in turn enforces more reactive organizational forms renewing the original trade-off between creative–reactive–decentralized and efficient–hier-archical–bureaucratic models of organization. Those approaches highlight both ICT and organizational impacts on the ability to innovate in process, product and organization.

Model

In order to analyze the impact of ICT use in firms on their probability and propensity to innovate, different levels of ICT use are defined and tested, with special attention given to measuring the impact of organizational innovation. Following the *Oslo Manual* we can define the innovation as 'the implementation of a new or significantly improved product or process, a new marketing approach, or a new organizational method in business practices, the workplace or in external relations. This covers both technological and non-technological innovations, and both the creation of new products and their diffusion.' Following this approach, the CIS2006 provides information for each type of innovation performed by firms during the period 2004–06:

- a product innovation is the introduction of a good or service that is new or significantly improved with respect to its characteristics or intended uses. This includes significant improvements in technical specifications, components and materials, incorporated software, user friendliness or other functional characteristics;
- a process innovation is the implementation of a new or significantly improved production or delivery method. This includes significant changes in techniques, equipment and/or software;
- an organizational innovation is the implementation of a new organizational method in the firm's business practices, workplace organization or external relations;
- a marketing innovation is the implementation of a new marketing method involving significant changes in product design or packaging, product placement, product promotion or pricing.

In this respect, two types of technological innovators and two types of non-technological innovators are considered. In the former group are:

- those that introduced new goods or new services;
- those that deployed new processes;

and in the latter:

- those who introduced major organizational change;
- those who introduced marketing innovation.

The innovative behavior of firms depends on several factors among which the model introduces ICT use variables. This approach suggests that different kinds of ICT do not have the same impact on different types of innovation.

A dichotomous variable describes each innovation implemented with value one if the firm has introduced the type of innovation considered during the last two years and zero otherwise. Only latent variables can be observed, but not the intensities of the different type of innovations. Finally, one should note that the CIS does not provide information relative to the positive/null or negative impact of the non-product innovations on firm performance. For product innovation, firms answered the following question: 'give the percentage of your total turnover in 2006 from goods and service innovations introduced during 2004–06 that were only new to your market or only new to your firm'. Due to the lack of information on spillovers for all innovations, impact on performances cannot be measured directly and are not analyzed in this work. In order to identify the ICT impact on the propensity to innovate, four binary response models (probit) are estimated. The 'generic model' can be expressed as follows: y^* is linked to the observed y by the measurement equation:

$$y_i = \begin{cases} 1 & \text{if} \quad y_i^* > \tau \\ 0 & \text{if} \quad y_i^* \leq \tau \end{cases}$$

y^* is a latent variable corresponding to the expected benefit from the innovative behavior. The binary indicator y_i equals unity if the firm has innovated. Let us remember that we will observe four separated regressions, one for each type of innovation. τ is called the threshold, and we make the identifying assumption that $\tau = 0$. ε is assumed to be normally distributed (mean equal to zero and variance equal to one) with probability density function:

$$\varphi(\varepsilon) = \frac{1}{\sqrt{2\pi}} e^{\left(-\frac{\varepsilon^2}{2}\right)}$$

and the cumulative density function:

$$\Phi(\varepsilon) = \int_{-\infty}^{\varepsilon} \frac{1}{\sqrt{2\pi}} e^{\left(-\frac{t^2}{2}\right)} dt$$

The probability that $y = 1$ (i.e., the firm innovates) is a function of the cumulative density function:

$$\Pr(y = 1 \mid x) = \Phi(x\beta) = \int_{-\infty}^{x\beta} \frac{1}{\sqrt{2\pi}} e^{\left(-\frac{t^2}{2}\right)} dt$$

where vector x contains firm characteristics.

Three remarks should be kept in mind regarding this model:

- the four cases are considered separately;
- a multinomial model cannot be used here because the dependent variable is not exclusive – for example, an entrepreneur can decide to innovate in product and in process;
- finally, one can notice that other specification has been tested; notably, in order to take into account potential endogeneity of the ICT variables, alternative estimation has been performed with a probit model with random effects.

Results obtained with this methodology do not improve on those obtained in the simplest case presented above. For commodity and clarity, only the results from the probit specification in cross-section have been retained (see Appendix: Probit equations with endogenous regressors).

Data and variables

Data

The sample used in this study comes from the merge of the community survey on ICT usage in enterprises for the year 2007 and the CIS2006. In order to ensure comparability across countries, for both surveys, European countries coordinated though Eurostat submit a standard core questionnaire with a common set of definitions and methodological recommendations.

ICT survey 2007

The design of the ICT survey allows assessment of the quality of access to ICT and how these technologies are used inside firms. This questionnaire is divided into modules and it covers a broad range of activities such as equipment and uses related to PCs, workstations and Internet,[2] e-commerce and other network systems allowing electronic/online purchases and sales etc.

The ICT survey has been conducted yearly since 2002. It is representative of firms with ten employees and more. This survey uses strata based on industry classification NACE[3] and covers the sections D, F, G, I and K, groups 55.1, 55.2, 92.1 and 92.2 and classes 65.12, 65.22, 66.01 and 66.03 (see Appendix and Eurostat[4] for details).

Community Innovation Survey 2006

The CIS2006 collects information about product and process innovation, as well as organizational and marketing innovations and their results during a two-year period. More precisely, it gives a clear picture about: innovation activity and expenditure, intramural research and experimental development (R&D), effects of innovation, public funding of innovation, innovation cooperation, sources of information for innovation, hampered innovation activity, patents and other protection methods and other important strategic and organizational changes in the enterprise. The first CIS (CIS1) was a pilot exercise, held in 1993, while the second survey (CIS2) was carried out in 1997/1998, the third survey (CIS3) was implemented in 2002 in Luxembourg, the CIS4 was carried out in 2005, based on the reference period 2004. The fifth survey: CIS2006 is the one used in this analysis. This survey focus on firm with at least ten employees and the industries covered are sections C, D, E, I, J, groups G51, K72, K74.2, K74.3 (see Appendix A13.1 and Appendix A13.2 for more details). After linking these two datasets, it is obvious that only the sections, groups or classes that are common in both surveys can be useful. We obtain a sample of 349 observations. Nevertheless, one should keep in mind that the 37 observations corresponding to the financial activities classification do not answer the e-commerce module.

Variables

The aim of this chapter is to bring to light the impact of ICT use on firms' propensity to innovate from an original sample of Luxembourgish firms. The main statistics presented hereafter describe in depth the content of this sample: general characteristics of the firms, variables related to innovation and, finally, ICT variables will be presented in the next paragraphs. Sample weighted is representative of the Luxemburgish firms of more than ten employees.

General characteristics

Table 13.1 gives an overview of the sample, depending on the size and the NACE, but also the main market scope of the firms.

One can notice that almost 95 percent are small and medium firms with less than 250 employees. The sample is well balanced, including firms from manufacturing, transport, telecommunication and financial services in equivalent proportion – that is, around 20 percent for each activity. More than half the firms are mainly present on national market, which is more limited. Moreover, more than a third of them have their main markets at European level and 40 percent have their main market out of the Grande Région (namely Luxembourg and regions of France, Belgium and Germany neighboring Luxembourg). This international aspect is characteristic of the Luxembourgish economy.

Innovation variables

Four different types of innovation are reported in the CIS. Table 13.2 reveals the percentage of firms declaring that they are active in each type of innovation. First, 60 percent of firms are innovative, regardless the type of innovation considered. This is not insignificant. Moreover,

Table 13.1   A sample of Luxembourgish firms

Variable	(%)
Size	
Firm from 10 to 19 employees	37.8
Firm from 20 to 49 employees	35.1
Firm from 50 to 249 employees	21.8
Firm with more than 250 employees	5.2
Main economic activity	
Manufacture Industry	21.6
Automobile and retails	19.6
Transports and communications	21.7
Financial	21.1
Other Business	16.0
Main market	
National market	52.7
Grande Region market	6.8
European market	33.5
Other market	7.0
obs. = 349	

Table 13.2 Innovativeness of the firms

	% of firms
All type of innovation	63.1
Product or service innovation	36.7
Process innovation	31.2
Organizational innovation	49.7
Marketing innovation	17.2
obs. = 349	

Source: STATEC, CIS2006-ICT2007 author's calculation.

more than 30 percent of firms declare that they have introduced a new product between 2004 and 2006, and more or less the same proportion has introduced innovation in their process – namely 'technological innovations'. Half of the sample recognizes an organizational change during the same period, while marketing innovation is the least frequent type of innovation implemented.

Table 13.3 combines previous information. Some interesting phenomena appear when crossing referencing information about innovative activities with main characteristics of the firms. First, small and medium-size firms (less than 250 employees) are much less frequently innovative than the biggest (250 employees and more). Therefore, considering the intermediate size, there is no clear linear relationship between firms' size and decision to innovate. Second, considering the main economic activities, firms from different NACE implement different types of innovation. Thus, manufacturers implement process and product innovation more often, whereas firms in transport and communications are more focused on organizational change, as well as the 'other business' sector. Finally, last but not least, focusing on the main market of firms, it appears that firms acting mainly in the European market are more innovative, whatever the type of innovation (except in marketing innovation).

ICT variables

One should bear in mind that, because it is a generic technology in continuous evolution, there is no clear definition of what ICT is and how to measure it. Indeed, 20 years ago, the number of firms that were employing ICT was very small.

Nowadays, as shown in Table 13.4, almost every firm in the sample has a local area network (LAN) and is connected to the Internet (95.9 percent) – even broadband is widespread (72.3 percent) – and,

Table 13.3 Propensity to innovate among firms' characteristics (size, main activity, main market)

	Innovative		Product innovation		Process innovation		Change in organization		Marketing innovation	
	%	%	%	%	%	%	%	%	%	%
	No	Yes	No	Yes	No	Yes	No	Yes	No	Yes
Main activity										
Manufacture Industry	37.9	62.1	62.8	37.2	64.2	35.8	56.2	43.8	84.5	15.5
Automobile and retails	40.5	59.5	65.1	34.9	90.8	9.2	54.8	45.2	72.0	28.0
Transports and communications	53.5	46.5	80.4	19.6	77.5	22.5	61.7	38.3	93.8	6.2
Financial activities	28.0	72.0	53.9	46.1	47.1	52.9	45.2	54.8	77.4	22.6
Other Business	20.5	79.5	50.8	49.2	64.7	35.3	28.1	71.9	86.0	14.0
Size										
Firm with 10 to 19 employees	38.5	61.5	74.9	25.1	76.2	23.8	55.1	44.9	87.4	12.6
Firm with 20 to 49 employees	40.0	60.0	60.8	39.2	67.0	33.0	48.7	51.3	83.5	16.5
Firm with 50 to 249 employees	36.3	63.7	57.3	42.7	64.5	35.5	52.8	47.2	79.9	20.1
Firm with more than 250 employees	7.0	93.0	20.6	79.4	44.6	55.4	15.7	84.3	56.9	43.1
Main market										
National market	37.9	62.1	66.6	33.4	76.9	23.1	51.0	49.0	82.0	18.0
Grande Region market	38.2	61.8	69.9	30.1	72.3	27.7	42.6	57.4	83.0	17.0
European market	35.8	64.2	55.0	45.0	61.4	38.6	44.8	55.2	83.1	16.9
Other market	33.8	66.2	70.7	29.3	39.9	60.1	78.6	21.4	87.8	12.2
Total	36.9	63.1	63.3	36.7	68.8	31.2	50.3	49.7	82.8	17.2

n = 349 observations.

Source: STATEC, CIS2006-ICT2007 author's calculation.

Table 13.4 Equipment and practices of adoption

	%
Intranet	60.8
Extranet	34.0
LAN	99.7
E-mail	97.4
Visio conference	17.2
Electronic forum	13.9
Electronic calendar	43.2
Project manager group	23.7
Internet access	95.9
Own a website	71.2
Secure protocol (SSL or TLS)	20.1
Open source software or O/S	24.1
Digital signature	21.4
ISDN connection	30.1
Broadband connection	72.3

n = 349 observations.

Source: STATEC, CIS2006-ICT2007 author's calculation.

moreover, over 70 percent of firms own a website. Nevertheless, looking to more advanced technologies shows that there is still progress to be made. Electronic calendar, visio- or video-conference and electronic forum are features not so often implemented. Also, with regard to security within the firm, only one firm in five uses a secure protocol, and the same proportion uses a digital signature. It is important for companies to protect themselves against potential risks. Finally, even considering Internet use, despite the fact that it is well known and has been widely available for more than a decade, only 40 percent of firms use it to purchase and 16 percent for selling. One should keep in mind that Luxembourg is a very small and open economy which could be more involved in e-commerce to overcome the borders and capture a broader market.

Providing information about uses of available equipment is an important feature of the survey. Reasons to use the Internet are shown in Table 13.5. The most frequent reasons to use Internet are, first, banking and services, second, market monitoring and, third, to receive products transmitted via Internet. Thus, 79 percent of firms use the Internet in order to benefit from banking and financial services, while 68 percent of firms monitor the market using the Internet. When firms adopt the Internet they provide multiple reasons; they mention at least two

Table 13.5　Internet use

	%
Reason to use Internet	
Banking and financial services	79.0
Training and education	24.5
Market monitoring (e.g. prices)	68.0
Receive products transmitted via Internet	60.5
Receive after sales support	45.3
Number of reason to use Internet	
None of those mentioned	7.4
1	12.5
2	25.8
3	16.7
4	24.8
5	12.7

reasons, over the five choices offered in the survey, in more than nine cases out of ten. On average, they give three reasons.

Several ICT variables have been constructed and tested but not retained in the model. Those variables are described in Appendix A13.3. The most useful and significant variable in linking ICT behavior and equipment to innovative activities is related to automatic links – that is, firms using a software application to manage order links automatically with different systems. The ICT survey refers to five systems listed below:

- internal system for reordering replacement supplies;
- invoicing and payment systems;
- your system for managing production, logistics or service operations;
- your suppliers' business systems (for suppliers outside your enterprise group);
- your customers' business systems (for customers outside your enterprise group).

The determinant of innovation product, process, marketing and of change in organization are shown in Table 13.6 – the results from the probit model with survey weights.

More than half of our sample has used software to manage order links for invoicing and payment systems.

Table 13.6 Proportion of firm with an application to manage order links automatically and type of links

	%
automatic link with your customers' business systems	27.6
automatic link for invoicing and payment systems	57.8
automatic link with your suppliers' business systems	21.7
automatic link with your system for managing production, logistics or service operations	36.4
automatic link with Internal system for re-ordering replacement supplies	22.1

Results

Table 13.7 reports the results of the models presented in the third section of this chapter. The first two columns show the results obtained for product and/or service innovation and for process innovation, known as technological innovation. The last two columns present results for organizational and marketing innovation, namely the non-technological innovations. All these regressions are based on the same weighted sample. First, the probability to be innovative increases significantly with the size regardless the type of innovation. This link between size and innovation ability is concave. R&D ratio expressed as R&D expenses over turnover has also a positive impact on probability to innovate for each type of innovation but marketing innovation. Second, from the five variables measuring ICT access and uses in the models – percentage of employees connected to Internet, using digital signature, access to broadband, having its own webpage on Internet and number of automatic IT links – the most frequently significant variable representing ICT is the number of automatic links. Indeed, it is the only ICT variable with positive impact for technological innovations. Digital signature has a positive impact on propensity to implement organizational change, while broadband has a negative impact on process implementation. Third, the percentage of highly qualified employees contributes significantly and positively to explaining the probability to innovate in product. Finally, regarding firms' activities, transport and telecommunication firms are significantly less innovative in marketing than manufacturing firms, whereas 'other business activities' are significantly more willing to implement organizational change.

Table 13.7 The determinant of innovation product, process, marketing, and from change in organization

Results from the probit model with survey weights	Product innovation	Process innovation	Change in organization	Marketing innovation
Percentage of employees connected to Internet	0.001	0.006	0.002	
	(–0.004)	(–0.004)	(–0.004)	(–0.006)
Digital signature	–0.275	–0.188	0.592*	0.376
	(–0.291)	(–0.284)	(–0.286)	(–0.259)
Broadband	–0.097	–0.665**	0.156	0.48
	(–0.241)	(–0.251)	(–0.25)	(–0.309)
Dummy own web page 2007	0.011	0.102	0.304	0.118
	(–0.279)	(–0.243)	(–0.244)	(–0.328)
Number of automatic links	0.176**	0.226***	0.094	0.170*
	(–0.064)	(–0.064)	(–0.063)	(–0.079)
Number of Internet uses 2007	–0.013	–0.129	–0.136	–0.079
	(–0.086)	(–0.089)	(–0.086)	(–0.093)
Percentage of employees with Higher education	0.009*	–0.002	0.003	0.011
	(–0.005)	(–0.005)	(–0.005)	(–0.006)
Ratio R&D	0.064**	0.162***	0.043**	0.009
	(–0.025)	(–0.044)	(–0.016)	(–0.013)
Main market is Europe	0.206	–0.242	0.245	–0.116
	(–0.237)	(–0.251)	(–0.233)	(–0.261)
Firm size: total number of employees	0.004***	0.002*	0.004**	0.003**
	(–0.001)	(–0.001)	(–0.001)	(–0.001)
Squared number of employees	–0.001**	0.001	–0.001**	–0.001**
	(0.001)	(0.001)	(0.001)	(0.001)
Automobile and retails	0.33	–0.539	0.366	0.487
	(–0.292)	(–0.299)	(–0.278)	(–0.316)
Transports and communications	–0.284	0.246	0.336	–0.752*
	(–0.274)	(–0.267)	(–0.244)	(–0.35)
Financial Activities	–0.044	0.635	0.149	–0.296
	(–0.396)	(–0.421)	(–0.433)	(–0.465)
Other business	0.177	–0.017	1.034**	–0.584
	(–0.394)	(–0.415)	(–0.389)	(–0.509)
Constant	–1.325***	–0.822*	–1.147***	–2.310***
	(–0.314)	(–0.332)	(–0.323)	(–0.444)

*p < 0.05, **p < 0.01, ***p < 0.001.

Source: STATEC, CIS2006-ICT2007 author's calculation.

Conclusion

Results presented here should be considered as the first step of a more general study about ICT, innovation and growth relationships. At this moment, main results are: on the one hand, there is a positive relationship between ICT use and propensity to innovate; nevertheless, on the other hand, estimating probit model with or without endogeneity correction emphasizes the weakness of those links. It seems that the relationship depends on ICT use intensity and it appears that different equipment and uses have different impact on each different kind of innovation.

These results are confirmed for other countries – for example, Abello and Pritchard (2008) for Australia and for other specifications in Luxembourgish data. Considering the results for Luxembourg, one can see Table A13.7 provided in appendix, as well as Nguyen Thi and Martin (2009). Nguyen Thi and Martin found also a positive link using an extended Crepon Duguet Mairesse model setting but also obtained various results depending on ICT uses and types of innovations considered. Identifying and measuring the impact of ICT use and equipment on propensity to innovate led to two difficulties.

First, it seems that each type of innovation is favored by different types of ICT. As it has been pointed out, definitions of ICT and advanced ICT, as well as radical innovation, are constantly changing. Second, Luxembourg is a small country with specific activities; these characteristics tend to make econometric estimation trickier. Thus, before going further in measuring the impact of ICT on innovation, the link between ICT pattern and mix of innovations has to be explored. Results provide inputs to build useful composite indicators for the next step modeling ICT, innovation and growth at firm level. Here, the extended Crepon Duguet Mairesse model should be revisited with comprehensive composite indicators.

In addition, this model allows assessment of the contribution of ICT to productivity of firms by including ICT investment as an input in the innovation process beside the R&D expenses.

Appendix

Table A13.1   Branches covered in the ICT survey 2007

NACE LUX REV 1.1	Section	Definition
10–14	C	mining and quarrying
15–37	D	manufacturing
40–41	E	electricity, gas, and water supply
45	F	construction
50	G	motor trade
51		wholesale trade
52		retail trade
55	H	hotels and restaurants
60–64	I	transport, storage, and communication
65–67	J	financial intermediation
70	K	real estate activities
71		renting of machinery and equipment without an operator
72		computer and related activities
73		research and development
73		research and development
74.1		legal, accounting, market research, consultancy, and management services
74.2		architectural and engineering activities
74.3		technical testing and analysis
74.4		advertising
74.5		labor recruitment and provision of personnel
74.6		investigation and security activities
74.7		industrial cleaning services
74.8		miscellaneous business activities n.e.c.

Table A13.2   Branches covered in CIS 2006

NACE LUX REV 1.1	Section	Definition
15–37	D	manufacturing
45	F	construction
50		motor trade
51	G	wholesale trade
52		retail trade
55.1+55.2	H	Hotels and other provision of short-stay accommodation
60–64	I	transport, storage, and communication
65.12+65.22	J	Monetary intermediation and other credit granting, except central banking
66.01+66.03	K	Insurance, except compulsory social security
70–74		Real estate, renting, and business activities

Probit equations with endogenous regressors

Different hypotheses have been tested through a series of 'probit equations with endogenous regressors' (Wooldridge, 2002, pp. 472–8). The probability of introducing an innovation with specific features (e.g., product, marketing, new-to-the-market, etc.) is modeled as a function of:

- the intensity of ICT use;
- the firm's size (number of employees); and
- the educational attainments of its employees (as a proxy of human capital).

The model was estimated through a 'two-stage conditional maximum likelihood' Rivers and Vuong, 1988 with firm or industry random effects. In order to control for the endogeneity of the ICT variable, we used and instrumental variable (IV) approach. We tested a number of ICT variables which are expected to be correlated to ICT use but not to innovation. The variable e-government turned out to be a valid instrument. In more formal terms, we started with the following model:

$$Inno_i^* = \beta_0 + \beta_1 \ln(size_i) + \beta_2 skills_i) + \sum_j \gamma_j D_{j,i} + u_i \qquad (A.1)$$

$$ICT_i = \delta_0 + \delta_1 \ln(size_i) + \delta_2 skills_i) + \delta_4 IV_i + v_i \qquad (A.2)$$

$$Inno_i = 1 \text{ if } Inno_i^* > 0 \; ; \; Inno_i = 0 \text{ otherwise} \qquad (A.3)$$

$$D_{j,i} = 1 \text{ if } ICT_i = j; \quad D_{j,i} = 0 \text{ otherwise} \qquad (A.4)$$

where i = 1,2,....,N indicates the firms; j = 1,2,...,Z the frequency of ICT use; (u_i, v_i) is assumed to have a zero mean, bivariate normal distribution and to be independent of all exogenous variables in (2). If u_i and v_i are correlated, ICT is endogenous and the probit estimates of all variables in (A.1) are biased. Under the assumption of joint normality of (u_i, v_i) we can write

$$u_i = \vartheta v_i + e_i \qquad (A.5)$$

where $e_i \sim N[0, Var(u_i) - cov(u_i, v_i)]$

Therefore, the above model can be rewritten as:

$$Inno_i^* = \beta_0 + \beta_1 \ln(size_i) + \beta_2 skills_i) + \sum_j \gamma_j D_{j,i} + \vartheta \hat{v}_i + e_i \qquad (A.6)$$

where $\hat{v}_i$ are the OLS residuals of equation (2). Equation (A.6) can be estimated by probit and the average partial effects (APEs) computed as the average of the partial effects (PEs) across. The model can be interpreted as a simultaneous model, where the decision to innovate and to use ICTs is taken jointly. In this sense, the model does not predict that ICT use is the cause of innovation, rather that ICTs are an enabler of innovation: firms use ICTs as a tool or a 'platform' for innovation.

Composite indicators for ICT equipment and use

Information about ICT needs to be summarized in order to be able to measure intensity and to qualify use and equipment of the firms. There is no clear and commonly admitted definition for ICT measurement of use and intensity. For the purpose of this analysis, composite indicators of ICT checked with Cronbach's Alpha were built. ICT use and equipment are measured using two scales:

- first, score_equipment is the score obtained by counting the number of different equipments available in the firm. Equipment taken into account includes: adoption of extranet, electronic forum, ERP, intranet and visio-/video-conference. This score evaluates to what extent a firm is intensively equipped for ICT or not.
- second, score_use is a composite indicator using reasons to use Internet. It indicates whether the firm is an intensive user of ICT or not. The score aggregates the following ICT use of Internet: for banking and financial services, for training or education, for market monitoring, receiving digital products, providing after-sales support, using open source. The resulting scale informs us about the motivation to use the Internet.

Table A13.1 presents the distribution of score obtained for both scales. It appears that 35 percent of the interviewed firms did not adopt any of the equipment included in the variable score_equipment. Moreover, 24.1 percent of our sample uses only one item of equipment of those proposed. Nevertheless, some firms (5.3 percent) adopted all of this equipment for their firm. Considering the number of reasons to use the Internet (score_use), about half of the sample uses the Internet for at least three reasons of the six available. Of the firms that adopt the Internet, it is those that make intensive use of it that most enjoy its benefits.

Table A13.3 Score variables

	%
Number of ICT equipment (score_equipment)	
0	35.0
1	24.1
2	15.5
3	12.2
4	7.9
5	5.3
Number of reason to use Internet (score_user)	
0	4.7
1	15.0
2	22.0
3	19.7
4	18.0
5	12.0
6	8.7

Notes

1. Therefore, OECD working parties undertook projects examining the impact of ICT on innovation so as to characterize the link between innovation and use of ICT within firms. This work derives from one of those projects undertaken with the Working Party on Indicators for the Information Society (WPIIS).
2. One should bear in mind that firms from the financial sector do not answer the e-commerce module.
3. NACE is the Statistical Classification of Economic Activities in the European Community. It is a European industry standard classification consisting of a six-digit code.
4. See *http://epp.eurostat.ec.europa.eu/cache/ITY_SDDS/en/inn_esms.htm*

References

Abello R. and G. Prichard (2008) 'Exploring Business Use of IT and Innovation using Linked FirmrLevel Data', *Australian Bureau of Statistics, presented as OECD mimeo to the Working Party of National Experts on Science and Technology Indicators*, 16–19 June 2008.

Asikainen, A.L. (2008) 'Innovation and Productivity in Luxembourg', *Economies et statistiques*, STATEC.

Askenazy P., D. Thesmar and M. Thoenig (2006) 'On the Relation Between Organisational Practices and New Technologies: The Role of (Time Based) Competition', *The Economic Journal*, Vol. 116, No. 508, pp. 128–54.

Benavente, J.M. (2006) 'The role of research and innovation in promoting productivity in chile', *Economics of Innovation and New Technology*, Vol. 15, No. 4–5, pp. 301–15.

Black, S.E. and L.M. Lynch (2001) 'How to Compete: The Impact of Workplace Practices and Information Technology on Productivity', *Review of Economics and Statistics*, Vol. 83, No. 3, pp. 434–45.

Bocquet, R. and O. Brossard (2007) 'The Variety of ICT Adopters in the Intra-firm Diffusion Process: Theoretical Arguments and Empirical Evidence', *Structural Change and Economic Dynamics*, Vol. 18, pp. 409–37.

Bresnahan, T.F., E. Brynjolfsson and L.M. Hitt (2002) 'Information Technology, Workplace Organization, and the Demand for Skilled Labor: Firm-Level Evidence', *The Quarterly Journal of Economics*, MIT Press, Vol. 117, No. 1, pp. 339–76, February.

Brynjolfsson, E. and L.M. Hitt (2000) 'Beyond Computation: Information Technology, Organizational Transformation and Business Performance', *Journal of Economic Perspectives*, Vol. 14, No. 4, pp. 24–48.

Bugamelli, M. and P. Pagano (2004) 'Barriers to Investment in ICT', *Applied Economics*, 36.

Castiglione C. (2009) 'ICT Investment and Firm Technical Efficiency', paper presented at EWEPA 2010, Pisa, June.

Greenan, N., J. Mairesse and A. Topiol-Bensaid (2001) 'Information Technology and Research and Development Impacts on Productivity and Skills', NBER.

Griffith R., E. Huergo, J. Mairesse and B. Peters (2006) 'Innovation and Productivity Across Four European Countries', *Oxford Review of Economic Policy*, 22.

Hempell, T. (2005) 'Does Experience Matter? Innovations and the productivity in German Services', ZEW, SSRN eLibrary, Mannheim.

Hempell, T. (2002) 'What's Spurious, What's Real? Measuring the Productivity Impacts of ICT at the Firm-level', *Empirical Economics*, 30.

Hempell, T., G. van Leeuwen and H. van der Wiel (2004) 'Innovation and Business Performance in Services: Evidence for Germany and the Netherlands', ZEW, SSRN eLibrary, Mannheim.

Hollenstein, H. (2004) 'Determinants of the Adoption of Information and Communication Technologies', *Structural Change and Economic Dynamics*, Vol. 15, No. 3, pp. 315–42.

Jefferson, G., B. Huamao, G. Xiaojing and Y. Xiaoyun (2006) 'R&D Performance in Chinese industry', *Economics of Innovation and New Technology*, Vol. 15.

Koellinger, P. (2008) 'The Relationship between Technology, Innovation, and Firm Performance: Empirical Evidence on E-Business', *Research Policy*, Vol. 37, No. 8, pp. 1317–28.

Lööf, H. and A. Heshmati (2006) 'On the Relationship between Innovation and Performance: A Sensitivity Analysis', *Economics of Innovation and New Technology*, Vol. 15.

Mansfield, E. (1963) 'The Speed of Response of Firms to New Techniques', *The Quarterly Journal of Economics*, Vol. 77.

Martin, L. and T.U. Nguyen Thi (2009) 'The Relationship between Innovation and Productivity Conditional to R&D and ICT Use', an empirical analysis for firms in Luxembourg Development.

Miguel Benavente, J. (2006) 'The Role of Research and Innovation in Promoting Productivity in Chile', *Economics of Innovation and New Technology*, Vol. 15.

OECD (2003) *ICT and Economic Growth*, OECD.

OECD EUROSTAT (2005) *'Oslo Manual: Guidelines for Collecting and Interpreting Innovation Data'*, 3rd Edition.

Pilat, D. (2004) 'The ICT Productivity Paradox: Insights from Micro Data', *OECD Economic Studies*, 38.

Rivers, D. and Quang H. Vuong (1988) 'Limited Information Estimators and Exogeneity Tests for Simultaneous Probit Models', *Journal of Econometrics*, Vol. 39, pp. 347–66.

Van der Wiel, H. and G. van Leeuwen (2003) 'Do ICT Spillovers Matter? Evidence from Dutch Firm-level Data', CPB Discussion Papers, p. 26.

Varian, H.R., J. Farrell and C. Shapiro (2004) *The Economics of Information Technology: An Introduction*, Cambridge, MA: Cambridge University Press.

Wooldridge, J. (2002) *Econometric Analysis of Cross Section and Panel Data*, MIT Press.

Index

GPSR Compliance
The European Union's (EU) General Product Safety Regulation (GPSR) is a set
of rules that requires consumer products to be safe and our obligations to
ensure this.

If you have any concerns about our products, you can contact us on

ProductSafety@springernature.com

In case Publisher is established outside the EU, the EU authorized
representative is:

Springer Nature Customer Service Center GmbH
Europaplatz 3
69115 Heidelberg, Germany